Fast Guns and War-Bonnets

Fast Guns and War-Bonnets
Two First Hand Accounts of the
American 'Wild West' Frontier
During the 19th Century

Thirty Years on the Frontier

Robert McReynolds

Seventy Years on the Frontier

Alexander Majors

Fast Guns and War-Bonnets
*Two First Hand Accounts of the American 'Wild West' Frontier
During the 19th Century*
Thirty Years on the Frontier
by Robert McReynolds
Seventy Years on the Frontier
by Alexander Majors

FIRST EDITION

First published under the titles
Thirty Years on the Frontier
and
Seventy Years on the Frontier

Leonaur is an imprint
of Oakpast Ltd

Copyright in this form © 2014 Oakpast Ltd

ISBN: 978-1-78282-271-4 hardcover)
ISBN: 978-1-78282-272-1 (softcover)

http://www.leonaur.com

Publisher's Notes
The views expressed in this book are not necessarily
those of the publisher.

Contents

Thirty Years on the Frontier   7

Seventy Years on the Frontier   151

Thirty Years on the Frontier

THEY CROSSED THE GILA AT FLOOD TIDE

Contents

In Days of Innocence	13
Out for a Fortune	17
Black Hills Days	20
The Custer Massacre	24
The Shadow Scout	29
Indian Fight in Colorado	34
A Cowboy Duel	39
Pleasant Halfacre's Revenge	42
Capturing Wild Horses	47
An Expedition That Failed	51
Across the Palm Desert	55
The Last Stand of a Dying Race	60
The Tragedy of the Lost Mine	67
The Land of the Fair God	71
Outlawry in Oklahoma	76
A New Land of Canaan	81
Told Around the Campfire	86
The Lone Grave on the Mesa	90

Under the Black Flag	93
In Cuban Jungles	97
Emulous of Washington	101
On the Round Up	104
The Egypt of America	110
In the Dome of the Sky	116
Where Nature is at Her Best	120
When the West was New	125

To
Louis Taliaferro
Colorado Springs
Colarado

1

In Days of Innocence

In the following pages I shall tell of much personal experience as well as important incidents which have come under my observation during thirty years on the frontier. As a cowboy, miner and pioneer, I have participated in many exciting events, none of which, however, caused me the prolonged grief that a certain bombshell affair did when I was a boy, resulting in a newspaper experience and habit of telling things, and eventually led to my coming West.

My grandfather's plantation in Kentucky and nearly opposite the town of Newburgh, on the Indiana side, was as much my home as was my mother's. She being a widow and having my brother and sister to care for, as well as myself, felt a relief from the responsibility of looking after me when I was at my grandfather's home.

The plantation faced the Ohio River, the wooded part of which had been a camping ground for rebel soldiers, until they were driven out by the shells of a Yankee gunboat. While hunting pecans in these woods one day, I stumbled on to an unexploded bombshell, and, boy-like, I wanted to see the thing go off. However, I was afraid to touch it until I had counselled with the Woods boys, whose father was a renter of a small tract of ground below the plantation. That night the three of us met and decided to explode the shell the following Sunday morning, after the folks had gone to church. I feigned a headache when grandmother wanted to take me in the carriage with them to church, but when I was satisfied they were well down the road, I hurried to the strip of forest a mile away, where the Woods boys were waiting. They had come in a rickety old buggy drawn by a white mule.

It was in autumn and as the leaves were dry on the ground, we were afraid to kindle a fire, and decided to take the shell near the tobacco barn, around which we could hide and watch it go off. Neither of the boys would handle it, so I lifted it into the buggy; then they were afraid to ride with it, and it was left to me to lead the mule to the tobacco barn. I hitched the animal to a sapling near the barn, while the other boys gathered up some kindling, and we made a pile of old fence posts, and when I had laid the shell upon the log heap, we lit the kindling with a match and all ran behind the barn, forgetting all about the mule. The wood was dry and was soon all aflame. Every little while one of us would peek around the corner to see if the thing was not about ready to explode. We were getting impatient, when the mule gave a great "hee haw" that called our attention to his peril. It was his last "hee haw," for in a second more the bomb exploded with a deafening noise, and fragments of the shell screamed like a panther in the air. We ran around to see the result of the explosion, and behold! it had spread that mule all over the side of the barn.

The things my grandfather said and did to me when he returned from church does not concern the public. But when he had finished, I was fully convinced that I was all to blame, and that I owed Mr. Woods $150 for his demolished mule.

Then followed long lectures from my mother and grandmother, and to add to my discomfiture was Mr. Woods' lamentations and his expressed regrets that it was not me, instead of his mule, that was blown up.

I was the owner of an old musket with which I spent most of my time hunting rabbits, using small slugs of lead for shot, which I chopped up with a hatchet. Two weeks before the bombshell episode, I had found a musket-ball, and I concluded to try a man's load in the gun on my next rabbit; I poured in a full charge of powder, but when I came to ram the ball home, it would go only half way down the barrel. I was afraid to shoot then, lest the gun might burst, and as I could neither get the ball out or farther down, I laid the barrel between two logs, tied a string to the trigger, and got behind a stump and pulled it off.

A few minutes later while I was examining my gun, grandfather came running out of the potato patch to find who was shooting at him. However, he was so thankful that matters were not worse, that I got off with a slight reprimand.

But this Sunday capped the climax. A council of my kinfolks was held that night, and decided that neither man nor beast was safe on that plantation if I remained. Their final verdict was that I should be sent to my mother's home in Newburgh, and there to learn the printer's trade, attend Frederick Dickerman's night-school, be made to pay for the mule, and my musket confiscated. I was paid $3 a week as printer's devil to start with, one dollar of which I might spend for my clothes, fifty cents for tuition in the night school, one dollar and twenty-five cents for the mule debt, and the other twenty-five cents I might spend.

Grandfather was very careful to see that I saved the mule money, and I used to think he took a special delight in collecting it from mother, to whom I paid it every week.

It took me nearly three years in that printing office to get out of debt. I was now eighteen years of age.

Life in the printing office was too monotonous; I wanted a more exciting scene of action. I used to watch the great river steamers come and go, and wondered if I could hold any kind of a position on one of them, except carrying freight, when by accident one day there came an opportunity. The steamer *Dick Johnson* was lying at the wharf loading hogsheads of tobacco, when the freight clerk was injured by a fall of the stage plank. The captain wanted someone to take his place, and my schoolmaster recommended me. Here was a chance to put in practice the bookkeeping I had studied under him. It was what I wanted—I could now get a glimpse of the outside world.

The position on the *Dick Johnson* was a stepping-stone, for in another year I was the mate of the steamer *Rapidan*, plying between Florence, Alabama, and Evansville, Indiana, and had thirty negroes under my control.

It was historic country through which we passed. The trees on the islands near Pittsburgh Landing yet showed signs of shot and shell fired by federal gunboats. Ofttimes some passenger who had been a participant on one side or the other at Shiloh, would entertain his listeners for hours with stories of the fight, until some of us younger officers became imbued with the war spirit.

The autumn of 1875 had come when yellow fever broke out aboard our boat, and we lay in quarantine two miles below Savannah, Tennessee, for a month. I stayed with the boat until we were released, and then went to my home in Newburgh, ill with malarial fever.

Stories of rich gold finds in the Northwest had been circulated through the newspapers, and one day I resolved to try my luck. The things we believe we are doing for the last time, always cause a pang of sorrow, and as I packed my valise on Sunday afternoon to leave forever the home of childhood, my feelings can be better imagined than described. My grandparents came over from their Kentucky home to bid me goodbye. When I was ready to start, grandfather took from his pocket a roll of bills, and placing them in my hands, said: "Here, Mackey, is your mule money, and I have added interest enough to make the sum total $500. I paid Mr. Woods for his mule, but I wanted to teach you a lesson. Profit by it, and make good use of the money, and say, Mackey, whatever you do in life, never insult a blind man, never strike a cripple and never marry a fool."

It was the last time I ever saw the noble old guardian of my youth. The first two of his parting injunctions I have religiously obeyed.

2

Out for a Fortune

My first view of the Nebraska plains was the next morning after leaving Omaha, and I thought I never saw anything half so grand. The February sun threw its beams aslant the mighty sea of plain over which so many white covered wagons had toiled on their way to the then wild regions of the West.

Small herds of buffalo and antelope were frequently seen from the car windows; the passengers fired at them and often wounded an antelope, which limped away in a vain attempt to join its mates. That night we witnessed the mighty spectacle of the plains on fire. The huge, billowy waves of flame leaped high against a darkened sky, and swept with hiss and roar along the banks of the shallow Platte. The emigrant train upon which I was aboard was crowded with people of all sorts. Many of them were home-seekers on their way to Oregon and California, while not a few adventurers like myself were bound for the Black Hills. A young man who went under the name of Soapy Wyatte, was working the train on a three-card *monte* game, and was very successful until he cheated a couple of ranchmen out of quite a sum of money. Then they organised the other losers, and were in the act of hanging him with the bell rope when he disgorged his ill-gotten gains and paid back the money. Men of his class were plentiful, but as a rule they were careful not to cheat the frontiersman, for when they did they usually got the worst of it.

Cheyenne at that time was a typical frontier town. Gambling houses, saloons and dance halls were open continuously, night and day. Unlucky indeed was the tenderfoot who fell into their snare. I soon secured transportation with a mule-train for Deadwood. There were thirty-three of us in the party. The wagons were heavily loaded with freight and the trail was in frightful condition; we ofttimes were compelled to walk.

I had bought a heavy pair of boots for the trip, but the sticky alkali mud made them so heavy that I soon cut off the tops. The next thing, I put my Winchester rifle and revolver in the wagon and then trudged along the best I could. The Sioux Indians were on the warpath and it was dangerous to get far away from the wagon train. Almost every freighter we met warned us against Red Canyon. The stage drivers reported "hold ups" and murders by organised bands of road agents. This kept us on the alert. At night there was a detail of eight, to divide up the night in standing guard. These men were selected from the most experienced plainsmen, of whom there were quite a number with us.

We were eight days out from Cheyenne, and several inches of snow had fallen during the night, but the sun rose clear on the biting cold of the morning. Suddenly we heard shots ahead. "Indians! Indians!" shouted one driver to another and then the wagons were quickly formed in a circle, the mules being unhitched and brought to the centre of the circle.

Then for the first time I saw the hideous forms of a band of half-naked savages mounted on their ponies in the distance. They were galloping in a circle around us, yelling their war cry, "*Hi-yi, Hip-yi, yi.*" They fell from their horses before the deadly aim of our men; their bullets came like the angry hum of hornets about our heads. Their numbers increased from over the foothills, whence they first came. There was a look of desperation upon the faces of our men, such as pen can not describe. James Morgan, who was standing near me in the act of reloading his Winchester, suddenly fell nerveless to the ground.

Our captain's voice rang out now and then, "Be careful there, boys; take good aim before you fire."

Two Indians circled nearer than the others. They were lying on their horses' necks and firing at us while they were at full gallop. I took aim at one and fired; others must have done so at the same time, for both of them fell from their horses. The fight lasted perhaps an hour, when the Indians withdrew to the hills. One of our men lay dead and two were wounded. I went to where the two Indians had fallen. There lay their forms, cold and stiff in death. The sunbeams were slanting over those snow covered hills. I felt an unaccountable terror as I looked upon them and the crimson snow which their life blood had stained. The raw north wind seemed to pierce my very heart. Night was coming on, and with it all the horrors of uncertainty. I lingered about the spot for some time, with a dreadful fascination mingled with terror. Human life had perished there; human souls had gone into the uncertainty of an unknown beyond. With my brain reeling with excitement of the day and sickened in heart, I returned to our wagons, where some of us walked outside the circle throughout the long watches of that wintry night.

When the morning sun rose clear above the snow-covered hills, we wrapped the body of the dead teamster in his blankets, and again took up the toilsome drive. The Indians had retired from the fight, probably for the reason that they saw another outfit of wagons coming far down on the plain. The wagons overtook us about 9 o'clock, and after that we had no more trouble with Indians.

Deadwood, at that time, was like all the frontier mining towns. Saloons, gambling houses and dance halls comprised the business of the place. The gulch was dotted with miners' cabins and dug-outs. There were a few stores, restaurants, and a bank, but as yet the town had not started a "regular" graveyard. The news of our fight soon spread up and down the gulch and many were the willing hands that offered their services in the burial of James Morgan, our teamster. They dug his grave on the hillside, where afterwards more than five thousand men were buried. They either fell from the deadly pneumonia, or from the bullets of each other in quarrels. When Morgan's grave was ready to be filled, someone suggested that a chapter from the Bible should be read, but none of us knew where to ask for one, in all Deadwood. Presently a boy said, "I will find one," and he soon returned with a young lady, who proved to be his sister. He handed the book to our bronzed captain of the mule train; he shook his head. Then someone asked her to read it. When she began, those grim frontiersmen bared their heads, and I fancied I saw the tears gather on more than one bronzed cheek as she knelt upon the frozen clay and offered up a prayer for the dead teamster's soul.

The adventurous spirits from far and wide were flocking to this new Eldorado. Wild Bill, the famous scout, Captain Jack Crawford, Texas Jack, and other equally noted scouts and Indian fighters, were there. They sought gold and adventure alike, only for the pleasure it would bring.

3

Black Hills Days

I knew Doc Kinnie was not a civil engineer, but he had a plan which looked good, and as I was almost broke, I consented to help him work it. There was a horseshoe bend in the creek which might be drained for placer mining by tunnelling through in a narrow place. I talked up the project with some of the boys, and they agreed to dig the tunnel while Doc did the civil engineering. Day after day they dug and blasted rock, while Doc stood around looking wise and encouraging the work. In about a month they were practically through to the other side of the creek. Then they began to call for Doc's measurements and calculations. "Never mind, you are not through yet," he would say, "I will let you know when to stop digging."

"But we can hear the water rushing," they would say.

"You fellows can't tell anything about it. Sounds of rushing water are always carried a long distance by rocks."

"But we are not in the rocks now, we are in a clay bank."

"Clay does the same thing; keep on digging."

Two days later and there was a commotion at the lower end of the tunnel, when a full head of water came rushing out, bearing with it men, wheelbarrows and shovels. They were nearly drowned, and half frozen, when they scrambled out of the creek. Mad as hornets, they sought their civil engineer, but he was nowhere to be found. The work was done. The prospects were good. When their clothes were dried and they had eaten dinner, they laughed over the incident and pardoned Doc's miscalculation. With pan and rocker, we now began to work the dry horseshoe bend. Nuggets weighing an ounce, and from that on down to the size of a pin head, were found. The fellows were honest, and made an even divide all around at the cleanup each night. In two months we had taken out over $6,000, and then sold

GENERAL GEORGE A. CUSTER

the claim to a placer mining company for $18,000 in cash—$3,000 apiece for the six of us. In two months we were all broke; the money had gone into wildcat speculation in mines. But who cared? Were the hills not full of gold, and all to be had for the digging?

I joined a party who went thirty miles to the northwest in search of new diggings, and the most that came of it was a laughable incident.

The great hills rose on every side, frowning darkly in the dense forest of pine. Our voices echoed from rock to rock, as we sat one noonday about our campfire, talking of possible finds, when, bareheaded, with hair dishevelled, blood flowing from a wound in his face, and a wildcat held to his chest in close embrace, Mark Witherspoon rushed into camp, yelling at the top of his voice. He was prospecting in a ravine a mile distant, when he saw something waving in the underbrush. Thinking it was mountain grouse, he advanced in hope of getting a shot, when a huge wildcat sprang at his throat.

As the forepaws of the animal struck his chest, he let fall his gun, and hugged the beast with all his strength to his chest with both arms. The head of the wildcat was drawn slightly backward by the tense pressure of his arms upon its back, while the claws were rendered practically powerless by the close embrace. So quick had been Witherspoon's action at the start, that he received only a slight wound on the face. In this predicament, he started on a run for the camp. He did not dare to let go and the wildcat wouldn't, so both held fast. The cat glared up fiercely at him with its yellow eyes, while its hot breath came into his face at every leap. Whenever the vicious beast made the slightest struggle, Witherspoon hugged the tighter, fearing at every step he might stumble and the deadly teeth be fixed in his throat.

In this manner he reached camp, and it was some seconds before he could make us understand that the cat was terribly alive, and that he was not holding it because he wanted to, or racing for the sake of the exercise. Finally one of the men despatched the animal with his revolver, and, to Witherspoon's inexpressible relief, the dead beast dropped from his arms. Before the boys got through telling the story afterwards, they made it out that Witherspoon had run nine miles with the wildcat.

Soon after our return to Deadwood, a man in an almost fainting condition came into town and announced that his companion had either been killed or captured by the Indians. A party was organised and was led by Wild Bill. It was not long before we came upon a scene that told what the poor fellow's fate had been, much plainer than words are able to portray. We found his blackened trunk fastened to a tree with rawhide thongs, while all around were evidences of the great torture which had been inflicted ere the fagots had been lighted.

When brought face to face with this, I stowed two cartridges safely away in my vest pocket, resolved to suicide rather than to fall into the hands of such miscreants. Then came the news of the Custer massacre. For many days afterward we patrolled the mountain tops, and kept bivouac fires lighted by night, as signals.

4

The Custer Massacre

The arrival at Fort Lincoln, on the Missouri River, of a party of Indians in 1874, who offered gold dust for sale, was the beginning of the cause that led to the great Sioux war in 1876, in which General Custer and his devoted soldiers were massacred on the Little Big Horn River on the 25th day of June of that year.

The gold which the Indians brought to Fort Lincoln, they said came from the Black Hills, where the gulches abounded with the yellow dust. The consequent rush of white men into that region was, in fact, a violation of the treaty of 1867, when Congress sent out four civilians and three army officers as peace commissioners, who gave to the old Dakota tribes, as the Sioux were then called, the vast area of land bounded on the south by Nebraska, on the east by the Missouri River, on the west by the 104th Meridian, and on the north by the 46th Parallel. They had the absolute pledge of the United States that they should be protected in the peaceable possession of the country set aside for them. This territory was as large as the state of Michigan, and of its interior little or nothing was known except to a few hardy traders and trappers prior to 1874.

With the advent of the gold seekers in 1875 the Indians saw that the greedy encroachments of the white man were but faintly resisted by the United States government, and that sooner or later it meant the total occupation of their country, and their own annihilation, and so with the traditional wrongs of their forefathers ever in mind, they determined to make a stand for their rights.

The scene of General Terry's campaign against these Indians lay between the Big Horn and Powder Rivers, and extended from the Big Horn Mountains northerly to beyond the Yellowstone River. A region barren and desolate, volcanic, broken and ofttimes almost impassable, jagged and precipitous cliffs, narrow and deep *arroyas* filled with massive boulders, alkali water for miles, vegetation of cactus and sagebrush—all these represent feebly the country where Custer was to contend against the most powerful, warlike and best armed body of savages on the American continent.

An army in this trackless waste was at that time at the mercy of guides and scouts. The sun rose in the east and shone all day upon a vast expanse of sagebrush and grass and as it set in the west cast its dull rays into a thousand ravines that neither man nor beast could cross; to go north or south could only be decided by personal effort. An insignificant turn to the wrong side of a little knoll or buffalo wallow would ofttimes lead the scout into ravine after ravine, or over bluff after bluff, until at last he would stand on the edge of a yawning canon, hundreds of feet in depth and with perpendicular walls. Nothing was left for him to do but to retrace his steps and find an accessible route.

Custer had been ordered by General Terry to proceed with his command, numbering 28 officers and 747 soldiers, up the Rosebud River, and if the trail of the Indians was not found at a given point, to then follow the course of the Little Big Horn. These instructions were followed, and on the 24th of June he turned westerly toward the Little Big Horn, where a large Indian village was discovered some fifteen miles distant. The trail they were on led down the stream at a point south of the villages. Major Reno with three companies was ordered to follow the trail, cross the stream and charge down its north bank, while Captain F. W. Benteen was sent with three companies to make a detour south of Reno.

The point where the little armies separated, many of their men never to meet again, the river wound its silvery course for miles in the narrow valley as far as the eye could reach; its banks were fringed with the elm and cottonwood, whose foliage hid from view a thousand Indian *tepees* beyond the river. Sharp eyes had noted the advancing columns, and quick brains had already begun to plan their destruction.

That night the three divisions made a silent bivouac beneath the stars which must have looked down like pitying eyes.

In the grey light of the morning, and with noiseless call to boots and saddles, they were stealing on toward the foe.

Reno proceeded to the river and crossed it, charged down its west banks and met with little resistance at first. Soon, however, he was attacked by such numbers that he was obliged to dismount his men, shelter his horses in a strip of woods and fight on foot. Finally, finding he would soon be surrounded, he again mounted his men, charged the enemy and recrossing the river, took a naturally fortified position on the top of a bluff.

Benteen, returning from his detour, discovered his position and drove away the Indians and joined him. Soon the mule train was also within his lines, making seven companies under his command.

Reno engaged the Indians soon after noon on the 25th and did some hard fighting until the evening of the 26th, when the enemy withdrew. After congratulations with their reinforcements the question uppermost in every mind was: "Where is Custer?"

They had heard heavy firing on the afternoon of the 25th and saw the black cloud of smoke settle like a pall over the valley, but Reno had his wounded to care for, and to have gone to the relief of Custer would have left them to be butchered. Neither could he divide his command, for such a course would have been suicidal.

Meanwhile the supply steamer, *Far West*, with General Terry on board, steamed up the Yellowstone on June 23rd and overtook Gibbon's troops near the mouth of the Big Horn on the morning of the 24th. At 5 o'clock on the morning of the 25th, Gibbon's column was marching over a country so rugged as to tax the endurance of the men to the utmost, and the infantry halted for the night, meantime General Terry pushed ahead with the cavalry and a light mountain battery. On the morning of the 26th, some Crow Indians reported to General Terry that a great fight had been going on the day before, and later scouts reported that a dense, heavy smoke was resting over the southern horizon far ahead, and in a short time it became visible to all.

So broken was the country and progress became so difficult that it was not until the morning of the 27th that Terry's relief column found the trail of Custer.

They had passed cautiously through a dense grove of trees and the head of the column entered upon a beautiful level meadow about a mile in width extending along the west side of the stream and skirted east and west by high bluffs. It was apparent at sight that this meadow had been the site of an immense Indian village and showed signs of hasty abandonment. Hundreds of lodge poles with finely dressed buffalo robes, dried meats, utensils and Indian trinkets were left behind. In a large *tepee* still standing were the stiffened forms of ten dead Indians. Every step of the march from here on showed signs of a desperate struggle. The dead bodies of Indian horses were seen; here and there were cavalry equipments, and soon the bodies of dead troopers, beside their frantic and still struggling, wounded horses gave evidence of a disastrous battle, and farther on was revealed a scene calculated to appal the stoutest heart. Here was a skirmish line marked by rows of slain with heaps of empty cartridge shells before them, and their officers lay dead just behind them.

Still farther on men lay in winrows, their faces still drawn with the awful desperation of a struggle unto death. Near the highest point of the hill lay the body of General Custer. There was a cordon of his brave defenders dead about him; his long hair was clotted with blood, while a great wound in his breast told how the brave soul had gone somewhere out into the wide waste and hush of eternity. Near him lay the body of his brother, Captain Custer, and some distance away another brother, Boston Custer, and his nephew, Armstrong Reed, a youth of 19. All were scalped except General Custer and Mark Kellogg, a correspondent of the *New York Herald*.

When the fight was at the hardest a Crow Indian with Custer wrapped himself in a dead Sioux Indian's blanket and made his escape; as he left the field he saw the squaws and Indian children rifling the dead of their trinkets and going about with their stone battle axes beating out the brains of the wounded; they danced about over the dead and dying, mutilating their bodies and singing the wild, weird strains of their battle songs.

When the welcome news of relief came to Reno's besieged command, strong men wept like children.

Among the first of his men to search among the fallen for a dead friend was one Charles Wilson, a blue-eyed, beardless trooper, a mere boy whose heart seemed to fairly break as he contemplated what must have been the awful death of his comrades. The man he was seeking was Jim Bristow, a tall, dark private whose last words to the young trooper were:

> Charley, my hour has come. We shall ride into this fight and you will come back alone. I want you to promise to take a little trouble for me when I am gone. You will find her face here in this locket upon my breast. I had thought to some day make her my wife, and that thought has gladdened my lonely life. Write to her, Charley, and tell her where is my resting place and that my spirit will wait for hers in that borderland twixt heaven and earth.

The boy answered, and his voice was low with pain. Just then the bugle sounded, and for an instant eye met eye and hand touched hand, and Jim Bristow rode away with Custer's column. This was the man young Wilson was searching for. The dead were so frightfully mutilated, their bodies bloated, blackened and swollen by the hot rays of the sun that they were buried as speedily as possible, on June 28th. Major Reno and the survivors of his regiment performed the last sad rites over their comrades and then a general retreat to the mouth of the Big Horn River was ordered.

5

The Shadow Scout

The bugle notes had died away, the cloud of battle smoke lifted from the valley and peaceful starlight shone over the rugged hills when a shadow crept out of a deep ravine and skulked into the valley of death and began dealing out retribution. Chief Dull Knife had much to say about it when he surrendered. He spoke in whispers when he referred to it, and he looked suddenly around, as if he feared it was softly stealing upon him to stab him in the back. Chief Gall's braves had something to say about it when they surrendered, and when white men asked them who or what the shadow was, they shook their heads and whispered:

"We kill 'em all, but yet there is one left. It is a white man; there is blood on his face and clothing; he carries a sabre and two revolvers, and the night wind blows his long black hair over his shoulders. It is a spirit sent by the Great Manitou to watch over the graves of the white soldiers."

White men saw the shadow, hunters, trappers and scouts who built their camp fires near that valley, through which the big mountain wolf skulked and prowled all night long, had felt the mysterious presence of the shadow or had seen it. They fled from their blankets at its soft step, and they had fired at it, and seen it glide off unharmed.

It was not a shadow of sentiment, but a being who sought vengeance for the butchery of the little band of heroes, for the brave comrades who grouped themselves about the noble Custer and fought to the death.

When the soldiers moved out of the valley, leaving so many graves behind them, the wolves rushed out from canon, ravine and den, to dig up the fresh earth and mutilate the dead. The shadow was there—a solitary, mysterious and vigilant sentinel to guard those sacred mounds.

Gathering Up the Dead at Wounded Knee

It screamed and gestured at the fierce beasts, it fired upon them with rifle and revolver and struck them with bright, keen sabre. The wolves ran here and there, from grave to grave, gnashing their teeth in anger, but the shadow closely pursued them. They formed in groups in the midnight darkness and waited for the shadow to tire out and fall asleep or go away, but it paced up and down over the graves, vigilant and unwearied, and daylight came to hurry the wild beasts to their lairs till another night.

Hunters and scouts had seen the sentinel-beat among the graves in the light of noon-day, when men could not be mistaken. The path ran from grave to grave, winding about to take in every one, and then it ran to the river and disappeared in a ledge of rocks. Scouts said it was a path beaten by human feet. The Indians said that a shadow or spirit alone could remain in that lonely spot, having only the company of wild beasts and the graves of the lonely dead.

Once when Red Cloud and a trusty few were scouting to learn the whereabouts of their white foes, they encamped in the valley for the night. The shadow stole among them as they slept, and when the fierce scream aroused the band from their slumbers, five of the red men had been murdered, each throat slashed across with a keen blade. The shadow stood and jeered at the living, who huddled together like frightened children. When they fled for their lives it pursued them with drawn sabre, and one of them had a scar on his shoulder to prove he had been struck with a blade. Next day when a full band of Indians rode into the valley to solve the mystery and secure revenge, they saw no living thing. The bodies of the dead warriors were cut and hacked and gashed. Five of the poor cavalrymen whose brains had been beaten out had been revenged.

Before the crown of a single grave had sunk down, Crazy Horse started to cross the valley at midnight with his lodges. The shadow confronted his band and mocked them, and as the red men hurried along in the darkness, vividly recalling the mad charge of the cavalry, the strange shadow skulked along with the column and fired shot after shot into the band. They fired at it and rushed out to capture it, but it disappeared, as shadows do. Two squaws, a child or two, an old man and two warriors fell by the bullets which the shadow fired. From that time the red men avoided the valley as white men avoid a pest. They would not cross it or skirt it, even at high noon when the sunshine beat down upon the graves.

Texas Jack, the famous scout in the employ of the army, and a companion, in the late autumn of 1876 crossed the lonely battleground and halted long enough to see that the graves had not been disturbed. They saw the path of the sentinel leading from grave to grave. They saw the skeletons of the red men slain by the shadow. They saw the shadow itself. They were leaving the valley when their ears were greeted by a wild laugh, and from a bed of rank grass and dry weeds a quarter of a mile away they saw the shadow beckon them to come forward. The shadow was a man—a tall, gaunt, heavy bearded and long-haired human being dressed in rags that once had been an army uniform. He held up in the air and shook at them a carbine and a sabre, and when they galloped away, he sent a leaden ball whistling over their heads.

This was the last time this trooper was seen alive, no doubt he was bereft of reason, and believed himself called upon to avenge his comrades and so lurked in the valley, living like the wild beasts around him and missing no chance to strike a blow.

Some years later, when peace was restored and Crow Dog with his son and two warriors were hunting buffalo on the Little Big Horn, they were themselves pursued by a hostile party of Crow Indians. They took refuge among the shelving rocks along the river. Far into the deep recesses, where the waves and winds for centuries had hollowed out a chamber, they found a skeleton. By its side lay a carbine, two revolvers and a long cavalry sabre; about the neck was a delicately wrought chain with a gold locket attached. This and some other trinkets they carried away. After a lapse of fourteen years from the time Custer and his soldiers fell, these same Sioux Indians were again on the war path in the Bad Lands of South Dakota. Custer's old regiment was there, too. Many of them had fought with Reno and Benteen on that fateful 25th of June, and by the chance of war it was a part of their command under Colonel Forsythe who fought the Battle of Wounded Knee. Among them was Charles Wilson, the beardless boy, who rode away with Reno, whilst his friend Jim Bristow followed Custer. No longer a boy, but a bronzed and bearded soldier who had stood the chance of fate in many an Indian fight.

After the battle, when they were gathering up the dead Indians frozen stiff by a four days' blizzard which raged with wild fury over the plain, there was found about the neck of a young warrior a locket and chain. Wilson curiously examined the trophy and found upon opening it, the photograph of Jim Bristow on one side and upon the other the sweet face of the girl who had promised to be his wife. The young brave from whose neck the locket was taken was found to be the son of Crow Dog, who had married into Big Foot's band, and this blood-stained bauble, which had at last found its way into the hands of Bristow's friend as he had intended when they parted, and all the circumstances connected with it, revealed at last the identity of the shadow-scout who kept the midnight vigils over the graves of Custer's heroic dead; who when the chill blasts of the northern winter had come, had crept into his lair among the rocks and far from the cottage where the voice of love had pleaded so long for his return, with the smoke of battle still before his eyes, and with the shouts and shots of that dreadful day still ringing in his ears, had died alone.

Wilson stood by my side a week later as a heavy army wagon rolled into Pine Ridge agency bearing the body of Sitting Bull, the great war chief, who had directed and led the fight on Custer's men. When the wagon halted, Wilson drew the canvas cover from the dead chief's form and gazed long at the bronzed, cruel face, which even in death, was magnificent in the strong drawn lines of unrelenting hatred. There was a cold glint of light in Wilson's eye as he took one last satisfied look at this dead monster of the plains and turned away to keep his word given fourteen years before to his comrade—Jim Bristow—the last survivor of that awful massacre on the Little Big Horn.

6

Indian Fight in Colorado

Old "Daddy" Stephenson sat in the shade of the ranch house, squinting his one eye toward the north, the other eye having been shot out a few years before. His squaw was boiling the leg of an antelope in a pot that swung under a tripod of sticks nearby, when "Doc" Kinnie and Charley Hayes rode up.

"Here's yer Injun," shouted "Doc," as he untied his lariat from a blanket and let the bloody head of an Indian roll on the ground near Stephenson's feet.

The old squaw came over, took a look, and, uttering a long, doleful sound like the cry of a wounded wolf, ran inside and grabbing her blanket, started for the hills, chanting a dismal wail peculiar to her people when in distress.

"You fellows have played billy hell; you've killed my brother-in-law," calmly remarked Stephenson as he refilled his pipe and again cast his one eye toward the north.

"And the best thing you can do is to hit the trail while you are wearing your scalps," he continued after a pause of several minutes.

At that moment the old man's half Indian boy and myself came up from the corral.

This incident furnished the cause for an ugly Indian fight which occurred on Rock Creek, northeastern Colorado, on June 12, 1877.

"Doc" Kinnie, Charley Hayes and myself had come from Deadwood to Cheyenne as an escort for a stage coach carrying the Wells-Fargo express, when Stephenson offered us better pay to work on his cattle ranch.

Four days before the incident of the bloody head, Stephenson had missed seven head of cattle and had struck the trail of one Indian who had driven them off. He rode to the ranch house in high rage and

CHARLES HAYES, "DOC" KINNIE, ROBERT MCREYNOLDS.
AFTER THE FIGHT

offered Kinnie and Hayes one hundred dollars if they would recover the cattle and kill the Indian. In five minutes they were in their saddles riding to the point where Stephenson indicated the trail. I did not join them, as Stephenson insisted that two were enough. Kinnie and Hayes had no difficulty in following the trail of the stolen cattle and were close on them the next evening. Not caring for a night attack they went into camp, eating their bacon raw rather than make a fire. They were in their saddles at the first grey streak of dawn and within an hour came upon two Indians eating their morning meal in a *cañon*, while the missing cattle were grazing five hundred yards beyond.

It was a complete surprise to the Indians, and in the *mêlée* that followed one of them was killed and the other made his escape. It then became a question of how best to prove to Stephenson that they had killed the Indian without the burden of taking him back.

Kinnie, who had been a medical student in Ohio before a certain escapade had caused him to emigrate to the west, suggested the amputation of the dead Indian's head as the handiest way, and also suggested that they keep quiet as to the Indian who got away, lest the old man should only want to pay one-half of the promised reward.

Hayes stood guard while Kinnie cut and twisted the Indian's neck until the head separated from the body. He then rolled it in the Indian's blanket and carried it on the pommel of his saddle until the afternoon, when he rolled the ghastly trophy out on the ground in front of Stephenson and his squaw wife.

"Seems to me if I had your kind of relations I would pay a better price and get them all killed off," said Hayes, as he returned from the corral.

This remark nettled Stephenson, who smoked his pipe awhile in silence. He then grew angry, ordered the three of us to hit the trail for Fort Morgan at once, saying that two thousand Cheyenne Indians would be down upon us as soon as his squaw could communicate with them. This we refused to do, as neither Kinnie nor Hayes, nor their horses were in condition for flight, besides the old man had not settled and we rightly guessed that he would like to get out of paying the one hundred dollars, as well as preserve his good standing with the Indians.

Later in the evening he was caught hiding a quantity of Winchester cartridges. That settled him. We knew then he wanted to see us slain, while he would endeavour to lay blame upon us. In five minutes he was bound hand and foot and laid upon a corner in the ranch house upon some blankets. The Indian boy was also bound and thrown into another corner for safe keeping. The log ranch house was then loop-holed and our horses were brought inside, also a quantity of hay, wood and water.

We were prepared for a siege. Kinnie and Hayes lay down to sleep, while I kept the first watch of the night. All light was extinguished and I constantly went from loop-hole to loop-hole, peering into the darkness for the approaching foe, while the old man lay upon his blankets, swearing like the old sinner he was. I lay down for some sleep in the after part of the night, leaving the others to watch.

It was daylight when I was awakened by rifle shots. They came from a hill upon whose crest rode forty Cheyenne warriors, bedecked in feathers and war paint and stripped for battle.

We made no reply to their shots, but led them to believe by our silence that the ranch house was deserted.

After *pow-wow*ing for an hour, six of them began advancing cautiously. We waited they were within a hundred feet of the house, when our rifles emptied three of the saddles, and two more were riderless before the sixth retreating Indian reached the main party, which by that time was in commotion and had begun a circling ride around the ranch house to prevent our escape.

For the remainder of the day they kept well out of reach of our rifles, but when night had gathered they stole away their dead and wounded under cover of darkness. The next morning there was no sign of them. We were not to be caught, however, by such a ruse, having played the same game ourselves the morning before. We felt sure they would be reinforced within two days with an overwhelming force that could easily storm the house and tear it down over our heads.

Our only hope was to get away, and we held a council of war in whispers. The old man and boy had been released at intervals to relieve the pain of the cords, but not a word was said to them of our plans. When darkness again came we saddled our horses, stored a quantity of provisions in our blankets, strapped them behind our saddles and filled our canteens with water.

The Indian boy was then liberated and given these instructions:

"Creep along the banks of the creek until you come to the lone cottonwood tree, one and one-half miles distant, then fire six shots from a revolver. This will draw the Indians to you, when you can explain that we have compelled you to do this. If you fail to fire the shots we will kill the old man and charge through the Indian lines anyway."

This command was delivered to the boy in a manner calculated to impress him with the earnestness of the threat, although it was not our intention to harm Stephenson, and yet the muzzle of a Winchester close to his head caused him to earnestly implore the boy to faithfully do as he was told.

From then the minutes dragged like hours. We watched anxiously from our loop-holes for the flash from the young Indian's revolver. Twenty minutes passed, then thirty, and no shot was fired. Was he playing us false, or had he been captured by the Cheyenne, who in turn might set a trap for us. Thirty-six minutes passed, then a spark flashed in the distance and we counted six shots. This was the critical moment and every ear was listening for the sounds of horses' hoofs. A few moments later we heard them, as they came out of the ravines. We saw them, too, as they skirted along the dim sky line. We waited a few minutes to give them time to reach the cottonwood tree and then led our horses out and rode rapidly away to the northwest, knowing that the clatter of our horses' hoofs would mingle with those of the Indian ponies and might readily be taken for those of their own horsemen.

Our rifles were in our saddle holsters and our heavy revolvers were in our hands, as we rode in silence. Kinnie was in the lead, while Hayes and I rode behind side by side. Not a word was spoken for more than five hours, until day was breaking, and by the red glow of the eastern sky we saw away down the plains the camp fires and white tents of a troop of cavalry from Fort Morgan. Kinnie burst out into a long, hearty peal of laughter.

"What the deuce has struck you now?" asked Hayes.

"I forgot to give daddy any change back," he replied, as he held up a well-filled pocketbook.

7
A Cowboy Duel

Tom Rawlins rolled out of his blankets from under the chuck wagon with the remark, "I suppose a man shouldn't be late at his own funeral," and walking over to the camp-fire, lit his pipe by the glowing embers.

Day was breaking, and by a solemn compact entered into with "Kid" Anderson the night before, he would be dead at sunrise.

A month before they had exchanged shots in a dance house in Ogallala, after quarrelling about a woman. The two cowboys met in North Platte the day before, for the first time since the affair, and each swore the other should die.

Many of us who were friends of the two men divided into factions and crowded about the principals. The declaration of war having been made on both sides, neither could withdraw without losing caste, as such was the custom in the 70's among the wild fellows of the plains, who put a cheap estimate on human life. Rawlins had seen four years' service in the Confederate Army, and at the close of the war had followed General Joe Shelby into Mexico and fought under the banner of Maxmilian. When Bazaine withdrew the French troops he secured his discharge and returned to Texas wearing the honourable scars of battle. "Kid" Anderson was inured to the life on the plains from his youth and had been in many an ugly Indian fight.

Someone suggested a duel, and no Indian ever conceived a more fiendish plan. Two Colt revolvers with handles exactly alike, one loaded, the other unloaded, were placed under a blanket with handles protruding. A silver dollar was tossed into the air, heads to win, tails to lose. The winner was to have the choice of the revolvers. If he drew the loaded one, he had the right to shoot the loser, who was to stand ten paces away with the unloaded weapon in his hand. Rawlins won the choice of revolvers and drew the empty one.

Anderson then spent a month's wages buying drinks for the boys, and kindly gave Rawlins until sunrise the next morning to live. Rawlins accepted his fate with stoicism and returned to camp, rolled in his blankets and slept soundly. Inured to danger for years, he knew sooner or later the end would come, and so gave himself but little concern about it.

It was the spring round up and there were fifteen outfits in camp within two miles of North Platte, and the round up would begin as soon as two more outfits arrived.

The news of the plan and chance of fate by which Rawlins was to lose his life had spread from one camp-fire to another during the night, and created an intense excitement.

Rawlins was standing by the fire, when I. P. Olive, one of the largest owners on the range, rode up.

"Look here, Rawlins, suppose you had won, would you shoot Anderson down like a dog this morning?"

"Certainly I would," he replied, "and he would not be the first dog I have killed, either."

"This thing cannot go on," said Olive, decisively. "If you men have got to kill each other you must do it in a civilized fashion. Your plan is too cold-blooded; it has given the shivers to the entire camp." He then rode over to the "Double Bar" camp, where Anderson lay sleeping.

"Get up from there, you wild ass of the plains," he shouted. "Rawlins is waiting to be killed. Are you going to do it?"

Anderson was on his feet in an instant, facing Olive in the dim light of the camp-fire.

"It is none of your business what I intend to do!" and his yellow eyes gleamed dangerously as his hand stole to the handle of his six-shooter. Olive was a dangerous man himself and had a record of killing four men in Texas. He saw danger in the manner he had approached Anderson, and using a more conciliatory tone, said:

"Give Rawlins a show for his life and we will all think the more of you for it."

Finding the sentiment of others who joined in with Olive strong against him, Anderson yielded to a change. This time the principals were to meet upon the plain a mile from camp, mounted and armed with revolvers. They were to fight within a circle of one hundred yards, outside of which they might retreat, reload and return to the combat.

It was a beautiful morning, all balm and bloom and verdure. The face of the sky was placid and benignant. The sun rose like a great golden disc on the purple and pearl of the distant sky line and clouds, airy and gossamer, floated away to the west.

The men stole away from camp in twos and threes, and were gathering on a knoll that overlooked the battle ground, while Rawlins and Anderson were selecting their horses from the *remudas*. Rawlins chose a Texas mustang, fleet of foot and supple as an Arab. Anderson chose a stocky built animal and appeared altogether indifferent as to any of his qualities. The two men were stationed at the edge of the circle formed of lariats with their backs toward each other.

Olive gave the word, "Ready!" The men grasped their bridle reins tightly and settled themselves in their stirrups.

"Wheel!" The trained horses turned as if upon pivots.

"Fire!" rang out Olive's clear voice of command.

Anderson rode forward a few paces and stopped. Rawlins dug his spurs into his animal's side, and came on with a rush, firing his revolver as he came. Four shots sped harmlessly over the plain.

The men were within a few feet of each other when Anderson fired his first shot. Rawlins reeled in his saddle a second, grasped the pommel, and bringing down his revolver sent a bullet through the brain of Anderson.

Both men fell from their horses, and there were two dead faces in the grass.

The horses dashed wildly away, with blood upon their trappings and sleek hides.

Two graves were dug, and the funeral was over before the sun had dried the dew upon the grass.

There was a girl in Nebraska without a lover, and a widowed mother in Texas without a son.

8

Pleasant Halfacre's Revenge

I was with a party of cowboys twenty-five miles west of Ogallala, Nebraska, in 1878, when a huge iron box was found in the sands of the Platte River by one of our party, which recalled a tradition of tragedy and revenge, unequalled in the annals of the west.

In one of those great bends of the Ohio River, opposite Three Mile Island and below the town of Newburgh, in Southern Indiana, there lived some forty years ago, a man who furnished cause for which his neighbors with one accord, joined in deporting him.

Pleasant Halfacre occupied a cabin in a small clearing, which opened on the south, facing the bayou which separated the island from the mainland on the Indiana side. On all other sides for a mile or more was a dense forest, where great hickory, pecan and beech trees furnished the winter provender for the grey squirrels, raccoons and opossums. In some places the woodland was low and swampy; there were great ponds where the water lilies grew and in winter the wild duck and Brant paused long in their southern flight to feed. The bayou abounded in catfish and silvery perch.

In this little oasis in a desert of toilers, Halfacre had lived for nearly a quarter of a century. His wife, a big buxom woman, was the mother of eight tow-headed children who, when anyone chanced to come, acted like scared squirrels. They would scamper away into the woods and coyly peep at the stranger from behind big trees, while the dogs kept up an incessant barking.

In summer, the woman and children would cultivate the small clearing with hoes, while Plez would catch catfish and sometimes work in the harvest field a few days for some neighbour. This he did only when dire necessity compelled. The very sight of an agricultural implement, he declared, would make him sweat. The man loved nature and in his simplicity, would go into raptures over the colouring of the gorgeous sunset, or wade about the ponds for hours for water lilies, or the great blue, bell-shaped flowers which grew upon the wild flag and *calimus* stalks.

He would bedeck his ragged garments with these flowers and, with a string of catfish, would emerge, a gorgeous spectacle, from the forest on his way to the Evansville market.

In winter his children would gather pecans and hickory nuts, while he would take the dogs and hunt raccoons and opossums, the meat of which furnished the family food, while the pelts brought a small price at the market.

In all the forty years of his life, Halfacre had not been twenty miles away from his home. He could neither read nor write and the world to him ended at the blue rim of the northern horizon beyond the cypress hills. The man was totally devoid of any sense of responsibility, either to his Creator, his neighbors or himself. Once when the good preacher, who held services at the "Epworth meeting house" twice a month, reproved him for some misdemeanour by threatening him with the hereafter, he replied, "The devil can't inflict any more punishment on me than I can stand, if he does, he will kill me." With this logic to soothe his conscience, and his love of idleness thoroughly gratified, Halfacre was very well contented.

For a long time the neighbors, for many miles around, had been missing articles of small value, the loss of which caused much delay in their work as well as vexation and annoyance.

A farmer would be all ready to go to market and when he came to hitch up, he would find the coupling bolt to his wagon gone, or perhaps the singletree would be missing; or if ploughing in the field he would take the horses out to where he had left the plough the night before and find that the clevis or some bolts had been stolen. The good matrons would have their dinner horns or bells taken away at night. Nothing of any considerable value was stolen and no organised search was made until one day, Farmer Beasley was floating down the bayou in a dinky boat when he came upon one of Plez Halfacre's children sitting on the bank eating mush and milk out of the blue flowered shaving mug which old Tippecanoe Harrison had presented to his grandfather, while another one of the Halfacre children sat upon a log, making a paw-paw whistle with his ancestor's razor.

This was too much for Farmer Beasley. He turned the dinky boat around, paddled back to Newburgh and swore out a search warrant for the Halfacre cabin.

In the loft they found a collection of articles which was a wonder to behold. There were grindstones, iron wedges for splitting rails, harrow teeth and a miscellaneous lot of plunder, enough to start a second hand store.

The word was passed and the next day the farmers began to assemble. They came by the score; some in wagons bringing the entire family and their dinners, and the day was spent identifying stolen articles.

Meantime, while all this was going on Pleasant Halfacre sat to one side, looking the very picture of dejection. A council was held and it was decided that if they sent Plez to jail, the county would have to support his family, and as taxes were already high, it was decided to deport him, his family and chattels.

Nearby, a house boat was found, which the owner offered to sell for twenty dollars. It was purchased and Halfacre, his family and effects were placed aboard and warned never to return, whereupon the boat was shoved out into the stream.

It was a sad blow and one the least expected. "To leave the cabin and go away where he should never again see the water lilies, out into the world where he just didn't know nobody." This was the burden of his lamentations as he sat upon the bow of the boat and wept.

Some of the women cried softly when they saw such evidence of his grief and love of home, humble and poverty stricken as it was, and they rode home in silence, wishing to forget the scene of the grief stricken man, who had said the birds would never sing so sweetly to him again.

When the word went around a day or two later, that Plez and his family were again living in the cabin, there was a general sigh of relief, and when the preacher spoke of forgiving "Those who trespass against us," there were some heartfelt Amens that went up from the holy corner of the "Epworth Church."

Winter had come and the Halfacres were discussed by the good dames who gathered at each others homes at quilting parties, and many were the articles of outgrown clothing that were sent to the destitute cabin.

There was a January thaw and the ice in the river was breaking up, when one morning in the grey dawn a barge came drifting down the stream amid the cakes of ice that were piling high upon the head of the island. A man was standing upon the deck, frantically calling for help, for it was certain the barge would be crushed in the great pack of ice when it struck the head of the island.

A crowd had followed along the shore, but none seemed to know what to do or to have the courage to venture to the man's rescue.

Suddenly Plez Halfacre was seen to launch a skiff from among a clump of willows and standing on the bow, fought his way through the ice floes with an oar, rescued the man from his perilous position and landed safely below the head of the island.

The barge was lost and Plez became the hero of the hour.

The rescued man proved to be a wealthy coal mine owner from the neighbourhood of Cannelton, and in his gratitude some days later he presented Halfacre with a cheque for $5,000.

Again a pressure of the neighbourhood was brought to bear, and Halfacre emigrated to the west. He started alone with his family from Omaha in a prairie schooner, intending to settle in the neighbourhood of Denver. When twenty-five miles west of Ogallala he left his family in camp one afternoon and wandered some miles away over the plain in search of antelope.

When he returned some hours later he found his wife and children slain by the Indians and their mutilated bodies lying about the smouldering ruins of his wagon. The horses had been driven away.

Wild with grief and rage, he did the best he could in burying his dead, and then made his way back to Omaha. He met with much sympathy from the pioneers along the route, but for this he seemed to care but little. He went about in a gloomy, abstracted way that caused people to say he was losing his mind.

One day he appeared at a blacksmith shop in Omaha, and ordered a big wagon box made of plow steel, which he paid for in advance. When it was completed he loaded it upon a wagon and covered it with a white cover, until it looked like an ordinary prairie schooner. Into this he loaded a barrel for water and provisions enough to last for six months. He also stored in the iron box, a large quantity of ammunition, with two or three rifles and revolvers. The sides, bottom and top of the box were loopholed, protected with iron slides.

When all was ready he purchased horses and drove to the place near the Platte river, where his family had been slain. Here he picketed his horses and deliberately built a camp-fire. He did not have long to wait for results. The Indians saw the smoke, and seeing only one man, they swept down upon his camp. He waited until they were reasonably near and went inside his iron box. When they came to within a few yards, he opened fire from the loop-holes, killing a number of them before they retreated. The Indians could not make out the situation, and that night they crept through the grass and tried to kindle a fire beneath his wagon. Halfacre was alert, and shot them from the bottom loop holes. After two or three assaults, in which they lost many of their number, the Indians went away and ever afterwards avoided the place, as they believed it protected by evil spirits.

Halfacre lived in his wagon for more than a year, making incursions into the Indian camps at night, where his rifle dealt death.

To the Indians, he was an avenging spirit and they spoke of him in whispers. His remains were found some miles away, long afterwards by soldiers, who believed he had frozen to death in a blizzard. The rusted relic on the banks of the Platte River, slowly disappearing beneath the quicksands, was the only memento left of the tragedies there enacted.

9
Capturing Wild Horses

Lying upon the plain with his shoulder dislocated and his foot tangled up in a lariat, O. E. Kimsey held the head of his fallen horse close to the ground, in No Man's Land, for four hours, to prevent him from rising and dragging him to certain death.

We had gone to No Man's Land, now Beaver County, Oklahoma, in 1887, to capture wild mustangs, to be sold to the ranchmen of Kansas and Colorado. We had become separated in our search for them. Kimsey was far out on the plain when his horse stumbled into a coyote hole and as he fell beneath the horse his shoulder was dislocated. In a moment he realised that his foot was tangled in his lariat, which hung from the pommel of his saddle, with one end tightly fastened there. The horse attempted to rise, but to allow him to do so would mean being dragged to death.

Kimsey threw his uninjured arm over the horse's head and held him down. To call for help was useless in that barren and uninhabited plain, and he could do nothing else but hold the horse's head close to the ground. Night was coming on and he saw the hungry coyotes gathering. His strength was failing as the hours dragged by. He had almost lost all hope when he thought he heard the tramp of a horse's hoofs, and he shouted loud and long. He was right. I was in search of him and came to his rescue.

Our trip lasted five months, and in capturing the wild mustangs we followed a different plan from the Texas hunters. The latter pursued the horses night and day, using relays of mounts, until the horses were exhausted, when they were driven into a corral.

We had started early in the spring, in time to reach the wild horse country just as the first grass was covering the plains with green.

The mustangs were then gaunt and thin from the hardships of

winter and the new grass was not nutritious enough to strengthen them quickly.

A boy kept camp for us while Kimsey and I followed the horses. A spring wagon, under which we could sleep at night, was filled with provisions and grain. A dozen of the best saddle horses that could be found, that were selected for fleetness and endurance, were a part of the outfit. There was no hurrah and wild pursuit when the horses first came in sight. We rode toward them leisurely and took precautions to alarm them as little as possible. At first it was difficult to approach closer than three or four miles. Each band was led by a stallion that circled round and round. Sometimes there were three or four stallions with a band of twenty or thirty mares and their foals. Generally, however, each band consisted of five to a dozen mares and a stallion. The moment we appeared the horses would begin to move. If they were followed close they would break into a gallop, keeping on the ridges from which they could view the surrounding country.

I know of nothing more fascinating than a band of moving wild horses. Their manes and tails are quite long and add grace to their movements as they sweep along in the wind. At a distance a tenderfoot imagines a wild horse to be a majestic animal, large in size, beautiful in colour, clean of limb and fleet of foot. At close range they are a disappointment, especially in the spring when their coats are rough. They have great endurance, some of them being able to carry a man 70 miles between suns, and their recuperative power is wonderful.

We pursued the largest band we could find, but, use the best precaution we could, the horses would take fright at first and run for ten or twelve miles before stopping. We tried to keep in sight of them if possible, and always made it a point to be close to them at sundown, as they sought water, and if not disturbed would remain near the spot all night. If startled they would move, and before morning would be many miles away. They were on the move at the first streak of dawn. After we followed them two or three days the mustangs grew less wary, and we began teaching them to drive.

A characteristic of the wild horse is that if an attempt is made to ride to the right of them, for the purpose of turning them to the left, they will invariably bolt to the right, and run directly across the path of their pursuers.

It requires much time and patience to teach them to run in the opposite direction. We won our first point when we taught the horses to be driven. We then began driving them in a circle, which at first had a large circumference. As the horses grew weaker from want of rest and food, the circle grew smaller until its diameter did not exceed a quarter of a mile. Meantime, we were using relays of fresh horses. Then they were taught another lesson. A long lariat was stretched on the ground, and in the path of the horses. Wild mustangs are very sagacious and quick to suspect a trap. The rope always frightened them greatly at first, but in time they grew accustomed to it, and could be driven across it. We were now ready for business. The lariat was strongly anchored in the ground by tying it to a buried log. The best horses were now brought out and saddled. Riding as swiftly as possible, we started the wild horses moving in a circle and kept after them until our own horses were exhausted. The boy then took our place and maintained the swift pace, while we saddled fresh horses. Before a great while a colt would give out and drift, toward the centre of the circle where it would be joined by its mother.

A band of wild horses will not desert one another and there was no longer any fear that the running horses would bolt from the circle in which they were moving. In the free end of the lariat a big running noose had been tied. As the circle grew smaller the horses would begin running over the noose. The boy kept close watch and gave a strong pull on the lariat when he saw that a horse had stepped into the noose. The horse would fall, snared by the foot. A heavy log chain about three feet long was fastened to one of its forelegs with a leather and the horse turned loose. The animal would spring to its feet and start away at a breakneck speed, only to turn a somersault, caught by the swinging chain encircling its forelegs.

When half a dozen horses had been caught in this manner the others would begin shying away from the noose, which was then abandoned for the time being. Then we would coil our lariats and ride straight into the midst of the band and rope them until the band was scattered.

The captured horses were then rounded up, and the lesson of teaching the others to pass over the rope was resumed. After a time, when their fear had abated, they would again pass over the rope without hesitancy. In this manner we caught one hundred and nine the first season. The work grew more difficult as the summer advanced; the grass was better, giving greater strength to the wild mustangs, while our own had become worn and thin with hard service. The captured horses soon became accustomed to being driven and herded and it was not difficult to move them across the plains to Kansas and Colorado, where they were sold. Kimsey usually selected the best ones and broke them to the saddle, an exciting and dangerous business.

Wild horses gave much trouble to ranchmen in those days. Tame horses are quick to follow wild ones away, but a wild horse never voluntarily forsakes the freedom of the plains for the corn fodder of the corral. The wild stallions are constantly seeking to increase their harem of mares. On the plains they do it through their ability as fighters and their superior generalship over weaker stallions. They resort to extreme violence in adding tame mares to their bands. I have seen a wild stallion gallop up to a herd of domestic horses, select a mare, and then begin manoeuvring to drive her away. Sometimes the mare is lying down and refuses to get up. The stallion throws back his ears and breaks for her at full speed.

If she does not move he seizes her with his teeth and bites her so violently that she is glad to spring to her feet. Once moving, she is lost, as the stallion keeps close behind, biting and pawing at her until she is driven into his band, when all of them gallop away. In time they drive away many horses, and in the old days ranchmen often united and killed wild stallions as they killed wolves. The stallions are constantly fighting among themselves, but as a rule without great injury to each other. Domestic stallions fight to the death, but the wild ones seem to know when they are worsted and the weaker ones run away. There were usually about as many wild stallions as mares, and as each successful stallion had from six to a dozen mares, there were necessarily a number of stallions who were freebooters on the plains. These were mostly old stallions, grown weak with age, and young ones not old enough to win their fights. I have seen as many as seventy-five such stallions in a band.

It was November when Kimsey and I sat in the Albany Hotel in Denver and divided almost $3,000 as the profits of our season's work.

"Where to now, Kimsey?" I asked.

"I go to San Antonio for the winter; and you?"

"To the C. C. Ranch, on the Cimarron," I replied.

10

An Expedition That Failed

Five men sat about a table in an upper room of the Coates House in Kansas City. The names of several of them I omit, as they will sleep easier. Upon the table was a plate of shining gold nuggets of a value of $1,600. Charley Cole, the owner, was a miner from the northwest.

He had met the party the day before, and offered to show them where the nuggets came from for $2,000, saying his reason for so doing was that he wanted to clean up and go to the Transvaal, then the Mecca of the gold-seeker.

This incident was in June, 188—.

Around that table a party was organised, but with the understanding that no money should be paid until the gold was found to our satisfaction, and with the further understanding that if Cole was deceiving us with the idea of leading us into a bandit trap to secure our money, he should be the first man shot.

To this he agreed and the next day the party was increased to six by a young doctor. Ten days later we were in Rawlins, Wyoming, where horses and a general outfit were purchased and the journey to the Wind River country in the Shoshone Indian reservation was begun.

July had come and the plains and valleys were beautiful in billowy green. Cole, always in the lead, headed west of Lander. There was nothing I could see about the man to indicate that he was other than he represented, although several of the party whispered suspicions as, day by day, we penetrated the wild and almost uninhabited country.

We entered the reservation at a point about thirty miles west of Lander, which town we had purposely avoided, not wishing to incite others to a gold hunt.

We broke camp and were riding down a beautiful valley one morning, when we came upon some antelope. I wounded one, and as it was getting away I spurred my horse after the antelope on the run. My horse stumbled into a badger hole, and the next thing I remember distinctly was the awful pain as the doctor of our party was setting my broken ankle.

My horse was also lame, but later in the day I made out to ride him five miles to the camp of some Shoshone Indians.

The pain in my limb was so great I could go no further, and as the Indians were friendly and hospitable, I begged to be left in their camp. A bed was made for me upon the ground in one of the *tepees*, and after giving me surgical attention, and leaving me such comforts as we carried, the party proceeded, at my request, for I knew it would be weeks before I could travel, and even then I would be a hindrance.

I felt secure from the kindly attention I had received from the Indians, who seemed desirous in many ways of alleviating my sufferings. Knowing that the Indian despises any manifestation of pain, I managed never to utter a groan, or show distress in my face, no matter how excruciating was Nature's process of healing.

After three or four days an Indian cut away the doctor's splints and bound my limb in a huge pack of wet clay. From that moment the pain grew less, and as I felt more like talking, the Indians would gather in the *tepee* and sit about like children. I made pictures to amuse them, taught them the game of mumbledy-peg, and in various ways won their simple affections.

The days had been dragging wearily, when the monotony was broken by an Indian wedding. Bright Eyes, a damsel of no exceeding beauty, was of that age when the consent of her father could be secured for her marriage for a consideration of ponies.

Several young bucks had been staking their ropes for the catch, each hoping he would be the fortunate one in securing her for a partner. Some of them had offered as high as nine ponies. But Wahne-a-tah, which means in English, "it is hurting him," came forward with a dozen ponies and secured the prize. A beef from the Agency had been secured and roasted, as well as other things good to the palate of a hungry Indian. At about 4 o'clock the bride was taken to a *tepee* set apart from the others, where some twenty squaw attendants dressed her out in a "rig" that for decoration resembled a general or an admiral's uniform.

Not wishing to get married at this time, she kept her attendants in tears by her lamentations. Someone in Lander had sold her father an old hearse as being just the thing for a family carriage. The top had been taken off, but the plumes remained, and into it she was loaded. The horses were gaily decorated and an Indian walked at the head of each horse. As she took her seat in the carriage, I obtained the first good view of the bride. A description of her dress is impossible, but it was a curious mixture of every colour imaginable. She had proceeded but a little way down the valley, when at breakneck speed came a buck and three squaws who were running to the bride.

The first squaw to reach the bride was to receive her raiment, the second a pony and the third a blanket. The bride was escorted to a *tepee* belonging to a relative of the groom. Here she was placed on a blanket and wrapped up until no part of her was visible and then carried to the *tepee* set apart for the happy couple. Arriving there she was unwrapped in the presence of the guests and her clothing immediately claimed by the squaw who came out best in the race. The bride was re-dressed, the groom summoned and seated on the blanket beside her. They were now married in the eyes of the Indians. Then came a feast, participated in only by the happy couple and the guests departed to the general feast.

Three weeks had passed when one day an officer of the Indian police came to our camp and through him I learned of Cole's former camp on a tributary of Wind River, and he said the gulches and sands of the stream were plentifully besprinkled with nuggets, that the reason white men were not there in multitudes was they were kept away by the Indian police.

He said that Cole was permitted to stay because he furnished the Indians with whisky. This Cole doubtless made from drugs.

At the end of another week my party returned without Cole. They came hastily and seemed in a hurry to get away. I asked if they found gold. They replied, "Yes, plenty of it, but Cole's treachery has defeated every plan." Beyond this they would say nothing.

As I was in no condition to accompany them and was as comfortable as circumstances would permit, they left me in the Indian camp. Here I remained for a month longer, when Red Jacket and Spotted Horse rode with me to Rawlins. Two truer hearts I never expect to find among any race. I had our photographs taken and made them presents, as well as sending a flour sack of candies back to the camp. When our train rolled away they stood on the platform and watched us out of sight.

The mystery of the fate of Cole was cleared some years later when I called on one of the parties in Kansas City. It seems they reached

Cole's cabin in the wilds of the Wind River country and that he showed them fine placer mines, and that after a few days he produced a vile decoction of whisky which he and a younger member of the party drank. A quarrel between the two men, crazed with the drink, ensued, in which Cole was killed.

11

Across the Palm Desert

An ancient fight—as ancient as the time dividing the bird from the serpent, a fight thousands of times repeated in the lonely places of the earth each year, but which man seldom sees, was witnessed by Mark Witherspoon and myself on the borders of the Palm Desert in California, where we had come in the search for gold. It was a struggle to the finish between an eagle and a big rattlesnake. Death was the referee, as he is in all the contests waged under nature's code of fang and claw.

There are two things men may not know, so it is said: "*The way of the serpent upon the rock; the eagle soaring in the sky.*" Each has a wonderful power which man does not understand—does not understand any more than he does why they always fight when they meet and that they always should and will, so long as there are serpents upon the rocks and eagles soaring in the sky. If there were no eagles, the rattlesnakes would have no enemy in the sky or upon the earth, save man, to fear. The eagle likewise has no fear of anything, unless it be the glistening yellow and brown poisonous creature of the rocks—the rattler.

Thus it lives forever—the death feud of the eagle of the Montezumas and the serpent father of the Moki's—the rattler.

How it began I did not see. I was standing near the top of a big stony crag that glistened in the bright light looking over the vast opens and great basins of the Palm Desert which we were to cross, when my attention was attracted by the flop of something striking the sands a hundred feet away. I could not see what it was, but a moment later I saw an eagle swoop down and rise slowly, holding within its mailed claws, a snake. The big bird soared up a hundred feet or more and shook the snake loose, which fell twisting and coiling with a distinctly

Truer Hearts I Never Expect to Find

audible "flop"—the noise that first attracted my attention. Again and again the bird swooped, arose with the serpent and dropped it, while Witherspoon drew closer and closer to watch.

Then the eagle—a young one, as we could tell by its size and plumage—struck and failed to rise. Witherspoon was now close enough to see everything that happened.

The young bird had almost exhausted itself in its struggles with the snake, and may, too, have been bitten by it. At any rate, it was upon the sands, its wings slightly spread, as if from the heat—its mouth open. The snake was recovering from its jolting fall, and slowly gathering its coils.

It rested a moment in position, and then struck the eagle, the fangs entering the corner of the bird's mouth, in the soft tissues at the base of the beak.

The eagle recovered from the shock, stood motionless a few seconds, while the rattler watched as only a rattler can, and spreading out its wings, toppled over.

Then the man—man who hates serpents as the eagle does—put forth his hand, using a power more wonderful than that of either. There was a puff of white smoke in the clear air and the report of a pistol rang among the glistening wind-polished rocks, and the snake was a mangled, bright, still thing that the ants began to gather about.

"It was unjust maybe," remarked Witherspoon. "The snake had won fairly—he was entitled to go his way, a terror for all the furry little bright things hereabouts." "But I couldn't help it." "Someway that slaying by poison, even if it is done in the open, doesn't seem fair." "Then, too, a man hates to see the emblem of his country's armies and navies, the triumphant eagle of thunderbolts, lying in the sunshine dead, and that by a serpent."

We had purchased a mustang in San Luis Obispo and loaded him with our stock of flour, bacon, frying pans, blankets, etc., and was resting on the borders of the Palm Desert, which we intended to cross the next morning, to the Mexican dry diggings, in the foothills of the Sierra Nevada Mountains, when the battle between the eagle and rattler furnished the topic of conversation all the afternoon. From San Luis Obispo we had taken the trail that led over the mountains and through the beautiful Santa Margarita Valley. Of all the places I have ever seen, I think this valley came the nearest to being an earthly paradise. It is seven miles in length, five in breadth, and is walled on all sides, except a narrow pass, by the lofty Santa Lucia Mountains. Through the centre of the valley flows the headwaters of the Salanis River. Giant live oak trees studded the valley at almost regular intervals, as if they had been planted by the hand of man.

The earth was a carpet of green verdure, with splashes of the yellow wild mustard and varied hues of the many different semi-tropical flowers. Two days after passing through this Eden, we began our toilsome march across an arm of the Palm Desert. When we reached the diggings we found a group of motley Mexicans, who good naturedly swarmed about us and showed us a camping place near a spring, but its waters were so impregnated with sulphates of magnesia and sodium, that we found it impossible to use it. We moved our camp about a mile further up the canyon, near the quarters of a sheep herder, where we found good water and were free from the Mexicans. They taught us, however, the art of dry washing the gold from the loose earth of the placer claim which we had staked off. Here, for more than three months, we toiled. When our supplies run short, we sent for more by the man who came once a week to bring provisions and look after his interests on the sheep ranch. I always pitied that sheep herder. He had several hundred to care for, and their continual bleating sounded dismally in the solitude of the mountains, and when he lighted his bivouac fire at night, it always seemed like a signal of distress.

From the red earth we gathered the golden grains, and when the stars came out at night, and the mountains took on their shadowy gloom, we talked of home two thousand miles away, and often wondered at the enigma of creation. Then came a time when by exposure to the damp and dews, and living upon poor food, we both began to fall sick. Medicine was out of the question, and so with our precious packet of gold dust upon our persons, we loaded our mustang with our camp equipments and took up our march toward San Luis Obispo.

It was in the early dawn of the morning when we started across the arm of the Palm Desert. The sun rose like a ball of fire in a cloudless sky and heated the sands until they parched and blistered our faces. By noon our water supply was exhausted, and soon after I threw away the Winchester which I carried, for I could no longer bear the burden. If it has not been found by some weary pilgrim it lies there today with its barrel as bright in that rainless valley as it was when I threw it down.

We walked in silence all that torrid afternoon. The poor mustang crept along, led by Mark, while we, with bloodshot eyes and fevered brains, could but feebly keep in sight the jutting mountain spur where we would find a haven of rest.

Exhausted, I sat down in the scant shade of a desert palm. Its sparse branches rattled in the hot wind like dried sunflower stalks, and then, in my imagination, I stood a few feet away and saw myself lying dead on the sands, with face drawn and withered and dead eyes staring at the skies.

I roused myself from the horrible dream and walked on. It was long after the sun had dipped beyond the mountain crest, and the Palm Desert was shrouded in the gloom of night, that we reached a pool of clear water, fed by a generous spring. We drank of its waters and bathed our fevered brows, and lay down in the warm sands to awake ever and anon in fitful dreams. It seemed I was buried in the stone coffins of Egypt, where I lay for a thousand years in torrid heat, with unquenchable thirst. Whenever I awoke, I drew myself to the edge of the pool, drank deeply of its refreshing waters, and fell asleep again, repeating the same thing perhaps twenty times during the night.

How soon we forget our troubles, and oh, how soon we forget that we have passed through the valley of the shadow, and that a merciful God has watched over our destinies. Within a week after this, when Mark and I came so near perishing on the Palm Desert, we had purchased new summer clothes and were sitting about the best hotel in San Luis Obispo, smoking fine cigars and playing the part of high-toned young gentlemen generally.

12

The Last Stand of a Dying Race

The Battle of Wounded Knee, South Dakota, occurred December 29, 1890. It was the last stand of a dying race, the last Indian battle fought on the soil of the United States.

Whatever views I may have held at the time, and whatever part I may have taken in the engagement is mitigated by previous experiences and circumstances; but with time there comes a belief that somebody grievously erred.

Nearly every nation in its decline has looked for the coming of a Redeemer to lead them back to the glory and valour of former days. This has been especially true of the Indian races. The few remaining Aztec tribes yet look for the coming of Montezuma, while the Indians in the mountains of Peru believe that Huascar will again appear and re-establish the magnificent empire of which the mailed heels of a conquering Pizarro host clanked the dying knell nearly four centuries ago.

In the autumn of 1890 there appeared in an Indian village in Nevada a man who was strange to them and to the neighbouring tribes. He told them a wondrous story. He had come from a far-off land beyond the setting sun, and was sent by the Great Spirit to rescue the redmen from the oppression of the paleface, to restore to them their hunting grounds and to populate the plains once more with the buffalo and the antelope. He taught them a new form of the death dance and made a garment, decorated it with hieroglyphics and blessed it, and said that it would turn the bullets of the white man. They received his tale with great rejoicing and started immediately to carry the tidings to the tribes on the plains to the east. Great enthusiasm among the Indians marked the progress of the march across the country, and when he reached the Rosebud Agency in South Dakota, so exag-

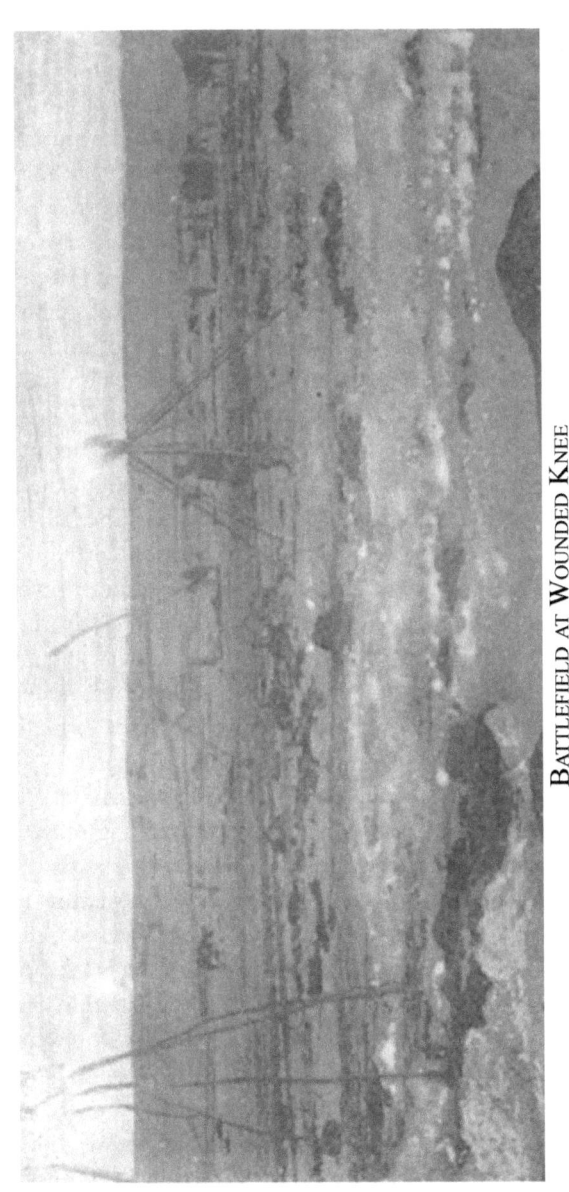

Battlefield at Wounded Knee

gerated were the wondrous stories that preceded him, he was fairly worshipped as a deity. Chiefs Red Cloud, Crow Dog and Two Strikes brought him before the Great Council at Pine Ridge Agency, some fifty miles distant from Rosebud.

For more than three months after his arrival thousands of the Sioux warriors kept up the ghost dance almost nightly. The quantities of unbleached domestic that they were purchasing at the agency stores and making up into "ghost shirts," together with the ammunition they were known to be hoarding convinced the agency authorities at Pine Ridge that an outbreak was imminent. A call was made for United States troops, but before any considerable number arrived hostilities had begun. A cattle herder was killed and a large herd of cattle belonging to the government was driven into the bad-lands. The same night Chief Red Cloud, who had become almost blind in his extreme old age, was taken forcibly from his home near the Pine Ridge agency building and made to lead the hostile attack on the Jesuit Mission some four miles distant. A desultory firing was kept up on the agency for some nights afterward, when a reinforcement of troops arrived and the hostiles withdrew to the natural fortresses of the bad-lands.

Chief American Horse appears to have doubted the divine origin of the Indian Messiah, and held in check some six or seven thousand of his people encamped on a creek near the agency. In the meantime General Miles arrived with a strong force of cavalry and artillery. Batteries were trained on the *tepees* of the Brule Sioux under American Horse, and they were ordered not to congregate, which order was respected up to the close of the campaign.

Rumours of Indian depredations were of every day occurrence. Settlers were fleeing from their homes and seeking refuge in the villages. So great was the terror in northwestern Nebraska that General John M. Thayer, then governor, ordered out the entire force of the National Guard, numbering about two thousand men, under Brigadier General Leonard W. Colby, to protect the Nebraska frontier.

The main body of hostiles was safely entrenched in the bad-lands and was only awaiting the springtime, when grass would furnish provender for their ponies; when they intended to begin their work of destruction on the white settlements.

Up to this time no Indian had been killed or wounded, although there was some heavy firing done in defence of the mission and the agency. This fact tended to strengthen their belief in the invulnerability of the ghost shirt which, by this time, was worn by all the warriors.

So great was their faith in the efficacy of this garment to turn the bullets of their white foe, that Big Foot and a band of about four hundred ventured to leave the stronghold and commit some petty depredations within thirty miles of Pine Ridge.

General Miles promptly dispatched Colonel Forsythe and a troop of two companies of the Seventh Cavalry to subdue them. It will be remembered that the Seventh was General Custer's old regiment that met the Indians on the Little Big Horn on that memorable 25th of June, 1876, when every man taking part in the engagement was massacred by this *same tribe of Sioux Indians* which this detachment under Colonel Forsythe was seeking. On the evening of the twenty-eighth of December, Colonel Forsythe came upon Big Foot's band. No resistance was offered at the time, although the demeanour of the braves foreboded the terrible tragedy soon to follow. The Indians were escorted some miles distant and ordered to go into camp on the banks of Wounded Knee Creek, which flows through a wide, open valley skirted for miles on either side by high, sandy bluffs and scant growth of fir, cedar and pine.

The Indians were made to pitch their *tepees* in a semi-circle and park their wagons and ponies behind them. The soldiers formed in a triangle in front of the semi-circle with a Hotchkiss gun under command of Sergeant Wingate in the centre of the triangle. The men stood by their guns throughout the bitter cold of the Dakota night, while the Indians were comfortably wrapped in their blankets within the shelter of the *tepees*. As the first rays of the sun were slanting across the bleak and cheerless plain, the shrill notes of a bugle rang out on the frosty air. It was the signal to arouse the Indian camp. They came from their *tepees* with blankets swathed about them, and desperation was stamped upon their faces. Big Foot, who was ill with pneumonia, was first carried out and laid upon a bed of fur in front of his *tepee*, and then two hundred and fifty braves seated themselves in rows about him.

Through an interpreter they were ordered by Captain Wallace to lay down their arms. They were armed mostly with Winchesters which were concealed beneath the blankets about them. Suddenly the medicine man of the tribe sprang to his feet and threw a handful of dirt into the air. It was a signal, and in another instant the deathlike shrieks—the Sioux war-cry, "*Hi-yi-hip-yi!*" echoed up and down the valley, and the blaze of two hundred Winchesters sent their deadly missiles into the faces of the soldiers not over thirty feet away. There was an instant of hush—then a crash of musketry, and the last Sioux Indian battle was on! There were wavering ranks of blue as men fell to the ground wounded or dying; frantic horses dashed riderless over the plain; forms in red blankets were running hither and thither as the deadly triangle poured a withering crossfire into the struggling mass about the *tepees*. There were swift retreats of small parties, followed by swifter pursuit of horsemen.

Indians were shot right and left as the mellow cadence of the bugle said, "Fire at will." Squaws were dashing right and left, attempting to stab the soldiers with their long, copper-handled scalping knives; boys kneeled on the ground and coolly fired rifles at the soldiers. They, too, were shot, and meanwhile the terrible Hotchkiss gun boomed death. Small fleeing parties gained the sand bluffs and shot the pursuing soldiers. A wagon, drawn by two ponies and loaded with bucks and squaws who were trying to get away, was struck by a six-inch shell and literally blown to pieces. Brave Captain Wallace was killed with a blow from a stone battle-axe as he was entering a *tepee*.

The field of carnage is a dreadful sight. The mind shrinks from contemplating it. Human life has there passed away. Agony and suffering is everywhere. Gloom is on men's faces and dark frowns on their brows. One wishes it were effaced from memory, for in years to come one must see in fancy and hear again in fitful slumber the dying shrieks and piteous cries of agony.

That evening the sun set behind a bank of crimson clouds. Sickening odours came from the smouldering *tepees*. Stark faces, stiffening in death, were turned to the skies. There, too, were the wounded with the dew of death already upon their brows. Strong lines were drawn upon the faces of the dead that told of the awful desperation of the soul at the moment they fell. Weapons were clutched in pulseless hands, and piteous was the sight of the struggling, wounded horses in their vain attempt to join their mates in the wild chase among the hills. Amid these scenes could be heard the prattle of childish voices about the Indian *tepees*. In the tenderness of their years and the savagery of their nature they were unable to comprehend the awfulness of the hour.

When darkness came over the scene like a pall, the booming gun had ceased, but the plains were aglow with the lurid fires in the high grass—a weird and fantastic scene. Two hours later and the crimson clouds, which at sunset had portended evil, burst into fury, and a blizzard, with icy winds and drifting snows, raged as if to aid the soldiers in their determination that no living thing should survive the day.

When, four days later, the winds had spent their fury, and General Colby was riding over the field with his party, a cry was heard from a snow-bank that covered the dead bodies of some squaws. A soldier dismounted and found an Indian *papoose* tied to its dead mother's back, and clasped in the child's arms was a soiled, little rag doll which the baby fought to retain. General Colby immediately had the little waif cared for and afterwards adopted her. The Indians named her "Ziutka Lanuni," which in the white man's tongue means "Lost Bird." She is now, (at time of first publication), living at the home of Mrs. L. W. Colby in Washington, D. C., a beautiful Indian girl, well educated, speaking the tongue of the white man, for she never had the opportunity to learn the language of her people.

A few days after the battle the great Sioux chief, Sitting Bull, was slain by the Indian police. The news of the battle spread among the hostile Indians. They learned that the much prized ghost shirt was no protection against the white man's bullets, and the closing scene of this drama occurred some weeks later when the hills about Pine Ridge agency fairly swarmed with returning hostiles.

No conquered general in the history of the world ever met the conqueror with haughtier mien than did Two Strikes, the untutored savage, chief of the hostile band, when he made his formal surrender to General Miles. Followed by half a dozen lesser chiefs, he strode majestically toward the agency school building in front of which stood General Miles and *aides* waiting to receive him. His magnificent form was erect, his head, proudly decked with the eagle feather, was thrown slightly back, while every muscle of his face was as tense as steel. His warrior robes were draped about his shoulders, while his arms were folded across a carbine upon his breast. With measured tread he approached and halted in front of General Miles and met the mild blue eye of that warrior with black, piercing eyes that fairly blazed fire.

Steadily the two men gazed at each other for more than a minute. The muscles of the Indian's face twitched and the proud lips essayed to speak—as though he would hurl a torrent of defiance and hatred into the conqueror's face. With one swift movement he laid the carbine at the general's feet, stood erect another instant gazing with defiant eyes—and strode away to join his people.

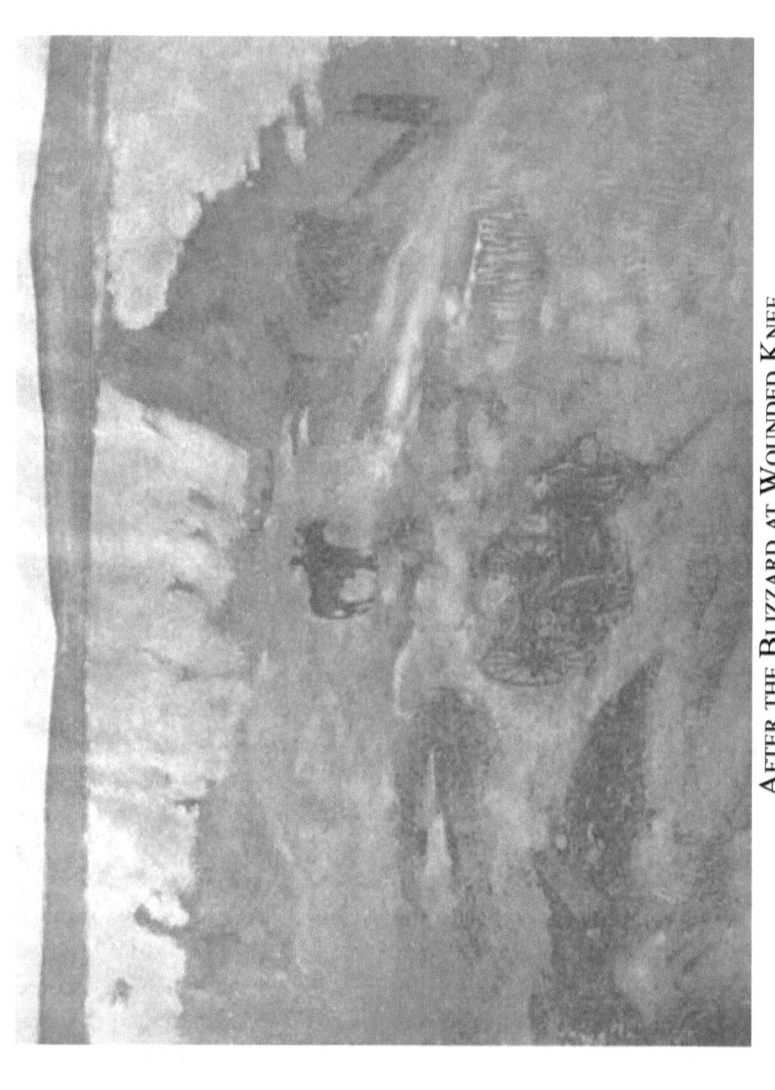

After the Blizzard at Wounded Knee

13

The Tragedy of the Lost Mine

In 1879, Capt. Charles Watt and Irwin Baker built a cabin in a gulch some miles distant from where Cripple Creek now stands. Baker had in his possession samples of very rich gold-bearing ore which he claimed to have brought from Arizona, where he and a Mexican had been driven out by Indians, as their reservation at that time extended over that region of country. The Mexican afterwards died of wounds received in the fight, and Baker was the sole possessor of the secret of the mine. He would sit for hours and tell how they had dug the white quartz which was threaded and beaded with strings of gold, and hoarded vast quantities of it under a great shelving rock which bore evidence of having at one time been the home of the Cliff Dwellers. And how he had carefully made a map of the country and intended when the Indian troubles were over to hire a sufficient force of men and burros to go there and bring away enough of the treasure to fix him in comfortable circumstances for the rest of his life. He often spoke of the map which he kept carefully concealed among his effects, which consisted of a valise and some mining tools.

In the fall of 1879 Baker concluded to make a trip to Leadville, which was then in the height of prosperity, and taking his rifle, blankets, and a few days' rations, set out on foot. He reached Leadville safely, and a few days later died of pneumonia. As no one claimed the few chattels, including the valise, which Baker left behind, Captain Watt as a matter of course took them. He searched everywhere for the map by which Baker set so much store, and not finding it, concluded it was concealed about his clothing and had been doubtless buried with him. And so years passed on, but the straight story the man had so often told around the cabin fire in the silence of night, was never forgotten by Watt, who, in the lonely hours among the towering peaks of the Rocky Mountains, had thought of it a thousand times.

But one day, the hand of Fate and Chance took a part.

Captain Watt needed a strip of leather. There was none to be found. Finally, his eye rested upon the old valise which had once been the property of Irwin Baker, which had tumbled about prospectors' cabins for the last ten years. It was worn out, but the sides would make the strip of leather the captain wanted. The first slash of his knife revealed between the outside and the lining a folded sheet of paper, yellowed with age, and a closer examination proved it to be the carefully prepared map which Irwin Baker had concealed ten years before. The lines were drawn with the skill of a civil engineer, and the places so plainly marked that a party instantly formed, believed they would have no difficulty in going straight to the lost mine.

Three others, myself and Captain Baker staked our time and money on the venture, and another month found us in the country called Coconino in Arizona through which the Colorado River crosses with many a curve and twist. It lies in the northern part of the great Colorado plateau and west of the Moqui country.

John Bowden, a young civil engineer, was one of our party. He had studied at Ann Arbor and also at the University of Minnesota. His field work covered about five years prior to joining us. He was not familiar with the Southwest, its climate and peculiar topography, but others of the party were, and in view of his knowledge of civil engineering he was considered a valuable man to us.

The sun shines in Coconino. It hangs day after day above Lava Butte, the Painted Desert, Shinumo Altar, and the Black Falls, as if it were a destroying angel, not the kindly orb that flashes in the northern belt, but a consuming, terrifying demon of the desert wastes from which there is no escape. Those who toil in the city's ways think the sun is hot, that the humidity is deadly, that pain such as theirs is unknown. They have never looked up to the solar star from the buttes of Coconino. There, blazing through the century-dried air all that is inhuman in stellar heat feeds upon the brain, the senses of man, until he staggers over the sands and falls to death.

Our party had made its way north of Mesa Butte, carrying provisions and water, making slow progress, enduring extraordinary discomforts. It was after we had camped at the Little Colorado on the south bank, that Bowden and I, acting upon the advice of Captain Watt, made some advance explorations to determine how best we should approach Lava Butte, which, according to Baker's map, was the key to the route to the lost mine.

We left one morning before sunrise and headed due north for the Painted Desert. We carried with our horses a two days' supply of water and provisions. It was impossible after ten o'clock in the morning to advance farther in the heat. We camped in the swale of a dry *arroya*, making such shade as we could, and waited for the coming of the late afternoon, when we might press on a little more. Bowden attempted some observations, but found that his sight was affected and that he must rest. In the evening and before we halted for the night, Lava Butte was in sight. After supper, Bowden said he would walk a distance under the stars; and that he would return to the camp within an hour.

He had not returned by midnight, and I dared not leave the horses and search for him, but I fired my rifle as a signal at short intervals throughout the night. The next day I tried to find him, firing my rifle now and then, until I had burned the last cartridge, and then I made a fire of dried cactus stalks, in hopes that the smoke would attract his attention, but all this failed. The water supply began to run short, the horses were suffering, and Bowden did not appear. I then headed back for camp on the Little Colorado, intending to follow our trail in the sands, but the hot winds had swept over the desert and obliterated most of them. I had depended upon Bowden's qualities as an engineer and had not taken as close an observation as I would otherwise. However, I remembered my experience in the Palm Desert of years before, and so urged my horse along through the torrid heat, always heading for a jutting butte where I thought our camp to be. At noon my horse died, and I lay in the shade of some rocks, giving myself up for lost, when, as the sun was going down and the shadows were creeping over the desert, I descried the relief party from our camp that was searching for us.

Bowden's body was found five miles from the camp he and I had made. He had walked in the night through the dead land, where, in starlight or sunlight, all things look alike. But there is so much white and so much grey, that to distinguish one object from another, to remember it, to say, "I will come back to this," is not possible. So when Bowden started to retrace his steps, he did not know where he was. The plain was all north, south, east and west.

He quite evidently had sat down and tried to collect his thoughts, for there were marks in the waste indicating the various positions he had taken. He had a small bottle of water with him, but no food.

No sound swept the plain. Bowden may have thought he was entombed in some vast charnel-house of the ages to which Time had brought Nature's remains and left them without burial. He was on the crest of one-time vast lava beds, a spot where fearful fires once raged beneath his feet. Here the last great battle of the peaks of the continent had probably been fought with thunderbolt and flame hurled from the bowels of the earth. And he was alone. Not even the wretched lizards of the lava region were moving. He called. No voice answered. He walked, but it was in a circle, and he came back time and time again to his starting point. He waited for the dawn—one hope that the sun's light might give him a trace of the camp. He saw the shade of the night grow deeper and deeper, and then the driving of this blackness back from the east and the coming there of a cold line of grey and then an insolent one of red and a savage yellow with that, and then, with one leap, the sun.

He must have scanned the plain, but there was no sight of camp. He called, he laughed, he cried. He drank his water to the last drop in the little bottle. He walked and ran. He returned to the spot where he had first become bewildered. He was hot and then cold, and the sun rose higher and higher; grew more pitiless with every advance. The white heat beat down on him; it rose in sheets before him. Now the lizards and the mean, creeping things came out, but they passed him by. They could wait. Others had preceded him. After a long time, Bowden threw his hands high in the air, far up to the sun god that was calling to him, although beating him down. He fell flat on his face, and there he slept his last sleep in the land where the sun shines forever and forever.

A week later and Captain Watt died of gastritis, and our party returned to Flagstaff and abandoned the search for the lost mine.

14

The Land of the Fair God

Captain David L. Payne was a born frontiersman. He left his home in Grant County, Indiana, in 1856, at the age of 20 years. He started west to fight the Mormons, and got as far as Doniphan County, Kansas. Here he found plenty of excitement and joined the Free Soil party. Five years later, when the border was aflame with fire and steel, he was among the first to enlist in the Union army. He served with distinction throughout the war. In 1865 he was honourably discharged at Ft. Leavenworth, with the rank of major. After this he went to Pueblo de Taos, New Mexico, and joined a party under Kit Carson, in an expedition against the Apaches. And after this he was known as the "Cimarron Scout."

I first met him in the Black Hills in 1876. He was then talking of Oklahoma, called by the Indians The Land of the Fair God. He claimed that the government had no title to the land. The next I noticed of him was in 1880, when he organised a band of raiders to invade Oklahoma and open it for settlement. His first company was thirteen strong. They went as far south as Fort Russell, on the Cimarron, leaving Arkansas City, April 30. They were captured and taken out by United States soldiers. But the brave pioneer was not to be daunted. His followers increased and they hovered upon the banks of the Arkansas River, awaiting the action of a dilatory congress at Washington until the country was thrown open to settlement, April 22, 1889.

Payne was like many other pioneers. He saw the land of promise, but dared not enter therein and live. Fate reserved this boon for others, while death decreed the brave soul should explore another bourne than this. While sitting at a breakfast table in Wellington, Kansas, December, 1884, he suddenly expired. Others may have felt as much interest in the opening of Oklahoma as Payne, but certainly none others devoted so much time and energy to the accomplishment of this work as he. He began the movement at a time when it was very unpopular, hence was the object of much unfavourable criticism and abuse, but he did not allow this to daunt him, and continued to surround himself with a class of followers who had the nerve to stand for the right.

On the opening day the people came. They represented every part of the Union—from the granite hills of Maine to the flowery borders of California, and from the northern lakes to the gulf. They formed one of the most cosmopolitan communities ever assembled in the United States, and as if by common consent all sectional prejudices were laid aside in one common interest of beginning life anew. When the shadows of night fell around and about them on that memorable day, Guthrie, the territorial capital, was a tented city. The rush for lands and lots was over; and men sat quietly about their bivouac fires discussing the exciting events of the day. It was a triumph for American manhood and education; that the day passed off peaceably, and a triumph for which Oklahomans may well feel proud when the turbulence of the times are considered. Practically there was no law save that administered by the United States military, until the organic act was effected, May 2, 1890, when Geo. W. Steele was appointed governor.

At the first session of the Territorial Legislature, a bill was introduced to remove the capital to Oklahoma City. When it was about to be placed upon its passage Arthur Daniels, the Speaker of the House, seized the bill and started on a run for the Santa Fe depot, where a special engine was waiting. Nearly all the members of the legislature started in pursuit, firing their revolvers at the fleeing speaker. He safely eluded them; and as the term of the legislature expired by law that night, the capital was saved to Guthrie.

Hammers and saws could be heard night and day. Men were building a city. In an incredible short space of time, palatial residences, business blocks and church spires rose upon what, a short time since, had been a barren plain. They had added another dot on the map.

The administration of Governor Steele was soon followed by the appointment of Governor A. J. Seay, an heroic figure on the federal side during the war of the rebellion, an able and kindly man whom history will revere. He was just the man for the times, for he always had a pleasant word or sound advice when occasion offered. He had the happy faculty of always looking at the bright side of life, and when speaking invariably put his audience in a good humour, as at the close of his term of office, in an address he said he always took an interest in the scriptural saying, "*If a man die, shall he live again?*" The crowd saw the point and gave a cheer for the retiring old hero so beloved by all.

About this time E. D. Nix was appointed United States marshal of the Territory. To Marshal Nix and his faithful deputies belong the credit of the suppression of outlawry in Oklahoma. At the time he was appointed in May, 1903, the country was overrun by a *banditti* that rivalled the noted James and Younger brothers, in Missouri. There was no safety for life or property outside the larger towns. Trains were held up, banks were looted, stores robbed, and travellers were murdered upon the highway.

To the young marshal, then only thirty years of age, it meant a long and bitter fight ahead, costing the lives of ninety-one deputy marshals, and over one and one-half million dollars to the government.

It was a fight to the death, but the young marshal was equal to the emergency, and the emergency confronted him. One by one the desperate bands were either captured or went down beneath the unerring aim of the faithful deputies; who were all skilled frontiersmen.

These men were inured to hardships, many had been on the cattle trails, and had burned cartridges in more than one Indian fight, some had been marshals of Abilene, Dodge City and other frontier towns in their days of lawlessness.

The time will come when men will paint them, write verses about them, as they deserve to be written about. These men who bared their breasts to outlaw's bullets, as did deputies Bill Tighlman, W. W. Painter, John Hixon, Heck Thomas, Ed Kelley, Chris Madson, Wm. Banks, Frank Canton, John Hale, Frank Rhinehart and many others and to the heroic dead, such as Tom Houston, Lafe Shadley, Dick Speed, Jim Masterson and nearly a hundred others who fell as nobly as any soldier upon the battlefield in country's cause, for it was in country's cause in which they fell. The graves of these dead heroes should be decorated, as they will be in time when Oklahomans stop long enough in their monied pursuits to give thought to services rendered by these noble lives.

A bushwhacking war was waged by the outlaws for more than three years. As soon as one leader bit the dust there was another to take his place. They were in bands of from ten to twenty and had their rendezvous in the dark forests of the Chickasaw Indian nation, the Grand River hills of the Osage Indian country or the Glass Mountains in the extreme west of Oklahoma. Often they would meet at a given

Chief Big Foot

point, do some daring act of train robbery, then scatter like quails with an agreed place of meeting; perhaps a hundred and fifty miles away. They were like the Insurgents of Cuba. No organised force could reach them. They knew every bridle path in the woods, or trail on the plains. Nothing prevailed but an Indian mode of warfare; but by long perseverance Marshal Nix's force conquered.

Bill Dalton was killed, Bill Doolin, Arkansan Tom, Tulsa Jack, George Newcomb, and Buck Weightman, alias, "Red Rock," all noted outlaw leaders in time bit the dust, while Bill Raidler fell "bleeding at every pore" from a shotgun in the hands of Marshal Heck Thomas.

Tearing open his shirt and looking at his bleeding breast as full of small holes as the lid of a pepper box, Raidler exclaimed, "Heck you damned scoundrel, haven't you any more respect for me; than to shoot me with bird shot," "Only used them for packing, my dear boy, only packing, you will find plenty of buck shot among them," said Heck, as he slipped the cold steel cuffs on Raidler's wrists.

15
Outlawry in Oklahoma

Bill Doolin, noted outlaw, was in the United States jail in Guthrie, Oklahoma. A chill, drizzling rain was falling and the night was dark. The half breed Indians and white border ruffians who had been his companions in the jail for the last two months, had grown tired of their card playing and had sullenly slunk off to their dirty bunks. Doolin had a cell of his own, but it had not yet been locked for the night and he had the freedom of the "bull pen." Near the front of the large room was a partition of steel bars. Outside this partition was a stove, near which a deputy marshal sat reading a novel. Another deputy was pacing the floor. Doolin was thinking of a night like this when he and his men lay in waiting at Red Rock for the Santa Fe express. How the chill rain dripped from their broad hats as they held a final whispered conversation just before the glaring eye of the headlight of the express flashed on them for an instant as the train rounded a curve, then the shrill whistle. How he blessed the dark night, and how he cursed the mud, for it would leave a trail, easy for the deputy marshals to follow.

It was action now, the panting engine had stopped at the water tank, the fireman had drawn down the great nozzle of the water pipe and was filling his tender. He struck the signal match across the butt of his revolver. Another instant and his men was swarming over the tender with revolvers at the heads of engineer and fireman. No time to lose. Uncouple the express car. All aboard, and the frightened engineer is compelled to run his engine five miles farther on and slow up at a creek crossing, where there are other men and horses. A demand is made of the express messenger to open his car, his answer is a bullet through the door. Then Raidler crawls under the car and begins sending Winchester bullets through the bottom of the car at random.

One of the bullets strikes the brave messenger in the head. They hear him fall with a groan. Quick, the dynamite, an explosion and the door of the express car is blown open. The pockets of the dead messenger are rifled, the key to the Wells-Fargo express box is found and next the iron chest is open. No time to count the big packages of currency and sealed bags of gold now. To the horses, and then to the Glass Mountains. For this and other crimes, death or imprisonment for life now awaited him. Oh, why did he let Bill Tighlman take him single handed at Eureka Springs where he thought he was safe in masquerading as an honest farmer from Texas.

A sudden pause in his thoughts, an idea struck Doolin, people knew they had gotten over $100,000 from the express company, and that money ought to be somewhere.

Doolin took a card from his pocket and a pencil and drew a map. Walking over to the iron grating he motioned to the guard.

"My heart hurts me tonight," he said, "and I am afraid I am going to die. I wouldn't mind all this so much if it wasn't for my boy with his mother over in the Osage nation, but I hate to see that boy go the way I have. If I could find a good man I'd make him my boys' guardian and fix him for life."

The guard stopped and came over to the iron grating.

"It is like this," continued Doolin. "I have got $30,000 in gold for some good man who will bring that boy up in the way he should go and be a father to him, get him interested in some profession, and make a man of him. I am done for sure and I believe I am going to die tonight, oh, how my heart hurts, why not you get my money and be a father to my boy, I believe you would do the honest thing by him, then I could die easier."

The guard looked over at his companion to see if he had heard. No, he was still reading the novel. He looked at Doolin and nodded. Then he drew close to the iron bars.

Doolin whispered, "I will trust you," and drew from his pocket the card on which he had drawn a map.

"Now stand close," he said, "and see if you can understand this,—here is the Bear Creek road in Pawnee county, here the ford, here a rock, ten feet to the south of this rock dig three feet and there is $30,000."

The guard did not quite understand and drew closer to the bars and took the card.

While he was waiting, a long thin hand reached through the grating to the handle of his six shooter and in a second he was peering down the muzzle of his own revolver in the hands of Bill Doolin.

"Keep perfectly quiet," said the outlaw, "you know me, open that bull pen door very quietly."

The guard silently obeyed. "Step in," said Doolin, the guard stepped inside. The next thing and he with the novel was staring into the quick blue eye of Doolin and the ugly thing he held cocked in his hand.

"This way boys," said Doolin, and the two guards followed him to his cell. When they were inside he locked the door, then he called for their cartridge belts and the revolver, which he with the novel still had about him.

In five minutes he was inside a heavy rain coat, had the guards' midnight lunches stored in its pockets, a heavy Winchester in his hands and a hundred rounds of ammunition belted about him. Out into the night, and on to the street where some belated revellers' horses were tied. He gathered up the reins of a fleet mustang and mounting into the saddle—"Richard was himself again."

★★★★★★

For two years, I had been in the government secret service. I had no visible means of support except that of a newspaper correspondent. My reports for Marshal Nix's office always went by a circuitous route, lest I be discovered, to have had my business known would have meant death. Even Marshal Nix never knew the real source of much information which reached his office.

I thought the outlaws were making a rendezvous at the little town of Ingrim, and I determined to see for myself. Going to the office of the *Daily Leader*, I secured a job at very poor pay to write up some towns in Oklahoma. Suddenly, under pretext of an affection in the head I became quite deaf. I knew better than go to the town of Ingrim first, lest I might excite suspicion. So I began at Tecumseh some thirty miles from Ingrim. I stayed in the town a week, solicited subscriptions and wrote up the prospects of the place, said many flattering things of the business men in my write-up, and when the papers came, I distributed them. The people were pleased with my work, but some complained at having to talk so loud to make me understand.

When I finished with Tecumseh, I rode with the mail carrier over to Ingrim. Sure enough here were my outlaws. They loafed about the only hotel and saloon, but were always on the alert. I appeared to take no notice of anything, but kept boring people to subscribe for my paper, interviewing merchants and writing up the town. The merchants, I discovered were glad to have the outlaws there, for they spent money like water, they paid big prices for their cartridges and bought heavy supplies of canned goods, which they sent away to be cached in the woods and hills for a time of need.

One day I was sitting alone on the hotel veranda reading, when I heard a man say to another, "I am going to see if that dam cuss is deaf or not." I heard his cat like step approaching, and then, click, click, he cocked his revolver at the back of my head.

It was a trying moment, but I did not move, I did not dare to, for had I quickly turned my head, I would have betrayed myself and lost my life.

When he was satisfied that I was deaf as a door nail, he invited me to drink. I excused myself, and I heard him tell the other man that I did not have the sense of a muskrat.

When I left town I owed the hotel man for my last days board, which I promised to send to him, I did this for effect, and went in an opposite direction from Guthrie.

Three days later and two emigrant wagons with farmer like men driving the teams came down the long red road that leads from the north into Ingrim.

An outlaw outrider saw them and rode casually down the road. He engaged the driver of the first wagon in conversation a moment, and riding to the side of the wagon he lifted the edge of the cover with his rifle, and there saw six armed deputy marshals on the hay inside. The outlaw wheeled his horse and rode furiously back to the village, waving his broad white hat as a signal.

The marshals hurried from the wagons and the battle was on.

Twenty minutes of sharp fighting and the outlaws were fleeing from the town on swift horses leaving one of their wounded behind, while the wagons that brought the marshals, carried four of their number back to Guthrie dead.

Almost at the same hour that afternoon, another tragedy was being enacted in the dark forests of the Osage Indian Nation. Deputy Heck Thomas had tracked Bill Doolin to his lair. He was sleeping under a rude shelter of branches in the forest, when the breaking of a twig awoke him. He saw Heck Thomas alone; not fifty feet away, and knew it was a duel to the death.

Leaping behind a barricade of logs he opened fire on Thomas who had sought the shelter of a tree. The duel lasted an hour, each jeering the other. Thomas held his hat to one side of the tree and when Doolin sent a bullet through it, he sank apparently helpless to the ground.

A long silence followed. Doolin again jeered the marshal. There was no answer. He came from behind his barricade to see the effect of his shot, and received a bullet through the brain.

It is worthy of mention here that when a company of Rough Riders for the Spanish war was organised in Oklahoma, a son of Marshal Tighlman and a son of Heck Thomas were among the first to enlist, and afterwards stormed the heights of San Juan hill with Colonel Roosevelt.

16

A New Land of Canaan

It was September of 1893. The Cherokee Strip, a large area of country in the Indian Territory, was about to be offered for settlement.

Guthrie, Oklahoma, was at this time filled with home-seekers who were camped about on vacant lots, in their wagons. They were men of good intentions. There was also a horde of gamblers and petty thieves who swarmed like ravening wolves scenting their prey. Saloons and gambling houses were open day and night, and many a poor fellow fell into the hands of these legalized bandits—to awaken from the effects of drugged liquor and find themselves robbed of every dollar they possessed, and their families without a day's provisions ahead.

Never was there an American town where morals were at a lower ebb than Guthrie was at that time. Street quarrels were frequent, and men shot each other down in cold blood for trivial offenses. There were contests over claims in Oklahoma proper, and it was no uncommon thing for a witness to be shot down after he had finished testifying in the land office. Or perhaps he was called to his door at midnight to stop a bullet, or was shot through a window while sitting at home with his family.

Highway robbery, burglary, thieving, perjury, gambling and whisky-drinking ran riot. Courtesans and harlots, with painted faces and tinselled dresses, plied their arts of conquest in open day; while city officials, not to be outdone in the practices of the hour, took all manner of bribes from all manner of men. This state of immorality generated a stench over the town that all the perfume of Arabia the Blest could not sweeten.

The Dalton gang of bandits was robbing Santa Fe trains in the Cherokee Strip, while more than one hundred and fifty United States marshals were searching for outlaws. When one was found, however, he was usually shot first and the warrant for his arrest read to the corpse.

The men assembled at Guthrie at this time were from all quarters of the United States, and represented almost every nationality. As one rider dashed up the street on a very fine horse, a gust of wind lifted his sombrero and landed it near where I stood. I picked it up and was in the act of handing it to him when he exclaimed: "Hello, Bob, you here!"

"Yes," I replied, scanning his face for an instant before recognising him. Then the face came back to me with pleasant memories. He was my old friend—Mark Witherspoon. The reunion was, indeed, pleasant to both of us, and it was late that night before we retired to our respective abodes.

Mark had jostled about from pillar to post, in all parts of the world; he had been in the mining camps of Australia and on the Rand in South Africa; he had grown rich several times and lost all again and again, and now he wanted an Oklahoma farm where, he concluded, he would settle down and live quietly. Just as though wild and impulsive natures like his could ever be content with a simple farming life. We agreed to make the run together and, if possible locate our farms beside each other.

When the opening day came, a blazing southern sun beat down upon the heads of more than one hundred thousand men drawn upon the line that marked the border of the new El Dorado. Most of the country on the southern border lay in high ridges, or in valleys and deep ravines, which, in some places, were 100 feet in depth, with precipitous ledges of rock on either side. The country was but sparsely covered with timber and nearly void of water at this season of the year. The few streams were impregnated with a mineral poison which had an evil effect for a long time on the systems of those who drank the water. Yet these men—many of whom had pioneered the plains of Nebraska and Kansas—were forced, by the conditions of the times, to seek new homes in this wild waste. For more than a year, more than 20,000 families had lived like rats in dugouts along the banks of the Arkansas River, to the north.

To say they lived is a mistake—they only existed. Parched corn and potatoes comprised the daily diet of hundreds. The winter of 1892 had been unusually severe for that section, and scant clothing and a lack of fuel added to the bitter suffering, while innumerable mounds of yellow earth stood silent monuments to those who braved the vicissitudes of the frontier in the hope of gaining homes.

In this new promised land there were some seventy Indian allotments to be made. These were located by government officials near townsites, for personal selfish purposes.

Then came an order from the Secretary of the Interior that all who would file on lands must register. That caused men to form in ranks miles long, to await their turn to register. It caused delay, and filled the pockets of government officials who, for pay, gave preference to the men of money. For days these men stood in line—a blazing sun above, and treeless, waterless plains about. Many sickened and were carried away to die, and, when the merciful night came, the others lay down on the bare, hard ground, to dream of happy homes—and shiver in the chill autumn darkness. The towns were platted by government employees. These plats contained false reservations for parks, and were sold to the men in line at a dollar each.

When we reached the line, a mighty caravan was there waiting, stretching as far as the eye could see, east and west, to the dim horizon on either side. Men were there with their families; in white covered wagons, in light running rigs and on horseback. Among them were the broad-hatted, swarthy fellows from the pampas and chaparrals of Texas. They were there from the deserts of New Mexico and Arizona. Old soldiers in the tattered blue of the Grand Army of the Republic were among the strugglers for homes. Just in front of all was another line, composed of the troops who were there to see that all kept back of the starting mark until the signal should be given. The gleam of the rifle could be seen in both lines. It was a thrilling scene; one upon which no man could look without mingled feelings of admiration and pity.

The signal for many to start to the eternal promised land came as the weary hours wore along. Worn with fatigue and exposure, and fainting from sunstroke and thirst, many fell from frantic horses that went dashing riderless over the plains. An officer rode down the line and halted near the railroad tracks. It was near noon, and an eager man took the action as a signal. There was a flash, a report. The man lay still in the sun-baked dust; a drunken soldier had taken a life and desolated a home. Some revolvers gleamed in the hands of angry Texans and in another moment the soldier lay writhing in the dust.

Just then an officer waved his sabre and the signal guns boomed down the line. Like a mighty tidal wave the dense mass of men, horses and wagons swayed for an instant and then went on with a rush. There were cries and shouts—and oaths and blasphemy from the drunken soldiers. The noise of rumbling wagons and the clatter of horses' hoofs sounded like the distant roar of cannonading. On surged the swaying line, horsemen dashing out in front here and there. Every little distance was to be found the wreck of a wagon that had been crushed in the rush. Other wagons were stalled in ravines, horses dropped from exhaustion, throwing their riders, who lay in gullies or on the rocky sides of the mountain ridges, with mangled limbs, begging for a drop of water. But the mad fever of the rush was on all and little heed was paid to suffering.

Our horses were in fine condition and were fleet of foot and ere long we were in the lead, in a wild race with the wind. We sighted a stream of clear running water, whose banks were fringed with trees, and a valley which stretched out for miles to the north. We reached a grove and found the cornerstone that marked the dividing line of two sections. We fired our Winchesters as a signal to the others that those claims were taken, and immediately commenced throwing up earth to show that improvements were under way. Then, tired out with the excitement of the day, we sat down under the trees to rest and talk it all over, and, in the late afternoon, fell asleep from sheer exhaustion.

It was dark when Mark suddenly awoke and aroused me with the shout: "Get up, for your life, get up! The plains are on fire!"

I was on my feet in an instant. The southern sky was aglow. Great tongues of flame were leaping through the inky blackness of the night, with a hiss and roar that sounded like the coming of a storm. We hurriedly mounted our frantic horses and rode swiftly into the northern darkness—whither, we knew not; our only thought was to distance the fire far enough to give us a chance to burn a space about us and thus find safety.

Suddenly I felt a falling sensation. Then there were pains in my head and mysterious, dreadful aches in my legs. Visions flitted before apparently unseeing eyes and at last I came to realise that I was lying on a cot in a tent. Mark came in and I asked him where I was.

"Never mind now," he said gently. Tomorrow came, and the next day, and still another, but Mark remained silent. Gradually my mind became normal and I distinctly recalled the last moments of consciousness; the prairie fire, the wild ride to safety. Mark then added the closing chapter. My horse had plunged into a rocky canon, fully 20 feet in depth. His horse had scented the danger and had reared, saving him from my fate. He back-fired the grass, and, in its light, saw me lying at the bottom of the *cañon*. Tenderly he cared for me during the night and in the morning got a doctor, who set the broken limb, and here I was convalescing.

17

Told Around the Campfire

"You knew Cora Belle Fellows, that white girl at Cheyenne Agency, South Dakota, who married a buck Indian, eh, Bill?"

"Yep," Bill Hawkins answered, "and I know what the results were, too.

"About a year after she had left a fashionable seminary in New York state and came among the redskins to teach them manners and the like, she surprised and shocked everybody by announcing her marriage to Chaska, a full blood Sioux, twenty-one years of age. Then her troubles began. She was frowned upon by both whites and Indians. She went with Chaska to his *tepee* and lived upon the coarse chuck furnished by Uncle Sam.

"Her escapade was commented upon by all the newspapers of the country at the time, and a museum man of Chicago induced her and Chaska to place themselves upon exhibition. For two years she was inspected by the public, which in the meantime had made her presents until she had a carload of furniture.

"Then she concluded to go back to the Agency and make a farmer out of Chaska, and so with the money earned in the museum, she and her Indian lord returned. She purchased land some miles from the agency and built a house.

"The agent and myself rode out there about six months after they had gone to housekeeping. We were both curious to know how they were getting along.

"It was a sight for your whiskers. Outside sat nearly all her furniture. The covers of plush had been ripped off for Indian horse trappings, the wood was stained and weather cracked.

"The house was without doors, worn blankets being hung instead. The floors were cold and bare. In a corner upon an old mattress lay

Cora Belle Fellows or Mrs. Chaska. An old squaw sat by her side, crooning some lingo over her new born kid. She did not want to talk and we went away. Chaska soon after left her and took a wife from his own tribe, leaving her to live in a *tepee* about the agency like any other squaw, feeding on Uncle Sam's grub.

"You might as well have tried to shove butter down a wildcat's neck with a hot awl as to have tried to talk that gal out of marrying the buck."

"Marrying is bad business, anyway, unless they are both hooked up right," observed the cook. "There is old Ben Berkley living over on the Cottonwood. He was pretty well fixed before he married that widder. She was a spiritualist or something of the sort, and used to go off in trances and have white lights coming around until she scared old Ben nearly to death. She was always running over the country telling people's future and leaving Ben at home to cook. He took to drinking and one day got the D. T.'s and thought a freight engine was chasing him up and down the alleys of the town, and he finally crawled under a barn to keep out of its way, when the boys rescued him. After that he would not drink any more, but poured the licker in his boots and would get as full as a tick by absorption.

"His wife had brought to the ranch a measly water Spaniel, which Ben used to amuse himself with by throwing cobs and sticks into the river and teaching the dog to swim in and get them and bring them back to him, not thinking of the great blessing it was finally to be to him.

"Ben had been blasting out a hole for a cyclone cellar with sticks of gun-cotton, when his wife took it into her head that she wanted a mess of fish.

"'No time to fish,' said Ben. 'Take a stick of that dynamite and go down to the creek where the water is still and blow out a mess for yourself.'

"His wife took the cartridge and lit the fuse, then gave the thing a toss into the creek. The dog was there and thinking she was playing with him, swam in and got the cartridge and came running up the bank to give it to her. Then she started to run over the ploughed ground, yelling at the top of her voice, 'Drap it, Tige! Drap it!' There was an explosion and a hole in the ground big enough to bury a horse. The dog had gone up higher than Elijah, while Mrs. Berkley was laying in a furrow with one leg injured by the cartridge. In a day or two the leg swelled up and old Ben sent for the cross-roads doctor, who decided that the injured leg would have to come off.

"The doctor went to town the next day to get some tools, and was so glad over getting a job that he filled up on cactus whiskey and came back and cut off the wrong leg. The sore leg got well afterwards, but, Gee-whiz! It tickled old Ben nearly to death, for she has to stay at home now."

"Story sounds fishy to me," remarked Ned Antler.

"Billy Bolton nearly lost his life for using that word," said Hank Pool. "You all know Billy runs a paper over at Woodward, on the Panhandle trail.

"There had been a hold-up in town, and Jim Belden was accused of it. After the trial before a justice of the peace, Belden was acquitted. In commenting on the affair in his paper the next day, Billy said Belden's story which secured his release sounded fishy. Belden was a bad man. He saddled his broncho, filled his saddle pockets with grub, and his skin full of whiskey and went over to Billy's printing office. He hitched the broncho in front, and with the paper in one hand and his Winchester in the other he went in and asked Billy what he meant by saying his story was fishy. Billy was taken by surprise, for he saw that Belden meant to kill him, as he was all ready to hit the trail.

"'Fishy,' says Billy. 'Aha, fishy, fishy. Why that's a compliment, my dear boy. Saint Peter used to fish and said so many good things that people used to call his sayings fishy. It was a favourite expression with Aristotle and Socrates, when they addressed Napoleon the Great, to say, 'I hope your royal majesty will speak some imperial fishy things today.' It is—ah, ahah, sort of an international *e pluribus unum* expression, a general sort of a *non compos mentis*, as it were, you understand.'

"'Oh, well, if that's all,' said Belden, 'it's all right, but I wouldn't use the word often if I were you, for some of the boys might not be as well posted as I am. Much obliged, Billy. I was just passing and thought I would subscribe for the paper for a year. Here is $2.00. Mail it to me at Lampassas."

"Bolton got off light," said Tom Tyler. "Over at Las Vegas two years ago a sheep man called 'Doc' Kinnie a liar and before the fellow could think twice Doc had his ear sliced off, and he went around afterwards using it for a beer check. He would call up the house and pay for the drinks with the sheepman's ear; he always redeemed it, though, for fear the owner would buy it back."

"Cut it out, boys, cut it out, get to roost in your blankets," said the boss. "We hit the trail at 5 o'clock in the morning and make the drive to Cimarron by noon."

An hour later, the fire had smouldered to embers, the stars twinkled in the great dark blue dome of the sky, a soft south breeze fanned the Oklahoma plains and all was silent, save the tramp of horses' hoofs as the outriders circled the herd of bedded cattle.

18

The Lone Grave on the Mesa

High upon the mesa northwest of Colorado City, Colo., and near the old cemetery used by the pioneers of the early sixties, there is a lonely grave, around which clings a romance of the early days, which is recalled by the phenomena which many persons say they have witnessed when passing at night.

As the story goes, Marie Tinville, the beautiful daughter of Victor Tinville lived with her parents in a cabin near Colorado City, in 1863. About that time Leon Murat, a dashing young fellow of about 20 years came out from St. Louis and found employment on her father's ranch. It was a case of love at first sight, intensified by isolated conditions and an almost constant companionship.

The cabin stood near the now famous Garden of the Gods, and many were the evenings the young people wandered among the towering rocks in the wondrous bright moonlight of that region, and talked of love, while the shadows of Pike's Peak shrouded the dreamy valley.

Love's young dream was rudely awakened one day in the autumn of 1864, by the call to arms to join Colonel Chivington in his campaign against the hostile Cheyenne and Arapahoe Indians, who were then murdering the settlers of Colorado.

Men were needed, and Leon was brave. He kissed his sweetheart goodbye and rode away with that avenging column of horsemen who fought the battle of Sand Creek in Colorado, November 29, 1864.

Murat's command did nearly three months' campaigning over the dry, heated plains before any effective work was accomplished.

Early in November a mounted column of 650 Colorado volunteers of Colonel Shoup's Third Regiment, 175 of the First Regiment and a few mounted Mexicans, formed the fighting force under Colonel Chivington. A large band of Indians was located on the banks of Sand Creek, about forty miles north of where Ft. Lyons now stands and near the village of Kit Carson.

Bent's Fort, a rude frontier structure of palisades, stood some miles below Ft. Lyons. It was to this point that Colonel Chivington led his men when he learned that Black Kettle and White Antelope with some three thousand braves, were encamped upon the banks of Sand Creek.

The column made prisoners of all whom they met, lest word should reach the Indians that they were pushing forward to the attack. At Bent's Fort a halt was made to rest riders and horses. On the night of the 28th the column headed for the encampment on Sand Creek, taking as a guide, a half breed son of Colonel Bent, and carrying in their rear a small brass cannon and ammunition wagon.

The night was cold and a bleak wind blew from the north. With jingle of spur and clank of sabre the column rode fours abreast through the darkness. The Indian guide led them through a shallow lake in the hope that the ammunition might become wet. When about half way through the lake Murat's horse floundered and wet him completely in the icy waters. The column rode on while Anthony Bott remained to assist him. After dividing his own dry clothing with Murat the two started to find the trail of the flying column in the darkness. They were favoured both by their knowledge of the plains and the instinct of their horses, but for five hours they were alone in the darkness of a hostile country.

They came up with their command in the grey dawn of the morning as they were forming for battle behind a ridge that overlooked the Indian camp. Here Colonel Chivington divided his men, sending a column of twos in opposite directions so as to surround the camp. The Indians were in their *tepees* when the cannon sent a crash of iron into their midst. The battle was on. Chief White Antelope came rushing from his *tepee* brandishing a rifle, urging on his followers. The encircling horsemen closing in on them emptied their rifles and revolvers into the confused mass of Indians.

Indian depredations had been so numerous in Colorado and the atrocities so cruel, that the men, many of whom had been victims of Indian raids and had lost their all, their families or friends being butchered, gave no quarter, and when the battle ended they felt even more justified when there was found within the *tepees* a number of scalps recently torn from the heads of white women and children. Nearly

1,000 Indians were killed when the firing ceased, and a crimson tide ebbed into the creek and reddened its waters with blood.

A squaw and a boy were found hiding in the tall grass. Murat shot the squaw and captured the boy. Bott bought the young Indian, intending to bring him up in civilization. The boy was standing by his side when, an hour later a pistol shot rang out from a group of men some yards away and the young Indian fell dead. Bott was angered, and drawing his own revolver, offered one hundred dollars to anyone who would point out the man who fired the shot. No one would tell.

Murat with a companion was trying to capture some of the Indians' horses far out on the plain, when one of Black Kettle's fleeing Indians rose from behind a hillock and shot him dead. White Antelope was killed, while a large number of Indians under Black Kettle escaped by scattering like quail over the plain and hiding in the grass.

While the battle was raging the families of many of the soldiers from Colorado City had gathered in the Anway Fort at that place, and a telepathic wave of horror spread over all. Many were praying and weeping, and all seemed to feel that a dreadful thing was being enacted in which their loved ones were taking part.

When the news of the battle reached the fort and the death of young Murat was announced, Marie Tinville fell in a swoon, after which her mind was a blank. From that time on her decline was rapid and in a few months she was laid in the lonely grave upon the mesa.

After that stories were told of strange things. A white light was seen about the grave, which vanished on close approach. Once old Ben Jordan an antelope hunter, came to town at night, his long hair fairly on end, saying that a white light had risen in front of him near the grave, out of which protruded a naked arm. The incredulous asked him what he had been drinking, but he stuck to the story as long as he lived.

George Birdsall, a young man of Colorado City, had heard the story and thought it all a joke. He recently went out one night to investigate. He saw no white light, but felt a peculiar rush of cold air and a touch upon the cheek as soft as if someone had gently kissed him.

19

Under the Black Flag

As the sun went down below the rolling glassy waters of the gulf of Mexico, I sat on the hatchway steps of the little steamer *Dauntless*, fully realising for the first time that perhaps before morning I would be swinging to the yard-arm of a Spanish man-of-war.

I was sick, anyway, and the abominable mixture of whiskey and garlic which Mark Witherspoon had given me as a preventive against yellow fever, had made the contemplation worse.

The *Dauntless* was loaded with arms and munitions of war for the Cuban Insurgents and if the Spaniards caught us we would doubtless share the fate of the crew of the *Virginius* at Santiago de Cuba in 1873.

I had credentials as a newspaper correspondent, but Mark Witherspoon and I had duly enlisted at Tampa, Florida, in the cause of Cuban liberty, and we were assigned to the third division of Garcia's army under command of General Ruloff.

Our little vessel hugged the Florida Keys for more than a week. Meantime we were reinforced by small parties of twos and threes, who came in open boats by night. The stores of rifles, ammunition and dynamite came by small sailing craft. We now numbered thirty-seven men. Eight of us were Americans, two were Germans and the others were Cubans from Tampa and Key West.

On the night we were ready to start the distinguishing lights of a revenue cutter were seen, so we lay close in a little cove and banked the fires in our furnace until four o'clock the next afternoon, when we slipped out and put for the high seas, headed straight for the coast of Cuba. When night fairly set in, there came small squalls and a drizzling rain. We had no signal lights out and every sound was muffled, even the funnel was so protected that not a spark could escape. All night long everybody was most keenly alert, and it was towards daylight that the irregular mountain lines of Cuba could be discerned, standing in shadowy relief against a darkened sky. On entering a little landlocked harbour we signalled with flash lanterns and were soon answered from the shore. Nearly a hundred insurgents met us, and the work of unloading quickly began.

During the morning we were reinforced by nearly a hundred more Cubans who brought ponies and pack mules. As soon as we were unloaded our vessel hoisted the Danish flag and with all possible speed put out for the high seas. Her hull was well down on the horizon when we took up our march inland. Our route lay over tortuous mountain trails over which our ponies climbed with the agility of goats. The trail was often dangerous in the extreme, for the slip of a pony's hoof would have sent both horse and rider hundreds of feet below. We had taken trails unknown to the Spanish soldiery.

When about fifty miles in the interior, we reached a plateau and here found encamped some eight hundred men under General Ruloff. From the very first I had but little confidence in him. He was a Polish Jew, well educated in military tactics, but unfitted to conduct a guerrilla warfare with men like us who were virtually fighting under the black flag.

Subsequent events proved this, for at the fight of Santo Esperitu we left our improvised hospital unguarded, and Captain Sandoval cut to our rear and captured it and after destroying much of our valuable stores, put every sick man to death.

Our rendezvous lay in the province of Puerto Principe and our line of action westward. After the fight at Santo Esperitu we never massed in action, but divided into companies of about one hundred, free to run or fight as our commander ordered.

Our detachment captured Captain Sandoval and a party of his men, and in view of his inhuman treatment of our prisoners, he was promptly shot. Sandoval went to his death as all other cowardly butchers do, trembling like a leaf in the wind.

We were ordered by Ruloff to burn all *azucaderos* (sugar mills) and to blow up with dynamite all railroad culverts and bridges and to destroy all telegraph lines. Our division frequently made rapid raids, always gaining ground westward. The division to which we were attached raided the town of San Lazaro which was defended by a small body of Spaniards. We routed them and captured some two hundred Mauser rifles and a large quantity of ammunition and other military stores. Our commander then ordered the execution of the *alcalde* (mayor) for having betrayed a number of insurgent sympathizers, causing them to be shot, and their families to be driven through the streets, beaten with sticks.

Early in November we were encamped near Nuevitas where we had lain inactive for several days. One afternoon scouts had reported an advancing column and we had chosen for our ambuscade the ruins of a stone building, now overgrown with vines and nearly hidden from view by a cactus thicket.

There was a hushed stillness in the dark forest that lay beyond the long yellow road, and in the cane fields that stretched away for leagues to our right. To the left the San de Cubitas mountains, with their covering of dense tropical vegetation, rose dark and silent. A lookout had climbed a tall *cebra* tree and was watching with a field glass. He suddenly gave the signal. Then the men were told in whispers each to select a man and to fire at a given order. The Cuban sun blazed hotly down that day. The air was close and stifling in our position behind the cactus thicket and our hearts beat quick and fast in those moments of waiting. There was the low rumble of horses hoofs, a cloud of yellow dust arose from down the road, and soon the Spanish column was almost abreast the 150 rifles that pointed from behind the stone wall. I peered over the sights of my Winchester and drew a bead on the breast of a young officer. He was chatting gaily with a companion and as he turned his face revealed a handsome countenance. It was a boyish face with the dawn of manhood just settling upon the brow.

Thoughts crowded each other in my mind just then: Perhaps the young man was a conscript, not here by his own choice to imperil his young life, and I, whom he had never wronged, an unsuspected foe, safely hid in the cactus thicket behind the stone wall, about to send his soul into eternity. I lowered my aim from his breast to his horse just behind the shoulder. The order came to fire. The trigger that would have pulled like a ton weight a second before pulled easily now. And so all through those dreadful volleys that we poured into the struggling ranks. For firing into a mass of men is a different thing from that of firing upon one man singly.

When the smoke of battle cleared away more than forty of the routed Spanish column lay dead or wounded in the road. I went to the place where the young trooper's horse had fallen and there lay the young officer pinioned underneath with a broken leg. I felt that I wanted to help him. I knew from the look on his manly face that in private life he would have been my friend, but to show a kindly feeling at that time would have made me a suspect among my comrades in arms. Their machetes flashed in the sunlight and their strokes falling swift and fast reddened the soil of Puerto Principe. Mark and I stood silent, helpless spectators of the horrors of war and revenge, wreaked by men, who in the remembrance of wrongs and outrage, were lost to any feeling of common humanity. There was only one act of kindness which I dared perform. In the pocket of his blood-stained blouse I found a letter. It was from his mother in Seville, and bore a mother's love and sister's prayer for his safe return. When I afterwards landed at Galveston, I sent it to his home, with an account of how he died upon the battlefield.

The blazing sun was yet high when we were in our saddles and moving away. I saw a vulture circling above the battlefield, one, two, then a dozen, then a score. These black-winged scavengers had scented death, and there let contemplation end. Night comes suddenly in the tropics, when the sun dips beyond the sea, but here and there in the valley were lights, lantern like at first, spreading soon like a long prairie fire. They were in the cane fields which our men were firing, and as the flames swept on, the bursting stalks sounded like a battle with light revolvers. It lit the night, and its glare and gloom added mystery to the dark forest beyond the road. Morning came and we were safely encamped amid the hills. The birds sang merrily and the sun dried the dew upon the tall, rank grass, and when it came roll call, two names were stricken off. They had reported the day before to the Great Commander of the great beyond.

20

In Cuban Jungles

Spies brought news of an encampment of Spanish infantry a day's march ahead. All was hustle in the Cuban insurgent camp. Twenty-eight Texans who had recently joined our command were allowed the privilege of leading our column to the attack. That day we followed circuitous mountain trails and encamped at night in the heart of a dense forest through whose trailing vines we made our way along the bridle paths. By 4 o'clock in the morning we were again in the saddle. There was no blare of trumpet or beat of drums to announce our coming as our column of horsemen stole from out the silent forest and wound along the road like a great creeping serpent to strike death.

The Spanish camp was beyond a small stream through which we were to charge. Halting a mile beyond their picket lines, saddle girths were tightened, weapons were looked to, and we formed in a column of fours. Americans to the front, and ready for the charge. Ten stalwart Cubans were selected to form the skirmish line two hundred yards in advance and engage the enemy when they reached the banks of the stream. The column was then to charge at a gallop and use the revolver and machete.

The first rays of the sun were gilding the mountain crests and awakening the flamingos around the lagoons when a Spanish sentry's rifle told the moment of action had come.

On pressed our column at double quick, while the increased firing ahead warned us that the Spanish camp was aroused. There was the heavy rattle of Mauser rifles, followed by the sharper report of Winchesters as our advance guard reached the stream and drew aside to let our column pass.

The little river flowed from the mountains and plunged over rock and cliff in wild tumult. Below the ford which we were crossing there were falls and as the Spaniards fired a volley that struck our column midway in the stream, they emptied many saddles, while wounded men were carried down to watery graves.

The Spaniards threw a double cordon of infantry at bayonet charge against our cavalry, but the Texans' revolvers opened a gap and the column rode through the demoralised camp, doing its fearful work. On the column plunged, fire leaping from the deadly revolvers on either side. When beyond the Spanish camp, the bugle sounded wheel, and back we rode among the panic stricken soldiers, dealing death until they broke in confusion, and gained the cover of the forest. We halted long enough to gather up our wounded and burn the supply train. An hour later and we were in full retreat to our rendezvous in the San de Cubitas mountains.

One evening Mark and I started for the vicinity of an *azucadero*, where we knew there was a patch of sweet potatoes. The night was dark, damp and chilly, and the road lay through a clearing of tall palms whose white trunks stood like ghostly sentinels. The silence was unbroken save by the sound of horses' hoofs, the croaking of frogs and the distant baying of dogs about some negro *casa*. We did not suppose there was a Spaniard within fifty miles of us, and as we rode our ponies silently along a horseman suddenly appeared in front of us, and in clear Castilian tones shouted: "*Quien vive!*"

"*Cuba Libre!*" cried Mark, drawing his machete and spurring his horse forward. At the same instant I discharged my revolver full in the sentinel's face. We wheeled our horses and rode quickly into the clearing, knowing better than to retreat by the road we came. It was well we did not, for soon a body of Spanish cavalry came tearing down the road, firing a volley ahead at random. We rode on through the clearing, being now cut off from our command. At length we came to a creek whose banks were steep and fringed on either side by trees, from whose branches hung a network of tangled vines and creepers. The water flowed sluggishly, as most streams in Cuba do. We determined to cross the creek at once, knowing that with the first streak of dawn we would be tracked, for we had left an easy trail in the soft soil.

We used our machetes with great difficulty to cut a path through the vines, and when we reached the water's edge swam our ponies across and cut our way through on the opposite bank where we lay down to await developments of the morning. Both of us must have fallen asleep, for we were startled by a loud *grito alto* from the other side of the creek. Peering through the bushes we saw a Spanish trooper gesticulating to a party of cavalry in the rear. In another second there was the simultaneous report of our two Winchesters and the trooper rolled from his horse. We hurriedly mounted our ponies amid the fusillade of bullets from the approaching squad of cavalry, and spurring our horses toward a cane field, we were soon hidden. A little later we abandoned our horses and started them off in another direction with a lashing, thinking thereby to gain time and elude our pursuers. Then we started for the *azucadero*.

It was our first intention to fire it, thinking its flames would attract the attention of our command and bring us relief. But as we came out of the cane field we saw a body of troopers crossing a bridge which spanned the creek. We did not think they saw us, and in our haste to find a hiding place we ran around the building to a well which supplied the boilers. Leaping on a platform we found a lot of empty sugar hogsheads standing on end near a lot of filled ones. We quickly rolled an empty beside them and turned the open end down, getting under it. The troopers had seen us and tracked us straight to the well. They supposed we had descended by means of the pump pipe and hidden our bodies in the water, for they began hurling stones in the water and with a mixture of Spanish oaths called us "*Perro Americano*" (dog American). Satisfied with their work of exterminating us in the well, they rode away.

Meanwhile we were couched in close quarters, with our revolvers tightly clenched, determined to sell out as dearly as possible. When they had gone, Mark whispered, "I am badly shot," indicating the spot by placing his hand upon his abdomen. The morning wore away and our situation was becoming unbearable. We were cramped and almost suffocated. Mark had swooned away twice in the agony of pain. Fortunately we had filled our canteens from the brackish waters of the creek, which alleviated our sufferings some. Yet it was past noon before we ventured out. I helped Mark inside the *azucadero*, where he laid down upon a pile of cane refuse, while I examined his wound. One look was enough. The contents of the abdomen were oozing out through the wound, and I knew that was a fatal sign. I carried a pocket case containing a few medicines for an emergency, among which was some morphine. I gave him an eighth grain tablet which relieved him some, but at times his pain grew so great that he begged me to shoot him.

We could hear distant firing during the afternoon, but the sounds were growing fainter and we knew our command was retreating. When night came on I gave Mark another tablet of morphine and lay down for some rest. The dreadful chill that always follows a gunshot wound had set in, but I had no blankets or other coverings with which to lessen his sufferings. Thoroughly exhausted myself, I soon fell asleep, and when I awoke late in the night, I was alone with the dead. For me to bury him was impossible, and I could not think of leaving him there a prey to the vultures. So I did what I should have wanted him to do for me had our places been reversed. Sorrowfully I left him alone in the now burning *azucadero* and while the flames of his funeral pyre were lighting the night, I started for the sea.

That day I fell in with a party of insurgents who were on their way to the coast to meet another filibustering vessel. As malaria and the effects of climate were telling heavily upon me, they kindly gave me aid in boarding the craft, by which I afterwards landed at the docks at New Orleans, feeling that I had done my share in the cause of Cuban liberty.

21
Emulous of Washington

"I don't know that I can tell you fellows about the first dollar I ever earned," said W. P. Epperson, the pioneer editor of the Colorado City ———, "but I do know the first and last lie I ever told."

"You ought to remember, seeing that it has not been over twenty minutes," said George Geiger.

"Twenty minutes be smashed!" yelled Epperson, reaching for his gun, "it's been twenty years this summer. My first lie was a trivial one about fishing, and the last happened in this way."

"Twenty years, did you say?" interrupted the hired man with an incredulous look.

"That's what I mean," and the veteran editor took another chew of Battle Ax, while a halo of white settled down about his head.

"In the autumn of 1885," he continued, "I stepped off a Union Pacific train at Silver Creek, Nebraska, and after a good supper I determined to drive across the country to Osceola, a distance of thirty miles. The driver of the livery rig was about the most handsomely attired imitation of a cowboy I had ever seen. He wore a new suit of corduroy with a broad *sombrero* and high-heeled boots with ornamented red tops, also a bright blue shirt and a rattlesnake skin necktie. I had him sized up for a green country boy from Indiana or Illinois who had seen but little of frontier life, and he confirmed my suspicions a little later as we were crossing the Platte River bridge by saying, 'I suppose if you knew what my business had been you would hesitate to ride with me alone on the plains at night.'

"It was getting dark and we were crossing a wide stretch of the then desolate plain that lay between the Platte River and Osceola. I was enjoying a cigar and felt at peace with all the world, when a devilish thought struck me, and I asked, 'What has been your business?'

"'Well, sir,' he replied, 'I have been a cowboy.'

"'The deuce you have,' said I, 'Shake, old man, you are a fellow after my own heart, and since you have been so kind to tell me your business, I will let you know who I am. I, sir, am Doc Middleton.'

"The fellow almost fell from his seat in surprise. Doc Middleton was the notorious outlaw whose depredations had become so terrorizing to the settlers of Nebraska that the State had offered a reward of $5,000 for his capture, dead or alive. I enjoyed the joke I was playing all the more when I saw the effect of my speech.

"'Just now,' I continued, 'I am trying to get away from a sheriff's posse; that is why I am making the cut across the country. They may overtake us, and if they do, there will be some heavy shooting.'

"'With this I drew a big Colt revolver from my overcoat pocket and I said I had two more like it in my valise. I also told him if they overtook us he must get down by the dashboard and drive for dear life, that he might get shot in the back, but that would be cowboy's luck.

By this time he was nervous and began looking backwards as he whipped the ponies up at a lively gait. I did not pretend to notice it and so kept up my lying.

"'The first man I ever killed,' I told him, 'was a one-eyed man in Utah, who called me a liar, and I threw his body over a cliff, and my conscience hurt me for full half an hour afterwards. After that I soon got so I loved to blow a man's head off just to see his brains fly.'

"It had grown quite dark, and having nothing better to do, I told him all the bloody stories I could think of and claimed them as my own experience until I became tired of the foolishness and lapsed into silence. We had made about half our journey and were passing a farm house set in a dense grove of trees. There were lights in the house and the young man broke the silence by asking, 'Please, dear Mister Doc Middleton, may I go in and get a drink of water? I think I have got a fever in my throat.'

"'Certainly, my boy, certainly,' I replied taking the lines. He slid off the rig and ran to the house, while I sat there like a fool holding the horses. About twenty minutes passed and he did not return. Then I noticed the lights in the house had been extinguished. I called loudly for the young man to return, and when it flashed over my mind that to him I was the outlaw Doc Middleton, and he might warn the farmer of my presence, who might even then be waiting to get a shot at me, I yelled again for him in fear, louder than before, but there was no response. The more I thought of my predicament, the more nervous I became, until the cold sweat stood out like beads on my face.

"I could stand it no longer, and seizing the whip, I cut the horses a lash and crouched down by the dashboard just as I had been instructing the young man to do. In the sudden dash, the horses broke one of the buggy springs, and I wandered on the plains until morning, for I had missed the Osceola road. It cost me $2 to have the spring mended and $5 to send a man back to Silver Creek with the rig, to say nothing of being scared within an inch of my life."

22

On the Round Up

The round-up of today, (1906), differs in no essential particular from that of former years, excepting in the number of cattle rounded up and the number of men and horses required in its working.

In 1900 I spent some months on a ranch in northern Colorado, where there are still large bunches of cattle.

For some days prior to the start the foreman had been busy preparing the wagon, rounding up saddle horses, hiring men and making final arrangements for the start.

When the day arrived everything was in a state of activity and as evening approached the corral was filled with horses. Each "waddie" was tolled off his string of mounts. Ten to each man, and after the summer on rich buffalo grass every horse was in a state that boded no good for the unaccustomed rider.

That night we ate our suppers at the chuck wagon at the round-up camp, after which the boys sat around a chip fire, telling stories and smoking.

The cowboy story differs from any I have ever heard, both in extravagance of statement and manner of telling. They relate to anything and everything that has ever come under his acute observation.

"I always had an especial desire to make governors my associates," said "Beaut" Bowers, "so with a view to a pleasant acquaintance I once called upon Governor Waite, presenting the compliments of Governor Rentfrow of Oklahoma and several other governors, none of whom had sent any compliments, but then they are so cheap I thought I could give him a few without their missing them.

"I had heard that he wanted to ride to his bridle bits in blood and I wanted to get into the swim, although I would rather it was beer.

"It was the governor's day to be out of sorts, and he did not seem inclined to talk. I wanted to talk and resolved to break the ice of his reserve in some manner. So when he asked how the people of Oklahoma stood the panic, I told him we had not felt it in the least. He seemed surprised at this and asked, "Why not!" I replied we were all too poor to own anything and had got beyond expecting it. "Well, poor people have to live; how do they manage for some money?" I told him when silver was demonetized we took to catching Keeley graduates and scraping the chloride of gold off them with a case-knife and had done fairly well.

"The old man stared at me and asked me if I had wheels in my head too. Everybody had been saying the old governor had wheels in his head until I believe he was afraid to pick his ears lest a cog clip the end of his finger off.

"I had recently been on Zack Mulhall's ranch in Oklahoma, where the Reverend Buchanan used to come and talk Populism to the boys until I got tired of it one night and stole his false teeth where he put them to soak in a tin cup. There was a lot of socialism too, in his talk that didn't go down, for on that ranch the first fellow up of a morning got the best socks, and that made me fall out with the idea of community of interests. But to humour the governor I spoke of the wide-spreading revolutionary sentiment in Texas and Oklahoma and hinted that they had their eyes turned eagerly on his movements, as it was their hope he might devise some way to lead the country out of the silver difficulty. He then showed me a letter from President Diaz, of Mexico. It suggested another pan-American congress in the interests of silver. "It's no use, though," he said, "the last assembly of the kind amounted to nothing. Eastern influences would soon retard any movement of the sort.'

"'If we are to continually be the back dooryard of the east,' I replied, 'the sooner we secede from it the better.'

"Here was a long pause, the old man looking at me intently to see if the wheels in my head were working, and I tried at the same time to discover if the machinery in his was all right.

"Seeing the point of vantage I continued: 'Divide the country from the Mississippi River, establish a new republic with our own capital, make Galveston our New York, with a national railroad to that point; coin our gold and silver, make banks a public trust, with any betrayal of it punishable as high treason. If we are going into revolution we must have something like this for our object, otherwise we will only terminate in anarchy. As Governor of Colorado call for a delegation of representative citizens from other states to meet here in convention and start the ball rolling.'

"I delivered this sentiment in round, strong terms, while the governor listened, apparently pleased.

"You will see all you want to of revolution before two years,' he quietly said, 'it is coming sure as fate and were I your age I would win fame and fortune by—'

"At this moment an unfortunate affair happened. An Indian had given me a white bulldog. That dog had more sense than half the people and I loved him like a brother. One day the dog got too close to the heels of a heifer and she kicked one eye out. He felt so bad over it that I wrote to an eye doctor to send me a glass eye for my dog. He wrote back that he did not deal in dogs' eyes, but sent me a bright blue human eye. One of the boys and I managed to fix it in and the dog was very proud of it, only it fit so tight he could not wink. He would lay for hours asleep with the glass eye staring with an expression of strangled innocence confronting the murderer. Where I went that dog went also, and all through the conversation with Governor Waite my dog lay on the floor asleep, but that glass eye kept staring at the governor's dog until he took it for an insult and came over to our part of the room for a scrap.

"In the *mêlée* of separating the dogs the governor jabbed his thumb in that glass eye and nearly cut it off. That made him so mad he would not talk any more and I may have to wander on through eternity guessing what he would have said. My dog felt so humiliated that he went home by the back alleys."

Other stories followed, relating to horses and daring deeds of their riders. It seemed like we had only slept a few moments when we were awakened by the call of the boss, "roll out," "roll out." In a short time every man of the twenty-five was on his feet, rolling up his bed and throwing it in a pile ready to be loaded on the wagon. All gladly answered to the call, "Chuck's ready!"

Each man took a plate and tin cup, knife, fork and spoon, and went to the Dutch ovens, where everything was cooked and helped himself. The breakfast consisted of bacon, potatoes, warm bread and black coffee. Seated on the ground Turk fashion, with plate on knees and cup by side, we ate our hearty meal.

After breakfast the bed wagon was loaded with its freight. The chuck wagon which was driven by the cook and drawn by six horses, pulled out for the next camp, followed by the wrangler with the bunch of unused saddle horses. Orders were given to the riders, the place of the next camp appointed. The range was divided into circles, beginning at the old camp and ending at the new. Riding the outside is the hardest of all. The boys took turns at this as each must use his best horse, start first and get in last. It is his business to round up all the cattle on the limits of the range and throw them toward the centre, where they will be taken up by the next man and so on until the whole is bunched together and driven to camp. Here they were held in a bunch until the foreman with his chosen riding men and trained cut horses went into the bunch and cut out the beef cattle and calves that had escaped branding and ear marking.

The beef cattle were then cut into a bunch by themselves and held by some of the men. After the beeves were out the calves were branded. The calves were roped from horseback, generally by both hind feet, then another rope was thrown over the head and the calf stretched out. Thus held by two horses the hot branding iron was applied. This required only a moment and "doggy" was on his feet making for the main bunch. So the work proceeded until the whole bunch had been worked.

The beef cattle were driven along with the wagons and night herded until five train loads had been gathered.

The unused saddle horses were herded and kept with the camp. They were brought to the wagons each morning by the wrangler. For a corral to catch the horses in, two long ropes were stretched out in the form of a triangle, using the wagon as one side, into which the bunch was driven. Each man then roped his horse for the day. A different horse is used each day, so that one horse is used only once in about eight or ten days, according to the number of horses a man has on his string.

I rode the outside one day with "Beaut" Bowers. We chose our stoutest horses, cinched on our hulls and rode in a steady lope from 5 o'clock in the morning until 2 o'clock in the afternoon.

When a bunch of cattle was found we started them in toward the centre on a full run. We took our slickers from behind our saddles and waved the cattle into a run, which carried them within the next rider's circle.

The cowboys are master hands at yelling, and cattle run at sight of a man on horseback much faster when he begins to yell.

Two or more men went on watch at sundown to keep the cattle from straying. Later in the evening the cattle become quiet and bed

Pueblo de Taos

down. If the night is still and nothing happens to disturb them, they will remain quiet all night. The stampede is one of the worst things that can happen, even now in these days of wire fences.

If the cattle are only a little scared they may be easily quieted, though sometimes they break away and the men on guard have to ride at breakneck speed through the night, over ground that is dangerous even in the day time. More than one fellow has met with a broken limb or ribs from such a mad ride.

When the cattle break away in this manner the men ride alongside of the bunch and gradually work up the leaders and sometimes even throw their horses over against them in an attempt to get them to "milling"—that is, get them to running in a circle. Once this is accomplished, the rest is more easy. The bunch is kept milling until exhausted, when they gradually slow down, and at last, after perhaps hours of hard riding, quiet down. Through the rest of the night they need close watching; they are nervous and may break away again. When the cattle become restless at night the boys sing and whistle and walk slowly around and around the bunch. The sound of the human voice seems to have a soothing effect on them.

When we had gathered five train loads of beef they were driven to the railroad station, where car after car was loaded.

23

The Egypt of America

Once I made a horseback ride from Trinidad, Colorado, to El Paso, following the old trail over the Glorietta mountains to Pueblo de Taos and thence by easy stages to El Paso, Texas, my object being to prospect for placer mines.

It is a wild, weird scene, when after crossing the Glorietta range, one finds himself in this storied valley of the Rio Grande, New Mexico, that mysterious land of sunshine, of eternal silence and (may I say) eternal sadness. Sunlight paints the landscapes in rarest tints of blues and greys, heightened by vermillion and bright ochre colourings on cliff and crag, whose silence of ages is broken only by the rumble of the train, to relapse again into its wonted quietude. The land has been asleep for over three hundred years, while the world's progress has been going on about her. Once she was aroused when the cattle men came from over the range and stocked her valleys, but the cattle did not do well. Then she laid down for another nap. These valleys are those of sadness like unto fabled regions of the hereafter, wherein ungodly spirits are destined to roam forever in isolation from kindred beings.

Sad-eyed Mexicans lean against the sunny side of their *adobe* huts—they are always leaning against something, as though their weak anatomies would not stand alone. They are poor, very poor, but proud. Let a stranger go to their *casas* and their hospitality is never wanting. A frugal meal of corn, beans and chile is divided with as free a hand as a minister's benediction. Sad-eyed sheep graze upon the scant vegetation of hill and valley, while the mournful, philosophic donkey does the work of the land,—and perhaps the thinking, too. When the shadows of night fall and the mountain range stands in dark relief against the sky the eye can trace the outlines of grotesque faces formed by irregular peaks and curves. Many of them have traditions old as the Sphinx, for the semi-civilization of the Aztecs that once inhabited this land dates hundreds of years before Cabeza de Vaca explored these valleys of the Pecos and Rio Grande.

The sacred fires of the Aztecs have died out in the ashes of the past, yet there are those living who still look for the coming of Montezuma. It seems that every race of people in their decline look for the coming of a redeemer. This belief is kept alive by the Pueblo Indians of these valleys, who bow to the sun from their housetops as he shines from over the mountain range at early morn. Like the men of Mars Hill, they believe in "the unknown God," whose name is too holy to be spoken. They hold sacred all animals living in or near water, which in this dry climate is the greatest blessing.

At Taos they have a tradition that at the flood a few faithful Pueblos gathered upon a mountain top and waited long and in vain for the waters to subside. At last a youth of royal blood and a beautiful virgin decorated with brilliant feathers, were let down from the cliff as an offering to the angry Deity. The waters soon fell, and the youth and maiden were transformed into statues of stone. With all the silence and sadness of this region, contentment seems to reign supreme, and if some genius with the pen of Washington Irving will study the simple ways of these Mexican people and write of their traditions he will do mankind a service and make himself famous.

Swiftly flows the Rio Grande along its shallow banks, from whence here and there runs an irrigating ditch which waters a patch of corn or vineyard, near the *adobe* houses which are scattered thickly along the banks of the river, from the Sangre de Christo mountains to the Mexican sea. Here for over three hundred years a semi-Spanish civilization has existed in a sweet contentment to which the Anglo-Saxon race was born a stranger. Here is the Egypt of America, teeming with the traditions of a simple people, content almost with breath alone.

The old mission of Las Cruces was among the first built by the Jesuits in this valley. Behind its altar were two crude paintings of Santo Domingo and Santa Rita, and between them the statuettes of the Virgin and St. Joseph. Beneath the whole was a painting, the scene of which the artist had located somewhere on the borderland between heaven and hell. Gilded saints were flying off in one direction while great horned toads and scorpions were pulling dark browed Mexicans and Indians into a sea of flames. At this mission was held the first Auto de Fa in New Mexico. An Apache chief had been made a prisoner and was set to work herding sheep. One day he lost one and the holy father said: "Son of the *infidel*, what did you do with that sheep?"

"I lost it," replied the Apache, "but you may take it out of my pay."

"Pay! what pay, you sacrilegious toad?"

"Why, out of my daily lashes."

"Holy saints protect us!" exclaimed the *padre*. "Theft, disbelief and the church itself defied! We will have Judaism here next. Away with him to the faggot fires."

Then, as the flames crept around the Apache chained to a stone post, he repented and the father baptised him and agreed to meet him up yonder, but did not offer to put out the fire. As about two hundred and fifty years have passed since then, (as at 1906), they have perhaps met and adjusted their differences by this time.

Cruel as these old religious zealots may have been at times, they did a world of good, for they semi-civilized the natives.

Beside the yellow waters of the Rio Grande and near the Sierra Blanco range, lies El Paso. Its streets were busy with traffic, and tall buildings rose majestically on either side. But the wind sweeps through the mountain pass and the dust storms darken the sky for days at a time. Like all other desert regions the chief boast of its inhabitants is climate and "this exceptionally bad weather only known heretofore to the oldest settler" grows irksome when one has heard it five hundred times in like regions. Around and about El Paso for three hundred miles north, south, east, and west, is desert, and to those who have never seen a desert country it is surprising how all conditions of life are changed. These conditions are harder than in humid countries. In our northern land between Canada and the Gulf, that which sustains life grows in abundance and few people there are who know what it is to be hungry. But here in El Paso there are many of the poorer classes who actually suffer for something to eat.

Within thirty minutes the entire scene had changed. I had crossed the river and was in El Paso del Norte, on the Mexican side of the Rio Grande. Narrow lane-like streets, white *adobe* buildings with heavily grated windows make the stranger feel that he has intruded on a convention of county jails. In half an hour I had gone backward three centuries. Silent, dark-browed figures walked the streets with Spanish cloak or serape wound majestically around them, donkeys laden with wood, peddlers with hogskins filled with *pulque*, strangely attired Mexicans, all formed a weird street scene not soon to be forgotten.

We Saw Smoke Signals

It was on the *plaza* here that General Bonito Juarez camped his little force of 150 men while he went to Washington to appeal to this government to enforce the Monroe doctrine in the midst of our own rebellion. When the American ultimatum went forth to France, Napoleon III withdrew his French troops. Then Juarez marched on to the City of Mexico gathering strength as he went. The unfortunate Maximilian fell into his hands and was executed on the "*Cerra de las Campus*" (The Hill of the Bells), near Queretaro on the 19th of June, 1867. General Bonito Juarez was a full blooded Aztec whom Fate seems to have ordained to bring about the political regeneration of his country.

It was a gala day in El Paso del Norte. A company of Rurales from the interior was to contest in a shooting match with the Carbine Rifles and bets were running high. Both sides did some good shooting at 500 yards and the Carbine Rifles won. Bets were paid freely and everybody was in a good humour.

I had formed the acquaintance of Captain Esperanza Provincio and at his invitation I fired a few shots, hitting the bull's eye each time with one of the Mexican carbines.

This excited everybody's attention and soon some Americans offered to bet that I could beat any man they had in their company shooting at 500 yards. The bets were taken and I was pitted against six crack shots belonging to the Carbine Rifles. I won in every instance and received a neat sum for my skill from my American friends who had won the Mexicans' money. Captain Provincio, not to be outdone in generosity, caused a handsome silver medal to be made which he afterwards presented to me with the compliments of his company.

The Military Band from Chihuahua discoursed sweet music in the *plaza* that night to a large crowd of citizens from both towns.

The Mexican *plaza* is the national chimney corner, where at evening a band plays wild, weird strains of martial music, and the young gather about the old to hear tales of daring and valour. It is the plaza where the traditions are kept alive and where the young are taught that the very acme of glory in life is the battlefield.

The soft effects of moonlight, the *plaza* with its green trees, fountains, and sauntering of *senors* and *senoritas* in the presence of the silver-toned bells of an old cathedral and the weird strains of martial music, form the pleasant remembrances of El Paso del Norte, since named Juarez.

In company with a Mexican miner named Martenez I rode westward along the Mexican border for two days, and thence toward the northwest to Gila River, when one morning we saw to the southward a column of smoke ascending. We knew it to be Indian signals and so rode our bronchos into a clump of bushes on the river banks in order to be out of sight.

On scanning the plain with my field glass I saw a column of dust rising far to the north like a pillar of smoke and rightly guessed it to be caused by a body of horsemen. From the speed they were making, I judged they were either pursuers or being pursued. In either event, we felt fairly safe, as our bronchos were in good condition, were splendid animals, and as we had used them well of late, we believed we could outdistance them if they proved to be hostile Indians. Nearer the cloud of dust approached and the closer I looked with my field glass until I discovered they were Apaches making all haste to reach the mountains. They crossed the Gila River, which was at flood tide, five hundred yards from where we were concealed and disappeared in the direction from whence we saw the smoke signals. We had made up our minds to remain in our hiding places until night, when I saw another dust cloud in the same direction as the first, and in a little while I made out that the dust was raised by a party of scouts and rode out to meet them. They were led by Captain Jack Crawford and were in pursuit of the murderous band of Apaches who had been killing ranchmen in the upper country.

The scouts continued on the pursuit, while we rode away in the direction of Silver City.

It was that band of marauding Apaches which we saw crossing the Gila River that furnished the cause for the Geronimo war, which broke out soon afterwards. It was not until March, in 1886, that General Crook captured Geronimo[1] and his band of Chiricahua Apaches, who escaped from him while they were being taken to Ft. Bowie. The chief and band were recaptured by General Nelson A. Miles in Mexico some months afterwards and sent to Fort Pickens, Florida. Geronimo and fourteen of his band were afterwards taken to Ft. Sill, Indian Territory. Here the cunning old chief spent most of his time playing *monte* with the soldiers.

---

1. *Geronimo* by Geronimo, the life of the famous Apache warrior in his own words is also published by Leonaur.

24

In the Dome of the Sky

There are three ways of reaching the summit of Pike's Peak—walking, riding a *burro*, or seated comfortably in one of the coaches of the Cog Road.

It was three o'clock in the afternoon when the car was pulled out of the yards at the foot of the peak. The strongly-built little engine puffed like a living thing, obedient to the task of drawing its heavy load. The wheels moved rapidly, and we ascended the steepest mountain railroad in the world. It wound about the mountain sides in little curves, climbing, always climbing higher and higher, until we shuddered at the dizzy heights as we looked down into the great yawning chasms thousands of feet below.

The air grew cooler in the deep mountain defiles densely wooded with fir, pine, cedar and quaking asp. A great fire once swept up these gorges and burned away the fir and pine in patches; in their place came the quaking asp, growing here and there in thickets.

Along the slopes and in the dells, wild flowers grew with the luxuriant profusion of a semi-tropical clime. There were columbines and tiger lilies growing at an altitude of ten thousand feet.

Nature has done some queer things in the mighty rocks which stand sentinel guard along the route.

One great boulder is named the Hooded Monk, because of its resemblance to the human head in a monk's cowl. There is a Gog and Magog. The Sphynx, the Lone Fisherman, and many other images of man, bird and beast, wrought by nature's hand in stone.

We glided by one of the loveliest glens in all the mountains; it was called Shady Springs. Here the oriole, the raven and the big blue jay of the mountains have built their nests and take their morning baths in waters clear as crystal from a spring that gushed from fern and moss covered banks.

Farther on to the right a stream plunges in wild, mad swirl of clear waters and dashing from rock to rock in foamy white, forms Echo Falls. An elephant's head in bass relief was here to be seen wrought in stone.

We rounded Cameron's Cone and Sheep Mountain and soon began the ascent of the "Big Hill," which has a rise of 1,300 feet to the mile.

Nearing timber line, the road ahead appears to be almost at an angle of 45 degrees.

Higher and higher; the great chasm below grew almost a mile deeper. On one side there were masses of square rock which looked like they were broken by human hands. Here, far above timber line, a variety of wild flowers blossomed, while among the rocks lived some of the strangest little animals, the whistling marmot, a fur animal about the size of an overgrown cat, and the *peka*, which has the legs of a rabbit and the head of a mountain rat; there were also minks, weasels, porcupines and mountain rats.

At the summit was where the magnificence of the great panorama burst upon our view. Northward, away down on the bluish haze of the horizon, rose the Arapahoe peaks—Long and Grey's Peak, with their white summits glistening in the setting sun. Northwest, Mt. Massive and Mt. Sheridan were outlined against the clear blue sky, while the green sward of the famous South Park, a hundred miles distant, lay between. College Range, Mt. Yale, Mt. Princeton, Mt. Ouray and Cavenaugh reared their rugged heads far to the west, while green mountain ranges of lesser note lay half way between them.

Far to the southwest, far as the eye could reach, faintly outlined against the sky, rose the snowy peaks of the Sangre de Christo and Sierra Blanco Mountains on the other side of the grand San Luis Valley.

Looking to the south, were the Spanish Peaks and range of Greenhorn Mountains, and a little to the southeast rose the snow-capped Gloriettas on the borders of New Mexico.

To the east, lay the mighty plains, stretching away to where the blue of the sky blended in coppery tones with the billowy green.

There were dark spots here and there that were dense forests of pine. The cloud banners hung above, in all the gorgeous colours of sunset in crimson, purple and gold.

A dark shadow crept out upon the plain toward the east, like the finger of a mighty giant. It moved rapidly along, covering the yellow sand lines that mark the course of old river beds, and finally, this shadow of Pike's Peak was covered by the shadows of other mountains lower down, until the plain was shrouded in the sable garb of eventide.

But westward, the gold and crimson of the sky lingered long above the distant peak of Mt. Ouray. The purple haze grew denser, and the silence of the hour was made more solemn by the mountains standing out in dark silhouette as the shadows of the night grew deeper and denser.

At such a time as this, one feels as though he stood upon the boundary of another world, while all about the wide white waste and hush of space, eternity and the infinite were calling to other glories, too great for the understanding of the human mind.

Here, in the very dome of the skies, in this clear air, the bright worlds seem to hover over, while the vault is strewn with stars, like isles of light in the misty sea above our heads. The purity of the heavenly prospect awakens that eternal predisposition to melancholy, which dwells in the depth of the soul, and soon the spectacle absorbs us in a vague and indefinable reverie. It is then that thousands of questions spring up in our mind, and a thousand points of interrogation rise to our sight—the great enigma of creation.

The harvest moon shed her yellow light over the distant plain, and gilded with a phosphorescent light the rocks and crags of the almost bottomless chasm below. The rocks took on fantastic shapes, while distant mountains rose in spectral form.

I sat throughout the night, watching the ever changing panorama, the most wondrous ever spread out to the gaze of man.

The moon and stars were bright above, while far down below storm clouds had formed where within their inky blackness the forked lightning played like so many fiery serpents.

There were thunderous crashes in the wild rocky pit below, where huge rocks were shivered by lightning bolts, while echo, echoing back the thunders of heaven's artillery, would seem as though a legion of imprisoned Joshuas were reaching upward again for that sun which would stand still no more over the plains of Agalon.

The shades of night grew deeper and then the blackness was driven back from the east by a flush of grey, gradually changing to a deep scarlet tinged with yellow and the sun burst above a dashing sea of clouds. There were purple and crimson waves below rising and falling in mighty billows. A shipless and shoreless ocean whose raging bosom claims no living thing.

An hour more and this purple sea of clouds has drifted on forever from the sight of human eyes.

The summer sun beamed once more upon the vast panorama. Far down upon the green *mesa* lay Lake Moraine, glistening in the morning light like a molten mass of silver.

Smoke was seen to rise from Denver and Pueblo, both fully sixty miles away. Some smelters in Cripple Creek and Victor could be seen with the naked eye, while the streets of Colorado Springs were but sandy marks like a checkerboard upon the plain.

I descended the peak on foot amid the beauteous scenes of green mountain defiles, where dashing waters sing eternal symphonies amid ferns and flowers, and the song of birds gladden the heart in their sweet echoes from rock to rock.

25

Where Nature is at Her Best

If one would view the wondrous surroundings of Manitou, in all their grandeur, let him some bright morning stroll up the long yellow road that winds its serpentine course through Williams Canon. A little brook with waters cold and clear as crystal, dashes along its pebbly bed beside the road, murmuring as it were, a song of regret at leaving its enchanted home on its journey to the sea. The road is known as Temple Drive, named so because many towering rocks look, at first glance, like ruined temples of India or of Egypt along the Nile.

At times the road narrows to barely carriage room between great high cliffs, and again abruptly brings the majestic panorama of the canon into view. High above, among the mountain crags is the Cathedral of St. Peter, like a massive ruin whose cornice, column and frescoed walls had fallen with decay ages past. A little farther and the Amphitheatre rises against the cliffs in hues of brown and yellow, with brighter streaks of golden ochre here and there, which fairly gleam and glisten in the morning sun. High above and in the background on either side are hills of emerald green, studded with cedar and pine, and dotted with flowers of gorgeous colour and of form, found elsewhere only in Alpine lands. There are towering rocks that rise a thousand feet above the road, which resemble the ruins of a Moorish citadel. There are towers, mosques and temples, with turrets and battlements, needing only the white-robed figure of the Arab in turban to make one fancy himself suddenly transported to that enchanting and mysterious land of *sultan* and slave. No sky of Tangiers was ever deeper, clearer or bluer, and no air of Geneva was ever purer or sweeter.

The road makes a sharp turn and traverses backward nearly half a mile, then turns again and runs in its original direction, climbing the mountain side like a great yellow serpent resting its head a thousand feet among the crags, where eagles build their nests; the white and red painted building that marks the entrance to the Cave of the Winds, does duty as the serpent's head. From this dizzy point of sight, the great mountain gorge with its grey and brown rocks, and the sloping foothills of green that stretch away to where fair Manitou lies cradled in the valley, form a wondrous panorama.

Eastward, down on the horizon, far as the eye can reach, stretch the mighty plains, westward the higher range of the eternal Rockies, and above all rises the snow-capped summit of Pike's Peak, about whose whitened crest float the fleecy clouds of the soft, still summer morning.

At the entrance of the Cave of the Winds one follows the guide into the dark pathway that leads into the subterranean chambers, where at some remote period a wild mountain cataract has whirled and plunged its maddening waters, in swirl and maelstrom into the black abyss of the earth. One is so suddenly transported from the gladsome and awe-inspiring scenes without, that the lamp and figure of the guide become spectral, his voice sounds in hollow tones and is echoed back from cavernous depths as though titanic monsters were repeating his words.

Knowing the cause, one bursts into a laugh, then the monsters laugh, too, long and loud, and still others take up the laugh, way down the black corridors, and high above in domes, as though all the imps of darkness were there to laugh at one in revenge for intrusion.

The guide flashes a magnesium light and the pilgrim beholds the wonders of Curtain Hall, which nature has ornamented with strangely coloured stalactites glistening here and there on the cavern walls, and again where they form a curtain of an intricate work and beauty as though wrought by maiden hands, amid scenes of love and apple blossoms. Mutely you follow the flaring lamp of the guide into the blackness of winding passages and across bridges that span bottomless pits opening into the very breast of the mountain, and when the magnesium light is again flashed, one sees the arching dome of the great canopy hall, its stalactite nymphs, Bed of Cauliflowers, Frescoed Ceiling, Lake Basin, Grandmother's Skillet, Bat's Wing, Prairie Dog Village and Fairy Scene; all presenting a picture weird and ghost-like in the moment of stillness, and heightened by the demoniacal, fiendish voices that repeat your every word.

On through other crooked subterranean passages where other demons mock the sound of your footsteps, through what the guide calls

Boston Avenue, one enters Diamond Hall. The lofty ceiling is decorated its entire length by graceful festoons and wreaths of coral and flowering alabaster. The walls sparkle and scintillate with the rainbow shades, thrown back from the myriad brilliants that stud these walls like diamonds set by hand in some antique mosaic work.

In these regions of darkness you are led by the guide until the Hall of Beauty is lit up to your astonished gaze. Crystal flowers of the most delicate design and exquisite workmanship hang in festoons from every nook and corner. Sparkling incrustations that rival the beauty of Arctic frosts and glitter in the bright light are sparkling on every side. Most wondrous of all there are a million stalactite figures in miniature that appear to be in a pandemonium of outlandish contortions. Maybe, who knows, but what the goblin spirits once lived here and worked out curious things in translucent stone, further down the black passages of earth and caught a glimpse of our ancestors in some of the great halls of torture way down below, and so reproduced the scene as Jack Frost has been wont to paint the leaves of summer on our frosted window panes.

The *Magi* of this dark abode, the guide in wide *sombrero*, black eyed and wearing a moustache fierce as a bandit of the Corsican isle, though harmless as a Kansas Populist, beckons on and leads the way. Here the Bridal Chamber, and there writhing reptiles, dancing devils, monkeys, beasts, birds in every form and riotous posture. Then as the weird wilderness is shut out in semi-darkness, one is inclined to ask of him with lamp and sombrero, "Mister, have I got 'em, or have you?"

The light flashes on Crystal Palace, where gems and jewels bedeck the walls, where huge chrysanthemums or chestnut burrs stand out in bold relief in fadeless crystal flowers moulded from tinted rock, and all seem to mutely plead for recognition as we pass. These silent beauties hidden away under the mountain slopes, where the rays of sun can never reach, speak with the beauty of their creation, to the soul with as great a love and power as the violet in the sequestered glens.

It is mysterious. It is strange. It is one of those unaccountable things in nature which no man can explain that here in the very bowels of the earth, human scenes have been reproduced and human passions portrayed.

Here perhaps centuries before man's eyes gazed upon the scene, we find in moulded stone, the head of a buffalo, the skeleton of a mastodon, the drapery of a palace, the bride at the altar, the face of sorrow, the Nymphs of Love, War and Poetry are depicted upon these stones.

Once more the light of day, the great chasm beneath, the turquoise skies above, and mighty plains beyond, brings one to the realm of the outer world.

The spectral figure of an hour ago is a pleasant faced young man, who bids you follow the winding path that leads around the mountain side some three hundred yards and which ends at the entrance to the Grand Caverns.

Desiring to see all, you meekly follow another guide through a dark labyrinth and find yourself in the mighty Rotunda of the Caverns. Here loyal hands have raised monuments to Lee, Grant and McKinley. They are built of fragments of stone cast by visitors to the memory of these heroes. The Imp, the guide, motions on; you are next within a mighty auditorium and as there comes upon you the awful silence and stillness of the hour, you hear musical notes, swelling and cadencing louder and louder until they break in thunderous tones within the cavernous depths, "*Nearer, Nearer, My God to Thee.*" High above, mid the domes of the cavern, the light shows the organist to be playing upon the stalactites which Nature has attuned to the same chords as instruments made by human hands. These stalactites are of crystal, and have the same resonant sound as though they were of finely tempered glass. Up and down the corridors of the cave, through winding passages and circling galleries above, come echoes of "*Nearer, My God to Thee,*" in waves and billows of sound, such as is only heard by artificial means in the Notre Dame of Paris.

Round about somewhere, in one of the chambers, near the entrance, the visitor is shown a human skeleton, as it was found at the time of the discovery of the cave. It belonged perhaps to that race of men known as the Cliff Dwellers, who once upon a time, when the world was new, lived, loved and reared a race of men in this fair region of the west whom Saxby, a western poet, touches with his magic pen, and beautifies the tradition of them when he says,

> *Dismantled towers and turrets broken,*
> *Like grim war-worn braves who keep*
> *A silent guard with grief unspoken*
> *Watch o'er the graves, by the canon weep,*
> *The nameless graves of a race forgotten*
> *Whose deeds, whose words, whose fate are one*
> *With the mist, long ages past, begotten of the sun*

The sun is now casting his shadows toward the east. From this point of sight we see the Midland trains creeping from tunnels like monster creatures of the Azotic period crawling from their lair. There are green valleys below, and there is also a long serpentine road leading to this side of the mountain by which visitors again reach the pleasant shades of Manitou. Silence, and even sadness, abound in the green-clad mountains beyond. They speak in whispers to themselves and you can understand them if you will. They tell you in sweet, soft voices of the song of birds, the lullaby of mountain brooks, and by gentle winds that sing a song of peace through cedar, fir and pine, that the love of nature, is the love of nature's God.

26

When the West was New

Thirty years have passed since I first crossed the plains, (as at 1906). The buffalo and antelope have disappeared and in their stead herds of cattle and sheep graze in countless thousands. Farms are tilled where raging fires swept the mighty plains in ungoverned fury; cities and towns rear their spires where once stood Indian *tepees*. The westward march of civilization has stretched across the continent and redeemed the desert. The soil has been made to yield its harvest and the eternal hills to give up their buried treasure. For the men who made the trails by which these things were done, life's shadows are falling toward the east. They braved the vicissitudes of the western wilderness as heroic as any soldier faced the battlefield; and the trails over which the pioneers slowly made their way across the desert wastes, were blazed with blood and fire. Women, too, on the frontier, volumes might be written of her sacrifices—Indians, poverty, years of patient toil, far from former home and friends, the luxuries of organised society denied, all for the purpose of earning a home and a competence for declining years.

It was my good fortune to become personally acquainted with many early pioneers of the west and number them among my warmest friends, and as I recall to mind some of their heroic deeds I feel that these chapters would be incomplete without a personal mention of a few of them.

★★★★★★

Captain Jack Crawford, the poet scout, is one of those noble characters whose memory will live so long as records exist of the pioneers who braved the vicissitudes of the frontier and made possible our Western civilization of today. A man of broad mind, daring and brave and yet with all the sweet tenderness of a child of nature, he became

Captain Jack Crawford

great by achievements alone. Others have gained a temporary fame by dime novel writers. Captain Jack, in comparison with others, stands out as a diamond of the first water. He has helped to make more trails than any scout unless it was Kit Carson. That was before the war. During that struggle he was wounded three times in the service of his country. When the war closed he was for many years chief of scouts under General Custer. He laid out Leadville in the Black Hills in 1876, and was of great service to the government in the settlement of the Indian troubles which succeeded the Custer massacre.

Captain Jack is one of the very few thrown together with the wild, rough element of the frontier who maintained a strictly moral character. I knew him in the "Hills" in 1876 and have known him ever since, and have always found him to be the same genial, whole-souled, brave Captain Jack.

★★★★★★

John McCoach, a pioneer of the sixties, was a among a party near the headwaters of Wind River, Wyoming, in August, 1866, who defeated a thousand warriors with the first Henri rifles used on the plains. The story is best told in Mr. McCoach's own language.

> Our mule trains consisting of thirty-eight wagons and forty-two men, left Fort Leavenworth, Kansas, in April, 1866, for Virginia City, Montana. We were all old soldiers and most of us had seen four years of war and, inured as we were to dangers, we cared but little for the hostile Indians of the plains.
> When we reached Fort Laramie, a big council of Indians was in progress, Chiefs Red Cloud, Spotted Tail, American Horse and others of lesser note were there to demand guns and ammunition from the government, saying they needed them with which to hunt game. Officials of high rank from Washington were there to listen to them and among the newspaper correspondents was Henry M. Stanley, who had been sent out by the *New York Herald*.
> After days of deliberation the Indians were refused the arms and they broke camp in bad humour.
> Before allowing our party to proceed the commander of the fort had us lined up for an inspection of our arms which were a miscellaneous collection all the way from an old muzzle-loading rifle to a modern musket. He told us we were too poorly armed to proceed, when the wagon boss took him to some of

the wagons and showed him 200 Henri rifles and abundant ammunition which we were freighting to gun dealers in Virginia City. He then allowed us to go.

I was herding the mules one afternoon near the headwaters of Wind River, when a party of Sioux Indians, led by Little Thunder, made a dash, intending to stampede the animals. One of them carried a rawhide bag containing some pebbles, which made a hideous noise. Despite their efforts, the mules broke for our camp of circled wagons. I tried to shoot the Indian with the rattle bag but missed. Then I dismounted and the next shot I cut the quiver of arrows from his back when he gave a long yell and throwing himself on the side of his pony, got away.

When I reached camp the rifles had been distributed. We were called from our slumbers the next morning at four o'clock and told to keep quiet and hold our fire.

With the first gray streak of dawn about one thousand warriors began to encircle us, riding at full speed and like a great serpent, drawing the coil closer about us with each revolution of the circle. Then the order came and forty-two blazing rifles with eighteen shots to each one dealt out death. Four years of war had taught the men the value of a steady nerve and deliberate aim and before the astonished Indians could retreat the plain was strewn with their dead and wounded.

These Indians had been at the Fort Laramie council and had seen us drawn up in line with our old assortment of guns for inspection and had counted on us being easy prey. They were the first Henri rifles used on the plains and caused the Indians to speak of us in whispers, as the white men who could load a gun once and then shoot all day. That morning we built our fires with arrows and cooked our breakfast. After that the Indians avoided us as though we were devouring monsters.

★★★★★★

The experience of John McCoach's party in surprising Little Thunder's braves with their Henri rifles, calls to mind a story often told in Fort Laramie of how General W. S. Harney fooled these same Sioux Indians under Little Thunder a few years previous to their attack on the McCoach outfit. Jake Smith, a soldier with General Harney in the 60's thus relates the story:

General Harney established his headquarters in Leavenworth,

Kansas. Little Thunder was at the head of the Sioux and sent word that he was willing either to fight or shake hands with the white soldier. Harney replied that if the Indian was without choice in the matter it might as well be fight; besides, as he remembered his orders, he was to whip some one. So Harney met Little Thunder and about a thousand war men on the North Platte in Nebraska. He whipped them good and some of the Indians' friends back East tried to make trouble for Harney because he had not had a long preliminary confab with Little Thunder. That Sioux band was a mild-mannered set long after Harney went back to Leavenworth.

It was after this fight that Harney threw the Society for the Protection of Western Savages into a particular frenzy. The wagon trail for Oregon and California led from Fort Leavenworth to Fort Kearney, Neb., then to Julesburg, in Colorado, from there to Fort Laramie, through old South Pass to Badger and then to Salt Lake. The trip by ox train took about one hundred days with good luck. I know of a party that was on the road 300 days, delayed by Indians and then snowbound. That wasn't a pleasant winter for a boy of 16.

Every now and then a band of Sioux would ride up to an ox train, kill if they felt like it and always drive away the stock. Soldiers would be sent out and have the pleasure of following the Indians' trail until the weather would make winter quarters necessary. Harney started from Leavenworth after one band, taking about 400 cavalrymen, or dragoons. The Indians loafed along ahead of him till they reached the mountains, and then Harney turned back. It was the old story, the Sioux said, and their scouts followed the soldiers until they were well into Kansas. Then the Sioux knew the country was clear for new operations.

Harney stopped on the Blue River in Northern Kansas near where Marysville now stands. A wagon train reached there from Leavenworth and Harney had all the freight unloaded—simply seized the train—then he put 400 soldiers into those wagons and in two were mountain guns. The great covers were pulled close and leaving a guard over the abandoned freight and horses, Harney started on his journey as a bull-whacker. Not a soldier or officer was permitted to put his head from under a cover in the day time, and only at night a few got leave to stretch their legs. All day they sat in those wagon beds, hot and dusty, playing cards, fighting and chewing tobacco for pastime. There were twenty-six of those wagons and they trailed along as if they were carrying dead freight; no faster nor slower than the ordinary freighters, and making camp at the usual places, forming the usual corral of wagons and herding stock at night. The train reached Fort Kearny and slowly went across the South Platte to Julesburg. Occasional Indian signs made Harney have hope.

The outfit was seventy miles on the way to Laramie when the big day came, and it came quick. Behind them on the trail the men on the outside saw a war party—some say there were five hundred Indians in it. Even if they hadn't been painted the fact that they were without women or children would have told the story. The train made the usual preparations for an Indian attack, throwing the wagons into a circle, or more of an ellipse, and unhooking the five lead yokes to each wagon. A front wheel of each wagon touched a hind wheel of the one in front and the tongues were turned to the outside. At the front end of the corral an opening about fifteen feet wide was left, but at the rear the opening into the corral was about fifty feet wide. That, also, was according to the freighters' methods; after a night camp the cattle would be driven into the corral through the big end to be yoked for the day.

Harney didn't have time to drive his oxen into the corral, or else he didn't want to. Only the five yoke of leaders were unhooked and they were then chained to the front wheel of their wagon. The space in the corral was all clear for the Indians, whose method of attacking a wagon train was to rush into the corral and do their shooting. They were a happy lot of braves this day; the war band started for the train when the corral was forming; they spread out like a fan and then came together again and started for the big opening as hard as their war ponies could carry them. A whooping, variegated mob with no more clothes than the paint gave it fell into the corral and then real fun began.

Those soldiers, who had been sweating under canvas for a few weeks wanted excitement and revenge. The tarpaulins went up and they shot down into that mess of braves as fast as they could load. The two mountain guns completed the surprise and the bucks hardly fired a shot before their ponies were climbing over one another to get out the way they came. It was the only real Indian panic. When the last Sioux brave able to ride disappeared across the prairie there was a big mess to clean up. In those days the Indians needed school all the year around. However, one old buck, a little chief, seemed to be impressed. He was near a mountain gun when the fire opened. 'Harney is the man who shot wagons at us,' is the way he told about it years later.

★★★★★★

Charles S. Stroble, "Mountain Charley," known as the cowboy painter, was adopted by the Ute Indians at the age of nineteen. I have often heard him tell the following experience:

> It was the most marvellous instance of daredevil bravery I ever witnessed. It happened in 1866 when I was living with the Utes west of the range in Middle Park, Colorado. They had adopted me a year or so before when I was twenty years of age. My name in Ute was Paghaghet, which means 'long-haired.'
> It was at this time that the old feud between the Utes and Arapahoes was at its height. Our scouts found the Arapahoes coming in from North Park in the endeavour to surprise some of the Utes' hunting parties. Our runners having come in and informed us, we soon collected a war party and started north to intercept our enemies.
> I was with the scouting party which went in advance, and I was the only white man in the entire tribe. We found the sign left by their scouts, and then concealed ourselves until our war party could come up. As soon as reinforcements arrived we deployed on either side of a gulch or *cañon*, with our horses hidden away among the rocks and timber in charge of horse-holders.
> We had not waited long when we sighted the advance of the Arapahoes down below us in the gulch. We were unnoticed, because we left no tracks in the gulch and had deployed some distance below.
> When the main body of the enemy had passed our place of concealment we opened fire on them from each side of the gulch, and they, not knowing our numbers, were panic-stricken. They wheeled and came tumbling back up the gulch in great confusion, and all the time subjected to our fire. To be sure, they were returning the fire wherever they caught sight of us, but we

had by far the best of them and peppered them hotly.

The Utes got about eight scalps, as the Arapahoes, although they carried their wounded with them in their flight, were in too big a hurry to look after the dead.

My Indian brother, Paah, or 'Black Tailed Deer," and Wangbich, the 'Antelope,' were with me behind some sheltering rocks, and on each side of me. As the Arapahoes were scurrying away through the canon below we noticed particularly one fine-looking young buck, wearing a splendid war bonnet, which flaunted bravely in the breeze. This fellow was singled out by Paah. At the crack of his rifle the Arapahoe threw out his arms and fell backward from his pony and the pony galloped away.

Paah, elated at the success of his shot, dropped his rifle and plunged down the steep side of the canon, which ran up here at an angle of about forty-five degrees, the other Indians passing all the time and letting loose at him a fusillade of rifle shots and flights of arrows. At length Paah got to his dead Arapahoe, planted his foot on the back of the man's neck, grasped both scalplock and side braids, gave them a turn on his wrist and with the aid of his knife secured the full scalp.

Then seizing the war bonnet, he came tearing up the side of the gulch, his trophies in one hand and his knife held dagger wise in the other, to assist him in making the steep ascent.

The arrows and bullets flew thickly about him, but, marvellous to tell, he arrived on the little flat space back of us without a scratch. Waving his bloody spoils above his head he essayed to give the Ute yell of victory, but he was so exhausted that he was only able to let out a funny squeak as he fell prostrate to avoid the shots that were now pouring in our direction. Wangbich and I covered him the best we could by emptying our six-shooters at the Arapahoes, and he finally succeeded in crawling to shelter.

On the return of our war expedition to the principal village we celebrated our victory in royal style. The Utes from other villages kept pouring in, and there was dancing afternoon and night for many days. This chief village was located under some high rocks on the Grand river, near a hot spring. The principal feature of the celebration was a scalp parade, a gorgeous affair in which all kinds of silvered ornaments, feathered and beaded costumes were worn. I afterward painted this splendid scene as it appeared to me and the picture is now hanging in the Iroquois club in Chicago.

★★★★★★

George P. Marvin says:

Possibly my experience in the bull-whacking days across the plains does not materially differ from that of other men who piloted six yoke of cattle hitched to eighty hundred of freight across the desert. Yet there were many incidents connected with life upon the plains that have never been written.

There was scarcely a day passed but something occurred that would furnish material upon which the writer of romance could build an interesting book of adventures.

In the freighting days of the early '60's, the overland trail up the Platte River was a broad road 200 or more feet in width. This was reached from various Missouri River points, as a great trunk line of railroad is now supplied by feeders. From Leavenworth, Atchison and St. Joe, those freighters who went the northern route crossed the Blue River at Marysville, Kansas, Oketo and other points, and travelled up the Little Blue, crossing over the divide and striking the big road at Dogtown, ten miles east of Fort Kearney. From Nebraska City, which was the principal freighting point upon the river from '64 until the construction of the Union Pacific railroad. What was known as the Steam Wagon road was the great trail. This feeder struck the Platte at a point about forty miles east of Kearney. It derived its name from an attempt to draw freight wagons over it by the use of steam, after the manner of the traction engine of today.

My first trip across the plains was over this route, which crossed the Big Blue a few miles above the present town of Crete, Nebraska. At the Blue crossing we were 'organised,' a detachment of soldiers being there for that purpose, and no party of less than thirty men was permitted to pass. Under this organisation, which was military in its character, we were required to remain together, to obey the orders of our 'captain,' and to use all possible precaution against the loss of our scalps and the freight and cattle in our care.

The daily routine of the freighter's life was to get up at the first peep of dawn, yoke up and if possible get 'strung out' ahead of other trains, for there was a continuous stretch of white covered wagons as far as the eye could reach.

With the first approach of day, the night herder would come to camp and call the wagon boss. He would get up, pound upon each wagon and call the men to 'turn out,' and would then mount his saddle mule and go out and assist in driving in the cattle.

The corral was made by arranging the wagons in a circular form, the front wheel of one wagon interlocking with the hind wheel of the one in front of it. Thus two half circles were formed with a gap at either end. Into this corral the cattle were driven and the night herder watched one gap and the wagon boss the other, while the men yoked up.

The first step in the direction of yoking up was to take your lead yoke upon your shoulder and hunt up your off leader. Having found your steer you put the bow around his neck and with the yoke fastened to him, lead him to the wagon, where he was fastened to the wheel by a chain. You then took the other bow and led your near leader with it to his place under the yoke. Your lead chain was then hooked to the yoke and laid over the back of the near leader, and the other cattle were hunted up and yoked in the same manner until the wheelers were reached. Having the cattle all yoked, you drove them all out, chained together, and hitched them to the wagon.

The first drive in the morning would probably be to 10 o'clock, or later, owing to the weather and distance between favourable camping grounds. Cattle were then unyoked and the men got their first meal of the day. The cattle were driven in and yoked for the second drive any time from 2 to 4 o'clock, the time of starting being governed by the heat, two drives of about five to seven hours each being made each day. The rate of travel was about two miles an hour, or from 20 to 25 miles a day, the condition of the roads and the heat governing.

This, then, was the regular daily routine, though the yoking up of cattle was often attended with difficulty. Many freighting trains started from the Missouri River with not more than two yoke of cattle in the six that comprised each team, that had ever worn a yoke before. Many had to be 'roped,' and not a few of the wildest, as the Texas and Cherokee varieties, were permitted to wear their yokes continually, for weeks.

While the bull-whacker's life was full of that adventure and romance that possessed its fascination, there were some very rough sides to it, though taking it all in all, it afforded an experience that few indeed would part with, and in after years there is nothing that I recall with more genuine pleasure than life in the camps upon the plains during the freighting days.

In an aggregation of men such as manned the prairie schooners of thirty odd years ago there were some very peculiar characters. This was especially true of those old 'Desert Tars,' who for the time made bull-wacking a profession and who were never so happy as when swinging a twenty-foot whip over a string of steers.

These droll people bore nicknames suggested by characteristics or conditions, and there were few indeed who responded to any other name, in fact, I have been intimately associated with men about the camp fire for months and never knew their real name.

A tall, slender person might be known as 'Lengthy' or 'Slim'; a short, stout one as 'Shorty' or 'Stub-and-Twist.' We had in one of our trains 'Kentuck,' who happened to hail from the Blue Grass State, also 'Sucker Ike,' who was from Illinois; 'Buckeye Bill' was from Ohio, while 'Hawkeye Hank' was from Iowa. 'Hoosier Dave' was from Posey County, while 'Yank' hailed from the far east; 'Mormon Jack' was an old-time bullwhacker who used to pass himself off for a Mormon when it suited his convenience; 'Bishop Lee' also played Mormon when we were over in the Salt Lake Valley; the man with red or auburn hair was invariably called 'Reddy,' 'Sandy' or 'Pinky,' while another whose facial architecture was of the Romanesque style would be called 'Nosey.'

These quaint characters would place a 'Wild West' comedy upon the boards without much acting. The costumes varied as much as their names. Some wore flannel shirts, some cotton of any and all colours, while others dressed in drilling jumpers. Their pants or overalls were held up by a belt, as suspenders were unknown. One character that was with us for a year or more, was a man called 'Scotty,' a native of Scotland, and a sailmaker by trade. He used to mend and patch his clothes and the clothes of the other boys, until it was difficult to tell the original goods. His strong point was 'foxing' clothes with canvas which he always carried for that purpose. He would take a new pair of pants and 'fox' them with white canvas, putting large patches over the knees, around the knees, around the pockets, in the seat and crotch, until they looked real artistic. He usually 'pinked' the edges of his patches or 'foxing,' and I have known the boys to pay his as much as $5 for 'foxing' a pair of heavy wool pants with duck.

By way of entertainment, every man could play a part. One could tell a good yarn, while another could sing a song, and all could play 'freeze-out.'

The songs sang about the campfires were not such as are rendered by opera companies of the present day. In fact, they have gone into disuse since the men who sang them and the occasion that gave them birth, have passed into history.

Among the popular melodies of the time was 'Betsey from Pike.' The first verse ran like this:

Oh, do you remember sweet Betsey, from Pike,
Who travelled the mountains with her lover, Ike;
With one yoke of cattle, a large yellow dog,
One full shanghai rooster and one spotted hog.'
Chorus—
Sing a Tu-ral Li-ural, Li-ural Li-a,
Sing a Tu-ral Li-ural, Li-ural, Li-a,
Sing a Tu-ral Li-ural, Li-ural, Li-a,
Why don't you sing Tu-ral, Li-ural Li-a.'

The chorus, when joined by twenty or more bullwhackers who always carried their lungs with them, was indeed thrilling, as was the last *stanza*, in fact every stanza from the first to the last.

The last verse ran like this:

The wagon broke down and the cattle all died,
That morning the last piece of bacon was fried.
Ike looked discouraged, and Betsey was mad,
The dog dropped his tail and looked wonderfully sad.

Another popular air of the day was:

My name is Joe Bowers,
 I had a brother Ike;
We came from old Missouri,
All the way from Pike, Etc., Etc.'

A song sang by a California miner who went by the euphonious sobriquet of "Sluice Box," never failed to elicit encore. It was descriptive of his adversities and trials through the sluice mining country, and the last lines that I remember were:

I stole a dog, got whipped like hell,
And away I went for Marysville.
Then leave, ye miners, leave,
Oh, leave, ye miners, leave.

Then the boys used to sandwich in Irish, German and negro melodies, besides drawing upon national and war songs. Among the latter, 'John Brown' and 'Dixie' were quite popular, but any song with a good, stiff chorus was the proper thing.

A parody on the 'Texas Ranger' was also a popular song, though not so lively and inspiring as the others, being lacking in a chorus. It was a sort of lament of a boy who at the age of eighteen ran away, 'joined Old Major's train,' and started for Laramie. They had a fight at Plum Creek, in which six of their men were killed by the Indians and buried in one grave. In his description of the fight he says:

We saw the Indians coming,
They came up with a yell,
My feeling that moment
No human tongue can tell.

I thought of my old mother,
In tears she said to me:
"To you they're all strangers;
You'd better stay with me."

I thought her old and childish,
Perhaps she did not know
My mind was fixed on driving,
And I was bound to go.'

We fought them full one hour
Before the fight was o'er,
And the like of dead Indians
I never saw before;'

And six as brave fellows
As ever came out West,
Were buried up at Plum-Creek,
Their souls in peace to rest.

In this connection I may say that less than thirty rods from the place where those six brave bull-whackers are buried, eleven others lie in one grave, killed by Indians.

The last time that I passed over the road at Plum Creek was in the spring of 1867. The railroad had been built beyond that point on the north side of the river, and the stage line had just been pulled off.

Bands of Indians were quite troublesome and as the little troop of soldiers stationed at Plum Creek had been removed, the station keeper had been frightened away, and the sole occupant of the place was a telegraph operator. I talked with him as we watched the Indians over on the hill and there was a picture of despair written upon his every feature. We told him that he ought not to stay and insisted upon his taking his traps and going with us. He wanted to, but felt it his duty to remain in charge of the telegraph office. I will never forget the parting with that man. He was a perfect stranger. I never saw him before, didn't even know his name, and our acquaintance only covered a few hours, but there was something terrible in the look of anxiety that he gave us as he refused to leave his post.

We were the last white men that that poor fellow ever looked upon. Even as our train pulled out the Indians were in sight upon the hills south of the station, and that evening they burned the station, and nothing was ever heard of the Plum Creek operator, who, knowing the fate that awaited him, remained at his post and was massacred by the merciless Sioux.

******

The frontier preacher had his share alike with others in hardship and adventure, as will be seen by the experience of the Rev. H. T. Davis.

> We said to the authorities of our church: 'We would like to go west and spend our lives in laying the foundations and building up the church on the frontier.' The way was at once opened, and in July, 1858, we landed at Bellevue, Nebraska. This was our first field of labour. We had no church organisation here at that time, so everything had to be made from the raw material. Notwithstanding this was the case, we really enjoyed the work.
>
> We shall never forget the first Nebraska blizzard we encountered. The day before was beautiful almost like a summer day.

Mrs. Davis had washed and hung out her clothes. We retired to rest, the soft balmy air, like a zephyr, was blowing from the south. About midnight the wind shifted to the north and it began to snow. In the morning the weather was freezing cold and the snow was piled in drifts many feet high around the house. We looked out and saw the clothes line but no clothes. We tried to find them, but in vain. They were gone. Not a shred was left save one or two small pieces. And we never saw or heard of them again. Our neighbors who were acquainted with Nebraska blizzards said: 'Your clothes were in Kansas long before morning.' Our wardrobe was not the most extensive, and we felt keenly the loss. Since then we have encountered many a blizzard, and we are never surprised at the awful havoc and devastation that follow in their wake.

Another thing that occurred that same winter we shall never forget. Although forty-one years have passed away since it took place, it stands out as vividly before us now as though it had happened but yesterday. The thought of that thrilling event even now causes our blood to tingle, our nerves to quiver, our heart to throb, and a lump to come into our throat, that produces anything but a pleasing sensation.

It was a race for life. We had friends in Omaha and we determined to go to visit them. The Missouri river is frozen over in the winter, and of course, is unnavigable. The whistle of the locomotive had never been heard on the prairies of Nebraska. The only way left for us to reach Omaha was by private conveyance. We procured a horse and sleigh for the purpose. After visiting a few days in Omaha we started home.

The day selected for our return was bright and clear. The snow was deep, and the weather bitter cold. The brilliant rays of the sun caused the snow in the road, on plain and hillside, to sparkle and glitter, and the whole country as far as the eye could extend shone like burnished silver. By my side, in the sleigh, sat my wife. It was our first winter in the territory. Everything was new and strange and wild, altogether different from anything we had ever seen before. The absence of timber made the snow-covered hills and plains appear dreary in the extreme, and created a feeling of loneliness that cannot be easily described.

After we had gone a few miles, looking back, my wife saw away in the distance an animal.

'What is that?' said she, somewhat agitated. I turned and looked. It was so far away I could not for the life of me distinguish just what it was. I replied: 'Oh, nothing but a dog from one of the farms by the wayside.'

But if it were only a dog I feared it. I never had any particular love for the canine race. And if that were only a dog my wife saw away in the distance I was extremely anxious to keep out of his way. So I urged my horse a little.

Reaching the top of the next hill my wife again looked back. Then she tucked the robe more closely about her. I looked into her face. She looked troubled and seemed quite nervous, but said nothing. I turned my head, and there in the road, away in the distance, I saw the same object. It seemed to be gaining on us. Again I urged my horse, encouraging him all I possibly could. A peculiar feeling instantly crept all over me. It was a strange sensation. My hand trembled and the whip quivered as I held it.

The fact had flashed over me that the object seen in the road behind us was not a dog but a buffalo wolf. The buffalo wolf of Nebraska was the same as the giant wolf of Oregon. It was the largest species of the gray wolf, and often attacked and killed buffaloes and on that account was called by trappers, Indian traders and the early pioneers of the west the 'buffalo wolf.' These wolves, when hungry, did not hesitate to attack man. They were large, strong, savage and dangerous in the extreme. I knew very well if it were one of these that had scented us out, and was on our trail, and should overtake us, there would be no hope whatever for our escape. The only hope of saving our lives was to reach the village before we were overtaken. Knowing how fleet of foot the wolf was, the hope seemed a forlorn one. I knew that not one moment's time could be lost—that my horse must be pushed to the last extremity of his strength. I tried to keep cool and not become frightened, but in vain. No one under such circumstances can keep from being frightened.

Silently we breathed a prayer to God for help. How natural it is to pray when in danger. Under such circumstances all men pray, believers in the Christian religion and unbelievers. All alike at times feel the need of supernatural help, and at such times call upon God for assistance. If at no other time, when in great danger, we pray—pray earnestly.

Seeing the wolf was rapidly gaining on us, I spoke sharply to my horse, and plied the whip anew. Faster and faster he flew over the hardened snow, and faster and faster our hearts beat with fear. The snow clods flew thick and fast from the hoofs of our flying steed. To these, however, we paid but little attention. Reaching the next rise, again we looked back, and to our surprise the wolf was nearer than ever. I felt that the only thing to do was to urge the horse until every nerve and muscle were taxed to their utmost tension. Our panting steed seemed to take in the situation, and if ever an animal made fast time it was our noble horse on that cold December day. Again my wife turned her anxious eyes toward our rapidly approaching foe and every time she looked back the trouble on her face deepened. She said nothing. Not a word was spoken. Her look, however, spoke volumes. My heart leaped into my throat, and I was too much frightened to speak.

Up one hill and down, then up another and down our galloping horse carried us. Again we turned our faces to the rear, and again were thrilled anew with fear. The wolf was only a short distance behind. The time had come when it seemed there must be a hand to hand grapple with the savage beast of prey. The top of the next hill was reached, and in full view, only a few rods away, rose the beautiful village of Bellevue. Descending the slope we looked back. The wolf had just reached the brow of the hill, and seeing the village, stopped for a moment, then turned aside. A moment afterwards our panting horse drove up to the parsonage and we were safe. A prayer of thanksgiving went up to God for deliverance.

Forty-one years have passed away since that eventful ride on the bleak prairies of Nebraska, but that race for life is as fresh on memory's page as if it had taken place but yesterday.

We have seen with our own eyes the buffalo path transformed into the public highway and the Indian trail to the railroad, with its fiery steed snuffing the breeze and sweeping with lightning speed from the Missouri River to the gold-washed shores of the Pacific.

★★★★★★

One of the hottest, bloodiest little fights on American soil occurred at Beecher Island, seventeen miles south of Wray, Colorado,

September 17, 1868, which Thomas Murphy, of Corbin, Kansas, had the honour of selecting as the place of defence.

Forsyth's Rough Riders, numbering fifty-four men, made as heroic a stand as the defenders of the Alamo, and from their rifle pits on the "Island of Death," in the Arickaree fork of the Republican River, defeated 1,000 Cheyenne Indians, in which their chief, Roman Nose, was killed.

At that time the Cheyennes were a devastating horde that swept over the plains of Kansas, Nebraska and Colorado. Major George A. Forsyth, who was with Sheridan on his ride from Winchester, and who has since become a general, was given permission by that general to organise a force against the marauding Indians. This he did, choosing a small body of picked men from plainsmen, hunters and ex-soldiers from Ft. Harker and Ft. Hayes.

Mr. Murphy recently gave me the following account of the fight.

On the 15th of September our little band of troopers arrived in the valley of the Arickaree and on the following morning at daybreak we were attacked by a rifle fire from the Indians, who had us almost surrounded. There was only one way out for retreat, but Major Forsyth shrewdly decided that it was done for the purpose of ambush, and instead of falling into the trap, took position on the small island in the river. We used our tin cups and plates to dig rifle pits in the sand. Our horses were hitched to the young cottonwoods on the island.

Roman Nose apparently had us in a trap. His riflemen were posted on the banks on either side of the island and poured a galling fire into the rifle pits all that day. Lieutenant Frederick H. Beecher, a nephew of the illustrious Henry Ward Beecher, was killed at the side of Major Forsyth. Dr. Mooers was hit in the forehead and mortally wounded. Several of the most valuable scouts also fell and many were wounded. Toward the close of the day Major Forsyth was wounded near unto death, but when merciful night came he rallied the men and gave directions for the fight the next morning.

At daybreak the second day Roman Nose led in person fully one thousand warriors on horseback, who rode up the shallow waters of the stream to attack the rifle pits. The charge was a magnificent one, but we poured volley after volley into their midst until Roman Nose fell and they retreated in confusion.

A second charge was made at 2 o'clock in the afternoon, but there was no longer a great war chief in command and the Indians broke within two hundred yards of the rifle pits. At 6 o'clock at night they made another charge from all sides, but our men deliberately picked them off before they set foot on the island, until the waters of the river were red with blood. The place was a very hornet's nest to the Indians and they withdrew baffled.

The casualties now amounted to twenty-three killed and wounded out of fifty-four men. Ammunition was running low and we were out of provisions, but there was plenty of horse meat, for our mounts had nearly all been killed. When darkness had settled down volunteers were called for to carry the news of our predicament to Fort Wallace. Peter Trudeau and Jack Stillwell volunteered. They skilfully ran the enemy's lines and brought relief seven days later.

Meanwhile the sufferings of the men were terrible. The horse meat had become putrid and unfit to eat. The days were hot and the nights were cold, and there was no surgeon to alleviate the sufferings of the sick and wounded.

Major Forsyth had given up hope of relief and begged us to leave him and cut our way out, but we said, "No, we have fought together, and if need be, we will die together." When relief came some of the men wept for joy.

It was I who suggested the island as a place of defence at the first attack. It was seconded by Jack Stillwell.

A reunion of Forsyth's men was held on the historic island September 17, 1905, when a monument given by the state of Colorado and the state of Kansas was unveiled, bearing the names of all who participated in that famous fight.

******

J. B. Sims, a pioneer of the sixties said:

> It seems to me people were happier in Colorado City in early days than now,.
>
> At Christmas times we had shooting matches, a horse race or two, plenty of Tom and Jerry, and usually wound up the day with a dance at the Anway Fort and a supper at Smith and Baird's hotel. Often half a dozen families would arrange a friendly dinner at some neighbour's house, and the hotel men would make a big dinner and invite the ranchmen to come in and enjoy the festivities.
>
> The pious people who were averse to horse-racing would generally pitch horseshoes and sometimes end the day in a big game of draw poker. There was not much money in circulation,

and the betting on a horse race was commonly a sack of flour, a side of bacon or a shotgun.

No, we never hung the horse-thieves on Christmas. Those festivities were held until the new year, so as to start the community off with good resolutions.

A premonition of danger warned me once of lurking hostile Indians on Cottonwood Creek on the morning of December 26, 1868, resulting in a preparation for battle that probably saved my life.

It was the day after Christmas. I was in the employ of the Beatty Brothers Cattle Company and was looking up some stray cattle near the head of the Cottonwood Creek, twenty miles north of Colorado City.

I had been riding through the timber and was about to emerge into the open when a premonition of danger came over me. The feeling was so strong that I loosened my Henri rifle from the saddle holster and looked to the two heavy Colt revolvers I carried about me.

Half an hour passed and while I had not yet seen anything, I could not shake off the feeling of approaching danger. Twenty minutes more and sure enough, from out of a ravine came about sixty Cheyenne and Arapahoe Indians in their war paint, riding rapidly toward me.

I instantly wheeled my horse and rode for a rocky butte about half a mile distant. My horse climbed the butte almost with the agility of a goat. As the bullets tore up the ground about us I led him behind some big rocks and then paid my respects to the advancing war party.

My Henri rifle carried eighteen shots. The repeating rifle being then unheard of by these Indians, was the greatest surprise they ever met. My first shot emptied a saddle, and then when they thought to rush me, two or three more went down. They could not understand the rapidity of my fire, and by the time I had emptied my rifle I had them on the run and out of range.

They advanced two or three times during the day and I became amused and allowed them to come within easy range, when I would turn loose as fast as I could work the rifle, and scatter them.

Late in the afternoon they gave me up as bad medicine and rode away toward Gomer's hill, where they killed a Mexican boy. They then swung back toward Palmer Lake and killed Mrs. Teeterman, who chanced to be alone on a ranch near the headwaters of Plumb Creek.

From that day I have never doubted the existence of an unseen power which may warn us of approaching danger.

★★★★★★

Antelope Jack, bronzed and grey, a grim warrior of the early frontier days, who made his home in Colorado City off and on for many years, would respond to no other name, whatever it may have been.

No one appeared to care much for old Jack, but Jack had a history that would have made him an idol in certain circles, for in 1874 he was one of the fourteen men who fought the Battle of Adobe Walls[1] in northwest Texas, one of the fiercest fought on the plains.

Long before Napoleon signed the Louisiana purchase treaty, and while all the vast territory lying south of it belonged to Mexico, a party of traders from Santa Fe established a fort in northwest Texas. It was of adobe or sun dried brick and had stood deserted in that arid region, almost intact, for perhaps more than one hundred years.

In 1874, when the extermination of the buffalo had become a military necessity in order to deprive the Indian of his commissary on his marauding expeditions, a party of buffalo hunters took up headquarters in the adobe walls and it being in the heart of the buffalo country, others came, and it was soon made a trading post.

The Comanches, Arapahoes and Apaches, ever jealous of their domain, formed a federation and proceeded against the settlements of northwest Texas and Kansas. A raid was planned on Adobe Walls. The time set for the attack was early dawn, when it was expected the men would be asleep.

The men, not apprehensive of danger, were asleep with the doors open, but "Bat" Masterson rose early that morning and upon going to the stream for water, caught sight of the advancing horde.

The men were quickly alarmed and the doors fastened. Two men asleep on the outside in wagons were killed.

The Indians rode their ponies up to the heavy doors and threw them on their haunches against them. The men inside barricaded the doors with sacks of flour and fired through loopholes in the faces of the savages, who numbered about five hundred.

---

1. *Billy Dixon & Adobe Walls* by Billy Dixon & Edward Campbell, *Life and Adventures of "Billy" Dixon* by Billy Dixon and *The Battle of Adobe Walls* by Edward Campbell Little is also published by Leonaur.

The battle raged all day and dead Indians and ponies were piled up to within a few feet of the doors.

One young brave, painted and bedecked with feathers, gained the roof and tore away the adobe covering until he could reach through with his revolver, which he fired at random below, filling the room with smoke. He was killed before he emptied his weapon. There were only fourteen guns of the defenders and at times every one had to be brought into action to resist the renewed attack against the doors.

Finally the doors parted until there was a wide aperture on both sides through which the Indians fired as they rode past, or hurled their arrows and lances.

Fixed ammunition was running low, but there was an abundance of powder, bullets and primers for reloading shells. Men were detailed for this work so that there was a volcano of fire belching from the fort all day.

Meanwhile, Minimic, the medicine man of the tribes, who had planned the fight, rode at a safe distance, urging on the Indians, saying the medicine he had made was good and they could not fail.

Finally, late in the day, his horse was hit by a sharpshooter and with this the Indians lost faith and withdrew.

"I was only busy like the rest," was all Antelope Jack would say of his courage on that day.

★★★★★★

The massacre at the White River Indian agency in Colorado, and the ambuscade of Major Thornburg's command by Utes in 1879, was the last of the serious troubles with the Indians in Colorado.

It was the cause, however, of a reign of terror on the plains, as it was thought to be the signal for a general uprising.

When the news reached the C. C. Ranch on the Cimarron River, I was especially interested in the fate of E. W. Eskridge, an *employé* of the White River Agency, who I would have joined within a short time, had the terrible affair resulting in his death not occurred.

I have never met any of the soldiers under Major Thornburg's command, nor any settlers who were in the vicinity at the time, and the best account I have been able to get of the massacre is the following by an unknown writer:

> The White River Utes had been ugly for some time, and had prepared for an outbreak. They committed many depredations among the settlers and cherished resentment against the agent,

Mr. Meeker. Only an hour before the attack upon the agency by Chief Douglass and twenty braves Meeker dispatched a message to Major Thornburg, known to be *en route*, in which he said:

> Everything is quiet here and Douglass is flying the United States flag.

At that hour Thornburg lay dead in Milk River Cañon, on the reservation. The writer was cruelly slain and mutilated within an hour, and the messenger, E. W. Eskridge, who carried the note, was shot down before he had proceeded two miles from the agency.

The attack on Thornburg was made at 10 o'clock on the morning of September 29. When the news reached Chief Douglass by courier he at once proceeded to execute his portion of the plot. He and his men went to the agency and began firing upon the *employés*, continuing until all were killed. The women, who were Mrs. Meeker, her daughter Josephine, Mrs. Price, wife of the agency blacksmith, and her little girl three years old, ran to the milkhouse and shut themselves in while the massacre went on. After the bloody work was completed the building was fired and they were forced out, to be taken captives.

Meeker's body was found a week later 200 yards from his house, with a log-chain about his neck, one side of his head mashed and a barrel stave driven through his body. Eight other bodies were found near by and four more on the road to the agency. The Indians stole all movable goods and packing the plunder on ponies fled, taking with them the captives. Through the influence and peremptory intervention of Ouray, head chief of the Ute nation, and after troublesome negotiations, Chief Douglass surrendered the captives, who were taken to Ouray's home, on the Southern Ute reservation, and reached Denver in November.

Major Thornburg's command, consisting of one company of the Fourth Infantry, Troop E, Third Cavalry, and Troops D and F, Fifth Cavalry, left Fort Steele, Wyoming, on the Union Pacific railroad, and marched over the mountains toward the agency to aid in quelling the threatened outbreak, but the Utes struck before the troops reached their destination and also intercepted and ambushed the command.

When the troops reached Bear River, sixty-five miles from the agency, they were visited in camp by Chief Captain Jack and several braves, who were most friendly, and were entertained at supper by Major Thornburg. The object of this call was to size up the force and to learn the route to be taken by the troops the next day. They offered to guide the troops to the agency, but this was declined.

The next morning about 10 o'clock, while the troops were in a narrow canon at the crossing of Milk River, fire suddenly opened upon them from the bluffs on all sides. No Indians could be seen, but bullets poured and smoke puffed from behind the rocks. Major Thornburg was killed while in front of his men.

Troop D was half a mile in the rear of the other troops with the wagon train at the time of the attack, and Lieutenant J. V. S. Paddock, in command, at once formed his wagons into a barricade and the other troops fell back to the improvised breastworks, where for six days the soldiers were besieged and nearly all their animals killed. On the morning of October 2 Captain Dodge, with a troop of the Ninth Cavalry, coloured, who had been on his way to the agency, reinforced the beleaguered men, but his force was not large enough to aid in repulsing the Utes. The first night Private Murphy of D troop volunteered to go through the lines for assistance. The heroic trooper made the ride to Rawlins, Wyo., a distance of 170 miles, in 24 hours, and telegraphed for help.

News of the plight of the Thornburg command reached Fort Russell on the morning of October 1, and General Wesley Merritt immediately ordered a relief expedition. Four troops of the Fifth Cavalry started at once to Rawlins by train, reaching there at 1 o'clock the next morning, where they were joined by four companies of the Fourth Infantry, and the troops began their long march to the relief of their comrades.

At dawn on the third day, with General Merritt ahead with the cavalry, the troops entered the valley of death and were greeted with cheers by the exhausted victims of treachery. The cowardly Utes withdrew when reinforcements arrived, and the troops were unable to follow them through the mountain trails.

On the road to Milk River the relief party came upon the remains of a wagon train which had been bound for the agency with supplies. All the men were murdered, stripped and partly burned. After General Merritt reached the agency Lieutenant W. B. Weir, of the ordnance department, while out on a scouting expedition, was surrounded by Utes and killed.

Of Major Thornburg's command thirteen were killed and forty-eight wounded.

Although the government made a long investigation of the Meeker and Thornburg massacres none of the leaders was ever punished. The only action taken was the removal of the White River Utes to a new reservation in Utah by an Act of Congress.

★★★★★★

In conclusion, we do not have to go to the annals of the past, nor to distant shores to find heroes and heroines. They are in our midst today, (at time of first publication). A nobler band of men and women never graced this planet than many of the men and women who laid the foundations of the state and the church on the frontier of the west.

Some of them lived in sod houses and dugouts, with barely enough to keep soul and body together, and for years had hard work to keep the wolf from the door. But they toiled on, undismayed by their hardships, and we today are reaping the reward of their toils and sufferings.

Seventy Years on the Frontier

Contents

Preface	157
To the Reader	160
Reminiscences of Youth	161
Missouri in Its Wild and Uncultivated State	169
A Silver Expedition	174
The Mormons	182
The Mormons' Mecca	198
My First Venture	204
Faithful Friends	211
Our War With Mexico	218
Doniphan's Expedition	222
The Pioneer of Frontier Telegraphy	229
An Overland Outfit	232
Kit Carson	236
Adventures of a Trapper	247
Trapping	252
An Adventure With Indians	254
Crossing the Plains	262
"The Jayhawkers of 1849"	272

Mirages	278
The First Stage into Denver	283
The Gold Fever	286
The Overland Mail	290
The Pony Express and its Brave Riders	299
The Battle of the Buffaloes	308
The Black Bear	313
The Beaver	324
A Boy's Trip Overland	328
The Denver of Early Days	335
The Denver of Today and Its Environs	339
Buffalo Bill from Boyhood to Fame	347
The Platte Valley	350
Kansas City Before the War	355
The Graves of Pioneers	360
Silver Mining	367
Wild West Fruits	371
How English Capitalists Got a	375
Foothold	375
Montana's Towns and Cities	381
California's Great Trees	385
The Flowers of the Far West	388
Colorado	396
The Surgeon Scout	406
Conclusion	409

DEDICATION.
AS A TRIBUTE OF MY SINCERE REGARD FOR
W. F. CODY
AS BOY AND MAN, MY FRIEND FOR TWO SCORE YEARS,
I DEDICATE TO HIM
THIS BOOK OF BORDER LIFE.
ALEXANDER MAJORS.

W. F. CODY "BUFFALO BILL."

Preface

As there is no man living who is more thoroughly competent to write a book of the Wild West than my life-long friend and benefactor in my boyhood, Alexander Majors, there is no one to whose truthful words I would rather accept the honour of writing a preface.

An introduction to a book of Mountain and Plain by Mr. Majors certainly need hardly be written, unless it be to refer to the author in a way that his extreme modesty will not permit him to speak of himself, for he is not given to sounding his own praise, being a man of action rather than words, and yet whose life has its recollections of seventy years upon the frontier, dating to a period that tried men's souls to the fullest extent, and when daring deeds and thrilling adventures were of every-day occurrence. Remembrance of seventy years of life in the Far West and amid the Rocky Mountains!

What a world of thought this gives rise to, when we recall that a quarter of a century ago there was not a railroad west of the Missouri River, and every pound of freight, every emigrant, every letter, and every message had to be carried by wagon or on horseback, and at the risk of life and hardships untold.

The man who could in the face of all dangers and obstacles originate and carry to success a line of freighter wagons, a mail route from the Atlantic to the Pacific, and a Pony Express, flying at the utmost speed of a hare through the land, was no ordinary individual, as can be well understood. And such a man Alexander Majors was. He won success; and today, on the verge of four score years, lives over again in his book the thrilling scenes in his own life and in the lives of others.

Family reverses after the killing of my father in the Kansas War, caused me to start out, though a mere boy, in 1855 to seek to aid in the support of my mother and sisters, and it was to Mr. Alexander Majors that I applied for a situation. He looked me over carefully in his kindly way, and after questioning me closely gave me the place of messenger boy, that was, one to ride with dispatches between the overland freighters—wagon trains going westward into the almost unknown wild dump of prairie and mountain.

That was my first meeting with Alexander Majors, and up to the present time our friendship has never had a break in it, and, I may add, never will through act of mine.

Having thus shown my claim to a thorough knowledge of my distinguished old friend, let me now state that his firm was known the country over as Majors, Russell & Woddell, but it was to Mr. Majors particularly that the heaviest duties of organising and management fell, and he never shirked a duty or a danger, as I well remember.

Severe in discipline, he was yet never profane or harsh, and a Christian and temperance man through all; he governed his men kindly, and was wont to say that he would have no one under his control who would not promptly obey an order without it was emphasized with an oath. In fact, he had a contract with his men in which they pledged themselves not to use profanity, get drunk, gamble, or be cruel to animals under pain of dismissal, while good behavior was rewarded. Every man, from wagon-boss and teamster down to rustler and messenger-boy, seemed anxious to gain the good will of Alexander Majors and to hold it, and today he has fewer foes than any one I know, in spite of his position as chief of what were certainly a wild and desperate lot of men, where the revolver settled all difficulties.

It was Mr. Majors' firm that originated and put in the Pony Express across the plains and made it the grand success it proved to be.

It was his firm that so long and successfully carried on the business of overland freighting in the face of every obstacle, and also the Overland Stage Drive between the Missouri River and Pacific Ocean, and in his long life on the border he has become known to all classes and conditions of men, so that in writing now his memoirs, no man knows better whereof he speaks than he does.

In each instance where he has written to his old-time comrades for data, he has taken only that which he knew could be verified, and has thrown out material sufficient to double his book in size, where he felt the slightest doubt that it could not be relied upon to the fullest extent.

His work, therefore, is a history of the Wild West, its pages authentic, and though many of its scenes are romantic and thrilling, it is what has hitherto been an unwritten story of facts, figures, and reality; and now, that in his old age he finds his occupation gone, I feel and hope that his memoirs will find a ready sale.

W. F. Cody,
"Buffalo Bill."

To the Reader

In preparing the material of my book, I desire here to give justice where justice is due, and express myself as under obligations for valuable data and letters, which I fully appreciate; and publicly thank for their kindness in this direction those whose names follow:

Col. W. F. Cody ("Buffalo Bill") of Nebraska.
Col. John B. Colton, Kansas City, Mo.
Mr. V. DeVinny, Denver, Colo.
Mr. E. L. Gallatin, Denver, Colo.
Judge Simonds, Denver, Colo.
Mr. John T. Rennick, Oak Grove, Mo.
Mr. Geo. W. Bryant, Kansas City, Mo.
Mr. George E. Simpson, Kansas City, Mo.
Mr. John Martin, Denver, Colo.
Mr. David Street, Denver, Colo.
Mrs. Nellie Carlisle, Berkeley, Cal.
Mr. A. Carlisle, Berkeley, Cal.
Mr. Green Majors, San Francisco, Cal.
Mr. Ergo Alex. Majors, Alameda, Cal.
Mr. Seth E. Ward, Westport, Mo.
Robert Ford, Great Falls, Mont.
Doctor Case, Kansas City, Mo.
Benj. C. Majors, May Bell P. O., Colo.
Prof. Robert Casey, Denver, Colo.
John Burroughs, Colorado.
Eugene Munn, Swift, Neb.
Rev. Dr. John R. Shannon, Denver, Colo.
Thos. D. Truett, Leadville, Colo.
Will C. Ferril.

   Yours with respect, Alexander Majors.

Chapter 1

Reminiscences of Youth

My father, Benjamin Majors, was a farmer, born in the State of North Carolina in 1794, and brought when a boy by my grandfather, Alexander Majors, after whom I am named, to Kentucky about the year 1800. My grandfather was also a farmer, and one might say a manufacturer, for in those days nearly all the farmers in America were manufacturers, producing almost everything within their homes or with their own hands, tanning their own leather, making the shoes they wore, as well as clothing of all kinds.

My mother's maiden name was Laurania Kelly; her father, Beil Kelly, was a soldier in the Revolutionary War, and was wounded at the Battle of Brandywine.

I was born in 1814, on the 4th day of October, near Franklin, Simpson County, Kentucky, being the eldest of the family, consisting of two boys and a girl. When I was about five years of age my father moved to Missouri, when that State was yet a Territory. I remember well many of the occurrences of the trip; one was that the horses ran away with the wagon in which my father, myself, and younger brothers were riding. My father threw us children out and jumped out himself, though crippled in one foot at the time. One wheel of the wagon was broken to pieces, which caused us a delay of two days.

After crossing the Ohio River, in going through the then Territory of Illinois, the settlements were from ten to twenty miles apart, the squatters living in log cabins, and along one stretch of the road the log cabin settlements were forty miles apart. When we arrived at the Okaw River, in the Territory of Illinois, we found a squatter in his little log cabin whose occupation was ferrying passengers across the river in a small flatboat which was propelled by a cable or large rope tied to a tree on each side of the river, it being a narrow but deep stream. The only thing attracting my special attention, as a boy, at that point was a pet bear chained to a stake just in front of the cabin where the family lived. He was constantly jumping over his chain, as is the habit of pet bears, especially when young.

From this place to St. Louis, a distance of about thirty-five miles, there was not a single settlement of any kind. When we arrived on the east bank of the Mississippi River, opposite the now city of St. Louis, we saw a little French village on the other side. The only means of crossing the river was a small flatboat, manned by three Frenchmen, one on each side about midway of the craft, each with an oar with which to propel the boat. The third one stood in the end with a steering oar, for the purpose of giving it the proper direction when the others propelled it. This ferry would carry four horses or a four-horse wagon with its load at one trip. These men were not engaged half their time in ferrying across the river all the emigrants, with their horses, cattle, sheep, and hogs, who were moving from the East to the West and crossing at St. Louis. Of course the current would carry the boat a considerable distance down the river in spite of the efforts of the boatmen to the contrary.

However, when they reached the opposite bank the two who worked the side oars would lay down their oars, go to her bow, where a long rope was attached, take it up, put it over their shoulders, and let it uncoil until it gave them several rods in front of the boat. Then they would start off in a little foot-path made at the water's edge and pull the boat to the place prepared for taking on or unloading, as the case might be. There they loaded what they wanted to ferry to the other side, and the same process would be gone through with as before. Reaching the west bank of the river we found the village of St. Louis, with 4,000 inhabitants, a large portion of whom were French, whose business it was to trade with the numerous tribes of Indians and the few white people who then inhabited that region of country, for furs of various kinds, buffalo robes and tongues, as this was the only traffic out of which money could be made at that time.

The furs bought of the Indians were carried from St. Louis to New Orleans in pirogues or flatboats, which were carried along solely by the current, for at that time steam power had never been applied to the waters of the Mississippi River. Sixty-seven years later, in 1886, I visited St. Louis and went down to the wharf or steamboat landing, and looking across to East St. Louis, which in 1818 was nothing but a wilderness, beheld the river spanned by one of the finest bridges in the world, over which from 100 to 150 locomotives with trains attached were daily passing. Three big steam ferryboats above and three below the bridge were constantly employed in transferring freight of one kind or another. What a change had taken place within the memory of one man! While looking in amazement at the great and mighty change, a nicely dressed and intelligent man passed by; I said to him:

"Sir, I stood on the other bank of this river when a little boy, in the month of October, 1818, when there was no improvement whatever over there" (pointing to the east shore). I also stated to him that a little flatboat, manned by three Frenchmen, was the only means for crossing the river at that time. The gentleman took his pencil and a piece of paper and figured for a few moments, and then turning to me said: "Do you know, sir, those three Frenchmen, with their boat, who did all the work of ferrying, and were not employed half the time, could not, with the facilities you speak of, in 100 years do what is now being done in one day with our present means of transportation."

Since that time, which was six years ago, (1887), another bridge has been built to meet the necessities of the increasing business of that city, which shows that progress and increase of wealth and development are still on the rapid march.

The next thing of note, after passing St. Louis, occurred one evening after we camped. My mother stepped on the wagon-tongue to get the cooking utensils, when her foot slipped and she fell, striking her side and receiving injuries which resulted in her death eighteen months later.

On that journey my father travelled westward, crossing the Missouri River at St. Charles, Mo., following up the river from that point to where Glasgow is now situated, and there crossed the river to the south side, and wintered in the big bottoms. In the spring of 1819 he moved to what afterward became La Fayette County, and took up a location near the Big Snye Bear River.

In February, the winter following, my dear mother died from the injuries she received from the accident previously alluded to. The Rev. Simon Cockrell, a Baptist preacher, who at that time was over eighty years of age, preached her funeral sermon. He was the first preacher I had ever seen stand up before a congregation with a book in his hand. Although my mother died when I was little more than six years of age, my memory of her is apparently as fresh and endearing as though her death had occurred but a few days ago. Many acts I saw her do, and things I heard her say, impressed me with her courage and goodness, and their memory has been a help to me throughout the whole career of my long life. No mother ever gave birth to a son who loved her more, or whose tender recollections have been more endearing or lasting than mine.

I have never encountered any difficulty so great, no matter how threatening, that I have not been able to overcome fearlessly when the recollection of my dear mother and the spirit by which she was animated came to me. Even to this day, and I am an old man in my eightieth year, I can not dwell long in conversation about her without tears coming to my eyes. There are no words in the English language to express my estimate and appreciation of the dear mother who gave me birth and nourishment. I would that all men loved and held the memories of their mothers more sacred than I think many of them do. One of the greatest safeguards to man throughout the meanderings of his life is the love of a father, mother, brother and sister, children and friends; it is a great solace and anchor to right-thinking men when they may be hundreds and thousands of miles away. Love of family begets true patriotism in his bosom, for, in my opinion, there is no such thing as true patriotism without love of family.

Returning to the events of 1821, we had in the neighbourhood of the Snye Bear River a great Indian scare. This happened in the month of August, when I was in my seventh year, after my father had built a log cabin for himself in that part of the country which afterward became Lafayette County, Mo. My mother had died the winter before, leaving myself, the eldest, a brother next, and a sister little more than two years old.

Mrs. Ferrin, a settler who lived on the outskirts of the little settlement of pioneers, was alone, except for a baby a year old. She left the child and went to the spring for water. When she had filled her bucket and rose to the top of the bank, she imagined she saw Indians. She dropped her bucket, ran to the cabin, took the child in her arms, and fled with all her might to Thomas Hopper's, the nearest neighbour. As soon as she came near enough to be heard, she shouted "Indians" at the top of her voice. Polly Hopper, a young girl of seventeen, hearing Mrs. Ferrin shouting "Indians," seized a bridle and ran to a herd of horses that were near by in the shade of some trees, caught a flea-bitten gray bell mare, the leader of the herd, she being gentle and easier to catch than the others, mounted the animal without saddle, riding after the fashion of men, and started to alarm the settlement.

My father was lying in bed taking a sweat to abate a bilious fever.

A family living near by were caring for us children, and nursing my father in his sickness. My brother and I were playing a little distance from the cabin when we heard the screams of the woman, shouting "Indians" with every jump the horse made, her hair streaming out behind like a banner in the wind. We were on the very outside boundary of the settlement, and some signs of Indians had been discovered a few days previous by some neighbours who were out hunting for deer. This fact had been made known to the little settlement, and the day this scare took place had been selected for the men to meet at Henry Rennick's to discuss ways and means for building a stockade for the protection of their families in case the Indians should make an attempt of a hostile nature. So the first thoughts of the families at home were to start for Rennick's, where the men were. This accounts for the young woman going by our house, as she had to pass our cabin to reach that place. My father, sick as he was, jumped out of bed when she passed giving the alarm, took a heavy gun from the rack, hung his shot pouch over his shoulder, took my little sister in his arms, and, like the rest, started for Rennick's, my little brother and I toddling along behind him.

A family living near by, consisting of the mother, Mrs. Turner, two daughters, a son, and a little grandson, also started for Rennick's. They would run for a short distance, and then stop and hide in the high weeds until they could get their breath. The old lady had a small dog she called Ging. He was on hand, of course, and just as much excited as all the rest of the dogs in the neighbourhood, and the people themselves. The screams of the girl Polly Hopper, and the ringing of the bell on the animal she was riding, aroused the dogs to the highest pitch of excitement. In those days dogs were a necessity to the frontiersman for his protection, and as much of a necessity on that account as any other animal he possessed, and consequently every settler owned from three to five dogs, and some more. They were the watch-guards against Indians and prowling beasts, both by night and day, and could not have been dispensed with in the settling of the frontier.

To return to our trip to Rennick's: When the old lady and her flock would run into the weeds to hide and regain their breath, this little dog Ging could not be controlled, for bark he would. The old lady when angry would use "cuss words," and she used them on this dog, and would jump out of her hiding-place and start on the trail again. Of course when the dog barked he exposed her hiding-place. They would run a little farther, and when their breath would fail, they would make another hiding in the weeds, but would scarcely get settled when the dog would begin his barking again. The old lady, with another string of "cuss words," would jump out of the weeds and try the trail again a short distance. This was repeated until they reached Rennick's almost prostrate, as the distance was considerably over a mile, and the day an exceedingly hot one about noon. My father, though sick, was more fortunate with his little group of children. When he felt about to faint, he would turn with us into the high weeds and sit there quietly, and, not having any dog with us to report our whereabouts, we were completely hidden by the high weeds, and had a hundred Indians passed they would not have discovered our hiding-place.

In due time we arrived safe at Rennick's, and strange to say, my father was a well man, and did not go to bed again on account of the fever.

When Polly Hopper reached Rennick's and ran into the crowd, she was in a fainting condition. The men took her off the horse, laid her on the ground, and administered cold water and other restoratives. She soon regained consciousness and strength, and of course was regarded as a heroine in the neighbourhood after that memorable day. One can well imagine the excitement among the men whose families were at home and exposed, as they thought, to the mercies of the savages. They scattered immediately toward their homes as rapidly as their horses would carry them, fearing they might find their families murdered. For hours after we reached Rennick's there continued to be arrivals of women and children, many times in a fainting condition, and all exhausted from the fright, the heat, and the speed at which they had run.

Mr. Rennick, who was one of the first pioneers, soon had more visitors than he knew what to do with, and more than his log cabin could shelter. These people remained in and around the cabin for two days, and until the men rode the country over and found the alarm had been a false one and there were no Indians in the neighbourhood.

One of the first occurrences of note in the early settlement of the West was the visitation of grasshoppers, in September, 1820, an occurrence which had never been known by the oldest inhabitants of the Mississippi Valley. They came in such numbers as to appear when in the heavens as thin clouds of vapour, casting a faint shadow upon the earth. In twenty-four hours after their appearance every green thing, in the nature of farm product, that they could eat or devour was destroyed. It so happened, however, that they came so late in the season that the early corn had ripened, so they could not damage that, otherwise a famine would have resulted. The next appearance of these pests was over forty years later, in Western Missouri, Nebraska, and Kansas, which all well remember, as there were two or three seasons in close proximity to each other in the sixties when Western farmers suffered to a great extent from their ravages.

For five years, from 1821 to 1826, nothing worthy of note occurred, but everything moved along as calmly as a sunny day.

In the month of April, 1826, a terrible cyclone passed through that section of the country, leaving nothing standing in its track. Fortunately the country was but sparsely settled, and no lives were lost. It passed from a south-westerly direction to the northeast, tearing to pieces a belt of timber about half-a-mile wide, in that part of the country which became Jackson County, and near where Independence was afterward located, passing a little to the west of that point.

The next cyclone that visited that country was in 1847; this also passed from the southwest to the northeast, passing across the outskirts of Westport, which is now a suburb of Kansas City. The third and last cyclone that visited that section of the country, about eight years ago, (at time of first publication), blew down several houses in Kansas City, and killed a number of children who were attending the High School, the building being demolished by the storm.

POLLY'S WARNING

CHAPTER 2

Missouri in Its Wild and Uncultivated State

There was about one-fourth of the entire territory of Missouri that was covered with timber, and three-fourths in prairie land, with an annual growth of sage-grass, as it was called, about one and one-half feet high, and as thick as it could well grow; in fact the prairie lands in the commencement of its settlement were one vast meadow, where the farmer could cut good hay suitable for the wintering of his stock almost without regard to the selection of the spot; in other words, it was meadow everywhere outside of the timber lands. This condition of things would apply also to the States of Illinois, Iowa, and some of the other Western States, with the exception of Missouri, which had a greater proportion of timber than either of the others mentioned. The timber in all these States grew in belts along the rivers and their tributaries, the prairie covering the high rolling lands between the streams that made up the water channels of those States.

Many of the streams in the first settling of these States were bold, clear running water, and many of them in Missouri were sufficiently strong almost the year round to afford good water power for running machinery, and it was the prediction in the commencement of the settlement of these States by the best-informed people, that the water would increase, for the reason that the swampy portions in the bottom lands, and where there were small lakes, would, by the settlement of the country, become diverted, its force to run directly into and strengthen the larger streams for all time to come. And to show how practical results overthrow theories, the fact proved to be exactly the reverse of their predictions. There has been a continuous slow decline in the natural flow of water-supply from the first settlement of the country.

Many places that I can now remember that were ponds or small lakes, or in other words little reservoirs, which held the water for months while it would be slowly passing out and feeding the streams, have now become fields and plowed ground. Roads and ditches have been made that let the water off at once after a rainfall. The result has been that streams that used to turn machinery have become not much more than outlets for the heavy rainfalls that occur in the rainy season, and if twenty of those streams, each one of which had water enough to run machinery seventy years ago, were all put together now into one stream, there would not be sufficient power to run a good plant of machinery. The numerous springs that could be found on every forty or eighty acres of land in the beginning, have very many of them entirely failed.

The wells of twenty or thirty feet in depth that used to afford any quantity of water for family uses, many of them in order to get water supplies have to be sunk to a much greater depth. Little streams that used to afford any quantity of water for the stock have dried up, giving no water supply, only in times of abundance of rain. All the first settlers in the State located along the timber belts, without an exception, and cultivated the timber lands to produce their grain and vegetables. It was many years after the forest lands were settled before prairie lands were cultivated to any extent, and it was found later that the prairie lands were more fertile than they gave them credit for being before real tests in the way of farming were made with them. The sage grass had the tenacity to stand a great deal of grazing and tramping over, and still grow to considerable perfection.

It required years of grazing upon the prairie before the wild grass, which was universal in the beginning, gave way, but in the timber portions the vegetation that was found in the first settling of the land gave way almost at once. In two years from the time a farmer moved upon a new spot and turned his stock loose upon it, the original wild herbs that were found there disappeared and other vegetation took its place. The land being exceedingly fertile, never failed to produce a crop of vegetation, and when one variety did appear and cover the entire surface as thick as it could grow for a few years, it seemed to exhaust the quality of the soil that produced that kind, and that variety would give way and something new come up.

The older the country has become, as a rule, the more obnoxious has been the vegetation that the soil has produced of its own accord.

But there has been in my recollection, which goes back more than seventy years, a great many changes in the crops of vegetation on those lands, showing to my satisfaction that there is an inherent potency in nature, in rich soil that will cover itself every year with a growth of some kind. If it is not cultivated and made to produce fruit, vegetables, and cereals, it will nevertheless produce a crop of some kind.

The first settlers in the Mississippi Valley were as a rule poor people, who were industrious, economizing, and self-sustaining. From ninety-five to ninety-seven *per cent* of the entire population manufactured at home almost everything necessary for good living. A great many of them when they were crossing the Ohio and Mississippi to their new homes would barely have money enough to pay their ferriage across the rivers, and one of the points in selling out whatever they had to spare when they made up their minds to emigrate was to be sure to have cash enough with them to pay their ferriage. They generally carried with them a pair of chickens, ducks, geese, and if possible a pair of pigs, their cattle and horses.

The wife took her spinning wheel, a bunch of cotton or flax, and was ready to go to spinning as soon as she landed on the premises, often having her cards and wheel at work before her husband could build a log cabin. Going into a land, as it was then, that flowed with milk and honey they were enabled by the use of their own hands and brains to make an independent and good living. There was any quantity of game, bear, elk, deer, wild turkeys, and wild honey to be found in the woods, so that no man with a family, who had pluck and energy enough about him to stir around, ever need to be without a supply of food. At that time nature afforded the finest of pasture, both summer and winter, for his stock.

While the people as a rule were not educated, many of them very illiterate as far as education was concerned, they were thoroughly self-sustaining when it came to the knowledge required to do things that brought about a plentiful supply of the necessities of life. In those times all were on an equality, for each man and his family had to produce what was required to live upon, and when one man was a little better dressed than another there could be no complaint from his neighbour, for each one had the same means in his hands to bring about like results, and he could not say his neighbour was better dressed than he was because he had cheated some other neighbour out of something, and bought the dress; for at that time the goods all had to come to them in the same way—by their own industry.

There was but little stealing or cheating among them. There was no money to steal, and if a man stole a piece of jeans or cloth of any kind he would be apprehended at once. Society at that time was homogeneous and simple, and opportunities for vice were very rare. There were very few old bachelors and old maids, for about the only thing a young man could do when he became twenty-one, and his mother quit making his clothes and doing his washing, was to marry one of his neighbour's daughters. The two would then work together, as was the universal custom, and soon produce with their own hands abundance of supplies to live upon.

The country was new, and when a young man got married his father and brothers, and his wife's father and brothers, often would turn out and help him put up a log cabin, which work required only a few days, and he and his spouse would move into it at once. They would go to work in the same way as their fathers had done, and in a few years would be just as independent as the old people. The young ladies most invariably spun and wove, and made their bridal dresses. At that time there were millions of acres of land that a man could go and squat on, build his cabin, and sometimes live for years upon it before the land would come into market, and with the prosperity attending such undertakings, as a general thing would manage in some way, when the land did come into market, to pay $1.25 per acre for as much as he required for the maintenance of his family.

Men in those days who came to Missouri and looked at the land often declined to select a home in the State on account of their having no market for their products, as above stated, everybody producing all that was needed for home consumption and often a surplus, but were so far away from any of the large cities of the country, without transportation of either steamboats or railroads, for it was before the time of steamboats, much less railroads—for neither of them in my early recollections were in existence—to make them channels of business and trade. Men in the early settlement often wondered if the rich land of the State would ever be worth $5 per acre.

Missouri at that time was considered the western confines of civilization, and it was believed then that there never would be in the future any white settlements of civilized people existing between the western borders of Missouri and the Pacific Coast, unless it might be the strip between the Sierra Nevada Mountains and the Pacific Ocean, which the people at that time knew but little or nothing about.

In 1820 and 1830 there were a great many peaceable tribes of Indians, located by the government all along the western boundary of Missouri, in what was then called the Indian Territory, and has since then become the States of Kansas, Nebraska, and Oklahoma Territory. I remember the names of many of the tribes who were our nearest neighbours across the line, and among them were the Shawnees, Delawares, Wyandottes, Kickapoos, Miamis, Sacs, Foxes, Osages, Peorias, and Iowas, all of whom were perfectly friendly and docile, and lived for a great many years in close proximity to the white settlers, even coming among them to trade without any outbreaks or trespassing upon the rights of the white people in any way or manner worth mentioning.

There was a long period existing from 1825 to 1860 of perfect harmony between these tribes and the white people, and in fact even to this day there is no disturbance between these tribes and their neighbours, the whites. The Indian troubles have been among the Sioux, Arapahoes, Cheyennes, Apaches, Utes, and some other minor tribes, all of which, at the present time, seem to have submitted to their fate in whatever direction it may lie. There is one remark that I will venture here, and it is this, that while the white people were in the power of the Indians and understood it, we got along with the Indian a great deal better than when the change to the white people took place. In the early days white men respected the Indian's rights thoroughly, and would not be the aggressors, and often they were at the mercy of the Indians, but as soon as they began to feel that they could do as they pleased, became more aggressive and had less regard for what the Indian considered his rights. Then in the early days Indians were paid their annuities in an honest way, and there was no feeling among them that they were mistreated by the agent whose duty it was to pay them this annuity.

I was acquainted with one Indian agent by the name of Major Cummings, who for a long time was a citizen of Jackson County, and for a great many years agent for a number of the tribes living along the borders of Missouri. There never was a complaint or even a suspicion, to the best of my knowledge, that he or his clerks ever took one cent of the annuities that belonged to the Indians. The money was paid to them in silver, either in whole or half dollars, and the head of every family received every cent of his quota. Therefore we had a long period of quiet and peace with our red brethren. It is only since the late war that there has been so much complaint from the Indians with reference to the scanty allowances and poor food and blankets.

CHAPTER 3

A Silver Expedition

In the summer of 1827 my father, Benjamin Majors, with twenty-four other men, formed a party to go to the Rocky Mountains in search of a silver mine that had been discovered by James Cockrell,[1] while on a beaver-trapping expedition some four years previous.

At that time, men attempting to cross the plains had no means of carrying food supplies to last more than a week, or ten days at the outside. When their scanty supply of provisions was exhausted, they depended solely upon the game they might chance to kill, invariably eating this without salt. These twenty-five men elected James Cockrell their captain, as he was the only man of the party who had crossed the plains. Being the discoverer of what he claimed was a rich silver mine, they relied solely upon him to pilot them to the spot. The only facilities for transportation were one horse each. Their scant amount of bedding, with the rider, was all the horse could carry. Each man had to be armed with a good gun, and powder and ball enough to last him during the entire trip, for the territory through which they had to pass was inhabited by hostile Indians. No cooking vessels were taken with them, as they depended entirely upon roasting or broiling their meat upon the fire.

When they could not find deer, antelope, elk, or buffalo they had to do without food, unless they were driven to kill and eat a wolf they might chance to get. When they reached the buffalo belt, however, 200 miles farther west, there was no scarcity of meat. The country where they roamed was 400 miles across, reaching to the base of the Rocky Mountains, and extending from Texas more than 3,000 miles, very far north of the Canadian line. The buffalo were numbered by

---

1. An uncle of Senator Cockrell of Missouri.

the millions. It often occurred in travelling through this district that there would be days together when one would never be out of sight of great herds of these animals. They stayed in the most open portion of the plains they could find, for the country was one vast plain, or level prairie. The grass called buffalo grass did not grow more than one and one-half to two inches high, but grew almost as thick in many places as the hair on a dog's back.

Other grasses that were found in this locality grew much taller, but one would invariably find the buffalo grazing upon the short kind, especially so in the winter, as the high winds blew the snow away from where this grass grew. There were millions of acres of this grass. The buffalo's teeth and under jaw were so arranged by nature that he could bite this short grass to the earth; in fact no small animal, such as a sheep, goat, or antelope, could cut the grass more closely than the largest buffalo. Strange to say this short grass of the prairie is rapidly disappearing, as the buffaloes have done. In crossing the plains with our oxen in later years we found it impossible for them to get a living by grazing on the portions of the plains where this grass grew.

The party in question soon reached the Raton Mountains not far from Trinidad, now on the Atchison, Topeka & Santa Fé Railroad. It is proper to state that after leaving their homes in Jackson and Lafayette counties, Mo., they travelled across the prairie, bearing a little south of west, until they reached the Big Bend, or Great Bend, as it is lately called, of the Arkansas River. At this point they found innumerable herds of buffalo, and no trouble in finding grass and water in plenty, as well as meat. They followed the margin of the river until they reached the foot-hills of the Rocky Mountains; then their captain told them he was in the region where he had discovered the mine. He found some difficulty in locating the spot, and after many days spent in searching, some of the party grew restless and distrustful, doubting as to whether he ever discovered silver ore, or if so, if he was willing to show them the location, and became very threatening in their attitude toward him. He finally found what he and they had supposed was silver ore.

This fact pacified the party and perhaps saved his life, as it was a long way for men to travel through peril and hardships only to be disappointed, or, as they expressed it, "to be fooled." They were disappointed, however, when they found nothing but dirty-looking rock, with now and then a bright speck of metal in it. Not one of them had ever seen silver ore, nor did they know anything about manipulating the rock in order to get the silver out of it. Many of them expected to find the silver in metallic form, and thought they could cut it out with their tomahawks and pack home a good portion of wealth upon their horses. They thought they could walk and lead their horses if they could get a load of precious metal to carry, as their captain had done a few years before, when he sold his beaver skins in St. Louis, took his pay in silver dollars, put them in a sack, bought a horse to carry it, and led him 300 miles to his home.

It must be remembered that this was the first prospecting party to look for silver that ever left the western borders of Missouri for the Rocky Mountains. After finding what they supposed was a silver mine, each one selected some of the best specimens and left for their homes. Everything moved along well with them until they arrived at about the point on the Arkansas River where Dodge City now stands. They camped one evening at the close of a day's travel, ate a hearty supper of buffalo meat, put their guard around their horses, and went to bed. Two men at a time guarded the horses, making a change every three hours during the night. This precaution was necessary to keep the Indians, who were in great numbers and hostile, from running off their horses. But on that fatal night the Indians succeeded in crawling on their bellies where the grass was tall enough to conceal them from the guard. It was only along the river bottoms and water courses that the grass grew tall.

When they got between the guard and the horses, they suddenly rose, firing their guns, shaking buffalo robes, and with war-whoops and yells succeeded in frightening the horses to an intense degree. Then the Indians who were in reserve, mounted on ponies, ran the horses off where their owners never heard of or saw them afterward. Part of the Indians, at the same time, turned their guns upon the men that were lying upon the bank of the river. They jumped out of their beds, over the bank and into the water knee-deep. The men, by stooping under the bank, which was four feet perpendicular, were protected from the arrows and bullets of the enemy. There they stood for the remainder of that cold October night. One of the party, a man named Mark Foster, when they jumped over the bank, did not stop, but ran as fast as he could go for the other side. The water was shallow, not being more than knee-deep anywhere, and in some places not half that depth. The bottom was sandy, and at that place the river was some 400 yards wide.

In running in the dark of the night, with the uneven bottom of the river, Mr. Foster fell several times. Each time it drew a yell from the Indians, who thought they had killed him, for they were shooting at him as he ran. After being three times ducked, he reached the other side and dry land. His clothes were thoroughly drenched, and his gun, which was a flint-lock and muzzle-loader, entirely useless. Just think of a man in that condition—his gun disabled, apparently a thousand wolves howling around him in all directions, the darkness of the night, the yelling of the Indians on the other side, and 400 miles from home; the only living white man, unless some of his comrades happened not to be killed. He remained there shivering with the cold the rest of the night. When daylight appeared he started to cross the river to the camp to find out whether his comrades were dead or alive. He reached the middle of the river and halted, his object being to see, if possible, whether it was the Indians or his party that he could see through the slight fog that was rising and slowly moving westward and up the river.

His comrades, who fortunately were alive, could hear, in the still of the morning, every step he made in the water. After standing a short time he decided that the men he saw moving about were Indians, and he was confirmed in the belief that all his party were killed, so he ran back to where he had spent such a doleful part of the night and there remained until the fog entirely cleared away. He then could see that the men at the camp from where he fled were his comrades. He returned within about sixty yards from where they were, stopped and called to my father, who answered him, after some persuasion from the rest of the party, for they all felt ugly toward him, thinking he had acted the coward in doing as he did. When my father answered his call, he asked if they would allow him to join them. After holding a consultation it was agreed that he might come. He walked firmly up to them and remarked:

"I have something to say to you, gentlemen. It is this: I know you think I have acted the d—d coward, and I do not blame you under the circumstances. When you all jumped over the bank I thought you were going to run to the other side, and I did not know any better until I had got so far out I was in greater danger to return than to go ahead. For, as you know, the Indians were sending volleys of bullets and arrows after me, and really thought they had killed me every time I fell. Now, to end this question, there is one of two things you must do. The first is that you take your guns and kill me now, or if you do not comply with this, that every one of you agree upon your sacred honour that you will never allude, in any way, or throw up to me the unfortunate occurrences of last night. Now, gentlemen, mark what I say. If you do not kill me, but allow me to travel with you to our homes, should one of you ever be so thoughtless or forgetful of the promise you must now make as to throw it up to me, I pledge myself before you all that I will take the life of the man who does it. Now, I have presented the situation fairly, and you must accept one or the other before you leave this spot."

The party with one accord, after hearing his story, agreed never to allude to it in any way in his presence, and gave him a cordial welcome to their midst. They treated him as one of them from that time on, for he was a brave man after all. Think of the awful experience the poor fellow had during the night, and in the morning, to reach an amicable understanding with his party. One can readily see that he was a man of very great courage and physical endurance, or he could not have survived the pressure upon him. It was a sad time for those twenty-five brave men for more reasons than one. Knowing that they were 400 miles from home, late in the fall, without a road or path to follow, no stopping place of any kind between them and their homes on the borders of the Missouri, which was as far as civilization had reached westward. The thought that impressed them most deeply was in reference to one of their comrades by the name of Clark Davis, whom they all loved and honoured. He was a man weighing 300 pounds, but not of large frame, his weight consisting more of fat than bone.

It was the universal verdict of the party that it would be impossible for him to walk home and carry his gun and ammunition as they all had to do. They would go aside in little groups, so he would not hear them, and deplore the situation. They thought they would have to leave him sitting in the prairie for the wolves to devour, or hazard the lives of all the rest of the party. Some actually wept over the thought of the loss of such a dear comrade and noble-hearted man. Should they chance to reach their own homes, for they were all men with families, the idea of telling his family that they were obliged to leave him was more than they felt their nerves could endure. In my opinion there never was a more brave and heroic group of men thrown together than were those twenty-five frontiersmen. All were fine specimens of manhood, physically speaking, between thirty and forty years of age, and with perfect health and daring to do whatever their convictions dictated.

They went to work and burned their saddles, bridles, blankets, in fact everything they had in camp that they could not carry with them on their backs. This they did to prevent the Indians from getting any more "booty." After all their arrangements were made for leaving their unfortunate camping-place, they started once more for their homes. They travelled at the rate of twenty to twenty-five miles per day. They could have gone farther, but for the fact that they had no trail to walk in. The grass in some places, and the drifting sand in others, made it exceedingly irksome for footmen.

My father was frequently asked after his return:

"Was there no road you could follow?"

He would answer:

"No, from the fact that the drifting sand soon filled every track of a passing caravan and no trace was left of a trail a few hours afterward."

A few years later on this shifting of sand discontinued, and grass and small shrubbery soon began to grow and cover many places that were then perfectly bare. One-half of the distance they had to walk was covered with herds of buffalo, the other half was through desolate prairie country, where game of any kind was seldom seen. It was on this part of their journey that they came near starvation. It only took them a few days after leaving the buffalo belt to consume what meat they had carried on their backs, as men become very hungry and consume a great deal of meat when they have long and tiresome walks to make. In the first week of their march their convictions in regard to Clark Davis were confirmed, as they thought, for his feet blistered in a terrible manner, his fat limbs became exceedingly raw and sore, so he of necessity would lag. Then they would detail of a morning when they started, a guard of five or six men to remain with him for protection from the Indians.

The rest of the party would walk on to some point they would designate for camping the next night, and he with his little guard would arrive some three or four hours later. This went on for seven or eight days in succession, each day they expecting the news from the guard that he had given up the hope of going any farther. But in time his feet began to improve, in fact his condition every way, and he would reach camp sooner each day after the arrival of the party. After they had passed the buffalo belt, where meat was abundant, and struck the starvation belt in their travels, Mr. Davis' fat proved a blessing and of great service. When fatigue and want were to be endured at the same time, he began to take the lead instead of the rear of the party. Several days before they reached home they would have perished, but for the fact that he alone had sufficient activity and strength to attempt to hunt for game, for they had seen none after leaving the buffalo. They had reached a place called Council Grove—now a city of that name—in the State of Kansas, about one hundred and thirty miles from their homes. After so many weeks of hard marching they thought they could go no farther, and some dropped on the ground, thinking it useless to make the attempt. At this juncture Clark Davis said:

"Boys, I will go and kill a deer."

My father said the very word was tantalizing to a lot of men who were almost dying of hunger. They did not know there was a deer in the country, or anything else that could be eaten, not even a snake, for cold weather was so near even they had disappeared. Davis, however, determined on his hunt, left his comrades, and had travelled only a few hundred yards until he saw two fine deer standing near. Directly the men in the camp heard the report of his gun, and as soon as he could reload they heard a second report, and then a shout, "Come here, boys! there is meat in plenty." You may imagine it was not long until every one joined him. They drank every drop of blood that was in the two deer, ate the livers without cooking, and saved every particle, even taking the marrow out of their legs. This meat tided them over until they were able to reach other food.

Never before in the history of the past, nor since that time, did 150 pounds of surplus fat—so considered until starvation overtook them—prove to be of such great value, and was worth more to them than all the gold and silver in the Rocky Mountains. When the test came, it was found to be one of nature's reservoirs that could be drawn upon to save the lives of twenty-five brave men when all else failed them. Mr. Davis, as well as the rest of the party, no doubt often wished it could be dispensed with, as after losing his horse he carried it with great suffering and fatigue, before they learned its use, and that it was to be the salvation of the party. We often hear it said that truth is stranger than fiction, and this certainly was one of the cases where it proved to be so.

They finally reached home without losing one of their party; but they all gave the man whom they expected to leave to the wolves in the start the credit of saving their lives. When Mr. Davis reached his family the first thing his wife did was to set him a good meal. When he sat down to the table he said, "Jane, there is to be a new law for the future of our lives at our table."

She said, "What is it, Clark?"

He answered, "It is this. I never want to hear you or one of my children say bread again."

"What then must we call it?" asked his wife.

"Call it bready," said he, "for when I was starving on the plains it came to me that the word bread was too short and coarse a name to call such sweet, precious, and good a thing, and whoever eats it should use this pet name and be thankful to God who gives it, for I assure you, wife, the ordeal I have passed through will forever cause me to appreciate life and the good things that uphold it."

The outcome of this trip was drawing the party together, like one family, and they could not be kept long apart. It is a fact that mutual suffering begets an endearment stronger than ties of blood. It was interesting to me as a boy to hear them relate their experiences in reference to their hard trials and forebodings that were undergone, with no beneficial results. Some of them sent their specimens to St. Louis to be tested for silver, but received discouraging accounts of its value. If a very rich mine had been found at that time it would not have been of any practical value, for they were more than thirty years ahead of the time when silver-mining could be carried on, from an American standpoint, with success. There was no one west of the Alleghanies with capital and skill enough to carry on such an enterprise, and there were no means whatever for transporting machinery to the Rocky Mountains.

CHAPTER 4

The Mormons

Nothing of very great note occurred in the county of Jackson, after the cyclone of 1826, until the year 1830, when five Mormon elders made their appearance in the county and commenced preaching, stating to their audiences that they were chosen by the priesthood which had been organised by the prophet Joseph Smith, who had met an angel and received a revelation from God, who had also revealed to him and his adherents the whereabouts of a book written upon golden plates and deposited in the earth. This book was found in a hill called Cumorah, at Manchester, in the State of New York. They selected a place near Independence, Jackson County, Mo., in the early part of the year 1831, which they named Temple Lot, a beautiful spot of ground on a high eminence. They there stuck down their Jacob's staff, as they called it, and said:

> This spot is the centre of the earth. This is the place where the Garden of Eden, in which Adam and Eve resided, was located, and we are sent here according to the directions of the angel that appeared to our prophet, Joseph Smith, and told him this is the spot of ground on which the New Jerusalem is to be built, and, when finished, Christ Jesus is to make his reappearance and dwell in this city of New Jerusalem with the saints for a thousand years, at the end of which time there will be a new deal with reference to the nations of the earth, and the final wind-up of the career of the human family.

They claimed to have all the spiritual gifts and understanding of the works of the Almighty that belonged to the Apostles who were chosen by Christ when on his mission to this earth. They claim the gift of tongues and interpretation of tongues or languages spoken in an unknown tongue. In their silent meetings, the one who had received the gift of an unknown tongue knew nothing of its interpretation whatever, but after some silence some one in the audience would rise and claim to have the gift of interpretation, and would interpret what the brother or sister had previously spoken. They also claimed to have the gift of healing by anointing the sick with oil and laying on of hands, and some claimed that they could raise the dead; in fact, they laid claim to every gift that belonged to the Apostolic day or age.

They established their headquarters at Independence, where some of their leading elders were located. There they set up a printing office, the first that was established within 150 miles of Independence, and commenced printing their church literature, which was very distasteful to the members and leaders of other religious denominations, the community being composed of Methodists, Baptists of two different orders, Presbyterians of two different orders, and Catholics, and a denomination calling themselves Christians. In that day and age it was regarded as blasphemous or sacrilegious for any one to claim that they had met angels and received from them new revelations, and the religious portion of the community, especially, was very much incensed and aroused at the audacity of any person claiming such interviews from the invisible world.

Of course the Mormon elders denounced the elders and preachers of the other denominations above mentioned, and said they were the blind leading the blind, and that they would all go into the ditch together. An elder by the name of Rigdon preached in the court house one Sunday in 1832, in which he said that he had been to the third heaven, and had talked face to face with God Almighty. The preachers in the community the next day went *en masse* to call upon him. He repeated what he had said the day before, telling them they had not the truth, and were the blind leading the blind.

The conduct of the Mormons for the three years that they remained there was that of good citizens, beyond their tantalizing talks to outsiders. They, of course, were clannish, traded together, worked together, and carried with them a melancholy look that one acquainted with them could tell a Mormon when he met him by the look upon his face almost as well as if he had been of different colour. They claimed that God had given them that locality, and whoever joined the Mormons, and helped prepare for the next coming of the Lord Jesus Christ, would be accepted and all right; but if they did not go into the fold of the Latter Day Saints, that it was only a matter of time when they would be crushed out, for that was the promised land and they had come to possess it. The Lord had sent them there and would protect them against any odds in the way of numbers.

Finally the citizens, and particularly the religious portion of them, made up their minds that it was wrong to allow them to be printing their literature and preaching, as it might have a bad effect upon the rising generation; and on the 4th of July, 1833, there was quite a gathering of the citizens, and a mob was formed to tear down their printing office. While the mob was forming, many of the elders stood and looked on, predicting that the first man who touched the building would be paralyzed and fall dead upon the ground. The mob, however, paid no attention to their predictions and prayers for God to come and slay them, but with one accord seized hold of the implements necessary to destroy the house, and within the quickest time imaginable had it torn to the ground, and scattered their type and literature to the four winds. This, of course, created an intense feeling of anger on the part of the Mormons against the citizens. At this time there were but a few hundred Mormons in the county against many times their number of other citizens. I presume there was not exceeding 600 Mormons in the county.

Immediately after they tore down the printing office they sent to the store of Elder Partridge and Mr. Allen, who was also an elder in the church, and took them by force to the public square, stripped them to their waists, and poured on them a sufficient amount of tar to cover their bodies well, and then took feathers and rubbed them well into the tar, making the two elders look like a fright. One of their names being Partridge, many began to whistle like a cock partridge, in derision. Now, be it remembered that the people who were doing this were not what is termed "rabble" of a community, but many among them were respectable citizens and law-abiding in every other respect, but who actually thought they were doing God's service to destroy, if possible, and obliterate Mormonism.

In all my experience I never saw a more law-abiding people than those who lived where this occurred. There is nothing, however, that they could have done that would have proved more effectual in building up and strengthening the faith of the people so treated as this and similar performances proved to do. For if there is anything under the sun that will strengthen people in their beliefs or faith, no matter whether it is error or truth, if they have adopted it as true, it is to abuse and punish them for their avowed belief in whatever they espouse as religion or politics.

A few months after the tearing down of the building, a dozen or two Mormons made their appearance one day on the county road west of the Big Blue and not far from the premises of Moses G. Wilson. Wilson's boy rode out to drive up the milk cows in the morning, and saw this group of Mormons and had some conversation with them, and they used some very violent language to the boy. He went back and told his father, and it happened that there were several of the neighbours in at the time, as he kept a little county store; and in those days men generally carried their guns with them, in case they should have a chance to shoot a deer or turkey as they went from one neighbour's to another. It so happened that several of them had their guns with them; those who did not picked up a club of some kind, and they all followed the boy, who showed them where they were.

When they got in close proximity to where the Mormons were grouped, seeing the men approaching with guns, the Mormons opened fire upon them, and the Gentiles, as they were called by the Mormons, returned the fire. There was a lawyer on the Gentile side by the name of Brazeel, who was shot dead; another man by the name of Lindsay was shot in the jaw and was thought to be fatally wounded, but recovered. Wilson's boy was also shot in the body, but not fatally. There were only one or two Mormons killed. Of course, after this occurrence, it aroused an intense feeling of hate and revenge in the citizens, and the Mormons would not have been so bold had it not been for their elders claiming that under all circumstances and at all times they would be sustained by the Almighty's power, and that a few of them would be able to put their enemies to flight. The available Mormon men then formed themselves into an organisation for fighting the battles of the Lord, and started to Independence, about ten miles away, to take possession of the town.

On their way, and when they were within about a mile of Independence, they marched with all the faith and fervour imaginable for fanatics to possess, encouraging each other with the words, "God will be with us and deliver our enemies into our hands." At this point they met a gentleman whom I well knew, by the name of Rube Collins, a citizen of the place, who was leaving the town in a gallop to go home and get more help to defend the town from the Mormon invasion. He shouted out as he passed them, "You are a d—d set of fools to go there now; there are armed men enough there to exterminate you in a minute."

They were acquainted with Collins, and supposed he had told them the truth; however, at that time they could have taken the town had they pressed on, but his words intimidated them somewhat, and they filed off from the big road and hid themselves in the brush until they could hold a council, and I presume pray for light to be guided by. During this time there were runners going in all directions, notifying the citizens that the Mormons were coming to the town to take it, and every citizen, as soon as he could run bullets and fill his powder horn with powder, gathered his gun and made for the town; and in a few hours men enough had gathered to exterminate them had they approached. In their council that they held they decided not to approach until they sent spies ahead to see whether Collins had told them the truth or not. They supposed he had, from the fact that they found the public square almost covered with men, and others arriving every minute.

As quickly as the citizens had organised themselves into companies (my father, Benjamin Majors, being captain of one of them), they then sent a message by two or three citizens to the Mormons, where they were still secreted in the *paw-paw* brush, and told them that if they did not come and surrender immediately, the whole party that was waiting for them in the town would come out and exterminate them. This message sent terror to their hearts, with all their claims that God would go before them and fight their battles for them. After holding another council they decided the best thing they could do was to go and surrender themselves to their enemies, which they did. I never saw a more pale-faced, terror-stricken set of men banded together than these seventy-five Mormons, for it was all the officers could do to keep the citizens from shooting them down, even when they were surrendering.

However, they succeeded in keeping the men quiet, and no one was hurt. They stacked all their arms around a big white-oak stump that was perhaps four feet in diameter, and at that time was standing in the public square. Afterward the guns were put in the jail house for safe keeping, and were eaten up with rust, and never to my knowledge delivered to them. They then stipulated that every man, woman, and child should leave the county within three weeks. This was a tremendous hardship upon the Mormons, as it was late in the fall, and there were no markets for their crops or anything else that they had. The quickest way to get out of the county was to cross the river into Clay, as the river was the line between the two counties. They had to leave

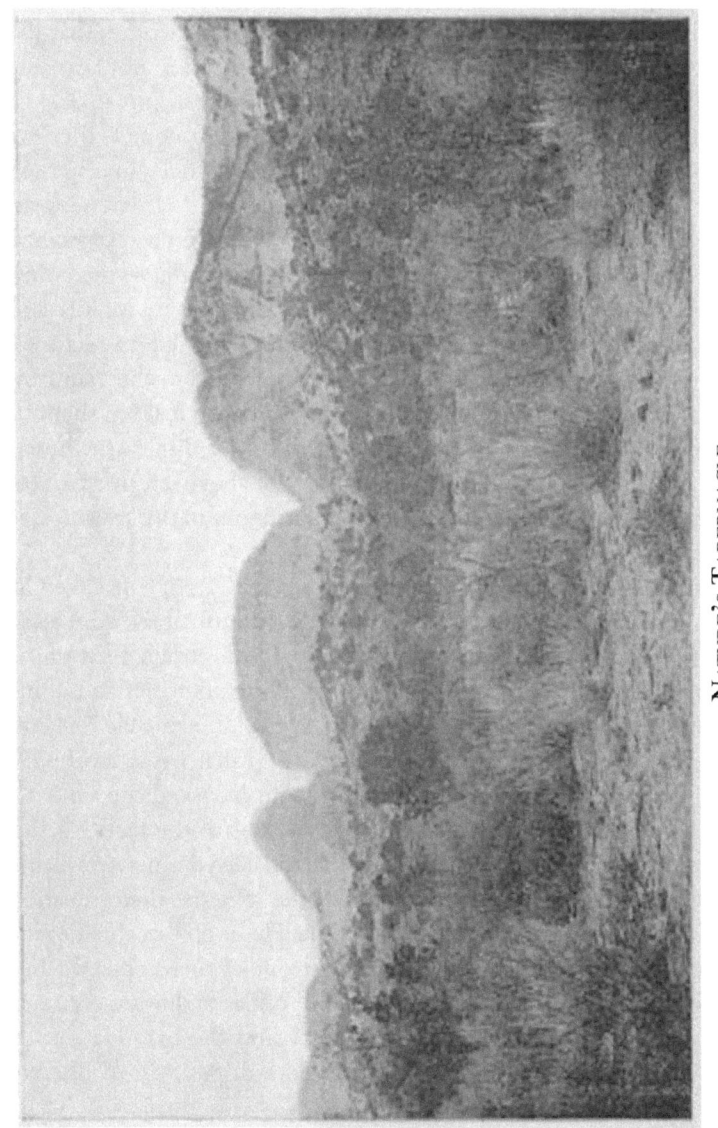

Nature's Tabernacle.

their homes, their crops, and in fact every visible thing they had to live upon. Many of their houses were burned, their fences thrown down, and the neighbours' stock would go in and eat and destroy the crop.

It has been claimed by people who were highly coloured in their prejudice against the Mormons that they were bad citizens; that they stole whatever they could get their hands on and were not law-abiding. This is not true with reference to their citizenship in Jackson County, where they got their first kick, and as severe a one as they ever received, if not the most severe. There was not an officer among them, all the offices of the county being in the hands of their enemies, and if one had stolen a chicken he could and would have been brought to grief for doing so; but it is my opinion there is nothing in the county records to show where a Mormon was ever charged with any misdemeanour in the way of violation of the laws for the protection of property. The cause of all this trouble was solely from the claim that they had a new revelation direct from the Almighty, making them the chosen instruments to go forward, let it please or displease whom it might, to build the New Jerusalem on the spot above referred to, Temple Lot. And, as above stated, whoever did not join in this must sooner or later give way to those who would.

I met a Presbyterian preacher, Rev. Mr. McNice, in Salt Lake City a number of years ago at the dinner table of a mutual friend, Doctor Douglas. It was on the Sabbath after hearing him preach a very bitter sermon against the Mormons, denouncing their doctrines and doings in a severe manner, and while we were at the dinner table, the subject of the Mormons came up, and I told him that I was thoroughly versed in their first troubles in Missouri, and he asked me what the trouble was. I told him frankly that it grew out of the fact that they claimed to have seen an angel, and to have received a new revelation from God which was not in accord with the religious denominations that existed in the community at that time. He hooted at the idea and told me he had read the history of their troubles there, and that they were bad citizens with reference to being outlaws, thieves, etc., who would pick up their neighbours' property and the like. He insisted that he had read their history, and showed a disposition to discredit my statements.

I then told him I was history, and knew as much about it as any living man could know, and that there were no charges of that kind against them; they were industrious, hard-working people, and worked for whatever they wanted to live upon, obtaining it by their industry, and not by stealing it from their neighbours. He then scouted at the idea that people would receive such treatment as they did merely because they claimed to have seen angels and talked with God and claimed to have a new revelation. I then referred him to the fact that fifty or sixty years previous to that time the public mind in America lacked a great deal of being so tolerant as it was at the time of our conversation; that not more than one hundred years ago some of the American people were so superstitious that they could burn witches at the stake and drag Quakers through the streets of Boston on their backs, with a jack hitched to their heels; that the Mormons today could go to Jackson County, Mo., and preach the same doctrines that they did then, and the result would be that they would be laughed at instead of mobbed as they were sixty years ago.

I was sitting in a cabin with my father's miller, a Mr. Newman, a Mormon, at the time of this trouble. Mr. Newman's mother-in-law, who lived with him, was named Bentley; she had a son in the company that surrendered at Independence, and who walked six miles that evening and came home. The young man walked in and looked as sad as death, and when asked what the news was he stood there and related what had taken place that day at the surrender. They all sat in breathless silence and listened to the story, and when he was through with his statement and said the Mormons had agreed to leave the county within three weeks, the old lady, who sat by the table sewing, raised her hand and brought it down upon the table with a tremendous thud, and said:

So sure as this is a world there *will be* a New Jerusalem built.

I relate this little incident to show that even after they had met with such a galling defeat how zealous even the old women were with reference to their future success. But it is my opinion that the more often a fanatic is kicked and abused, the stronger is his faith in his cause, for then they would take up the Scriptures and read the sentences expressed by Christ:

But before all these they shall lay their hands on you and persecute you, delivering you up to the synagogues and into prisons, being brought before kings and rulers for my name's sake.

But take heed to yourselves, for they shall deliver you up to councils, and in the synagogues ye shall be beaten; and ye shall be brought before rulers and kings for my sake for a testimony against them.

From such passages they have always drawn the greatest consolation, and one would ask one another, "Where are the people the blessed Lord had reference to?" Another brother, with all the sanctity and confidence imaginable for a fanatic to feel, would answer, "Well, brother, if you do not find them among the Latter Day Saints you can not find them upon the face of this green earth, for we have suffered all the abuses the blessed Lord refers to in the Scripture you have just quoted."

I have said before that the Mormons all crossed the Missouri into Clay County, where they wintered in tents and log cabins hastily thrown together, and lived on mast, corn, and meat that they would procure from the citizens for whom they worked in clearing ground and splitting rails, and other work of a like character.

In the spring they were determined to return to their homes, although they were so badly destroyed, and claimed again as before that God would vindicate them and put to flight their enemies. The people of Jackson County, however, watched for their return, and gathered, at the appointed time, in a large body, on the opposite side of the river to where the Mormons, were expected to congregate and cross back into the county. Their spies came to the river, and seeing camps of the citizens, who had gathered to the number of four or five hundred strong (I being one of the number) to prevent their crossing, then changed their purpose and sent some of their leading men to locate in some other part of the State, for the time being, with the full understanding, however, that at the Lord's appointed time they would all be returned to Jackson County, and complete their mission in building the city of the New Jerusalem. The delegation they sent out selected Davis and Colwell counties as the portion of the State where they would make their temporary rally until they became strong enough for the Lord to restore them to their former location.

During that spring the citizens of Jackson County, feeling that there had been, in many cases, great outrages perpetrated upon the Mormons, held a public meeting at Independence and appointed five commissioners, whose duty it was to meet some of the leading elders of the Mormons at Liberty, the seat of Clay County, and make some reparation for the damages that had been done to their property the fall before in Jackson County. They met, but failed to agree, as the elders asked more and perhaps wanted to retain the titles they had to the lands, as they thought it would be sacrilege to part with them, for that was the chosen spot for the New Jerusalem.

During the time that elapsed between the commissioners crossing the river in the morning and returning in the evening, the ferryman (Bradbury), whom I have often met, a man with a very large and finely developed physique, a great swimmer, was supposed to be bribed by the Mormons to bore large auger-holes through the gunwales of his flatboat just at the water's edge. The boat having a floor in it some inches above the bottom, there could be no detection of the flow of the water until it was sufficiently deep to cover the inner floor. The commissioners went upon the boat with their horses, and had not proceeded very far from the shore until they found the water coming up in the second floor and the boat rapidly sinking. This, of course, produced great consternation, for the river was very high and turbulent. Bradbury, the owner of the ferry, said to his two men:

"Boys, we will jump off and swim back to the shore."

As above stated, he was a great swimmer, and had been known to swim the Missouri upon his back several times not long before this occurred. When the water rose in the boat so that it was necessary for the commissioners to leave it, three of them caught hold of their horses' tails, after throwing off as much clothing as they could before the boat went down with them. The other two men who could swim attempted to swim alone, but the current was so turbulent that they were overcome and were drowned. Those who hung on to the tails of their horses were brought safely to shore. One of the men drowned was a neighbour of my father's and as fine a gentleman and good fellow as ever lived. His name was David Lynch.

I remember well their names, and was well acquainted with two of the men who were pulled through by their horses, S. Noland and Sam C. Owens, the foremost merchant of the county, a man who stood high in every sense, and of marked ability.

This occurrence put the quietus on any further attempt to try to settle for the damages done the Mormons when driven from the county, for it caused in the whole population the most intense feeling against them, and they never were remunerated.

When Bradbury jumped off the boat he swam for the shore, but was afterward found dead, with one of his hands grasping the root of a cottonwood tree, so there was no opportunity for trying him for the crime, or finding out how it was brought about. It was supposed that he was bribed, as no one knew of any enmity he had against the commissioners.

The town the Mormons started, which they selected for their home in Paris County, they called Far West. This was the first experience that the people of Western Missouri had with the emigrants of the Eastern or New England States. Brigham Young, who afterward became the leader of the Mormons, was from Vermont, and many others composing the early pioneers of the Mormon church were from the New England States; some, however, from Ohio and Illinois, as well as some proselytes from Missouri. Up to the time of their appearance in Western Missouri the entire population was from some one of the four States—Virginia, North Carolina, Tennessee, or Kentucky.

It has been claimed by some that one of the causes of the dissatisfaction was that the Mormons were Abolitionists. This, however, played no part in the bitter feeling that grew up between them and their neighbours, for at the time of their coming to Jackson County there were but very few slaves, the people generally being poor farmers who lived from the labour of their own hands and that of their families. And then, when the Mormons were driven entirely from Missouri to Illinois, which was a free State, they soon got into difficulty with their neighbours there, as they had done in Missouri. It is claimed now, universally, by the people of this country that polygamy, or the plurality-wife system, is the only objection that good citizens can have to Mormonism.

This was not the cause of their difficulties or their trouble in Illinois and Missouri, as they had never, up to the time they left Nauvoo, Ill., proclaimed polygamy as being a church institution. And as I have previously stated, it was their clannishness, as is natural for a church to do, more or less, only they carried it to a greater degree than other denominations. Also the new doctrine they were preaching, stating that they were the only and chosen people of God, and that they had the key of St. Peter, which was lost during the dark ages and was revealed again to Joseph Smith, their prophet; that the Lord would stand by them and enable them to prevail in their undertakings as against any array of opposition, no matter how much greater the numbers might be than their own.

They built up the city of Far West, of several thousand people, and while there increased very rapidly, having missionaries in many parts of the country preaching their doctrine. As quickly as an individual would accept their faith, they would at once rally to the headquarters, and in the course of a few years they had put a great deal of the prairie lands into cultivation and increased their numbers until they were so formidable that when they began to be odious to their neighbours by showing a hostile attitude toward any power that might interfere with them, they got into trouble much in the same way as they did in Jackson County.

A party of Gentiles and Mormons met at a point called Horn's Mill, and became involved in a quarrel, when there were some killed on both sides. This created such a feeling in the community that both Mormons and Gentiles felt insecure, living neighbours to each other as they were, and the trouble went on until it culminated in the Governor, Lilburn W. Boggs, calling out a portion of the militia of the State and ordering them to Far West, the Mormon centre. The Mormons were drilling continuously, and increasing their facilities for fighting, when the militia reached the place designated, and organising, placed themselves in battle array. The Mormons were also drawn up in long lines, and for a short time it looked as if a bloody battle was unavoidable, but before any engagement occurred the Mormons again surrendered. They then agreed to leave the State of Missouri, and in April, 1839, the last of the band left Far West, moved across the Mississippi into Illinois, where they afterward located and built the city of Nauvoo, but with no better results with the people in the free State than they experienced in Missouri. This shows that slavery had nothing to do with the hard feelings and prejudice they aroused in every community in which they lived.

The Mormons' new village was named Nauvoo, which means Peaceful Rest. While there, having increased to fifteen thousand souls, they built a temple to the Lord, which was, perhaps, the finest building that had ever been erected in the State up to that time. During the year 1844, trouble arose between them and the Gentiles, to suppress which the militia was called out, and in June of that year a writ was sworn out for the arrest of the Mormon prophet, Joseph Smith. His brother Hiram and Elder Taylor, who, after Brigham Young's death, became president of the church, accompanied him to Carthage, Ill., where he went to give himself up. Arriving at Carthage, all three were put in jail, where a mob succeeded in killing the two brothers and seriously wounding Taylor, who carried some of the bullets in his body during the remainder of his life. On the death of Joseph Smith, Brigham Young was chosen by the church as its prophet, president, and leader.

After three severe experiences in establishing settlements in Missouri and Illinois, they determined in their councils to emigrate farther west and start a colony which would be composed of Latter

Day Saints, where they would be entirely distinct and separate from any antagonizing elements. At that time Salt Lake Valley, being under Spanish dominion and a thousand miles from any white settlement, was ultimately chosen as the spot best suited for their purpose.

After leaving Nauvoo, Ill., they went to Council Bluffs, Iowa (called by them Kaneville), travelling through the State of Iowa, and undergoing the greatest hardships and sufferings any people were ever called upon to endure, being without money, some of them without the proper means of transportation, destitute of almost all the necessities of life, and a great many sick on account of exposure to the elements. Arriving at the place above named, on the Missouri River, they went into winter quarters, and the next spring planted and raised crops in that vicinity, the greater number of the emigrants remaining there for the next two years.

In the spring of 1847, at the time war was being carried on between the United States and Mexico, Brigham Young started west with a band of from seventy to seventy-five pioneers, having, I believe, an impression that in Salt Lake Valley might be found the Mecca of their hopes. They arrived in Salt Lake Valley on the 21st day of July of that year. Previous to this, in 1846, at the call of the President for troops for the Mexican War, Brigham Young raised a regiment of a thousand volunteers to go to Mexico, under a stipulation with the United States Government that, when the war was over, the survivors should receive their discharges in California. This agreement was made in view of the fact that they had already resolved to go west into Spanish territory.

The treaty of peace between the United States and Old Mexico, at the close of the war, resulted in the Government of Mexico giving up to the United States all the territory possessed by it lying north of the present boundary line between the two countries, so that, after all the exertions the Mormons had made to effect a settlement on Spanish territory, in less than a year they found themselves still in the United States, where they have ever since remained, having built cities and towns on the colonising plan in every available portion of the Territory of Utah, and having quite a number of colonies in other Territories, with one at present established in Mexico, as I have lately been informed.

I have met in later years and become familiarly acquainted with many of the leading spirits of the Mormon church, and have had large business transactions with Brigham Young and many other prominent

Mormons, among whom were Captain Hooper, General Eldridge, Ferrimore Little, William Jennings, John Sharp, Lew Hills, Gen. Daniel H. Wells, Wilford Woodruff (now president of the Mormon church), Joseph Smith, and George Q. Cannon, and a fairer, more upright set of gentlemen I never met.

I have heard all the leading elders of the Mormon Church preach, including Brigham Young, Heber Kimball, George Q. Cannon, George A. Smith (the historian), John Taylor, Orson Pratt, and Elder Woodruff, who is now president of the church.

Orson Pratt was the ablest expounder of the Scriptures, particularly of the prophecies, in the Mormon church. He was the man chosen by Brigham Young and his counsellors to discuss the subject of polygamy, from a Bible standpoint, with the Rev. John P. Newman, who was at that time pastor of one of the Methodist churches in Washington, D. C. I, among many other Gentiles, was present and heard the discussion, which took place in the Mormon Tabernacle.

President Young, as he was invariably called by his own people, was the boldest, most outspoken man I ever saw in the pulpit. I remember hearing him one Sabbath day when he was preaching in the Tabernacle, which seats 13,000 people, and on that day was packed to its full capacity, there being probably one hundred and fifty or more strangers present—excursionists from the East on their way to California, who had stopped over Sunday to visit the Mormon church, and listen to the immense organ and singers, but whose greatest desire was to hear Brigham Young expound the Mormon doctrine. These strangers were given the most prominent seats by the ushers, and this is the only church in which I remember strangers having precedent over the regular church members in being seated.

When Brigham Young was well along in his discussion, it occurred to him that the strangers present would want to know the size of his family, as that was a question often asked by visitors, so he ceased his discourse and said: "I suppose the strangers present would like to know how many wives and children I have," and then proceeded to say he had sixteen wives and forty-five living children, having lost eight or ten children, I believe. He then proceeded to finish his discourse.

I was present on another occasion when he was preaching to a very large congregation, and he said to them:

> Brethren, we have thieves, scoundrels, perjurers, and villains in our church, but the day will come when the tares will be sepa-

rated from the wheat and burned up with unquenchable fire; if this were not so, however, we could not claim to be the church of Jesus Christ, for he said that the kingdom of God was like a great net, which, being cast into the sea, brought all manner of fishes to the shore.

He was the only preacher I ever heard make such remarks to his own people, and recognise the church as being the true one because of the tares that grew among the wheat.

The Mormon church taught regeneration through baptism by immersion. In the commencement of their service a chapter from either the Old or New Testament was generally read, and during the discourse frequent reference was made to the Book of Mormon and to Joseph Smith, their prophet.

President Young was one of the smartest men, if not the ablest man, it was ever my fortune to meet. He was a man well posted on all subjects relating to the business interests of the country, and especially to his own people. His bishops and himself settled all manner of difficulties arising out of business or church matters without the assistance of courts, and he always insisted that every difficulty should be settled by arbitration of the members of the community in which the disputants lived.

In the ten years I lived in Salt Lake City, which was from 1869 to 1879, I never heard any talk among the Mormons about the gift of speaking the unknown tongue, or the interpretation thereof, as they claimed to have in Missouri. They, however, claimed to possess all the gifts of the Apostolic age and, as I have stated in another place, the keys of St. Peter. They believed in church authority, as do the Catholics, and in a personal God; they differ widely, however, from their Catholic brethren when they come to the marriage relation, the Mormons believing their bishops and elders should each have many wives, the Catholics, on the other hand, denying marriage to their priests.

Mormon communities, like all others, are made up of those who are reliable and those who are not—in other words, the good and the bad. Polygamy, which was practiced among them for more than a quarter of a century, they claimed upon scriptural authority was practiced in the Apostolic days. Let that be as it may, perhaps there never was a time in the march of civilization when to adopt such a practice would have been in more direct opposition to the moral sense of the civilized world than the present one of the nineteenth century.

In by-gone days, when the people depended upon their own and home productions for their living, the larger a man's family, with every one a worker, the easier it was for him to get along. Not so now, however, but it is just the reverse.

The Mormons[1] believed that church and state should be one, and that the laws of God should be the laws of the land; therefore many of them persisted in practicing polygamy after Congress passed laws prohibiting it, preferring, as they said, to practice the higher law in disobedience to the laws made by men, and many of them have gone, singing and dancing, to the penitentiary, consigned there by the courts for violating the statutes because of their belief.

---

1. For further reading about the Mormons '*Tell it All*' by Fanny Stenhouse and *Wife No. 19* Ann Eliza Young are both also published by Leonaur.

CHAPTER 5

The Mormons' Mecca

The new Mormon temple marks the history of the Church of Jesus Christ of Latter Day Saints from the day when Brigham Young and his few followers first set foot in the new promised land. It is a work commenced in the wilderness, and completed forty years afterward.

The laying of the cap-stone of the temple recorded the culmination of a work the Mormon people have been eagerly anticipating for nearly two generations. It recalls, too, many chapters of history abounding in interest. It tells a tale of patience, industry, and unswerving devotion to an object and a religious principle.

It is forty years ago, (at time of first publication), since the corner-stones of this temple were laid, and although there have been occasional lapses of time when nothing was done, and often only a few men employed, the work has practically been going on continuously.

Not more than a few days after the arrival of the Mormon pioneers in the Great Salt Lake Basin, the prophet, Brigham Young, was strolling about in the vicinity of his camping-place in company with some of the apostles of his church. The days previous had been employed in exploring the valley to the north and south. These explorations satisfied them that there was no more favourable location to commence the building of a new city in the wilderness than the one on which they had first pitched their tents. The night when Brigham took that stroll was at the end of a perfect day in July. Looking to the south the valley stretched away into magnificent distances and beautiful vistas as lovely as eye ever beheld.

Over in the west was the Great Salt Lake, with its huge islands rising from the mirrored surface of its waters, and burying their mountainous heads in the white of the clouds and the blue of the sky. In the east were the cold and rugged ranges of the Wasatch. To the north were the brown hills that guarded the city in that direction. It was a scene to inspire beautiful and poetic thoughts, and Brigham gazed about him, apparently delighted with the sublimity of the glorious prospect.

Turning his eyes to the east he struck his cane into the earth and said, "Here is where the temple of our God shall rise." Not a word of dissent was heard to his proclamation. There were no suggestions that better sites might be had. Brigham had issued his edict, and when he had spoken it was law to his people, so solemn that all indorsed it. From that moment the Temple Square was looked upon as sacred to the purpose to which it had been dedicated.

Remembering with what matchless courage this great Mormon leader had conducted his insignificant army across the desert from the Missouri River, and through the mountain defiles into this then wilderness, it is impossible to still the thought, "Did his imagination's eye peer through the mist of years and see the gray and solemn pile which is now the temple?"

But that July night when Brigham Young struck his cane on the ground was in 1847, and nothing was done toward building the temple until six years afterward. Still it is doubtful if the original intention had ever been abandoned.

At first it was intended to build it of adobe, but when a mountain of granite, fine in its quality and most beautiful in colour, was found some miles from the city, that material was substituted. On a panel just above the second-storey window of the east end of the temple is this inscription:

> HOLINESS TO THE LORD.
> THE HOUSE OF THE LORD
> BUILT BY
> THE CHURCH OF JESUS CHRIST
> OF
> LATTER DAY SAINTS.
> COMMENCED APRIL 6, 1853,
> COMPLETED
> ——— ———

Below the word "completed" there is a blank line where, when the last piece of stone has been chiselled and the frescoer has applied the last touch of his brush, a date will be cut into the marble slab. That date may not be inscribed for two or three years yet, for there is still very much to do on the interior.

April 6, 1853, was a bright day in the history of Zion. Not only was the semi-annual conference of the Mormon church in session, but the corner-stone of the great temple was to be laid with imposing ceremonies. The first company of Mormon pioneers to enter the Salt Lake Valley only numbered 143, but six years afterward the city had a population of nearly 6,000 people. It was a city, too, peculiar and unique in its customs and the character of its residents. By that time Utah had many large settlements, and from the most remote of these the saints came to assemble at the centre stake of Zion. They came wearing their brightest and best garments and their happiest faces. Presumably their souls were possessed of that sweet peace which passeth all understanding. A grand procession was formed in honour of the ceremony about to be celebrated.

An old program of that parade, and the exercises of the day, is yet in existence, and it is notable that the church dignitaries were the most conspicuous figures in the pageant. There were the presidents, apostles, and bishops, the high priests, the counsellors, the elders, and all the lesser degrees of Mormon ecclesiastical authorities.

Flags were flying, bands were playing—there were two bands in Utah, even then. Four corner-stones were laid, four dedicatory prayers offered, in which the Almighty was invoked to bless the building then begun, and four orations were delivered.

There are many conflicting stories in regard to the designer of the temple. A man by the name of Truman C. Angell was the first architect, and he drew the plans, but it was in the fertile genius of Brigham Young that the ideas of form and arrangement were conceived. These he submitted to Angell, who elaborated them. Doubtless Brigham had based his conceptions on the descriptions he had read of Solomon's temple, but however much of the plans he may have cribbed, to him belongs the credit. He claimed the design of the temple, even to the smallest detail, had been given him by a revelation from God.

Angell devoted his life to this building. After him two or three others directed the construction, but for the past four or five years Don Carlos Young, a son of Brigham's, has been the architect.

For many years the progress was exceedingly slow. The foundations were sunk sixteen feet below the surface. There was a great yawning hole to be filled with rock, every one of which had to be pulled by ox teams. Many people remember how slowly the building rose. They say it was several years before the walls could be seen above ground. But there was no hurry and nothing was slighted, for the temple when completed was intended to be as enduring as the mountains from which the stone it was built of was quarried.

No better illustration of the infinite patience, the ceaseless industry, and the religious zeal of the Mormon people could be given than they have manifested in this work. It was a stupendous undertaking. They possessed no modern mechanical appliances; everything had to be done by the crudest methods. Considering these difficulties, and the immense character of the work, it inspires wonder and admiration.

The temple quarries are in a mountain-walled *cañon* called Little Cottonwood, twenty-two miles from the city. For many years, or until 1872, every stone had to be hauled that distance by ox teams. The wagons were especially constructed for that purpose, and some of the stones were so large that four or five yoke were required to pull the load. How slow and expensive a building of this magnitude must have been, when such methods were employed, can readily be appreciated. But in 1872 a branch railroad was built from the Temple Square to the quarries; since then the construction has been more rapid and less expensive.

Figures only give a suggestion of its gigantic proportions. It is only when seen from a distance that its massiveness manifests itself. Then it towers above the other tall buildings of the city like a mountain above the level plain—it stands out solemn, grand, majestic, and alone. It is 99 feet wide and 200 feet long. The four corner towers are 188 feet high; to the top of the central western tower is 204 feet. The main, or eastern tower, is 211 feet to the top of the great granite globe, and on that the statue of the angel Gabriel stands, the figure itself being 14 feet high. Above all these points are the supplementary spires, on which the electric lights will be fixed. The lights on these sky-piercing spires will be interesting, for they will be so powerful as to penetrate the darkest corner of the valley, and will be like unto a beacon to a watching mariner. That on the main, or eastern spire, will be placed below the statue of the angel, and will be reflected upward, surrounding the figure with a brilliant halo.

In the designing of the temple, no startling architectural innovations seem to have been attempted. The exterior has a poverty of ornamentation, yet perhaps that is the most attractive feature. But the interior is exceedingly interesting. There are all manner of eccentricities and queer unexpected places. In the four corner towers are winding stone staircases reaching to the roof, each having 250 steps. These were all cut by hand at a cost of $100 apiece, and they are anchored in walls of solid masonry. The largest room is in the top storey, and is 80 x 120 feet and 36 feet high. This is to be used as an assembly hall, and will have a capacity to seat 1,000 people. The other rooms are much smaller. There is the fount-room, where baptisms are performed, for the Mormons, like the Baptists, believe in immersion. They baptise for the remission of sins, and the living, acting as proxies, are baptised for the dead.

As understood, if a person has some dear friend or relative who has passed into the beyond without having had the saving rite of baptism administered, the living can attend to that little formality so as to insure the dead a peaceful sojourn in the agreeable climate of the hereafter.

The uninitiated do not understand the purposes of Mormon temples. They are not intended to be used for public worship. Services of that character are never held in them. They are designed to be used for the meeting of the priesthood and for the performances of ordinances and ceremonies of marriage, baptisms, etc., and for the administering of ecclesiastical rites—the conferring of priestly degrees. Thousands of people have seen this great monument which has been built by this peculiar people to their more peculiar religion, and have described the impressions it made on them. Some, in a too-pronounced enthusiasm, have declared it to be a wonder in architecture—a triumph in its way—as something grand, almost marvellous in its conception. It is not. There is little that is exceptionally remarkable about it. True, there is much to impress one, but it is rather its bigness and general appearance of solemnity than anything else. Then there is something in its historical associations, the great difficulties overcome, and the great zeal displayed in its construction that inspires admiration.

Rudyard Kipling, who once saw it, in a vein of his keenest satire characterized it as "*architecturally atrocious, ugly, villainously discordant, contemptuously correct, altogether inartistic and unpoetical,*" and other adjectives equally as forcible and uncomplimentary. But he was probably more severe than just in his criticism. There is nothing about it to shock the artistic eye, and there are a few things to please.

A word about the statue that is perched on the topmost pinnacle. Certainly that is pleasing to the artistic soul. It is the work of a finished sculptor, who is even now not wholly unknown to fame. He is C. E. Dallin, and was born in Salt Lake City not much over thirty years ago, (as at 1893). But the statue: It is not of marble, but of hammered copper, covered with gold. To the eye it looks as if it were made entirely of that metal. It is a very fascinating piece of work, and on its high pedestal it glistens in the sunlight as if made of fire. One prominent Mormon has said the statue is not intended to represent Gabriel, but the angel Moroni proclaiming the gospel to all the world. It was the angel Moroni, it will be remembered, who showed the golden plates to Joseph Smith from which the Book of Mormon was written.

From Dallin's boyhood he began to display the artistic bent and temperament of his nature. Before he ever had any instruction, he modelled in clay with such success as to attract attention to his work. Then he went abroad to study, and at the Paris Salon of 1888 he received the medal of "Honourable Merit" for his "Peace Signal," that being a full-sized figure of an Indian brave on horseback holding his lance in such a manner as to be a signal to his fellow warriors at a distance that all was well. He has also done other meritorious work, and is at present engaged on a statue to be built on one of the corners of the Temple Square in honour of Brigham Young and the Mormon pioneers.

There have been many extravagant statements made concerning the cost of this temple. Figures have been placed as high as $6,000,000, which is nearly double its actual cost. As it stands today, $3,000,000 have probably been expended, and not more than half a million will be required to complete it.

The laying of this cap-stone practically completes the temple. There is not another stone to be laid, all that remains to be done being confined to the interior, and that is mostly in a decorative way. In its fulfilment there is great rejoicing in the hearts of the Mormon people. It has been a work requiring the toil of years, the manifestation of much self-denial, and the display of religious earnestness and sincerity almost without a parallel.

CHAPTER 6

My First Venture

When I grew up and became a married man, with daughters who were to be clothed and educated, I found it impossible to make, with the labour of one man on a farm, sufficient money to meet my growing necessities. I was raised on a farm and had always been a farmer, but with increasing expenses I was compelled to go into business of some kind, where I could accumulate a sufficiency for such purposes.

As I was brought up to handle animals, and had been employed more or less in the teaming business, after looking the situation all over, it occurred to me there was nothing I was so well adapted for by my past experience as the freighting business that was then being conducted between Independence, Mo., and Santa Fé, New Mexico, a distance of 800 miles.

At that time almost the entire distance lay through Indian Territory, where we were likely, on a greater portion of the trail, to meet hostile Indians any moment.

Being a religious man and opposed to all kinds of profanity, and knowing the practice of teamsters, almost without an exception, was to use profane and vulgar language, and to travel upon the Sabbath day, another difficulty presented itself to my mind which had to be overcome.

After due reflection on this subject I resolved in my innermost nature, by the help of God, I would overcome all difficulties that presented themselves to my mind, let the hazard be whatever it might. This resolve I carried out, and it was the keynote to my great success in the management of men and animals.

Having reached this determination, and being ready to embark in my new business, I formulated a code of rules for the behaviour of my *employés*, which read as follows:

While I am in the employ of A. Majors, I agree not to use profane language, not to get drunk, not to gamble, not to treat animals cruelly, and not to do anything else that is incompatible with the conduct of a gentleman. And I agree, if I violate any of the above conditions, to accept my discharge without any pay for my services.

I do not remember a single instance of a man signing these "ironclad rules," as they called them, being discharged without his pay. My *employés* seemed to understand in the beginning of their term of service that their good behaviour was part of the recompense they gave me for the money I paid them.

A few years later, when the Civil War had commenced, I bound my *employés* to pay true allegiance to the Government of the United States, while in my employ, in addition to the above.

I will say to my readers that, had I had the experience of a thousand years, I could not have formulated a better code of rules for the government of my business than those adopted, looking entirely from a moral standpoint. The result proved to be worth more to me in a money point of view than that resulting from any other course I could have pursued, for with the enforcement of these rules, which I had little trouble to do, a few years gave me control of the business of the plains and, of course, a widespread reputation for conducting business on a humane plan.

I can state with truthfulness that never in the history of freighting on the plains did such quiet, gentlemanly, fraternal feelings exist as among the men who were in my employ and governed by these rules.

It was the prevalent opinion, previous to the time I started across the plains, that none but daring, rough men were fit to contend with the Indians and manage teamsters upon those trips. I soon proved to the entire contrary this was a great mistake, for it was soon observable that both men and animals working under this system were superior, and got along better in every way than those working under the old idea of ruffianism.

It is my firm conviction that where men are born commanders or managers there is no need of the cruelty and punishment so often dealt out by so many in authority. With men who have the key of government in their natures there is little trouble in getting *employés* to conform strictly to their duty.

Nebraska City in overland freighting days.

I have seen, to my great regret and dislike, such cruelty practiced by army officers in command, and managers upon steamships on the seas and steamboats on the rivers, as well as other places where men were in charge of their fellow beings and had command over them, as should receive the most outspoken protest, and ought not to be tolerated in Christendom.

If men in charge would first control themselves and carry out, in their management of others, the true principles of humanity and kindness, pursuing a firm and consistent course of conduct themselves, wearing at the same time an easy and becoming dignity, it would do away with all the cruelties that have so often shocked humanity and caused needless suffering to those who were compelled to endure them. I found that an ounce of dignity on the plains was worth more than a pound at home or in organised society.

With all the thousands of men I had in my employ it was never necessary to do more than give a manly rebuke, if any one committed any misdemeanour, to avoid a repetition of the offense.

In all my vast business on the plains I adhered strictly as possible to keeping the Sabbath day, and avoided travelling or doing any unnecessary work. This fact enabled me to carry out perfectly the "iron-clad rules" with my *employés*. When they saw I was willing to pay them the same price as that paid for work including the Sabbath day, and let them rest on that day, it made them feel I was consistent in requiring them to conduct themselves as gentlemen.

In later years, when my business had so increased and the firm of Majors & Russell was formed, I insisted on carrying my system of government and management into the business of the new firm, and the same course was pursued by the firm of Russell, Majors & Waddell as I have above narrated. Notwithstanding the disagreeable features mentioned, I selected this avocation, and on the 10th day of August, 1848, with my first little outfit of six wagons and teams, started in business.

At that time it was considered hazardous to start on a trip of that kind so late in the season; but I made that trip with remarkable success, making the round run in ninety-two days, the quickest on record with ox teams, many of my oxen being in such good condition when I returned as to look as though they had not been on the road. This fact gave me quite a reputation among the freighters and merchants who were engaged in business between the two points above mentioned.

I was by no means the first to engage in the trade between Mexico and the United States, for as early as 1822 Captain Rockwell started in the trade, carrying goods in packs on mules.

The next notable era in the line of this trade was the introduction of wagons in the year 1824. This, of course, was an experiment, as there were no beaten roads, and the sand on some portions of the route was so deep (the worst part being in the valley of the Cimarron) that it was doubted whether wagons could be used with success. But the experiment proved to be so much superior to packing that it did away entirely with the former mode; and wagon-makers at St. Louis and Independence, Mo., commenced to build wagons adapted solely to that trade.

It was not long after the adoption of wagon trains on that route until there was a wide and well-beaten road the entire distance, the country over which it passed being level plains, requiring no bridges; but little work of any kind was necessary to keep the thoroughfare in good travelling condition.

On a large portion of the route there was an abundance of grass and water for the work animals. In those early days a belt of at least 400 miles was covered with herds of buffalo.

This crossing with large and heavy trains so well established the route that, by the year 1846, the people on the west border of Missouri were equipped and prepared in every way for transporting the supplies for Colonel Doniphan's army, when he was ordered to cross from Fort Leavenworth, Kan., to Santa Fé, N. M., at the commencement of the war between the United States and Mexico.

To return to my own operations in the freighting business, it will be seen by the foregoing dates mentioned in this article that two years later I made my first start, and I met on my outward-bound trip many of the troops of Colonel Doniphan returning home, the war being over and peace having been made between the two countries.

I continued in the freighting business continuously from 1848 to 1866, most of the time in the employ of the United States Government, carrying stores to different forts and stations in the Western Territories, New Mexico, Colorado, and Utah. Having freighted on my own account for about seven years, in 1855 I went into partnership with Messrs. Russell & Waddell, residents of Lexington, Lafayette County, Mo., my home being still in Jackson County, Mo. We did business three years under the firm name of Majors & Russell. In 1858, when we obtained a contract from the government for transporting supplies to Utah, the name of the firm was changed to Russell, Majors & Waddell.

At this time freighting for the government had increased enormously on account of General Johnston, with an army, having been sent to Utah. All of the supplies for the soldiers and much of the grain for the animals had to be transported in wagons from the Missouri River. However, one of the conditions of the contract the firm made with the government, through the quartermaster-general at Washington, was that they should have another starting-point other than Fort Leavenworth, the established depot for supplies going west.

I made this proposition to General Jessup, knowing, from my long experience in handling that kind of business, that it would be next to impossible to handle the supplies from one depot, as there were not herding grounds within a reasonable distance to keep such a vast number of cattle as the business would require when conducted from one point.

My partner, Mr. Russell, remarked to me that if he had to make a station higher up the river I would have to go and attend to it, for he could not. My answer was I would willingly do so, for I knew that loading hundreds of thousands of pounds of supplies daily would create a confusion at one point as would retard the business.

It was then and there agreed between the quartermaster and ourselves that one-half the entire stores should be sent to another point to be selected by his clerk and myself.

Immediately after the contract was signed I went to Fort Leavenworth, and with Lieutenant Dubarry of the Quartermaster's Department set out to locate another point. We travelled up the Missouri River as far as Plattsmouth, when we concluded Nebraska City, Neb., was the most available point upon the river for our business. I at once arranged with the citizens of that town to build warehouses, preparatory to receiving the large quantities of supplies the government would soon begin to ship to that point.

The supplies sent to Utah in the year 1858 were enormous, being over sixteen million pounds, requiring over three thousand five hundred large wagons and teams to transport them. We found it was as much as we could do to meet the government requirements with the two points in full operation.

As agreed, I took charge of the new station and moved my family from my farm, nine miles south of Kansas City, Mo., to Nebraska City, where I bought a home for them and commenced to carry out my part of the agreement.

The firm of Russell, Majors & Waddell conducted the business for two years, and in the spring of 1860 I bought out my partners and continued the business in my own name that year.

In Nebraska City I found a very intelligent, enterprising, and clever people, among whom were S. F. Knuckle, J. Sterling Morton, Robert Hawk Dillon, Colonel Tewksberry, McCann, Metcalf, Rhodes, O. P. Mason, Judge Kinney, Rinkers, Seigle, and a great many others of integrity and enterprise. I never did business more pleasantly than with the gentlemen whom I met during my residence of nine years there.

CHAPTER 7

Faithful Friends

To one who has had to make friends of the brute creation, it is natural for him to claim companionship with those domestic animals with which he is constantly drawn by day and night, such as horses, oxen, mules, and dogs. The dog is most thoroughly the comrade of those who dwell upon the frontier, and a chapter regarding them will not, I feel, be uninteresting to the reader.

I have always been a great admirer of a good dog, but my knowledge of them is a general one, such as you and a great many other Western men have. I have never made him a scientific study, but I think he is the only domestic animal, and I don't know but the only animal that takes a joint ownership in all of his master's property so far as he can comprehend it, whether it be personal, portable, or realistic; in other words, the man owns the dog and his other property, and the dog seems to claim or own the man and all of his other effects, so far as he can comprehend them.

I had a Shepherd dog that would not allow a stranger to take hold of me or my horse, saddle, bridle, rope, spurs, gun, or anything else that he thought belonged to us, without making a fuss about it, and he seemed to think stepping upon a rope or blanket, or anything of that kind, was just the same as taking hold with the hands, and yet he was very good-natured with strangers otherwise.

He was very fond of playing with other dogs, especially young ones on the pup order, but if they ever took any freedom with our joint property, there was sure to be trouble. He would not allow them to take hold of, or sleep on, or lay down in the shade of a horse, wagon, buggy, or do anything that he thought was taking too much liberty with his peculiar rights. He would go almost any distance to hunt anything that I would lose, and was very quick to pick up anything that I would drop, and give it to me without mussing it, whether I was walking or on horseback.

He was a good retriever, either on land or water, and would cross a river to get a goose or duck if it fell on the opposite side after being shot. He would also take hold of one hind leg of a deer or antelope and help me all he could to drag it home or to where I would leave my horse, but he was more help in driving and handling stock than in any other way. He would also go after a horse that would get away, with a bridle or rope on, and catch him by the rein or rope and bring him back if he could lead him, or if not, he would try and hold on until I would come up. He had a great many other minor tricks to make sport for the boys in camp, such as speaking, jumping, waltzing, etc., and he would also carry in wood to make fires with, and thus save the men trouble.

I have also had experience with the Newfoundland and the Setter dogs, and found them fully as easy to train and as faithful as the Shepherd dog I have written about. A Newfoundland that I brought down from Montana with me would do almost anything that it was possible for a dog to do. When living in Salt Lake City I saw my daughter send him after an apple once when she was sitting in a room up stairs. He went down and found the doors all fastened, so he came back and went out at an upstairs window and onto a lower roof and from there down on a common rung ladder to the ground and out into some one's orchard, got an apple, and returned the same way, and did it quicker than any boy could possibly have performed the same thing. But of course he knew where the ladder was, and had climbed up and down it many times before that. I used to see the children in our neighbourhood sending this dog over in the orchards after apples, while they remained at the fence outside, and he would keep going and returning with the apples until they were satisfied. The people never objected that owned the fruit, as they thought it so smart in the dog to steal for the children that which he did not eat himself.

It came to my knowledge once of a dumb beast that showed the intelligence of a human being.

He was only a dog, but a remarkably clever one. He belonged to the class known as Shepherd dogs, which are noted for their sagacity and fidelity. His master was a little Italian boy called Beppo, who earned his living by selling flowers on the street.

Tony was very fond of Beppo, who had been his master ever since he was a puppy, and Beppo had never failed to share his crust with his good dog. Now, Tony had grown to be a large, strong dog, and took as much care of Beppo as Beppo took of him. Often while standing on the corner with his basket on his arm, waiting for a customer, Beppo would feel inclined to cry from very loneliness; but Tony seemed to know when the "blues" came, and would lick his master's hand, as much as to say: "You've got me for a friend. Cheer up! I'm better than nobody; I'll stand by you."

But one day it happened that when the other boys who shared the dark cellar home with Beppo went out early in the morning as usual, Beppo was so ill that he could hardly lift his head from the straw on which he slept. He felt that he would be unable to sell flowers that day. What to do he did not know. Tony did his best to comfort him, but the tears would gather in his eyes, and it was with the greatest difficulty that he at last forced himself to get up and go to the florist, who lived near by, for the usual supply of buds.

Having filled his basket, the boy went home again and tied it around Tony's neck; then he looked at the dog and said: "Now, Tony, you're the only fellow I've got to depend on. Go and sell my flowers for me, and bring the money home safe; don't let anyone steal anything."

Then he kissed the dog and pointed to the door.

Tony trotted out to the street to Beppo's usual corner, where he took his stand. Beppo's customers soon saw how matters stood, and chose their flowers, and put their money into the tin cup in the centre of the basket. Now and then, when a rude boy would come along and try to snatch a flower from the basket, Tony would growl fiercely and drive him away.

So that day went safely by, and at nightfall Tony went home to his master, who was waiting anxiously for him, and gave him a hearty welcome. Beppo untied the basket and looked in the cup, and I should not wonder if he found more money in it than ever before. This is how Tony sold the rosebuds, and he did it so well that Beppo never tired of telling me about it.

A farmer's dog who had been found guilty of obtaining goods under false pretences is worthy of mention. He was extremely fond of sausages, and had been taught by his owner to go after them for him, carrying a written order in his mouth. Day after day he appeared at the butcher-shop, bringing his master's order, and by and by the butcher became careless about reading the document.

Finally, when settlement day came, the farmer complained that he was charged with more sausage than he had ordered. The butcher was

River scene at Nebraska City

surprised, and the next time Lion came in with a slip of paper between his teeth he took the trouble to look at it. The paper was blank, and further investigation showed that whenever the dog felt a craving for sausage, he looked around for a piece of paper, and trotted off to the butcher's. The farmer is something out of pocket, but squares the account by boasting of the dog's intelligence, which enabled him to deliberately steal for him, and deceive the butcher to do so.

While in Edinburgh, Scotland, where my wife and I remained for a year, our apartments were cared for by an English maid, who owned a very fine Scotch terrier. Whenever she would come to our rooms the dog accompanied her, and soon became very much attached to me, and would come into our apartments whenever an opportunity offered, to pay his respects to me. My wife had a great aversion to dogs of all kinds, and particularly objected to having one in the room with her, as she declared she could feel fleas immediately upon the appearance of a canine, no matter how far away they were from her.

One morning, while I was quietly reading, my wife being busy in another part of the room, the dog slipped in and succeeded in establishing himself under my chair, without either of us being aware of his presence; but before many minutes had passed my wife discovered him, and remonstrated with me at once for allowing him to come in, when I knew so well how she detested him. I assured her of my ignorance as to his presence, but said nothing whatever to the dog. He arose with a crestfallen air, and with his tail tucked between his legs, walked slowly across the room, stopping in the doorway to look once at Mrs. Majors, with the most reproachful, abused expression I have ever seen on any creature's face.

After that he always endeavoured to make his calls upon me when Mrs. Majors was absent, and would often come up and wait in one end of the hall until he would see her go into the adjoining room, when he would come to see me, but immediately upon hearing her opening the door of the other room, he would make a break for the door, making his escape before she would reach the room; and this, too, when she had never been unkind to him except in what she said of him.

One morning while the landlady and her servant were "doing up" our sleeping apartment, the dog as usual accompanying the servant, Mrs. Majors stepped into the room to speak to the landlady, and the servant, knowing the dog's fondness for me, said:

"Prince, ask Mrs. Majors if you can't go in to see Mr. Majors."

He turned around, went up to Mrs. Majors and commenced jumping up and down in front of her, asking as plain as dogs can speak for the coveted permission. My wife could not help laughing, and said, "Well, sir, you have won me over this time; you can go," whereupon he made a rush for the other room, leaped upon my lap, and seemed fairly wild with joy. I could not understand his unusual demonstrations until Mrs. Majors came in and explained.

A friend who owned a very fine dog was one morning accosted by a neighbour, who accused the dog of having killed several of his sheep in the night. The owner said he thought it was a mistake, as he had never known the dog to be guilty of such tricks, and after some discussion it was decided to examine the dog's mouth, and if wool was found sticking in his teeth, they would believe him guilty, and the man who had lost the sheep could kill him. They called the dog up while talking about it, and the master opened his mouth, and to his grief, found the evidence of his crime between his teeth. The neighbour knew the man's attachment for the dog, and not wishing to kill him in his presence, said he would defer the execution until a more convenient time. The dog heard the conversation, appeared to understand the situation perfectly, and when the neighbour tried later to find him, he had disappeared, and neither the owner nor the neighbour ever heard of him again. He fled to parts unknown, thus showing his wisdom by putting himself out of harm's way.

It is hardly possible to say enough in the praise of the dog family, especially regarding their services to the pioneers in the settlement of the Mississippi Valley and frontier. At that time, bears, panthers, wolves, and small animals of prey were so thick that without the aid of dogs the stock, such as pigs, lambs, poultry, and such small animals, would have been completely destroyed in one single night. The dogs were constantly on guard, night and day, storm or sunshine, and upon the approach of an enemy, would warn the pioneers, giving them a sense of security against danger. They knew by the smell, often before hearing or seeing an enemy, and would give out the warning long before the pioneers themselves could have known of the proximity of the wild beasts.

As a rule those faithful friends and protectors of our race have not been appreciated, more especially, as above stated, in the settlement of the frontier, for without them it would have been impossible for the pioneers to have saved their stock and poultry from the ravages of the wild beasts. I could write a volume upon the sagacity, faithfulness, and intelligence of these remarkable animals, as during my life in the Wild West I learned to fully appreciate them.

CHAPTER 8

Our War With Mexico

On the 18th of June, 1846, A. W. Doniphan was elected colonel of the regiment that he commanded in the Mexican War. In his speech at Independence, Jackson County, Mo., on July 29, 1837, he declared he had not been a candidate for office for seven years, and did not expect to be for the next seventy years to come. The passage by the American Congress of the resolutions of annexation, by which the republic of Texas was incorporated into the Union as one of the States, having merged her sovereignty into that of our own Government, was the prime cause which led to the war with Mexico. However, the more immediate cause of the war may be traced to the occupation by the American army of the strip of disputed territory lying between the Nueces and the Rio Grande.

Bigoted and insulting, Mexico was always prompt to manifest her hostility toward this government, and sought the earliest plausible pretext for declaring war against the United States. This declaration of war by the Mexican government, which bore date in April, 1846, was quickly and spiritedly followed by a manifesto from our Congress at Washington, announcing that a state of war existed between Mexico and the United States. Soon after this counter declaration, the Mexicans crossed the Rio Grande in strong force, headed by the famous generals, Arista and Ampudia. This force, as is well known, was defeated at Palo Alto on the 18th, and at Resaca de la Palma on May 9, 1846, by the troops under command of Major-General Taylor, and repulsed with great slaughter. The whole Union was in a state of intense excitement. General Taylor's recent and glorious victories were the constant theme of universal admiration.

The war had actually begun; and that, too, in a manner which demanded immediate action. The United States Congress passed an act about the middle of May, 1846, authorising President Polk to call into the field 50,000 volunteers designed to operate against Mexico at three distinct points, namely: The southern wing, or the "Army of Occupation," commanded by Major-General Taylor, to penetrate directly into the heart of the country; the column under Brigadier-General Wool, or the "Army of the Centre," to operate against the city of Chihuahua; and the expedition under the command of Colonel (afterward Brigadier-General) Kearney, known as the "Army of the West," to direct its march upon the city of Santa Fé.

This was the original plan of operations against Mexico, but subsequently the plan was changed. Major-General Scott, with a well-appointed army, was sent to Vera Cruz, General Wool effected a junction with General Taylor at Saltillo, and General Kearney divided his force into three separate commands; the first he led in person to the distant shores of the Pacific. A detachment of nearly eleven hundred Missouri volunteers, under command of Col. A. W. Doniphan, was ordered to make a descent upon the State of Chihuahua, expecting to join General Wool's division at the capital, while the greater part was left as a garrison at Santa Fé, under command of Col. Sterling Price. The greatest eagerness was manifested by the citizens of the United States to engage in the war, to redress our wrongs, to repel an insulting foe, and to vindicate our national honour and the honour of our oft-insulted flag.

The call of the president was promptly responded to, but of the 50,000 volunteers at first authorised to be raised, the service of about 17,000 only were required. The cruel and inhuman butchery of Colonel Fannin and his men, all Americans, the subsequent and indiscriminate murder of all Texans who unfortunately fell into Mexican hands; the repeated acts of cruelty and injustice perpetrated upon the persons and property of American citizens residing in the northern Mexican provinces; the imprisonment of American merchants without the semblance of a trial by jury, and the forcible seizure and confiscation of their goods; the robbing of American travellers and tourists in the Mexican country of their passports and other means of safety, whereby they were in certain instances deprived of their liberty for a time; the forcible detention of American citizens, sometimes in prison and other times in free custody; the recent blockade of the Mexican ports against the United States trade; the repeated insults offered our national flag; the contemptuous ill treatment of our ministers, some of whom were spurned with their credentials; the supercilious and menacing air uniformly manifested toward the government, which with characteristic forbearance and courtesy had endeavoured to maintain a friendly understanding; Mexico's hasty and unprovoked declaration of war against the United States; the army's unceremonious passage of the Rio Grande in strong force and with hostile intentions; her refusal to pay indemnities, and a complication of lesser evils, all of which had been perpetrated by the Mexican authorities, or by unauthorised Mexican citizens, in a manner which clearly evinced the determination on the part of Mexico to terminate the amicable relations hitherto existing between the two countries, were the causes which justified the war.

On the 18th day of August, 1846, after a tiresome march of nearly 900 miles in less than fifty days, General Kearney with his whole command entered Santa Fé, the capital of the province of New Mexico, and took peaceable possession of the country, without the loss of a single man or shedding a drop of blood, in the name of the United States, and planted the American flag in the public square, where the stars and stripes and eagle streamed above the Palacio Grande, or stately residence of ex-Governor Armigo.

On the 29th of July, 1847, Captain Ruff was dispatched by General Smith with a squadron composed of one company of the Second Dragoons under Lieutenant Hawes and his own company of mounted riflemen, in all eighty-six men, to attack the town of San Juan de los Llanos. In this engagement the Mexicans lost forty-three killed and fifty wounded. Only one American was wounded and none killed. At the Battle of San Pascual, on the morning of the 6th of December, General Kearney commanding, with Captains Johnson, Moore, and Hammond as principal aids, drove the enemy from the field. Loss not known. American loss, seventeen killed and fourteen wounded. On the 5th of November, 1846, a small detachment of forty-five volunteers, commanded by Captains Thompson and Burrows, met and totally defeated 200 Californians on the plains of Salinas, near Monterey. American loss, four killed and two wounded.

On the 8th of January General Kearney and Commodore Stockton, with 500 men, met the insurgents, 600 strong, to dispute the passage of the River San Gabriel. This action lasted one hour and a half. The next day the Mexicans were again repulsed. Their loss on both days estimated in killed and wounded not less than eighty-five; American, two killed and fifteen wounded. A battle commanded by Doniphan was fought on Christmas day at Brazito, twenty-five miles from El Paso. Mexican loss was seventy-one killed, five prisoners, and 150 wounded, among them their commanding general, Ponce de Leon. The Americans had none killed and eight wounded. On the 27th the city of El Paso was taken possession of without further opposition. On the 13th a battle with the Indians occurred. Americans lost none; Indians had seventeen killed and not less than twenty-five wounded. On the 19th of January, Governor Bent was murdered with his retinue. On the 24th Colonel Rice encountered the enemy. Our loss was two killed and seven wounded. The Mexicans acknowledged a loss of thirty-six killed and forty-five prisoners.

On the 3rd of February, met the enemy at Pueblo de Taos. The total loss of the Mexicans at the three engagements was 282 killed—wounded unknown. Our total was fifteen killed and forty-seven wounded. On the 24th, in an engagement at Las Vegas, the enemy had twenty-five killed, three wounded; our loss, one killed, three wounded. At Red River Cañon we were vigorously attacked by a large body of Mexicans and Indians; Americans lost one killed and several wounded; Mexicans and Indians, seventeen killed, wounded not known. At Las Vegas Major Edmondson charged the town; there were ten Mexicans slain and fifty prisoners taken. On the 9th of July a detachment of Captain Morin's company was attacked; five of our men killed and nine wounded. On the 26th of June Lieutenant Love was attacked and surrounded by Indians; they cut their way through with a loss of eleven; the Indians lost twenty-five. On the 27th of October Captain Mann's train was attacked; American loss, one killed, four wounded; Indian loss not known.

CHAPTER 9

Doniphan's Expedition

On Sunday, the 28th of February, a bright and auspicious day, the American Army, under Colonel Doniphan, arrived in sight of the Mexican encampment at Sacramento, which could be distinctly seen at the distance of four miles. His command consisted of the following corps and detachments of troops:

The First Regiment, Colonel Doniphan, numbering about eight hundred men; Lieutenant-Colonel Mitchell's escort, ninety-seven men; artillery battalion, Major Clark and Captain Weightman, 117 men, with light field battery of six pieces of cannon; and two companies of teamsters, under Captains Skillman and Glasgow, forming an extra battalion of about one hundred and fifty men, commanded by Major Owens of Independence, making an aggregate force of 1,164 men, all Missouri volunteers. The march of the day was conducted in the following order: The wagons, near four hundred in all, were thrown in four parallel files, with spaces of thirty feet between each. In the centre space marched the artillery battalion; in the space to the right the First Battalion, and in the space to the left the Second Battalion. Masking these, in front marched the three companies intending to act as cavalry—the Missouri Horse Guards, under Captain Reid, on the right; the Missouri Dragoons, under Captain Parsons, on the left; and the Chihuahua Rangers, under Captain Hudson, in the centre. Thus arranged, they approached the scene of action.

The enemy had occupied the brow of a rocky eminence rising upon a plateau between the river Sacramento and the Arroya Seca, and near the Sacramento Fort, eighteen miles from Chihuahua, and fortified its approaches by a line of field-works, consisting of twenty-eight strong redoubts and entrenchments. Here, in this apparently secure position, the Mexicans had determined to make a bold stand, for the pass was the key to the capital. So certain of the victory were the Mexicans, that they had prepared strings and handcuffs in which they meant to drive us prisoners to the City of Mexico, as they did the Texans in 1841. Thus fortified and entrenched, the Mexican Army, consisting, according to a consolidated report of the adjutant-general which came into Colonel Doniphan's possession after the battle, of 4,220 men, commanded by Major-General Jose A. Heredia, aided by Gen. Garcia Conde, former Minister of War in Mexico, as commander of cavalry; General Mauricia Ugarte, commander of infantry; General Justiniani, commander of artillery, and Gov. Angel Trias, brigadier-general, commanding the Chihuahua Volunteers, awaited the approach of the Americans.

When Colonel Doniphan arrived within one mile and a half of the enemy's fortifications (a reconnaissance of his position having been made by Major Clark), leaving the main road, which passed within the range of his batteries, he suddenly deflected to the right, crossed the rocky Arroya, expeditiously gained the plateau beyond, successfully deployed his men into line upon the highland, causing the enemy to change its first position, and made the assault from the west. This was the best point of attack that could possibly have been selected. The event of the day proves how well it was chosen.

In passing the Arroya the caravan and baggage trains followed close upon the rear of the army. Nothing could exceed in point of solemnity and grandeur the rumbling of the artillery, the firm moving of the caravan, the dashing to and fro of horsemen, and the waving of banners and gay fluttering of guidons, as both armies advanced to the attack on the rocky plain; for at this crisis General Conde, with a select body of 1,200 cavalry, rushed down from the fortified heights to commence the engagement. When within 950 yards of our alignment, Major Clark's battery of six-pounders and Weightman's section of howitzers opened upon them a well-directed and most destructive fire, producing fearful execution in their ranks. In some disorder they fell back a short distance, unmasking a battery of cannon, which immediately commenced its fire upon us.

A brisk cannonading was now kept up on both sides for the space of fifty minutes, during which time the enemy suffered great loss, our battery discharging twenty-four rounds to the minute. The balls from the enemy's cannon whistled through our ranks in quick succession. Many horses and other animals were killed and the wagons much shattered. Sergeant A. Hughes of the Missouri Dragoons had both his legs broken by a cannon ball. In this action the enemy, who were drawn up in columns four deep, close order, lost about twenty-five killed, besides a great number of horses. The Americans, who stood dismounted in two ranks, open order, suffered but slight injury.

General Conde, with considerable disorder, now fell back and rallied his men behind the entrenchments and redoubts. Colonel Doniphan immediately ordered the buglers to sound the advance. Thereupon the American Army moved forward in the following manner, to storm the enemy's breastworks:

The artillery battalion, Major Clark in the centre, firing occasionally on the advance; the First Battalion, commanded by Lieutenant-Colonels Jackson and Mitchell, composing the right wing; the two select companies of cavalry under Captains Reid and Parsons, and Captain Hudson's mounted company, immediately on the left of the artillery; and the Second Battalion on the extreme left, commanded by Major Gilpin. The caravan and baggage trains, under command of Major Owens, followed close in the rear. Colonel Doniphan and his aids, Captain Thompson, United States Army, Adjutant De Courcy, and Sergeant-Major Crenshaw acted between the battalions.

At this crisis a body of 300 lancers and *lazadors* were discovered advancing upon our rear. These were exclusive of Heredia's main force, and were said to be criminals turned loose from the Chihuahua prisons, that by some gallant exploit they might expurgate themselves of crime. To this end they were posted in the rear to cut off stragglers, prevent retreat, and capture and plunder the merchants' wagons. The battalion of teamsters kept these at bay. Besides this force there were a thousand spectators—women, citizens, and rancheros—perched on the summits of adjacent hills and mountains, watching the event of the day.

As we neared the enemy's redoubts, still inclining to the right, a heavy fire was opened upon us from his different batteries, consisting in all of sixteen pieces of cannon. But owing to the facility with which our movements were performed, and to the fact that the Mexicans were compelled to fire plungingly upon our lines (their position being considerably elevated above the plateau, and particularly the battery placed on the brow of the Sacramento Mountain with the design of enfilading our column), we sustained but little damage.

When our column had approached within about 400 yards of the enemy's line of field-works, the three cavalry companies, under Captains Reid, Parsons, and Hudson, and Weightman's section of howitzers, were ordered to carry the main centre battery, which had considerably annoyed our lines, and which was protected by a strong bastion. The charge was not made simultaneously, as intended by the colonel; for this troop having spurred forward a little way, was halted for a moment under a heavy crossfire from the enemy, by the adjutant's misapprehending the order. However, Captain Reid, either not hearing or disregarding the adjutant's order to halt, leading the way, waved his sword, and rising in his stirrups exclaimed: "Will my men follow me?"

Hereupon Lieutenants Barnett, Hinton, and Moss, with about twenty-five men, bravely sprang forward, rose the hill with the captain, carried the battery, and for a moment silenced the guns, but were too weak to hold possession of it. By the overwhelming force of the enemy, we were beaten back, and many of us wounded. Here Maj. Samuel C. Owens, who had voluntarily charged upon the redoubt, received a cannon or musket shot, which instantly killed both him and his horse. Captain Reid's horse was shot under him, and a gallant young man of the same name immediately dismounted and generously offered the captain his.

By this time the remainder of Captain Reid's company, under Lieutenant Hocklin, and the section of howitzers under Captain Weightman and Lieutenants Choteau and Evans, rose the hill, and supported Captain Reid. A deadly volley of grape and canister shot, mingled with *yager* balls, quickly cleared the entrenchments and redoubt. The battery was retaken and held. Almost at the same instant Captains Parsons and Hudson, with the two remaining companies of cavalry, crossed the entrenchments to Reid's left and successfully engaged with the enemy. They resolutely drove him back and held the ground.

All the companies were now pressing forward, and pouring over the entrenchments and into the redoubts, eagerly vying with each other in the noble struggle for victory. Each company, as well as each soldier, was ambitious to excel. Companies A, B, C, and a part of Company D, composing the right wing, all dismounted, respectively under command of Captains Waldo, Walton, Moss, and Lieutenant Miller, led on by Lieutenant-Colonels Jackson and Mitchell, stormed a formidable line of redoubts on the enemy's left, defended by several pieces of cannon and a great number of well-armed and resolute men. A part of this wing took possession of the strong battery on Sacramento Hill, which had kept a continued cross-firing upon our right during the whole engagement. Colonels Jackson and Mitchell and their captains, lieutenants, non-commissioned officers, and the men generally, behaved with commendable gallantry. Many instances of individual prowess were exhibited. But it is invidious to distinguish between men, where all performed their duty so nobly.

Meanwhile the left wing, also dismounted, commanded by Major Gilpin, a gallant and skilful officer, boldly scaled the heights, passed the entrenchments, cleared the redoubts, and, with considerable slaughter, forced the enemy to retreat from its position on the right. Company G, under Captain Hughes, and a part of Company F, under Lieutenant Gordon, stormed the battery of three brass four-pounders strongly defended by embankments and ditches filled by resolute and well-armed Mexican infantry. Some of the artillerists were made prisoners while endeavouring to touch off the cannon. Companies H and E, under Captains Rodgers and Stephenson, and a part of Hudson's company, under Lieutenant Todd, on the extreme left, behaved nobly, and fought with great courage. They beat the Mexicans from their strong places, and chased them like bloodhounds. Major Gilpin was not behind his men in bravery—he encouraged them to fight by example.

Major Clark, with his six-pounders, and Captain Weightman, with his howitzers, during the whole action rendered the most signal and essential service, and contributed much toward the success of the day. The gallant charge led by Captain Reid, and sustained by Captain Weightman, in point of daring and brilliancy of execution, has not been excelled by any similar exploit during the war.

General Heredia made several unsuccessful attempts to rally his retreating forces, to infuse into their minds new courage, and to close up the breaches already made in his lines. General Conde, with his troop of horse, also vainly endeavoured to check the advance of the Missourians. They were dislodged from their strong places, and forced from the hill in confusion.

The rout of the Mexican Army now became general, and the slaughter continued until night put an end to the chase. The battle lasted three hours and a half. The men returned to the battlefield after dark, completely worn out and exhausted with fatigue. The Mexicans lost 304 men killed on the field, and a large number wounded, perhaps not less than five hundred, and seventy prisoners, among whom was Brigadier-General Cuilta, together with a vast quantity of provisions, $6,000 in specie, 50,000 head of sheep, 1,500 head of cattle, 100 mules, twenty wagons, twenty-five or thirty *caretas*, 25,000 pounds of ammunition, ten pieces of cannon of different calibre, varying from four to nine pounders; six culverins, or wall pieces; 100 stand of small colours, seven fine carriages, the general's escritoire, and many other things of less note. Our loss was Major Samuel C. Owens, killed, and eleven wounded, three of whom have subsequently died.

Thus was the army of Central Mexico totally defeated, and completely disorganised, by a column of Missouri volunteers. The Mexicans retreated precipitately to Durango, and dispersed among the ranchos and villages. Their leaders were never able to rally them.

In this engagement Colonel Doniphan was personally much exposed, and by reason of his stature was a conspicuous mark for the fire of the enemy's guns. He was all the while at the proper place, whether to dispense his orders, encourage his men, or use his sabre in thinning the enemy's ranks. His courage and gallant conduct were only equalled by his clear foresight and great judgment. His effective force actually engaged was about nine hundred and fifty men, including a considerable number of amateur fighters, among whom James L. Collins, James Kirker, Messrs. Henderson and Anderson, interpreters, Major Campbell, and James Stewart, deserve to be favourably mentioned. They fought bravely. It was impossible for Captains Skillman and Glasgow to bring their companies of teamsters into the action. They deserve great honour for their gallantry in defending the trains. The soldiers encamped on the battlefield, within the enemy's entrenchments, and feasted sumptuously upon his viands, wines, and pound-cake.

There they rested.

Colonel Doniphan, not like Hannibal loitering on the plains of Italy after the Battle of Cannæ when he might have entered Rome in triumph, immediately followed up his success and improved the advantage which his victory gave him. Early the next morning (March 1st) he dispatched Lieutenant-Colonel Mitchell, with 150 men under command of Captains Reid and Weightman, and a section of artillery, to take formal possession of the capital, and occupy it in the name of his Government. This detachment, before arriving in the city, was met by several American gentlemen escaping from confinement, who represented that the Mexicans had left the place undefended, and fled with the utmost precipitation to Durango. The Spanish consul, also, came out with the flag of his country to salute and acknowledge the conqueror. This small body of troops entered and took military possession of Chihuahua without the slightest resistance, and the following night occupied the Cuartel, near Hidalgo's monument, which stands on the Alameda.

Meanwhile Colonel Doniphan and his men collected the booty, tended the captured animals, refitted the trains, remounted those who had lost their steeds in the action, arranged the preliminaries of the procession, and having marched a few miles encamped for the night. On the morning of March 2nd Colonel Doniphan, with all his military trains, the merchant caravan, gay fluttering colours, and the whole *spolia opima*, triumphantly entered the city to the tunes of "Yankee Doodle" and "Hail Columbia," and fired in the public square a national salute of twenty-eight guns. This was a proud moment for the American troops. The battle of Sacramento gave them the capital, and now the stars and stripes and serpent eagle of the model republic were streaming victoriously over the stronghold of Central Mexico.

CHAPTER 10

The Pioneer of Frontier Telegraphy

It is thirteen years since, (at time of first publication), Edward Creighton, the pioneer of frontier telegraphy, died, and that he is so well and honourably remembered in the Omaha of today—aye, his memory respected by the thousands who have gone there since he was no more—but illustrates how great was his service to the community, how broad and enduring a mark he made upon his time. No man did so much to sustain Omaha in its early and trying days as Edward Creighton. His career was a notable one in its humble beginning and splendid triumph in the flush of manhood. He was born in Belmont County, Ohio, August 31, 1820, of Irish parentage.

His early days were passed upon a farm, but at the age of twenty he took the contract for building part of the national stage road from Wheeling, W. Va., to Springfield, Ohio. He continued in the contracting business, but it was not until 1847 that he entered upon that branch of it in which he achieved his greatest success and laid the foundation of his after fortunes. In that year he received the contract for and constructed a telegraph line between Springfield and Cincinnati. To this business he devoted his time and energies for five years, being successfully engaged in the construction of telegraph lines in all parts of the country, completing the line from Cleveland to Chicago in 1852. In 1856, while engaged in telegraph construction in Missouri, Mr. Creighton visited Omaha, and his brothers, John A., James, and Joseph, and his cousin James, locating there, he returned to Ohio, where he wedded Mary Lucretia Wareham of Dayton, and in 1857 he also went to Omaha and located. He continued in the telegraph construction business, completing, in 1860, the first line which gave Omaha connection with the outer world *via* St. Louis.

For years Mr. Creighton entertained a pet project—the building of a line to the Pacific Coast—and in the winter of 1860, after many conferences with the wealthy stockholders of the Western Union Company, a preliminary survey was agreed upon. In those days the stage-coach was the only means of overland travel, and that was beset with great danger from Indians and road agents. In the stage-coach Mr. Creighton made his way to Salt Lake City, where he enlisted the interest and support of Brigham Young, the great head of the Mormon church, in his project. It had been arranged to associate the California State Telegraph Company in the enterprise, and on to Sacramento, in midwinter, Mr. Creighton pressed on horseback.

It was a terrible journey, but the man who made it was of stout heart, and he braved the rigors of the mountains and accomplished his mission, and in the spring of 1861 he returned to Omaha to begin his great work. Congress, meanwhile, had granted a subsidy of $40,000 a year for ten years to the company which should build the line. Then a great race was inaugurated, for heavy wagers, between Mr. Creighton's construction force and the California contractors who were building eastward, to see which should reach Salt Lake City first. Mr. Creighton had 1,100 miles to construct and the Californians only 450, but he reached Salt Lake City on the 17th of October, one week ahead of his competitors.

On October 24th, but little more than six months after the enterprise was begun, Mr. Creighton had established telegraphic communication from ocean to ocean. He had taken $100,000 worth of the stock of the new enterprise at about eighteen cents on the dollar, and when the project was completed the company trebled its stock, Mr. Creighton's $100,000 becoming $300,000. The stock rose to 85 cents, and he sold out $100,000 worth for $850,000, still retaining $200,000 of the stock. He continued in the telegraphic construction business until 1867, when his great cattle interests, in which he had embarked in 1864, and his great plains freighting business, established before the building of the Union Pacific and continued even after its completion, to the mining regions of Montana and Idaho, exacted his attention.

During all these years of great business success, Mr. Creighton was firm in his allegiance to Omaha. He was the first president of the first national bank in the city, and was ever ready to aid, by his means, and counsel, and enterprise, the furthering of Omaha's interests. He commanded the confidence of all the people, his sterling integrity and unwavering fidelity combining with his generous and charitable nature to make him a very lovable man. No man has an unkind word to say of Edward Creighton, and his memory is revered to this day as an upright, just, and kind man, who, out of his own sterling qualities, had wrought a successful and honourable career. He was stricken with paralysis and died November 5, 1874. To his memory Creighton College was erected and endowed by his widow, in response to his own wish, expressed during his lifetime, to found a free institution for the non-sectarian education of youth—the institution to be under Catholic control.

CHAPTER 11

An Overland Outfit

The organisation of a full-fledged train for crossing the plains consisted of from twenty-five to twenty-six large wagons that would carry from three to three and a half tons each, the merchandise or contents of each wagon being protected by three sheets of thin ducking, such as is used for army tents. The number of cattle necessary to draw each wagon was twelve, making six yokes or pairs, and a prudent freighter would always have from twenty to thirty head of extra oxen, in case of accident to or lameness of some of the animals. In camping or stopping to allow the cattle to graze, a corral or pen of oblong shape is formed by the wagons, the tongues being turned out, and a log chain extended from the hind wheel of each wagon to the fore wheel of the next behind, etc., thus making a solid pen except for a wide gap at each end, through which gaps the cattle are driven when they are to be yoked and made ready for travel, the gaps then being filled by the wagon-master, his assistant, and the extra men, to prevent the cattle from getting out.

When the cattle are driven into this corral or pen, each driver yokes his oxen, drives them out to his wagon, and gets ready to start. The entire train of cattle, including extras, generally numbered from 320 to 330 head and usually from four to five mules for riding and herding. The force of men for each train consisted of a wagon-master, his assistant, the teamsters, a man to look after the extra cattle, and two or three extra men as a reserve to take the places of any men who might be disabled or sick, the latter case being a rare exception, for as a rule there was no sickness. I think perhaps there was never a set of labouring men in the world who enjoyed more uninterrupted good health than the teamsters upon the plains. They walked by the side of their teams, as it was impossible for them to ride and keep them moving with regularity.

The average distance travelled with loaded wagons was from twelve to fifteen miles per day, although in some instances, when roads were fine and there was a necessity for rapid movement, I have known them to travel twenty miles. But this was faster travelling than they could keep up for any length of time. Returning with empty wagons they could average twenty miles a day without injury to the animals.

Oxen proved to be the cheapest and most reliable teams for long trips, where they had to live upon the grass. This was invariably the case. They did good daily work, gathered their own living, and if properly driven would travel 2,000 miles in a season, or during the months from April to November; travelling from 1,000 to 1,200 miles with the loaded wagons, and with plenty of good grass and water, would make the return trip with the empty wagons in the same season. However, the distance travelled depended much upon the skill of the wagon-masters who had them in charge. For if the master was not skilled in handling the animals and men, they could not make anything like good headway and success. To make everything work expeditiously, thorough discipline was required, each man performing his duty and being in the place assigned him without confusion or delay.

I remember once of timing my teamsters when they commenced to yoke their teams after the cattle had been driven into their corral and allowed to stand long enough to become quiet. I gave the word to the men to commence yoking, and held my watch in my hand while they did so, and in sixteen minutes from the time they commenced, each man had yoked six pairs of oxen and had them hitched to their wagons ready to move. I state this that the reader may see how quickly the men who are thoroughly disciplined could be ready to "pop the whip" and move out, when unskilled men were often more than an hour doing the same work. The discipline and rules by which my trains were governed were perfect, and as quick as the men learned each one his place and duty, it became a very pleasant and easy thing for him to do.

Good moral conduct was required of them, and no offense from man to man was allowed, thus keeping them good-natured and working together harmoniously. They were formed into what they called "messes," there being from six to eight men in a mess, each mess selecting the man best fitted to serve as cook, and the others carrying the water, fuel, and standing guard, so that the cook's sole business when in camp was to get his utensils ready and cook the meals.

We never left the cattle day or night without a guard of two men, the teamsters taking turns, and arranging it so that each man was on guard two hours out of the twenty-four, and sometimes they were only obliged to go on guard two hours every other night. This matter they arranged among themselves and with the wagon-master. The duty of the wagon-master was about the same as that of a captain of a steamboat or ship, his commands being implicitly obeyed, for in the early stages of travel upon the plains the men were at all times liable to be attacked by the Indians; therefore the necessity for a perfect harmony of action throughout the entire band. The assistant wagon-master's duty was to carry out the wagon-master's instructions, and he would often be at one end of the train while the master was at the other, as the train was moving. It was arranged, when possible, that no two trains should ever camp together, as there was not grass and water sufficient for the animals of both, and thus all confusion was avoided.

The average salary paid the men was $1 a day and expenses. Most of the travelling in the early days of freighting was done upon what was called the Santa Fé road, starting from Independence, Mo., and unloading at Santa Fé, N. M. The rattlesnakes on that road, in the beginning of the travel, were a great annoyance, often biting the mules and oxen when they were grazing. At first, mules were used altogether for travelling, but they would either die or become useless from the bite of a rattlesnake, and the men would sometimes be sent ahead of the caravan with whips to frighten the snakes out of the pathway, but later on, the ox-teamsters, with their large whips, destroyed them so fast that they ceased to trouble them to any great extent.

It has been claimed by men that the snakes and prairie-dogs, who were also found in great numbers upon the plains, lived in the same houses, the dog digging the hole and allowing the snake to inhabit it with him; but I do not think this is correct. Men came to this conclusion from seeing the snakes when frightened run into the dog-holes, but I think they did it to get out of the way of danger, and they lived, too, in the houses that had been abandoned by the dogs. It is a fact that the prairie dogs would only live in one hole for about a year, when they would abandon it and dig a new one, leaving the old ones to be taken possession of by the rattlesnakes and prairie owls. As far as I have been able to find out, there is no creature on earth that will live with a rattlesnake. They are hated and feared by all living animals.

The following are the names of the men who were employed on our trains, in one capacity and another:

Dr. J. Hobbs,   Jim Lobb,
Alex Lobb,   Aquila Lobb,
Joel Dunn,   Mitchell Wilson,
Hank Bassett,   George W. Marion,
N. H. Fitzwater,   George Bryant,
Tom A. Brawley,   Peter Bean,
James L. Davis,   William Hickman,
A. W. Street,   Joel Hedgespeth,
Charles Byers,   Nathan Simpson,
R. D. Simpson,   Ben Tunley,
Hiram Cummings,   John Ewing,
Rev. Ben Baxter,   A. and P. Byram,
Frank McKinney,   John T. Renick,
John D. Clayton,   William Wier,
Frank Hoberg,   Gillis of Pennsylvania,
David Street,   Joel Lyal,
Albert Bangs,   Elijah Majors,
Aquila Davis,   Samuel Poteete,
William Hayes,   George A. Baker,
James Brown,   William Dodd,
Mr. Badger,   Green Davis,
John Scudder,   Jackson Cooper,
Samuel Foster,   Robert Foster,
Chat. Renick,   John Renick,
Mr. Levisy,   Dick Lipscomb,
James Aiken,   Johnson Aiken,
Stephen De Wolfe,   Linville Hayes,
Sam McKinny,   Ben Rice,
Ferd Smith,   Henry Carlisle,
Alexander Carlisle,   Robert Ford,
Joseph Erwin,   Daniel D. White,
Johnny Fry,   Alexander Benham,
Luke Benham,   Benjamin Ficklin,
           John Kerr.

CHAPTER 12

Kit Carson

Kit Carson, as he was familiarly known and called, was born in Madison County, Ky., on the 24th of December, 1809.

During the early days of Carson's childhood his father moved from Kentucky to Missouri, which State was then called Upper Louisiana, where Kit Carson passed a number of years, early becoming accustomed to the stirring dangers with which his whole life was so familiar.

At the age of fifteen years he was apprenticed to a Mr. Workman, a saddler. At the end of two years, when his apprenticeship was ended, young Carson voluntarily abandoned the further pursuit of a trade which had no attractions for him, and from that time on pursued the life of a trapper, hunter, and Indian fighter, distinguishing himself in many ways and rendering invaluable service to the Government of the United States, in whose employ he spent a large part of his life, in which service he had risen to the rank of colonel and was brevetted brigadier-general before his death, which occurred at Fort Lyon, Colo., on the 23rd of May, 1868, from the effects of the rupture of an artery, or probably an aneurism of an artery in the neck.

Carson as a trapper, hunter, and guide had no superior, and as a soldier was the peer of any man.

The following from the *Life of Kit Carson* will be found most interesting reading regarding this great scout:

> With fresh animals and men well fed and rested, McCoy and Carson and all their party soon started from Fort Hall for the rendezvous again, upon Green River, where they were detained some weeks for the arrival of other parties, enjoying as they best might the occasion, and preparing for future operations.

A party of a hundred was here organised, with Mr. Fontenelle and Carson for their leaders, to trap upon the Yellowstone and the headwaters of the Missouri. It was known that they would probably meet the Blackfeet, in whose grounds they were going, and it was therefore arranged, that while fifty were to trap and furnish the food for the party, the remainder should be assigned to guard the camp and cook. There was no disinclination on the part of any to another meeting with the Blackfeet, so often had they troubled them, especially Carson, who, while he could be magnanimous toward an enemy, would not turn aside from his course if able to cope with him; and now that he was in a company which justly felt itself strong enough to punish the 'thieving Blackfeet,' as they spoke of them, he was anxious to pay off some old scores.

They saw nothing, however, of these Indians; but afterward learned that the smallpox had raged terribly among them, and that they had kept themselves retired in mountain valleys, oppressed with fear and severe disease.

The winter's encampment was made in this region, and a party of Crow Indians which was with them camped at a little distance on the same stream. Here they secured an abundance of meat, and passed the severe weather with a variety of amusements, in which the Indians joined them in their lodges, made of buffalo hides. These lodges, very good substitutes for houses, were made in the form of a cone, spread by means of poles spreading from a common centre, where there was a hole at the top for the passage of smoke. These were often twenty feet in height and as many feet in diameter, where they were pinned to the ground with stakes. In a large village the Indians often had one lodge large enough to hold fifty persons, and within were performed their war dances around a fire made in the centre. During the palmy days of the British Fur Company, in a lodge like this, only made instead of birch bark, Irving says the Indians of the North held their 'primitive fairs' outside the city of Montreal, where they disposed of their furs.

There was one drawback upon conviviality for this party, in the extreme difficulty of getting food for their animals; for the food and fuel so abundant for themselves did not suffice for their horses. Snow covered the ground, and the trappers were obliged to gather willow twigs, and strip the bark from cottonwood trees, in order to keep them alive. The inner bark of the cottonwood is eaten by the Indians when reduced to extreme want. Besides, the cold brought the buffalo down upon them in great herds, to share the nourishment they had provided for their horses.

Spring at length opened, and gladly they again commenced trapping; first on the Yellowstone and soon on the headwaters of the Missouri, where they learned that the Blackfeet were recovered from the sickness of last year, which had not been so severe as it was reported, and that they were still anxious and in condition for a fight, and were encamped not far from their present trapping grounds.

Carson and five men went forward in advance 'to reconnoitre,' and found the village preparing to remove, having learned of the presence of the trappers. Hurrying back, a party of forty-three was selected from the whole, and they unanimously selected Carson to lead them, and leaving the rest to move on with the baggage, and aid them if it should be necessary when they should come up with the Indians, they started forward eager for a battle.

Carson and his command were not long in overtaking the Indians; and dashing among them, at the first fire killed ten of their braves; but the Indians rallied and retreated in good order. The white men were in good spirits, and followed up their first attack with deadly results for three full hours, the Indians making scarce any resistance. Now their firing became less animated, as their ammunition was getting low, and they had to use it with extreme caution. The Indians, suspecting this from the slackness of their fire, rallied, and with a tremendous whoop turned upon their enemies.

Now Carson and his company could use their small arms, which produced a terrible effect, and which enabled them to again drive back the Indians. They rallied yet again, and charged with so much power and in such numbers, they forced the trappers to retreat.

During this engagement the horse of one of the mountaineers was killed, and fell with his whole weight upon his rider. Carson saw the condition of the man, with six warriors rushing to take his scalp, and reached the spot in time to save his friend. Leaping from the saddle he placed himself before his fallen companion, shouting at the same time for his men to rally around him, and with deadly aim from his rifle, shot down the foremost warrior.

The trappers now rallied around Carson and the remaining five warriors retired, without the scalp of their fallen foe. Only two of them reached a place of safety, for the well-aimed fire of the trappers levelled them with the earth.

Carson's horse was loose, and as his comrade was safe, he mounted behind one of his men and rode back to the ranks, while by general impulse the firing on both sides ceased. His horse was captured and restored to him, but each party, now thoroughly exhausted, seemed to wait for the other to renew the attack.

While resting in this attitude, the other division of the trappers came in sight, but the Indians, showing no fear, posted themselves among the rocks at some distance from the scene of the last skirmish, and coolly waited for their adversaries. Exhausted ammunition had been the cause of the retreat of Carson and his force, but now, with a renewed supply, and an addition of fresh men to the force, they advanced on foot to drive the Indians from their hiding places. The contest was desperate and severe, but powder and ball eventually conquered, and the Indians, once dislodged, scattered in every direction. The trappers considered this a complete victory over the Blackfeet, for a large number of their warriors were killed, and many more were wounded, while they had but three men killed and a few severely wounded.

Fontenelle and his party now camped at the scene of the engagement, to recruit their men and here bury their dead. Afterward they trapped through the whole Blackfeet country, and with great success, going where they pleased without fear or molestation. The Indians kept off their route, evidently having acquaintance with Carson and his company enough to last them their lifetime.

With the smallpox and the white man's rifles the warriors were much reduced, and the tribe, which had formerly numbered 30,000, was already decimated, and a few more blows like the one dealt by this dauntless band would suffice to break its spirit and destroy its power for future and evil.

During the battle with the trappers the women and children of the Blackfeet village were sent on in advance, and when the engagement was over and the braves returned to them so much reduced in numbers, and without a single scalp, the big lodge that had been erected for the war dance was given up for the wounded, and in hundreds of Indian hearts grew a bitter hatred for the white man.

An express, dispatched for the purpose, announced the place of the rendezvous to Fontenelle and Carson, who were now on Green River, and with their whole party and a large stock of furs, they at once set out for the place upon Mud River, to find the sales commenced before their arrival, so that in twenty days they were ready to break up camp.

Carson now organised a party of seven and proceeded to a trading post called Brown's Hole, where he joined a company of traders to go to the Navajo Indians. He found this tribe more assimilated to the white man than any Indians he had yet seen, having many fine horses and large flocks of sheep and cattle. They also possessed the art of weaving, and their blankets were in great demand through Mexico, bringing high prices on account of their great beauty, being woven in flowers with much taste. They were evidently a remnant of the Aztec race.

They traded here for a large drove of fine mules, which, taken to the fort on the South Platte, realised good prices, when Carson went again to Brown's Hole, a narrow but pretty valley, about sixteen miles long, upon the Colorado River.

After many offers for his services from other parties, Carson at length engaged himself for the winter to hunt for the men at this fort, and, as the game was abundant in this beautiful valley, and in the *cañon* country farther down the Colorado, in its deer, elk, and antelope reminding him of his hunts upon the Sacramento, the task was a delightful one to him.

In the spring Carson trapped with Bridger and Owens, with passable success, and went to the rendezvous upon Wind River, at the head of the Yellowstone, and from thence, with a large party of the trappers at the rendezvous, to the Yellowstone, where they camped in the vicinity for the winter without seeing their old enemy, the Blackfeet Indians, until midwinter, when they discovered they were near their stronghold.

A party of forty was selected to give them battle, with Carson, of course, for their captain. They found the Indians already in the field to the number of several hundred, who made a brave

Kit Carson's grave.

resistance until night and darkness admonished both parties to retire. In the morning, when Carson and his men went to the spot whither the Indians had retired, they were not to be found. They had given them a 'wide berth,' taking their all away with them, even their dead.

Carson and his command returned to camp, where a council of war decided that, as the Indians would report at the principal encampment the terrible loss they had sustained, and others would be sent to renew the fight, it was wise to prepare to act on the defensive, and use every precaution immediately; and accordingly a sentinel was stationed on a lofty hill near by, who soon reported that the Indians were upon the move.

Their plans matured, they at once threw up a breastwork, under Carson's directions, and waited the approach of the Indians, who came in slowly, the first parties waiting for those behind. After three days a full thousand had reached the camp about half a mile from the breastwork of the trappers. In their war paint, stripes of red across the forehead and down either cheek, with their bows and arrows, tomahawks and lances, this army of Indians presented a formidable appearance to the small body of trappers who were opposed to them.

The war dance was enacted in sight and hearing of the trappers, and at early dawn the Indians advanced, having made every preparation for the attack. Carson commanded his men to reserve their fire till the Indians were near enough to have every shot tell; but, seeing the strength of the white men's position, after a few ineffectual shots, the Indians retired, camped a mile from them, and finally separated into two parties, and went away, leaving the trappers to breathe more freely, for, at the best, the encounter must have been of a desperate character.

They evidently recognised the leader who had before dealt so severely with them, in the skill with which the defence was arranged, and if the name of Kit Carson was on their lips, they knew him for both bravery and magnanimity, and had not the courage to offer him battle.

Another winter gone, with saddlery, moccasin-making, lodge-building, to complete the repairs of the summer's wars and the winter's fight all completed, Carson, with fifteen men, went past Fort Hall again to the Salmon River, and trapped part of the season there, and upon Big Snake and Goose Creeks, and selling his furs at Fort Hall, again joined Bridger in another trapping excursion into the Blackfeet country.

The Blackfeet had molested the traps of another party who had arrived there before them, and had driven them away. The Indian assailants were still near, and Carson led his party against them, taking care to station himself and men in the edge of a thicket, where they kept the savages at bay all day, taking a man from their number with nearly every shot of their well-directed rifles. In vain the Indians now attempted to fire the thicket; it would not burn, and suddenly they retired, forced again to acknowledge defeat at the hands of Kit Carson, the 'Monarch of the Prairies.'

Carson's party now joined with the others, but concluding that they could not trap successfully with the annoyance the Indians were likely to give them, as their force was too small to hope to conquer, they left this part of the country for the north fork of the Missouri.

Now they were with the friendly Flatheads, one of whose chiefs joined them in the hunt, and went into camp near them with a party of his braves. This tribe of Indians, like several other tribes which extend along this latitude of the Pacific, have the custom which gives them their name, thus described by Irving, in speaking of the Indians upon the Lower Columbia, about its mouth:

> A most singular custom prevails not only among the Chinooks, but among most of the tribes about this part of the coast, which is the flattening of the forehead. The process by which this deformity is effected commences immediately after birth. The infant is laid in a wooden trough by way of cradle; the end on which the head reposes is higher than the rest. A padding is placed on the forehead of the infant, with a piece of bark above it, and is pressed down by cords which pass through holes upon the sides of the trough. As the tightening of the padding and the pressure of the head to the board is gradual, the process is said not to be attended with pain. The appearance of the infant, however, while in this state of compression, is whimsically hideous, and its little black eyes, we are told, being forced out by the tightness of the bandages, resemble those of a mouse choked in a trap.

About a year's pressure is sufficient to produce the desired effect, at the end of which time the child emerges from its bandages a complete flathead, and continues so through life. It must be noted, however, that this flattening of the head has something in it of aristocratic significance, like the crippling of the feet among the Chinese ladies of quality. At any rate it is the sign of freedom. No slave is permitted to bestow this deformity upon the head of his children. All the slaves, therefore, are round-heads.

In December, 1846, after a severe battle with the Mexicans and the condition of General Kearney and his men had become desperate, a council of war was called. After discussing a variety of measures, Carson showed himself "the right man in the right place." He said, "Our case is a desperate one, but there is yet hope. If we stay here we are all dead men; our animals can not last long, and the soldiers and marines at San Diego do not know of our coming, but if they receive information of our condition, they will hasten to our rescue. I will attempt to go through the Mexican lines, then to San Diego, and send relief from Commodore Stockton."

Lieutenant Beale of the United States Navy at once seconded Carson, and volunteered to accompany him. General Kearney immediately accepted the proposal as his only hope, and they started at once, as soon as the cover of darkness hung around them. Their mission was to be one of success or of death to themselves and the whole force. Carson was familiar with the customs of the Mexicans, as well as the Indians, of putting their ears to the ground to detect any sound, and therefore knew the necessity of avoiding the slightest noise. As it was impossible to avoid making some noise wearing their shoes, they removed them, and putting them under their belts crept over bushes and rocks with the greatest caution and silence. They discovered that the Mexicans had three rows of sentinels, whose beats extended past each other, embracing the hill where Kearney and his men were held in siege.

They were doubtless satisfied these could not be eluded, but they crept on, often so near a sentinel as to see his figure and equipment in the darkness, and once, when within a few yards of them, discovered one of the sentinels, who had dismounted and lighted his cigarette with his flint and steel. Discovering this sentinel, Kit Carson, as he lay flat on the ground, put his foot back and touched Lieutenant Beale, as a signal for him to be still, as he was doing. The minutes the Mexican was occupied in this way seemed hours to our heroes, who momentarily feared they would be discovered. Carson asserted they were so still he could hear Lieutenant Beale's heart beat, and, in the agony of the time, he lived a year. But the Mexican finally mounted his horse and rode off in a contrary direction, as if guided by Providence to give safety to these courageous adventurers.

For full two miles Kit Carson and Lieutenant Beale thus worked their way along upon their hands and knees, turning their eyes in every direction to detect anything which might lead to their discovery; and, having passed the last sentinel and left the lines sufficiently far behind, they felt an immeasurable relief in once more gaining their feet. But their shoes were gone. In the excitement of this perilous journey neither had thought of his shoes since he first put them in his belt, but they could speak again and congratulate themselves and each other that the great danger was passed, and thank heaven that they had been aided thus far. But there were still many difficulties in their path, which was rough with bushes, from the necessity of having to avoid the well-trodden trail, lest they be discovered. The prickly pear covered the ground, its thorns penetrated their feet at every step, and their road was lengthened by going out of the direct path, though the latter would have shortened their journey many a weary mile.

All the day following they pursued their journey onward without cessation, and into the night following, for they could not stop until they were assured relief was to be furnished their anxious and perilous conditioned fellow soldiers.

Carson pursued so straight a course and aimed so correctly for his mark that they entered the town by the most direct route, and answering "friends" to the challenge of the sentinel, it was known from whence they came, and they were at once conducted to Commodore Stockton, to whom they related their errand, and the further particulars we have already narrated.

Commodore Stockton immediately detailed a force of nearly two hundred men, and, with his usual promptness, ordered them to go to the relief of their besieged countrymen by forced marches. They took with them a piece of ordnance, which the men were obliged themselves to draw, as there were no animals to be had for this work.

Carson's feet were in a terrible condition, and he did not return with the soldiers; he needed rest and the best of care or he might lose his feet; but he described the position of General Kearney so accurately that the party sent to his relief could find him without difficulty, and yet had the commodore expressed the wish, Carson would have undertaken to guide the relief party upon its march.

Lieutenant Beale was partially deranged for several days from the effects of the severe service, and was sent on board a frigate lying in port for medical attendance, and he did not fully recover his former health for more than two years.

The relief party from Commodore Stockton reached General Kearney without encountering any Mexicans, and very soon all marched to San Diego, where the wounded soldiers received medical assistance.

CHAPTER 13

Adventures of a Trapper

Fifty years ago, when Kansas City consisted of a warehouse and there was not a single private residence of civilized man between the Missouri River and San Francisco, S. E. Ward, a trapper, landed from a steamer at Independence. He was a penniless youth of eighteen years, direct from the parental home in Virginia, filled with eager desire to gain a fortune in the far West. Now, at sixty-eight years of age, Mr. Ward is almost twice a millionaire and one of the most respected citizens of Western Missouri. He is one of the pioneers that are left to speak of the struggles and triumphs of early Western life. The family home is a spacious two-story brick house, 2½ miles south of Westport, on the old Santa Fé trail. The house stands upon a farm of 500 acres at the edge of the great prairie which stretches away through Kansas to the base of the Rocky Mountains. On this very spot where he now lives Mr. Ward camped more than once on his return from trading expeditions, years ago, in the Southwest.

He has had experiences that do not fall to the ordinary lot of man. Thrown by circumstances into a new country in his earlier life, he has travelled thousands of miles alone through the mountains and across the prairies, and often spent weeks without meeting a single human being. Exposed to snow, sleet, and rain, with no shelter but a buffalo robe, and at times with starvation staring him in the face, the chances seemed slight indeed of ever coming out alive. During his experience in the West he met Fremont in his expedition through the mountains, saw Brigham Young on the Platte River as he was on his way to found a Mormon empire, passed through the stormy period of the Mexican War, the California gold excitement, the Civil War, and witnessed the opening of the Pacific Railroad, and the mighty influx of population on the plains of the great West.

The first seven years of his life on the frontier were passed largely in intercourse with Indian tribes, extending from the Red River on the south to the upper waters of the Columbia and Yellowstone on the north. Hunting, trapping, and trading were the only occupations open to white men west of the Missouri River in those days. In little bands of from two to twelve the hunters and trappers roamed through the vast region with but little fear of the redskins. The Indians had not contracted the vices of civilization, and were a different race of people from what they are today. The cruelties we read of as practiced by them in later years were unknown. I never knew of a prisoner being burned at the stake, and ordinarily the hunter felt as safe in an Indian country as in his own settlement. The Indians were armed with bows and arrows, not more than one in fifty being the possessor of a gun. When an Indian did use a gun it was usually a light shotgun that proved ineffective at any great distance. An experienced frontiersman considered himself safe against any small number of Indians.

By means of the sign language we were able to talk with the Indians upon all subjects; and as they were very great talkers and inveterate story-tellers, many is the hour I have passed seated by the camp-fire hearing their adventures or the legends of their nations. I have often wondered why the sign language, as recognised and perfected by the Indians, was not adopted among civilized people instead of the deaf and dumb alphabet. The Indian's method of communicating his ideas is much more impressive and natural. The Cheyennes and Arapahoes were especially noted for their skill in sign language.

In some respects the Indians were superior to the whites as hunters. They knew nothing of trapping beaver until taught by the whites, but they could give valuable points on bagging the large game on the plains. Forty or fifty years ago the plains were swarming with buffalo. I have often seen droves so large that no eye could compass them. Their numbers were countless. The Indian hunter riding bare-backed would guide his horse headlong into the midst of the herd, singling out the fattest and in an instant sending the deadly arrow clean through his victim. In a single day's hunt they sometimes killed 3,000 to 4,000 buffalo. The dead bodies would lie scattered over the prairie for miles. It required the greatest diligence to save the skins and dry the meat for use in winter. They made wholesale slaughter of antelope by forming a "surround." This required the presence of several hundred Indians to make a complete success.

Early in the morning the men and boys would form a circle miles in diameter, riding round and round, making the circle smaller at every revolution and growing closer together. All the game within the ranks was gradually collected into a body which was driven to an enclosure formed by weeds piled high up at the sides, behind which were the women and old men. As the game passed the reserve force these bobbed up and set up unearthly shrieks and yells that caused the frightened animals to plunge forward over a precipice to which the enclosure conducted. The slaughter was terrible. Indians stationed below gave the quietus to such game as made the descent with but slight injury. At the close of the day a great feast was held, and nobody enjoys a feast more than an Indian.

I have been asked if marriage was a success among the aborigines. I never heard it hinted that it was otherwise. The Indian had the privilege of taking as many wives as he was able to support, and if he married the oldest sister in a family, all the remaining sisters were considered his property as they became of age. Under favourable circumstances, in some tribes, a warrior took a new wife every two or three years. A separate lodge was provided for each wife, as the women would fall out and scratch each other if kept together. A peculiarity in the Indian family relations was that as soon as a wife found herself to be with child her person was considered sacred, and she lived apart from all the rest of the household until the child had been born and had weaned itself of its own accord. This exclusion extended even to the master of the house, and was never violated. The children were fairly idolised among the more advanced tribes. The parents seemed to live for their children, more particularly when the children were boys.

An Indian's wealth was known by the number of his horses. There were both rich and poor Indians, but the latter were never allowed to want when there was anything to be had. After a great hunt the poor man was granted the privilege of taking the first carcasses nearest the camp.

Some Indians kept their lodges nicely painted and beyond criticism as to cleanliness. The lodges were renewed every year, as frequent moving and exposure to weather made the skins leaky. The Indians' range extended anywhere that game and food for their animals could be found. It was a rare occurrence for them to remain a month in a single vicinity. The monotony of hunting and moving was varied by occasional forays upon an unfriendly tribe, stealing their horses, and carrying off scalps and prisoners. Unless these captives were children they were put to death. The children were usually adopted and treated with the greatest kindness. The older prisoners, both men and women, were dispatched with little ceremony. The killing was usually deferred for several days after the prisoners were brought into camp. A young Pawnee Indian who was killed by a party of Comanches was taken into the open air, his hands were tied to his legs, and he was shot through the heart. He uttered not a word or groan.

After the killing, a warrior stepped forward and raised the dead Pawnee's scalp, then the war dance was held. A Crow Indian was dispatched even more expeditiously. Trapper Ward called on the captain in the lodge where he was confined, and they talked together by signs. He said he knew he must die, but felt perfectly resigned to his fate, as he would inflict the same penalty on his enemies if he had the chance. While they were talking, a warrior appeared at the door and made a motion. The Crow stepped forward and was shot within a few feet of the spot he had occupied the moment before. After the scalping and war dance he was tied up in a standing position, with his hands stretched as far apart over his head as possible, making a ghastly spectacle, and left as a warning to all the enemies of his executioners.

The winter of 1838 and 1839, Mr. Ward says, was vividly impressed upon his mind, being his first experience as a trapper. After a journey of 600 miles from Independence, he arrived at Fort Bent, and early in the fall the different hunting and trapping parties started out for a long sojourn in the mountains. He was fortunate in being one of a party of twelve, of which Kit Carson was a member. They made headquarters in Brown's Hole, on the Colorado River, where it enters the mountains. Trapping proved hard work, but he never enjoyed life more, and knew no such thing as sickness. Their clothes were made (by their own hands) of buckskin. Their food was nothing but meat cooked on a stick or on the coals, as they had no cooking utensils. Antelope, deer, elk, bear, beaver, and, in case of necessity, even the wolf, furnished a variety that was always acceptable to eat. At night they gathered round a roaring fire, in comfortable quarters, to listen to the stories which such men as Kit Carson could tell.

At the close of three months a successful trapper was often able to show a pack of 120 beaver skins, weighing about 100 pounds. As he made two trapping expeditions during the year, in the spring and fall, he would show 200 pounds, worth $6 per pound, as his year's work. In addition to this, the musk-stones of the beaver were worth as much as the skins, so that some of them made $3,000 per year as trappers.

It was a poor trapper that did not earn half as much. But few of them ever saved any money. The traders from the States charged them enormously for supplies, and Western men were inveterate gamblers. Sugar was $1.50 per pound, coffee the same, tobacco $5 per pound, and a common shirt could not be bought for less than $5, while whisky sold for over $30 a gallon. With flour at $1 per pound, and luxuries in proportion, it was a question of but a few days at the rendezvous before the labour of months was used up. The traders were often called upon to fit out the men upon credit, after a prosperous season.

Chapter 14

Trapping

To be a successful trapper required great caution, as well as a perfect knowledge of the habits of the animals. The residence of the beaver was often discovered by seeing bits of green wood and gnawed branches of the basswood, slippery elm, and sycamore, their favourite food, floating on the water or lodged on the shores of the stream below, as well as by their tracks or foot-marks.

These indications were technically called "beaver signs." They were also sometimes discovered by their dams thrown across creeks and small, sluggish streams, forming a pond in which were erected their habitations.

The hunter, as he proceeded to set his traps, generally approached by water, in his canoe. He selected a steep, abrupt spot in the bank of the creek, in which he excavated a hole with his paddle, as he sat in the canoe, sufficiently large to hold the trap, and so deep as to be about three inches below the surface of the water, when the jaws of the trap were expanded. About two feet above the trap, a stick, three or four inches in length, was stuck in the bank. In the upper end of this stick the trapper cut a small hole with his knife, into which he dropped a small quantity of the essence of perfume, which was used to attract the beaver to the spot. This stick was fastened by a string of horse-hair to the trap, and with it was pulled into the water by the beaver. The reason for this was that it might not remain after the trap was sprung, and attract other beavers to the spot, and thus prevent their seeking other traps ready for them.

This scent, or essence, was made by mingling the fresh castor of the beaver with an extract of the bark of the roots of the spice-bush, and then kept in a bottle for use. The making of this essence was kept a profound secret, and often sold for a considerable sum to the younger trappers by the older proficients in the mysteries of beaver-hunting. Where trappers had no proper bait, they sometimes made use of the fresh roots of the sassafras or spice-bush, of both of which the beaver was very fond.

It is said by old trappers that the beaver will smell the well-prepared essence the distance of a mile, their sense of smell being very acute, or they would not so readily detect the vicinity of man by the scent of his trail. The aroma of the essence, having attracted the beaver to the vicinity of the trap, in his attempt to reach it he has to climb up on the bank where it is sticking. This effort leads him directly over the trap, and he is usually caught by one of his fore legs.

The trap was connected by an iron chain, six feet in length, to a stout line made of the bark of the leather wood, twisted into a neat cord fifteen or twenty feet in length. These cords were usually prepared by the trappers at home, or at their camps, for cords of hemp or flax were scarce in the days of beaver-hunting. The end of the line was secured to a stake driven into the bed of the creek under water, and in the beaver's struggles to escape he was usually drowned before the arrival of the trapper. Sometimes, however, he freed himself by gnawing off his own leg, though this rarely happened.

When setting the trap, if it was raining, or there was a prospect of rain, a leaf, generally of sycamore, was placed over the essence stick to protect it from the rain.

The beaver was a very sagacious and cautious animal, and it required great care in the trapper in his approach to his haunts to set his traps, that no scent of his hands or feet should be left on the earth or bushes that he touched. For this reason the trapper generally approached in a canoe. If he had no canoe it was necessary to enter the stream thirty or forty yards below where he wished to set his trap, and walk up the stream to the place, taking care to return in the same manner, lest the beaver should take alarm and not come near the bait, as his fear of the vicinity of man was greater than his appetite for the essence.

Caution was also required in kindling a fire near the haunts of the beaver, as the smell of smoke alarmed them. The firing of a gun, also, often marred the sport of the trapper.

Thus it will be seen that, to make a successful beaver hunter, required more qualities or natural gifts than fall to the share of most men.

CHAPTER 15

An Adventure With Indians

In the early part of June, 1850, I loaded my train, consisting of ten wagons drawn by 130 oxen, at Kansas City, Mo., with merchandise destined for Santa Fé, N. M., a distance of about eight hundred miles from Kansas City, and started for that point. After being out some eight or ten days and travelling through what was then called Indian Territory, but was not organised until four years later, and was then styled Kansas. Arriving one evening at a stream called One Hundred and Ten, I camped for the night. I unyoked my oxen and turned them upon the grass. Finding the grass so good and the animals weary with the day's work, I thought they would not stroll away, and therefore did not put any guard, as was my custom.

At early dawn on the following morning I arose, saddled my horse, which, by the way, was a good one, and told my assistant to arouse the teamsters, so they could be ready to yoke their teams as soon as I drove them into the corral, which was formed by the wagons. I rode around what I supposed to be all the herd, but in rounding them up before reaching the wagons, I discovered that there were a number of them missing. I then made a circle, leaving the ones I had herded together. I had not travelled very far when I struck the trail of the missing oxen; it being very plain, I could ride my horse on a gallop and keep track of it.

I had not travelled more than a mile when I discovered the tracks of Indian ponies. I then knew the Indians had driven off my oxen. I thought of the fact that I was unarmed, not thinking it necessary to take my gun when I left the wagons, as I only expected to go a few hundred yards. We had not yet reached the portion of the territory where we would expect to meet hostile Indians, so I went ahead on the trail, thinking it was some half-friendly ones that had driven my

An Adventure with Indians.

oxen away, as they sometimes did, in order to get a fee for finding and bringing them back again.

I expected to overtake them at any moment, for the trail looked very fresh, as though they were only a short distance ahead of me. So on and on I went, galloping my horse most of the time, until I had gone about twelve miles from my camp. I passed through a skirt of timber that divided one portion of the open prairie from the other, and there overtook thirty-four head of my oxen resting from their travel.

About sixty yards to the east of the cattle were six painted Indian braves, who had dismounted from their horses, each one leaning against his horse, with his right hand resting upon his saddle, their guns being in their left. I came upon them suddenly, the timber preventing them from seeing me until I was within a few rods of them. I threw up my hand, went in a lope around my oxen, giving some hideous yells, and told the cattle they could go back to the wagons on the trail they had come. They at once heeded me and started. I never saw six meaner or more surprised looking men than those six braves were, for I think they thought I had an armed party just behind me, or I would not have acted so courageously as I did. So I followed my cattle, who were ready to take their way back, and left the six savages standing in dismay. The oxen and myself were soon out of sight in the forest, and that is the last I saw of the six braves who had been sent out by their chief the night before to steal the oxen.

Very soon after I got through the timber and into the prairie again I met, from time to time, one or two Indians trotting along on their ponies, following the trail that the cattle made when their comrades drove them off. When within a short distance of the herd they would leave the trail and leave plenty of space to the cattle, fall in behind me, and trot on toward the six braves I had left. I will say here that I began to feel very much elated over my success in capturing my cattle from six armed savages, and being given the right-of-way by other parties also armed. But I did not have to travel very far under the pleasant reflection that I was a hero; when I was about half-way back to the wagons I looked ahead about half-a-mile and saw a large body of Indians, comprising some twenty-five warriors, who proved to be under the command of their chief, armed and coming toward me. I then began to feel a little smaller than I had a few minutes previous, for I was entirely unarmed, and even had I been armed what could I have done with twenty-five armed savages?

My fears were very soon realised, for when they arrived within a few hundred yards of me and the chief saw me returning with the cattle he had sent his braves to drive off, he commanded his men to make a descent upon me, and he undertook the job of leading them. They raised a hideous yell and started toward me at the top of their horses' speed. If my oxen had not been driven so far and become to some extent tired, I would have had a royal stampede. The animals only ran a few hundred yards until I succeeded in holding them up. By this time the Indians had reached me and my cattle. The braves surrounded the cattle, and the chief came at the top of his horse's speed directly toward me, with his gun drawn up in striking attitude. Of course I did not allow him to get in reaching distance. I turned my horse and put spurs to him; he was a splendid animal and it was a comparatively easy matter for me to keep out of the reach of the vicious chief, who did not want to kill me, but desired to scare me, or cause me to run away and leave my herd, or disable me so I could not follow him and his band if they attempted to take the cattle.

This chasing me off for some distance was repeated three times, I returning in close proximity to where his braves surrounded the cattle on every side, some on foot holding their ponies, others on horseback. Those who had alighted were dancing and yelling at the tops of their voices. The third time I returned to where the chief and one of his braves, armed with bow and arrows, were sitting on their horses, some distance from the cattle and in line between me and the group of braves. When I got within thirty or forty yards of him he beckoned me to come to him, for all the communication we had was carried on by means of signs; I did not speak their language nor they mine. I rode cautiously up side by side, a short distance from the chief, with our horses' heads in the same direction. When I had fairly stopped to see what he was going to do, his brave who was on the opposite side from me slid off his horse, ran under the neck of the chief's, and made a lunge to catch the bridle of my horse. His sudden appearance caused the animal to jump so quick and far that he had just missed getting hold of the rein.

Had he succeeded in the attempt they would have taken my horse and oxen and cleared out, leaving me standing on the prairie. When he found he had failed in his attempt, he returned to his horse, mounted, and he and the chief rode slowly toward me, for I had reined up my horse when I found I was out of reach. I sat still to see what their next manoeuvre would be. The brave changed from the left of the chief to the right as they came slowly toward me. When they got within a few feet of me, with the heads of our horses in the same direction, they reined up their ponies and the brave suddenly drew his bow at full bend, with a sharp-pointed steel in the end of the arrow. He aimed at my heart with the most murderous, vindictive, and devilish look on his face and from his eyes that I ever saw portrayed on any living face before or since. Of course there was no time for doing anything but to keep my eye steadfast on his. To show the influence of the mind over the body, while he was pointing the arrow at me I felt a place as large as the palm of my hand cramping where the arrow would have struck me had he shot.

While in this position he pronounced the word "say" with all the force he could summon. I did not at that time understand what he meant. The chief relieved my suspense by holding up his ten fingers and pointing to the oxen. I then understood that if I gave him ten of my animals he would not put the dart through me. I felt that I could not spare that number and move on with my train to its destination, and in a country where I had not the opportunity of obtaining others, so I refused. He then threw up five fingers and motioned to the cattle. Again I shook my head. He then motioned me to say how many I would give, and I held up one finger. The moment I did so he gave the word of command to his braves, who were still dancing and screaming round the cattle, and they, whirling into line, selected one of the animals so quickly that one had hardly time to think, and left thirty-three of the oxen and myself standing in the prairie. I had held them there so long, refusing to let them go without following them, I think they were afraid some of my party would overtake me. There was no danger of that had they only known it, for on my return I found all my men at the wagons wondering what had become of me. I had left the camp at daylight and it was after noon when I returned.

In conclusion, I will say that never at any time in my life, and I have encountered a great many dangers, have I felt so small and helpless as upon this occasion, being surrounded by twenty-five or thirty armed savages and with whom I could communicate only by signs. To surrender the animals to them was financial ruin, and to stay with them was hazarding my life and receiving the grossest abuse and insults. The effect of passing through this ordeal, on my mind, was that I became so reduced in stature, I felt as if I was no larger than my thumb, a hummingbird or a mouse; all three passed through my mind, and I actually looked at myself to see if it was possible I was so small.

No one can tell, until he has been overpowered by hostile savages, how small he will become in his own estimation. However, when they left me, I at once came back to my natural size and felt as if a great weight had been lifted from me.

Although the Indians were nothing more nor less than specimens of nature's sons, without any education whatever of a literary nature, they were very shrewd and quick to see and take up an insult. They were remarkable for reading faces, and although they were not able to understand one word of English, they could tell when looking at a white man and his comrades when in conversation about them, almost precisely what they were saying by the shadows that would pass over their faces, and by the nodding of heads and movement of hands or shoulders, for the reason that they talked with each other and the different tribes that they would meet by signs, and it was done generally by the movement of the hands.

They had but few vices, in fact might say almost none outside of their religious teachings, which allowed them to steal horses and fur skins, and sometimes take the lives of enemies or opposing tribes. Persons who were not thoroughly acquainted with Indian character and life might wonder why there were so many different tribes—or bands, as they were sometimes called—and if it could be there were so many nationalities among them. This is accounted for solely and truly upon the fact that when a tribe grew to a certain number it became a necessity in nature for them to divide, which would form two bands or tribes and at that point of time and condition it became necessary for the one leaving the main tribe to have a name to designate themselves from the family that they had of necessity parted from, for as soon as a tribe reached such a proportion in numbers that it was inconvenient for them to rendezvous at some given point easy of access, their necessities in such cases demanded a new deal or different arrangements; hence the different names by which tribes were called.

These tribes differed in their methods of living according to the conditions with which they were surrounded. Indians who lived along the Atlantic Coast and made their living from fishing, as well as from hunting, were very different from the Indians of the plains and Rocky Mountain regions, who live almost solely upon buffalo and other varieties of game that they were able to secure.

The Indians from the Atlantic and Mississippi valleys were more dangerous, as a rule, when they came into a combat with white soldiers, than were the Indians of the plains and Rockies. The Shawnee and Delaware Indian braves a hundred years ago, when my grandfather was an Indian fighter in Kentucky, were considered equal to any white soldiers and proved themselves in battle to be so. Their mode of warfare, however, was not on horseback, as was the mode of warfare with the Indians of the plains. They were "still" hunters, as they might be called, and when they met with white men in battle array, would get behind trees, if possible, as a protection, and remain and fight to the bitter end. When these tribes became overpowered, it was easy, compared with the Indians of the plains, to bring them under some of the conditions of civilization; therefore the Cherokees, Seminoles, Chickasaws, Choctaws, Shawnees, Delawares, Wyandottes, Kickapoos, Sacs, Foxes, the Creeks, and many others whose names I can not now recall, have become somewhat civilized, and many of them semi-civilized tribes, but the Indians of the plains and Rocky Mountain regions have been very slow to accept what we term civilization.

They seem somewhat like the buffalo and other wild animals that we have never been able to domesticate. It looks to one like myself that has known them for so many years, that before they are civilized they will become almost exterminated; that is to say that civilized life does not agree with them, and they die from causes and conditions that such life compels them to exist under, and in my opinion the day will come when there will be few, if any, in the near future, left of the tribes that were known to belong to the territory west of the Mississippi River and extending to the Pacific Coast. There was often among the wildest tribes of America many good traits. If they found you hungry and alone and in distress, as a rule they would take care of you, giving you the very best they had, and never with a view of charging you for their kindness. If they had a grudge against the white race for some misdemeanour some white man may have committed, they might kill you in retaliation.

For this reason white men always felt, when they were among them, that their safety depended largely upon how the tribe had been treated by some other white man, or party of white men. As far as I know, throughout the entire savage tribes retaliation is one of the laws by which they are governed. The women, as a rule, were very generous and kind-hearted, and I know of one case where a friend of mine, Judge Brown of Pettis County, Mo., had his life saved and his property restored to him through the instrumentality of an Indian woman. The Indians were at that time quite hostile toward the whites, and had held council and determined to kill him, as they had him a prisoner and at their mercy. This woman seemed to be one of great influence in the tribe, and when the braves held their council and decided to take his life and property, she rose to her feet and plead for the life of my friend.

Of course he could not understand a word she said, but he saw in her face a benevolence and kindness that gave him heart, for he had about despaired of ever living another hour. From the way in which she looked, talked, and gestured, he felt certain that she was assuming his cause, and he in relating the circumstances to me and others said he never saw a greater heroine in the appearance and conduct of any woman in his life. Of course this he had to judge largely of from appearances, as the Indians judge of the white people that I before alluded to.

CHAPTER 16

Crossing the Plains

Everything worked along smoothly on my westward way, after my adventure with the Indians, until I reached Walnut Creek, at the Big Bend of the Arkansas River. At that point the buffalo, running past my herd of oxen in the night, scattered them, part running with the buffalo and crossing the river where it was very high, it being the season of the year when the channel was full of water, from the melting of the snow in the mountains from which it received its waters. The next morning, as before, at the One Hundred and Ten, I found a portion of my herd missing, but not so many this time as to prevent me from travelling. I had the teams hitched up, some of them being a yoke of oxen minus, but sufficient remained to move the wagons, and I started my assistant, Mr. Samuel Poteet, one of the most faithful of my men, on the road with the teams, and I took my extra man to hunt for the missing oxen.

We crossed the river where it was almost at swimming point and at the place where the buffalo had crossed the night before, for we had followed their trail for several miles. After losing the trail, for they had so scattered we could not tell which trail to take, we wandered around for a time in the open prairie, expecting Indians to appear at any moment; but in that we were happily disappointed. I finally found my cattle all standing in a huddle near a pond. We soon surrounded them and started driving them to the river, crossed them and reached the road, following the train, until we overtook it a little before sundown that evening. From that point there was nothing to trouble or disturb our movements until we reached the Wagon Mounds, beyond the borders of New Mexico, now a station upon the Atchison, Topeka & Santa Fé Railroad.

There we came upon the ruins of a stage-coach which had been burned; the bones and skeletons of some of the horses that drew it, as well as the bones of the party of ten men who were murdered outright by the Indians. Not one escaped to tell the story, and they were, I think, a party of ten as brave men as could be found anywhere. Whether there were any Indians killed while they were massacring this party is not known, for it was some few days before the news of the affair was known, as there was little travel over the road at that season of the year.

This party had passed me on the road some weeks before, and being able to travel three times as far per day as I could, had reached the point of their fate several weeks before, so we could see nothing but the bones the wolves had scratched out of the ground where they had been buried. In fact there was nothing to bury when we found them. The wolves would not even let them lie at rest. It seemed there was no flesh the wolves could get hold of they were so fond of as the flesh of an American or white man, and, strange to say, they would not eat a Mexican at all. It frequently happened that when the Indians killed a party on the Santa Fé Road there were both Mexicans and Americans left dead upon the same spot. When found the bodies of the Americans would invariably be eaten, and the bodies of the Mexicans lying intact without any interference at all.

There were various speculations with travellers along that road as to why this was so. Some thought it was because the Mexicans were so saturated with red pepper, they making that a part of their diet. Others thought it was because they were such inveterate smokers and were always smoking cigarettes. I have no suggestions to make on the subject any further than to say such was a fact, and there are many American boys today who would not be eaten by wolves, so impregnated are they with nicotine.

After passing this gloomy spot at the Wagon Mounds, which almost struck terror to our hearts to see the bones of our fellow-men who had been swept away by the hand of the savages, without a moment's warning, we pursued our way to Santa Fé, N. M., and delivered my freight to the merchants. They paid me the cash, $13,000 in silver—Mexican dollars—for freighting their goods to that point, a distance of 800 miles from the place of loading at Kansas City, Mo. I returned home without any further drawbacks or molestations on that trip.

On arriving home I found that Maj. E. A. Ogden of Fort Leavenworth desired to send a load of Government freight to Fort Mann, 400 miles west on the same road I had just travelled over, at about the point on the Arkansas River where Fort Dodge now stands. I agreed with him on terms at once, and loaded my wagons for that point. Lieutenant Heath of the United States Army was in command of the little post at Fort Mann. I arrived in good time, with everything in good order, and when the government freights were unloaded he expressed a desire that I should take my entire train and go south about twenty-five miles, where there was some large timber growing near a stream called Cottonwood, for the purpose of bringing him a lot of saw-logs to make lumber for the building of his post.

A more gentlemanly or clever man I never met in the United States Army or out of it—thoroughly correct in his dealings, and kind and courteous as could be. I made the trip and brought him a fine lot of cottonwood and walnut saw-logs, for these were the only kinds of timber that grew along the stream, unloaded them at his camp and returned home without losing any men or animals. The men were all in fine health and good spirits, as men generally are when everything moves successfully in their business, and particularly a business which hangs upon so many contingencies as our trips across the plains did.

In the year 1851 I again crossed the plains with a full outfit of twenty-five wagons and teams. This trip was a complete success; we met with no molestations, and returned home without the loss of any animals, but, owing to the cholera prevailing to some extent among the men who were on the plains, I lost two men by that disease. Several would have died, perhaps, but for the fact that I had provided myself with the proper remedies before leaving Kansas City. In 1852 I corralled my wagons, sold my oxen to California emigrants, and did no more work upon the plains that year. In 1853 I bought a new supply of work-cattle and again loaded my wagons at Kansas City for Santa Fé, N. M., as I had previously been doing. I was very successful in my operations that year, meeting with no loss of men and no animals worth mentioning.

I also made a second trip that year from Fort Leavenworth to Fort Union, in New Mexico, returning to my home near Westport, Mo., late in November. During the year 1854 I also went upon the plains as a freighter, changing my business from freighting for the merchants in New Mexico to carrying United States Government freights. At this time I added to my transportation, making 100 wagons and teams for that year, divided into four trains. Everything moved along this year in a most prosperous way, without loss of life among my men, but I lost a great many of my work-cattle on account of the Texas fever. The loss was not so great, however, as to impede my travelling. The Government officers with whom I came in contact at either end of the route were well pleased with my way of doing business as a freighter, for everything was done in the most prompt and business-like manner.

In 1855 W. H. Russell of Lexington, Mo., and I formed a partnership under the name and style of Majors & Russell. That year we carried all the Government freight that had to be sent from Fort Leavenworth to the different posts or forts. The cholera prevailed among our men that year. Not more than two or three died, however, but quite a delay and additional expense were caused on account of this dire disease among our teamsters, with a train load of freight for Fort Riley. This was in June, and the train was almost deserted. Another train was entirely deserted, the sick men being taken to some of the farmers in the neighbourhood, the well ones leaving for their homes, our oxen scattering and going toward almost every point of the compass. It was not long, however, until we got straightened again, and the train started for its destination.

Not long after this Maj. A. E. Ogden, the United States quartermaster at Fort Leavenworth, was taken with the cholera, and died at Fort Riley. A more honest, straightforward, and Christian gentleman could not be found in any army, or out of it. He had more excellent qualities than are generally allotted to man, and his death was much mourned by all who had the pleasure of his acquaintance. He left a very estimable wife and several children to mourn his death.

After the cholera disappeared that year, the freighting business moved along nicely and resulted in a prosperous year's work, after all the drawbacks in the early part of the season.

We also did a large business in freighting in 1856. I think that year we had about three hundred to three hundred and fifty wagons and teams at work, and our profits for 1855 and 1856 footed up about three hundred thousand dollars. This sum included our wagons, oxen, and other freighting and transportation outfits, valuing them at what we thought they would bring the beginning of the freighting season the next year.

In 1857 the government extended the contract to Majors & Russell for one year longer, and it was during this year the United States Government determined to send an army to Utah to curtail the power that Brigham Young was extending over the destiny of that country; many complaints having reached Washington through the Government officials who had been sent to the Territory to preside as judges in the United States Courts. This resulted in a very great increase of transportation that year, and great difficulties were encountered, to begin with, which required quite an increase in the facilities for transportation, which had to be very hurriedly brought together. Before all the Government freight reached Fort Leavenworth, it became too late for trains to reach the headquarters of the army before cold weather set in, in the high altitude of Fort Bridger and that portion of the country where the army was in winter quarters; therefore many of the animals perished on account of having to be kept, under army orders, where grass and water were sometimes scarce, and they suffered more or less from severe cold weather. The result was great loss of the work-animals and an entire loss of the previous two years' profits.

A party of Mormons, under command of Col. Lott Smith, had been sent out by the Mormon authorities in the rear of Johnston's army to cut off his supplies. They captured and burned three of our trains, two on the Sandy, just east of Green River, and one on the west bank of Green River. They gave the captain of each train the privilege of taking one of his best wagons and teams and loading it with supplies, to return home or back to the starting point. They committed no outrage whatever toward the men, and, as soon as the captain of each train told them he had all the food necessary to supply him to get back to the starting point, they told him to abandon the train, and they were set on fire and everything burned that was consumable.

The captains of the trains, with their teamsters, returned to the States in safety. The cattle were driven off by the Mormons, and those that were not used for beef by the hungry men were returned in the summer to the company after peace had been made between the Mormons and the government. The loss to the army was about five hundred thousand pounds of government supplies. This loss put the army upon short rations for that winter and spring, until they could be reached with supplies in the spring of 1858.

That spring, our firm, under the name of Russell, Majors & Waddell, obtained a new contract from the United States Government to carry Government freight to Utah for the years 1858-59. That year the Government ordered an immense lot of freight, aggregating 16,000,000 pounds, most of which had to be taken to Utah. We had to increase the transportation from three or four hundred wagons and teams we had previously owned to 3,500 wagons and teams, and it required more than forty thousand oxen to draw the supplies; we also employed over four thousand men and about one thousand mules.

Our greatest drawback that year was occasioned by floods and heavy rains upon the plains, which made our trains move tardily in the outset. We succeeded admirably, however, considering the vast amount of material we had to get together and organise, which we could not have done had we not had so many years' experience, previous to this great event, in the freighting enterprise; and especially was this so with me, for I had had, previous to this, a great many years' experience in handling men and teams, even before I crossed the plains ten years before. We succeeded this year in carrying everything to the army in Utah, fifty miles south of Salt Lake City, to Camp Floyd, the headquarters of Sidney Johnston's command, a distance of 1,250 miles.

After unloading the wagons at Camp Floyd, they were taken to Salt Lake City and placed as near as they could stand to each other in the suburbs of the city, and covered many acres of ground, where they remained for one year or more, when our agent sold them to the Mormon authorities for $10 apiece, they having cost us at the manufacturers' $150 to $175 apiece. The Mormons used the iron about them for the manufacture of nails. The oxen we sent to Skull Valley and other valleys near Camp Floyd, known to be good winter quarters for cattle and mules. During the year 1859, while our teams were at Camp Floyd we selected 3,500 head as suitable to drive to California and put on the market, and they were driven to Ruby Valley, in Nevada, where it was intended they should remain, that being considered a favourable winter locality; and in the spring of 1860 they were to be driven to California, the intention being to let them graze on the wild oats and clover in the valleys of the Sacramento, and convert them into beef-cattle when fully ready for the market.

A very few days after the herders reached the valley with them, which was late in November, a snow-storm set in and continued more or less severe, at intervals, until it covered the ground to such a depth that it was impossible for the cattle to get a particle of subsistence, and in less than forty days after the animals were turned out in the valley they were lying in great heaps frozen and starved to death. Only 200 out of the 3,500 survived the storm. They were worth at the time they were turned into the valley about $150,000, as they were a very superior and select lot of oxen. This was the largest disaster we met with during the years 1858 and 1859.

In 1857 the Indians attacked the herders who had charge of about one thousand head on the Platte River, west of Fort Kearney, which is now called Kearney City, in Nebraska, killing one of the herders

A ROUGH TRAIL.

and scattering the cattle to the four winds. These were also a complete loss.

We had very little trouble with the Indians in 1857, 1858, and 1859 in any way, owing to the fact that Johnston's army, consisting of about five thousand regulars, besides the teamsters, making in all about seven thousand well-armed men, had passed through the country in 1857, and they had seen such a vast army, with their artillery, that they were completely intimidated, and stayed at a very respectful distance from the road on which this vast number of wagons and teams travelled. Each one of our wagons was drawn by six yoke, or twelve oxen, and contained from five to six thousand pounds of freight, and there was but one wagon to each team. The time had not yet come when, what was afterward adopted, trail wagons were in use. This means two or three wagons lashed together and drawn by one team. Twenty-five of our wagons and teams formed what was called a train, and these trains were scattered along the road at intervals of anywhere from two to three miles, and sometimes eight to ten miles, and even greater distances, so as to keep out of the way of each other.

The road, until we reached the South Pass, was over the finest line of level country for travelling by wagons, with plenty of water and grass at almost every step of the way. Crossing the South Platte at what was then called Julesburg, and going across the divide to North Platte, at Ash Hollow, we continued in the valley of the North Platte to the mouth of the Sweetwater, and up that stream until we passed through the South Pass. After passing that point it was somewhat more difficult to find grass and water, but we were fortunate enough all along the road to get sufficient subsistence out of nature for the sustenance of our animals, and were not obliged to feed our oxen. They did the work allotted to them, and gathered their own living at nights and noon-times.

In the fall of 1857 a report was sent by the engineers who were with General Johnston's army at Fort Bridger, and who had crossed the plains that year, to the Quartermaster's Department at Washington, stating it was impossible to find subsistence along the road for the number of animals it would require to transport the freight necessary for the support of the army. General Jessup, who was then Quartermaster of the United States Army at Washington, and as fine a gentleman as I ever met, gave me this information, and asked me if it would deter me from undertaking the transportation. I told him it would not, and that I would be willing to give him my head for a football to have kicked in Pennsylvania Avenue if I did not supply the army with every pound that was necessary for its subsistence, provided the government would pay me to do it. We satisfied him after the first year's work had been done that we could do even more than I assured him could be done.

There is no other road in the United States, nor in my opinion elsewhere, of the same length, where such numbers of men and animals could travel during the summer season as could over the thoroughfare from the Missouri River up the Platte and its tributaries to the Rocky Mountains. In fact, had it been necessary to go east from the Missouri River, instead of west, it would have been impossible in the nature of things to have done so, owing to the uneven surface of the country, the water being in little deep ravines and, as a rule, in small quantities, often muddy creeks to cross, at other times underbrush and timber that the animals could have roamed into and disappeared, all of which would have prevented progress had we started with such an enterprise east instead of west.

But the country west of the Missouri River for hundreds of miles, so far as making roads for travel of large numbers of animals is concerned, is as different from the east as it is possible for two landscapes to be. The whole country from the west border of the Missouri, Iowa, and Arkansas was thoroughly practical, before inhabited by farmers, for carrying the very largest herds and organisations of people on what one might term perfectly natural ground, often being able to travel hundreds of miles toward the sunset without a man having to do one hour's work in order to prepare the road for the heaviest wagons and teams.

The road from Missouri to Santa Fé, N. M., up the Arkansas River, a distance of 800 miles, was very much like the one up the Platte River, and over which millions of pounds of merchandise were carried, and where oxen almost invariably, but sometimes mules, did the work and subsisted without a bite of any other food than that obtained from the grasses that grew by the roadside.

The roads all running west from the Missouri River came up the valleys of the Platte, Kansas, or Arkansas rivers, running directly from the mountains to the Missouri River. These rivers had wide channels, low banks, and sandy bottoms, into which a thousand animals could go at one time, if necessary, for drink, and spread over the surface, so as not to be in each other's way, and whatever disturbance they made in the water, in the way of offal or anything of that kind, was soon overcome by the filtering of the water through the sand, which kept it pure, and thousands of men and animals could find purer water on account of these conditions.

Then again the first expedient in the way of fuel was what was called buffalo chips, which was the offal from the buffalo after lying and being dried by the sun; and, strange to say, the economy of nature was such, in this particular, that the large number of work-animals left at every camping-place fuel sufficient, after being dried by the sun, to supply the necessities of the next caravan or party that travelled along. In this way the fuel supply was inexhaustible while animals travelled and fed upon the grasses.

This, however, did not apply to travel east of the Missouri River, as the offal from the animals there soon became decomposed and was entirely worthless for fuel purposes. This was altogether owing to the difference in the grasses that grew west of the Missouri River on the plains and in the Rocky Mountains and that which grew in the States east of the Missouri. Thus the fuel supply was sufficient for the largest organisations of people who, in those days, were travelling on the plains. Armies, small and great, that found it necessary to cross the plains, found sufficient supply of this fuel, and it seemed to be a necessity supplied by nature on the vast open and untimbered plains lying between the Missouri River and the Rocky Mountains, far beyond the Canadian line to the north, without which it would have been practically impossible to have crossed the plains with any degree of comfort, and in cold weather would have been absolutely impossible.

The small groups of timber growing along the streams would soon have been exhausted if used for fuel, and there would have been nothing to supply those who came later.

History records no other instance of like nature, where an immense area of country had the same necessity and where that necessity was supplied in such a manner as on the vast plains west of the Missouri River. These chips would lay for several years in perfect condition for fuel.

CHAPTER 17

"The Jayhawkers of 1849"

In this year a number of gentlemen made up a party and started for the far West. During that fearful journey they were lost for three months in the "Great American Desert," the region marked on the map as the "unexplored region." General Fremont, with all the patronage of the government at his command, tried to cross this desert at several points, but failed in every attempt. This desert is bounded by the Rocky Mountains and Wasatch range on the east and the Sierra Nevada on the west. From either side running streams sink near the base of the mountains, and no water exists except alkali and the hot springs impregnated with nitre.

The party arrived at Salt Lake late in the season of '49. It was thought by the older members of the company to be too late to cross the Sierra Nevada by the northern routes. No wagon had ever made the trip to the Pacific Coast by way of the Spanish Trail from Santa Fé to the Pacific, but it was determined to undertake this perilous journey. Captain Hunt, commander of the Mormon Battalion in the Mexican War, agreed to pilot the train through to Pueblo de los Angeles for the sum of $1,200. The weather south being too warm for comfortable travel, the party remained in Salt Lake City two months, leaving that place October 3, 1849. Upon their arrival at Little Salt Lake, a few restless comrades, angry that the party did not go through by the northern route, formed a band and determined to cross the desert at all hazards, and thus save hundreds of miles' travel via Los Angeles route. The sufferings they endured can not be described.

The survivors have since been scattered through the country, and have never come together since they separated at Santa Barbara, on the Pacific, February 4, 1850, until the twenty-third anniversary of their arrival was celebrated at the residence of Col. John B. Colton.

The following letter will explain:

Galesburg, Ill., January 12, 1872.

Dear Sir: You are invited to attend a reunion of the "Jayhawkers of '49," on the 5th day of February next at 10 o'clock in the forenoon, at my house, to talk over old times and compare notes, after the lapse of twenty-three years from the time when the "Jayhawkers" crossed the "Great American Desert."

In the event that you can not be present, will you write a letter immediately on receipt of this, to be read on that occasion, giving all the news and reminiscences that will be of interest to the old crowd?

Yours fraternally,

John B. Colton.

A short sketch of the party's wanderings may not be amiss. On the 5th of April, 1849, a large party of men, with oxen and wagons, started from Galesburg, Ill., and vicinity for the then newly discovered gold-fields of California. To distinguish their party from other parties who went the same year, they jestingly took the name of "Jayhawkers," and that name has clung to them through all the years that have come and gone.

They encountered no trouble until after leaving Little Salt Lake, when taking the directions given them by Indian Walker and Ward—old mountaineers, who gave them a diagram and told them they could save 500 miles to the mines in California by taking the route directed—the Jayhawkers branched off from the main body. They found nothing as represented, and became lost on the desert, wandering for months, traversing the whole length of the Great American Desert, which Fremont, with all the aid of the government at his call, could not cross the shortest way, and laid it down on the map as the "unexplored region."

They cut up their wagons on Silver Mountain and made of them pack-saddles for their cattle. Here thirteen of their number branched off, on New Year's day, taking what jerked beef they could carry, and started due west over the mountains, which the main party could not do on account of their cattle, but when they came to a mountain they took a southerly course around it. Of these thirteen, but two lived to get through, and they were found by ranch Indians in a helpless condition, and brought in and cared for. They had cast lots and lived on each other until but two remained. When questioned afterward in

ALEXANDER MAJORS.
R. H. HASLAM ("Pony Bob"). PRENTISS INGRAHAM.
JOHN B. COLTON. W. F. CODY ("Buffalo Bill").

regard to their trip, they burst into tears and could not talk of it.

The main body of Jayhawkers kept their cattle, for they were their only hope; on these they lived, and the cattle lived on the bitter sagebrush and grease-wood, except when they occasionally found an oasis with water and a little grass upon it. The feet of the cattle were worn down until the blood marked their every step. Then the boys wrapped their feet in raw hides, as they did their own. Many died from exposure, hunger, and thirst, and were buried in the drifting sands where they fell, while those who were left moved on, weak and tottering, not knowing whose turn would be next. But for their cattle, not a man could have lived through that awful journey. They ate the hide, the blood, the refuse, and picked the bones in camp, making jerked beef of the balance to take along with them. People who are well fed, who have an abundance of the good things of life, say: "I would not eat this; I would not eat that; I'd starve first." They are not in a position to judge. Hunger swallows up every other feeling, and man in a starving condition is as savage as a wild beast.

After many desert wanderings and untold suffering, they at last struck a low pass in the Sierra Nevada Mountains, and emerged suddenly into the Santa Clara Valley, which was covered with grass and wild oats and flowers, with thousands of fat cattle feeding, a perfect paradise to those famished skeletons of men. There were thirty-four of the party who lived to reach that valley, and every one shed tears of joy at the sight of the glorious vision spread before them and the suddenness of their deliverance.

The boys shot five head of the cattle, and were eating the raw flesh and fat when the ranch Indians, hearing the firing, came down with all the shooting irons they could muster, but seeing the helpless condition of the party, they rode back to headquarters and reported to Francisco, the Spaniard who owned the ranch and cattle. He came down and invited them to camp in a grove near his home, bade them welcome, and furnished the party with meat, milk, grain, and everything they needed, and kept them until they were recruited and able to go on their way. Verily, he was a good Samaritan. They were strangers, and he took them in; hungry, and he fed them; thirsty, and he gave them drink. In the grand summing up of all things, may the noble Francisco be rewarded a thousandfold.

They reached the Santa Clara Valley the 4th of February, 1850, and on that day each year they celebrate their deliverance by a reunion, where in pleasant companionship and around the festive board they recount reminiscences of the past, and live over again those scenes, when young and hopeful, they lived and suffered together.

There are but eleven of the survivors of that party alive today, (1893), and these are widely scattered east of the Rocky Mountains and on the Pacific Slope. Some are old men, too feeble to travel, and can only be present in spirit and by letter at the annual reunions. Gladly would every Jayhawker welcome one and all of that band, bound together by ties of suffering in a bond of brotherhood which naught but death can sever.

The names and residences of the original party are as follows:

John B. Colton, Kansas City, Mo.
Alonzo C. Clay, Galesburg, Ill.
Capt. Asa Haines, Delong, Knox County, Ill.,
    died March 29, 1889.
Luther A. Richards, Beaver City, Neb.
Charles B. Mecum, Perry, Greene County, Iowa.
John W. Plummer, Toulon, Ill., died June 22, 1892.
Sidney P. Edgerton, Blair, Neb., died January 31, 1880.
Edward F. Bartholomew, Pueblo, Colo., died February 13, 1891.
Urban P. Davidson, Derby P. O., Fremont County, Wyo.
John Groscup, Cahto, Mendocino County, Cal.
Thomas McGrew, died in 1866, in Willamette Valley, Ore.
John Cole, died in Sonora, Cal., in 1852.
John L. West, Coloma, Cal., since died.
William B. Rude, drowned in the Colorado River,
    New Mexico, in 1862.
L. Dow Stevens, San José, Cal.
William Robinson, Maquon, Ill., died in the desert.
—— Harrison, unknown.
Alexander Palmer, Knoxville, Ill., died at Slate Creek,
    Sierra County, Cal., in 1853.
Aaron Larkin, Knoxville, Ill., died at Humboldt, Cal., in 1853.
Marshall G. Edgerton, Galesburg, Ill., died in Montana
    Territory in 1855.
William Isham, Rochester, N.Y., died in the desert.
—— Fish, Oscaloosa, Iowa, died in the desert.
—— Carter, Wisconsin, unknown.
Harrison Frans, Baker City, Baker County, Ore.
Capt. Edwin Doty, Naples, Santa Barbara County, Cal.,

died June 14, 1891.
Bruin Byram, Knoxville, Ill., died in 1863.
Thomas Shannon, Los Gatos, Santa Clara County, Cal.
Rev. J. W. Brier, wife, and three small children, Lodi City, San Joaquin County, Cal.
George Allen, Chico, Cal., died in 1876.
Leander Woolsey, Oakland, Cal., died in 1884.
Man from Oscaloosa, Iowa, name not remembered, died in California.
Charles Clark, Henderson, Ill., died in 1863.
—— Gretzinger, Oscaloosa, Iowa, unknown.

A Frenchman, name unknown, became insane from starvation, wandered from camp near the Sierra Nevada Mountains, captured by the Digger Indians, and was rescued by a United States surveying party fifteen years after.

The following are today, (as at time of first publication), the sole survivors of the Jayhawk party of 1849:

John B. Colton, Kansas City, Mo.
Alonzo G. Clay, Galesburg, Ill.
Luther A. Richards, Beaver City, Neb.
Charles B. Mecum, Perry, Iowa.
Urban P. Davidson, Derby, Wyo.
John Groscup, Cahto, Cal.
L. Dow Stevens, San Jose, Cal.
Rev. J. W. Brier and Mrs. J. W. Brier, Lodi City, Cal.
Harrison Frans, Baker City, Ore.
Thomas Shannon, Los Gatos, Cal.

The last reunion of the Jayhawkers was held at the home of Col. John B. Colton of Kansas City, Mo., just forty-four years after the arrival of the party upon the Pacific Slope.

Of the eleven survivors there were but four able to be present, but the absent ones responded to their invitations with their photographs and letters of good will.

Among the invited guests to meet these old heroes were Col. W. F. Cody (Buffalo Bill), Col. Frank Hatton of the Washington Post, General Van Vliet, Capt. E. D. Millet (an old ranger), and the writer, who wishes the remnant of the little hero band may yet live to enjoy a score more of such delightful meetings.

Chapter 18

Mirages

About September 1, 1848, on my way from Independence, Mo., to Santa Fé, N. M., I met some of the soldiers of General Donaldson's regiment returning from the Mexican War on the Hornather or dry route, lying between the crossing of the Arkansas and Cimarron. It was about noon when we met. I saw them a considerable distance away. They were on horseback, and when they first appeared, the horses' legs looked to be from fifteen to eighteen feet long, and the body of the horses and the riders upon them presented a remarkable picture, apparently extending into the air, rider and horse, forty-five to sixty feet high. This was my first experience with mirage, and it was a marvel to me.

At the same time I could see beautiful clear lakes of water, apparently not more than a mile away, with all the surroundings in the way of bulrushes and other water vegetation common to the margin of lakes. I would have been willing, at that time, to have staked almost anything upon the fact that I was looking upon lakes of pure water. This was my last experience of the kind until I was returning later on in the season, when one forenoon, as my train was on the march, I beheld just ahead the largest buffalo bull that I ever saw. I stopped the train to keep from frightening the animal away, took the gun out of my wagon, which was in front, and started off to get a shot at the immense fellow, but when I had walked about eighty yards in his direction, I discovered that it was nothing more nor less than a little coyote, which would not have weighed more than thirty pounds upon the scales.

The person who imagines for a minute that there is nothing in the great desert wastes of the Southwest but sand, cacti, and villainous reptiles is deluded. It is one of the most common fallacies to write down these barren places as devoid of beauty and usefulness. The rhymester who made Robinson Crusoe exclaim, "Oh, solitude, where are the charms that sages have seen in thy face?" never stood on a sand-dune or a pile of volcanic rock in this South-western country just at the break of day or as the sun went down, else the rhyme would never have been made to jingle.

To one who has never seen the famous mirages which Dame Nature paints with a lavish hand upon the horizon that bounds an Arizona desert, it is difficult to convey an intelligent portrait of these magnificent phenomena. And one who has looked upon these incomparable transformation scenes, the Titanic paintings formed by nature's curious slight-of-hand, can never forget them. They form the memories of a lifetime.

Arizona is rich in mirage phenomena, which, owing to the peculiar dryness of the atmosphere, are more vivid and of longer duration than in other parts. The variety of subjects which from time to time have been presented likewise gives them an unusual interest. Almost every one who has lived in the Territory any length of time, and one who has merely passed through, especially on the Southern Pacific Route, is familiar with the common water mirage which appears at divers places along the railroad. The most common section in which this phenomenon may be seen is between Tucson and Red Rock, and through the entire stretch of the Salton Basin from Ogilby to Indio.

Here in the early morning or in the late afternoon, if the atmospheric conditions be right, lakes, river, and lagoons of water can be seen from the train windows. Ofttimes the shimmering surface is dotted with tiny islands, and the shadows of umbrageous foliage are plainly seen reflected in the supposed water; yet an investigation shows nothing but long rods of sand-drifts or saline deposits.

Animals as well as men are deceived by these freaks of the atmosphere. Many instances are recorded where whole bands of cattle have rushed from the grazing grounds across the hot parched plains in pursuit of the constantly retreating water phantom, until they perish from exhaustion, still in sight of running brooks and surging springs. Prior to the advent of the railroad through this region, when overland passengers passed by on the old Yuma road to San Diego, scores of adventurous spirits perished in chasing this illusive phantom. It is said that one entire company of soldiers was thus inveigled from the highway and perished to a man.

One of the most interesting sights of this class is to be seen almost any time of the year in Mohave County, down in the region of the Big Sandy. Here for leagues upon leagues the ground is strewn with volcanic matter and basalt. It is one of the hottest portions of the continent, and except in the winter months it is almost unendurable by man or beast.

At a point where the main road from the settlements on the Colorado to Kingman turns toward the east, there are a number of volcanic buttes. At these buttes just before sunrise the famous cantilever bridge which spans the Colorado River near the Needles, seventy miles distant, is plainly visible, together with the moving trains and crew. The train has the appearance of being perhaps an eighth of a mile distant, and every motion on board, the smoke, the escaping steam, are as natural and vivid as though not a hundred yards away.

At this same point huge mountains are seen to lift themselves up bodily and squat down again in the highway. Near these buttes, which are known as the Evil Ones, away back in the sixties a small force of cavalry was making its way from Fort Yuma to Fort Whipple. Owing to the extreme heat during the day, and as a further precaution against the hostile Indians, they were obliged to march at night, finding shelter in some mountain *cañon* during the day.

Shortly after daybreak, as they were preparing to go into camp, a whole legion of painted devils appeared on their front and hardly a quarter of a mile distant. The troops were thrown into confusion, and an order was immediately given to break ranks, and every man concealed himself behind the rocks, awaiting the attack which all felt must necessarily end in massacre.

For some minutes the Indians were seen to parley and gesticulate with each other, but they gave no signs of having noticed their hereditary foe. The unhappy troopers, however, were not kept in suspense long. As the great red disk of the day began to mount slowly up over the adjoining mountains, the redskins vanished as noiselessly and as suddenly as they had appeared.

Used as they were to treachery, and fearing some uncanny trick, the soldiers maintained their position throughout the long hot day, nor did they attempt to move until late in the night. Some weeks later it was learned from captives that on that very morning a band of nearly one thousand Chinhuevas and Wallapais were lying in wait for this same command but ninety miles up the river, expecting the soldiers by that route.

The most remarkable of all the mirages which have been witnessed in Arizona, at least by white man's eyes, was seen some years ago by an entire train-load of passengers on the Southern Pacific Railroad, near the small eating station of Maricopa, thirty-five miles below Phoenix. The train was due at the eating station at 6.30 a. m.

At 6.15 o'clock it stopped at a small water-tank a few miles east. During this stop the trainmen and such of the passengers as were awake were amazed to see spring out of the ground on the sky a magnificent city. The buildings were of the old Spanish and Morisco architecture, and were mostly adobe. Spacious courtyards lay before the astonished lookers-on, filled with all varieties of tropical fruits and vegetation.

Men and women clothed in the picturesque garbs of Old Spain were seen hurrying along the narrow, irregular streets to the principal edifice, which had the appearance of a church. Had the astonished spectators been picked up bodily and landed in one of the provincial towns of Seville or Andalusia, they would not have seen a more dazzling array of stately *senoras* and laughing black-eyed *muchachas* of the land of forever *manana*.

But the vision lasted much less time than it takes to write of the strange occurrence. It vanished as mysteriously as it came. Of course all of the hysterical women fainted. That is one of woman's prerogatives, in lieu of an explanation.

This phenomenon remained unsolved for two or three years. About that time, after the mirage was seen, a young civil engineer who was among the witnesses was engaged on the Gulf coast survey from the headwaters below Yuma to Guaymas. In the course of his labours he found himself at the old Mexican pueblo of Altar, and there he saw the original of the picture in the sky seen three years before near Maricopa Station. The distance, as a buzzard flies, from Maricopa to Altar is more than a hundred miles.

The native tribes are very superstitious concerning the mirage, and when one is once observed, that locality receives a wide berth in the future.

In the secluded Jim-Jam Valley of the San Bernardino Mountains there are the most marvellous mirages known to the world. The wonderful mirages of the Mojave Desert have been talked about a great deal, and they are entitled to all the prominence they have had. But those of the Jim-Jam Valley are far more wonderful than these.

It is called Jim-Jam Valley because of the strange things seen there, and I defy any man, however sound of mind he may be, to go in there and not think he has "got 'em" before he gets out.

This valley is about twenty-five miles long by fifteen miles wide. It is uninhabited. It is bordered by the main San Bernardino range on the east, and by a spur of the Sierra Magdalenas on the west. There is no well-defined trail through the heart of it. The valley is a desert. The surrounding mountains are terribly serrated and cut up. The peaks are jagged. Altogether the surroundings are weird and forbidding.

Leaving Fisk's ranch on the trail at the foot of the Sierra Magdalenas, you climb an easy grade to Dead Man's Pass, the entrance to the valley.

Go in, and pretty soon you see lakes, and running rivers, and green borders, and flying water-fowl. Willows spring up here and there, and in the distance you see water-lilies.

What you behold contrasts finely with the rugged mountains, and you are charmed with it, and go on thinking you have struck an earthly paradise. Indian camps appear in view, and little oarsmen propel fantastic crafts upon the waters. Advancing still farther, dimly outlined forms may be seen, and the pantomime reminds you of a strange hobgoblin dance.

Sometimes a storm brews in the valley, and then the scene is all the more terrible. Forked lightning blazes about, and strange, uncouth animals, differing from any you have ever read about, are to be seen there.

These phenomena are seen for a stretch of about fifteen miles, up and down the middle of the valley principally, and they have been viewed by a great many people. They can not understand why the forms of the mirage, if such it may be called, are so much more strange there than on the Mojave Desert.

Everybody is in awe of the valley, and there are mighty few men, however nervy they may be ordinarily, who care to go there a second time.

CHAPTER 19

The First Stage into Denver

In the winter of 1858, while my partner, Mr. W. H. Russell, John S. Jones, a citizen of Pettis County, Mo., and myself were all in Washington, D. C., which was about the time that the Pike's Peak excitement was at its highest pitch, Messrs. Jones and Russell conceived the idea (I do not know from which one it emanated), and concluded to put a line of daily coaches in operation between the Missouri River and Denver City, when Denver was but a few months old. They came to me with the proposition to take hold of the enterprise with them.

I told them I could not consent to do so, for it would be impossible to make such a venture, at such an early period of development of this country, a paying institution, and urgently advised them to let the enterprise alone, for the above stated reasons. They, however, paid no attention to my protest, and went forward with their plans, bought 1,000 fine Kentucky mules and a sufficient number of Concord coaches to supply a daily coach each way between the Missouri River and Denver. At that time Leavenworth was the starting point on the Missouri. A few months later, however, they made Atchison the eastern terminus of the line and Denver the western.

They bought their mules and coaches on credit, giving their notes, payable in ninety days; sent men out to establish a station every ten to fifteen miles from Leavenworth due west, going up the Smoky Hill fork of the Kansas River, through the Territory of Kansas, and direct to Denver.

The line was organised, stations built and put in running shape in remarkably quick time.

They made their daily trips in six days, travelling about one hundred miles every twenty-four hours. The first stage ran into Denver on May 17, 1859. It was looked upon as a great success, so far as putting the enterprise in good shape was concerned, but when the ninety days expired and the notes fell due they were unable to meet them. And in spite of my protests in the commencement of the organisation as against having anything to do with it, it became necessary for Russell, Majors & Waddell to meet the obligation that Jones & Russell had entered into in organising and putting the stock on the line. To save our partner we had to pay the debts of the concern and take the mules and coaches, or, in other words, all the paraphernalia of the line, to secure us for the money we had advanced.

The institution then having become the property of Russell, Majors & Waddell, we continued to run it daily. A few months after that, we bought out the semi-monthly line of Hockaday & Liggett, that was running from St. Joseph, Mo., to Salt Lake City, thinking that by blending the two lines we might bring the business up to where it would pay expenses, if nothing more.

This we failed in, for the lines, even after being blended, did not nearly meet expenses. Messrs. Hockaday & Liggett had a few stages, light, cheap vehicles, and but a few mules, and 110 stations along the route. They travelled the same team for several hundreds of miles before changing, stopping every few hours and turning them loose to graze, and then hitching them up again and going along.

I made a trip in the fall of 1858 from St. Joseph, Mo., to Salt Lake City in their coaches. It was twenty-one days from the time I left St. Joseph until I reached Salt Lake, travelling at short intervals day and night. As soon as we bought them out we built good stations and stables every ten to fifteen miles all the way from Missouri to Salt Lake, and supplied them with hay and grain for the horses and provisions for the men, so they would only have to drive a team from one station to the next, changing at every station.

Instead of our schedule time being twenty-two days, as it was with Hockaday & Liggett, and running two per month, we ran a stage each way every day and made the schedule time ten days, a distance of 1,200 miles. We continued running this line from the summer of 1859 until March, 1862, when it fell into the hands of Ben Holliday. From the summer of 1859 to 1862 the line was run from Atchison to Fort Kearney and from Fort Kearney to Fort Laramie, up the Sweet Water route and South Pass, and on to Salt Lake City.

This is the route also run by the Pony Express, each pony starting from St. Joseph instead of Atchison, Kan., from which the stages started. We had on this line about one thousand Kentucky mules and

300 smaller-sized mules to run on through the mountain portion of the line, and a large number of Concord coaches. It was as fine a line, considering the mules, coaches, drivers, and general outfitting, perhaps, as was ever organised in this or any other country, from the beginning.

And it was very fortunate for the government and the people that such a line was organised and in perfect running condition on the middle route when the late war commenced, as it would have been impossible to carry mails on the route previously patronised by the government, which ran from San Francisco *via* Los Angeles, El Paso, Fort Smith, and St. Louis, for the Southern people would have interfered with it, and would not have allowed it to run through that portion of the country during the war.

It turned out that Senator Gwin's original idea with reference to running a pony express from the Missouri River to Sacramento to prove the practicability of that route at all seasons of the year was well taken, and the stage line as well as the pony proved to be of vital importance in carrying the mails and Government dispatches.

It so transpired that the firm of Russell, Majors & Waddell had to pay the fiddler, or the entire expense of organising both the stage line and the pony express, at a loss, as it turned out, of hundreds of thousands of dollars. After the United States mail was given to this line it became a paying institution, but it went into the hands of Holliday just before the first quarterly payment of $100,000 was made. The government paid $800,000 a year for carrying the mails from San Francisco to Missouri, made in quarterly payments.

The part of the line that Russell, Majors & Waddell handled received $400,000, and Butterfield & Co. received $400,000 for carrying the mails from Salt Lake to California. During the war there was a vast amount of business, both in express and passenger travelling, and it was the only available practicable line of communication between California and the States east of the Rocky Mountains.

CHAPTER 20

The Gold Fever

During the winter of 1858-59 the public generally, throughout the United States, began to give publicity to a great gold discovery reported to have been made in the Pike's Peak region of the Rocky Mountains.

From week to week, as time passed, more extended accounts were given, until the reports became fabulous.

The discovery was reported to have been made in Cherry Creek, at or near its junction with the South Platte River, and one of the newspapers at the time, published in Cleveland, Ohio, came out, giving a cut which was claimed to be a map of the country. Pike's Peak was given as the central figure. The South Fork of the Platte River was represented as flowing out from the mountain near its base, and Cherry Creek as coming out of a gorge in the mountain's side, and forming a junction with the Platte in the low lands, at which point Denver was designated.

Reports went so far as to state that gold was visible in the sands of the creek-bed, and that the banks would pay from grass roots to bed rock.

People became wild with excitement, and a stampede to Pike's Peak appeared inevitable.

The great question with the excited people was as to the shortest, cheapest, and quickest way to get to the country, with little thought of personal safety or comfort, or as to how they should get back in the event of failure. But the problem was soon believed to have been solved to the satisfaction of all concerned.

A brilliant idea took possession of the fertile brain of an energetic Buckeye citizen, and a plan was conceived and to an extent put in execution. A canal-boat which had been converted into a steam tug was secured, not only for the purpose of transporting the multitudes from Cleveland to Denver, but to transport the millions of treasures back to civilization, or, as it was then put, "to God's country." Passengers were advertised for at $100 per head; the route given as follows: From Cleveland, Ohio, via the lake to Chicago, thence via Illinois Canal and River to the Mississippi River, then to the mouth of the Missouri River and up the Missouri to the mouth of the Platte River, and, thence up the Platte to Denver, and it was with pride that this boat was advertised as the first to form a line of steamers to regularly navigate the last named stream.

Of course this trip was never made, for in fact, at certain seasons of the year, it would be difficult to float a two-inch plank down the river from Denver to the Missouri, and yet this is but illustrative of the hundreds of visionary, crude and novel plans conceived and adopted by the thousands of so-called Pike's Peakers who swarmed the plains between Denver and the border during the early part of 1859.

Having caught the fever, and there being no remedy for the disease equal to the gold hunter's experience, horses and wagon were secured and, with travelling companions, the trip was made by land. Many novel experiences to the participants occurred during that trip.

At Leavenworth one of my companions concluded to economize, which he did by piloting six yoke of oxen across the plains for me. He drove into Denver in the morning and drove out of it in the evening of the same day, fully convinced (as he himself stated) that all reports of the country were either humbugs or greatly exaggerated, and that he had seen and knew all that was worth seeing and knowing of that land. I suggested the advisability of further investigation before moving on, but not being favourable to delay, and suiting himself to his means, he secured an ox and cart that had been brought in from the Red River of the North, and loading it with all necessary supplies headed for Denver, with a determination so aptly and forcibly expressed in the usual motto, "Pike's Peak or bust." All went well until he reached the Little Blue River in Kansas, when he "busted," or at least the cart did, and the result was the location of a ranch on that stream and an end to his westward career.

Thus Kansas is largely indebted for her early and rapid settlement to the discovery of gold in Colorado, and to the misfortunes of many of the Pike's Peakers who, for some cause, failed to reach the end desired, and who were thus compelled to stop and become settlers of that now great State.

Shortly before the time of which I write, June, 1859, Horace Greeley passed through Leavenworth en route for Denver, and thousands of people were to be found in every principal town and city, from St. Louis to Council Bluffs (there was no Omaha at that time), who were awaiting his report, which was daily expected, and for once, at least, the New York *Tribune* was in demand on the borders. I may say here that Horace Greeley was *dead-headed* through to California.

In the early part of July came a favourable report in the *Tribune*, and at that time a shipment of gold was made from Denver and put on exhibition in one of the banks at Leavenworth.

Thus new life was given to the immigration movement, and soon the towns along the border were largely relieved of their floating population, and the plains at once became alive with a moving, struggling mass of humanity, moving westward in the mad rush for the goldfields of Pike's Peak.

Among my friends an association was formed and the following party organised, viz.: Alfred H. Miles and his wife, their son George T., and two daughters, Fannie D. and Emma C. Miles, with William McLelland and P. A. Simmons.

They outfitted with two wagons, four yoke of oxen, two saddle-mules, one cow, and all supplies presumed to be sufficient for at least one year. On the first day of August, 1859, they moved out from Leavenworth, happy and full of "great expectations" for the future. Forty-nine days were spent in making the drive, and then they landed in Denver on the eighteenth day of the following month. And here let me say, that I believe this party of seven proved an exception to the rule, in this, that every member of it became a permanent settler, and for the last thirty-three years they have been actively connected with, and identified in, the various departments of life and business, both public and private.

All are yet living and residents of the State, (at time of first publication), except Mrs. Miles, who recently passed to a higher life, respected and loved by all who knew her; and I here venture the opinion that no other party of emigrants in this country, of equal number, can show a better record.

Many novel events occurred on this trip also, but to mention all the new and novel experiences incident to an expedition of that kind would require more than the allotted space for a chapter. I will, therefore, confine the account to one incident alone which will make manifest the radical changes that are sometimes wrought in the individual lives of people, in a sometimes radically short space of time. Two of the ladies of the party before mentioned arrived in Leavenworth about one month previous to their departure on this trip. They were just graduated from a three years' course of study in a female seminary, and in thirty days from that time they were transported from their boarding-school surroundings to the wilds of the Great American Desert, and after passing into the timberless portion of the great desert, the great query with them was as to how and where they were to secure fuel necessary for culinary purposes; and when informed that it would be necessary to gather and use buffalo chips for that purpose, their incredulity became manifest, and their curiosity was rather increased than satisfied.

When called upon to go, gunny-sack in hand, out from the line of travel to gather the necessary fuel, it was difficult to persuade them they were not being made the victims of a joke; but when finally led into the field of "chips," and the discovery made of their character, the expression upon the face of each would have been a delight to an artist and amusing to the beholder; and to say that the distance between the chip-field and the camp was covered by them in the time rarely, if ever, covered by the native antelope, is to speak without exaggeration.

As before stated, all of the seven members of this party, on their arrival in Denver, became residents and actively identified in the various departments of life and business, and to each and every one there is no spot on the face of this globe that is quite so good, so grand, and so dear as the Centennial State, of which Denver is the centre of their love.

Chapter 21

The Overland Mail

Over thirty-two years ago, when a bachelor occupied the President's mansion at Washington, and there was no Pacific Railroad and no transcontinental telegraph line in operation over the Great American Desert of the old schoolbooks, and the wild Indian was lord of the manor—a true native American sovereign—St. Joseph, Mo., was the western terminus of railway transportation. Beyond that point the traveller bound for the regions of the Occident had his choice of a stage-coach, an ox-team, a pack-mule, or some equally stirring method of reaching San Francisco.

Just at that interesting period in our history—when the gold and silver excitement, and other local advantages of the Pacific Coast, had concentrated an enterprising population and business at San Francisco and the adjacent districts—the difficulty of communication with the East was greatly deplored, and the rapid overland mail service became an object of general solicitude. In the year 1859 several magnates in Wall Street formed a formidable lobby at Washington in the interests of an overland mail route to California, and asked Congress for a subsidy for carrying the mails overland for one year between New York and San Francisco.

The distance was 1,950 miles. Mr. Russell proposed to cover this distance with a mail line between St. Joseph, Mo., and San Francisco, that would deliver letters at either end of the route within ten days.

Five hundred of the fleetest horses to be procured were immediately purchased, and the services of over two hundred competent men were secured. Eighty of these men were selected for express riders. Light-weights were deemed the most eligible for the purpose; the lighter the man the better for the horse, as some portions of the route had to be traversed at a speed of twenty miles an hour. Relays were established at stations, the distance between which was, in each instance, determined by the character of the country.

These stations dotted a wild, uninhabited expanse of country 2,000 miles wide, infested with road-agents and warlike Indians, who roamed in formidable hunting parties, ready to sacrifice human life with as little unconcern as they would slaughter a buffalo. The Pony Express, therefore, was not only an important, but a daring and romantic enterprise. At each station a sufficient number of horses were kept, and at every third station the thin, wiry, and hardy pony-riders held themselves in readiness to press forward with the mails. These were filled with important business letters and press dispatches from Eastern cities and San Francisco, printed upon tissue paper, and thus especially adapted by their weight for this mode of transportation.

The schedule time for the trip was fixed at ten days. In this manner they supplied the place of the electric telegraph and the lightning express train of the gigantic railway enterprise that subsequently superseded it.

The men were faithful, daring fellows, and their service was full of novelty and adventure. The facility and energy with which they journeyed was a marvel. The news of Abraham Lincoln's election was carried through from St. Joseph to Denver, Colo., 665 miles, in two days and twenty-one hours, the last ten miles having been covered in thirty-one minutes. The last route on the occasion was traversed by Robert H. Haslam, better known as "Pony Bob," who carried the news 120 miles in eight hours and ten minutes, riding from Smith's Creek to Fort Churchill, on the Carson River, Nevada, the first telegraph station on the Pacific Coast.

On another occasion, it is recorded, one of these riders journeyed a single stretch of 300 miles—the other men who should have relieved him being either disabled or indisposed—and reached the terminal station on schedule time.

The distance between relay riders' stations varied from sixty-five to one hundred miles, and often more. The weight to be carried by each was fixed at ten pounds or under, and the charge for transportation was $5 in gold for each half of an ounce. The entire distance between New York City and San Francisco occupied but fourteen days. The riders received from $120 to $125 per month for their arduous services. The pony express enterprise continued for about two years, at the end of which time telegraph service between the Atlantic and Pacific oceans was established. Few men remember those days of excitement and interest. The danger surrounding the riders can not be told. Not only were they remarkable for lightness of weight and energy, but their service required continual vigilance, bravery, and agility. Among their number were skilful guides, scouts, and couriers, accustomed to adventures and hardships on the plains—men of strong wills and wonderful powers of endurance. The horses were mostly half-breed California mustangs, as alert and energetic as their riders, and their part in the service—sure-footed and fleet—was invaluable. Only two minutes were allowed at stations for changing mails and horses. Everybody was on the qui vive. The adventures with which the service was rife are numerous and exciting.

The day of *the first start*, the 3rd of April, 1860, at noon, Harry Roff, mounted on a spirited half-breed broncho, started from Sacramento on his perilous ride, and covered the first twenty miles, including one change, in fifty-nine minutes. On reaching Folson, he changed again and started for Placerville, at the foot of the Sierra Nevada Mountain, fifty-five miles distant. There he connected with "Boston," who took the route to Friday's Station, crossing the eastern summit of the Sierra Nevada. Sam Hamilton next fell into line, and pursued his way to Genoa, Carson City, Dayton, Reed's Station, and Fort Churchill—seventy-five miles.

The entire run, 185 miles, was made in fifteen hours and twenty minutes, and included the crossing of the western summits of the Sierras, through thirty feet of snow. This seems almost impossible, and would have been, had not pack trains of mules and horses kept the trail open. Here "Pony Bob"—Robert H. Haslam—took the road from Fort Churchill to Smith's Creek, 120 miles distant, through a hostile Indian country. From this point Jay G. Kelley rode from Smith's Creek to Ruby Valley, Utah, 116 miles; from Ruby Valley to Deep Creek, H. Richardson, 105 miles; from Deep Creek to Rush Valley, old Camp Floyd, eighty miles; from Camp Floyd to Salt Lake City, fifty miles; George Thacher the last end. This ended the Western Division, under the management of Bolivar Roberts, now in Salt Lake City.

Among the most noted and daring riders of the Pony Express was Hon. William F. Cody, better known as Buffalo Bill, whose reputation is now established the world over. While engaged in the express service, his route lay between Red Buttes and Three Crossings, a distance of 116 miles. It was a most dangerous, long, and lonely trail, including the perilous crossing of the North Platte River, one-half mile wide, and though generally shallow, in some places twelve feet deep, often

A FRONTIER VILLAGE.

much swollen and turbulent. An average of fifteen miles an hour had to be made, including changes of horses, detours for safety, and time for meals. Once, upon reaching Three Crossings, he found that the rider on the next division, who had a route of seventy-six miles, had been killed during the night before, and he was called on to make the extra trip until another rider could be employed. This was a request the compliance with which would involve the most taxing labours and an endurance few persons are capable of; nevertheless, young Cody was promptly on hand for the additional journey, and reached Rocky Ridge, the limit of the second route, on time. This round trip of 384 miles was made without a stop, except for meals and to change horses, and every station on the route was entered on time. This is one of the longest and best ridden pony express journeys ever made.

Pony Bob also had a series of stirring adventures while performing his great equestrian feat, which he thus describes:

> About eight months after the Pony Express commenced operations, the Piute war began in Nevada, and as no regular troops were then at hand, a volunteer corps, raised in California, with Col. Jack Hayes and Henry Meredith—the latter being killed in the first battle at Plymouth Lake—in command, came over the mountains to defend the whites. Virginia City, Nev., then the principal point of interest, and hourly expecting an attack from the hostile Indians, was only in its infancy. A stone hotel on C Street was in course of erection, and had reached an elevation of two stories. This was hastily transformed into a fort for the protection of the women and children.
>
> From the city the signal fires of the Indians could be seen on every mountain peak, and all available men and horses were pressed into service to repel the impending assault of the savages. When I reached Reed's Station, on the Carson River, I found no change of horses, as all those at the station had been seized by the whites to take part in the approaching battle. I fed the animal that I rode, and started for the next station, called Buckland's, afterward known as Fort Churchill, fifteen miles farther down the river. This point was to have been the termination of my journey (as I had been changed from my old route to this one, in which I had had many narrow escapes and been twice wounded by Indians), as I had ridden seventy-five miles, but to my great astonishment, the other rider refused to go on.

"Pony Bob."

The superintendent, W. C. Marley, was at the station, but all his persuasion could not prevail on the rider, Johnnie Richardson, to take the road. Turning then to me, Marley said:
'Bob, I will give you $50 if you make this ride.'
I replied:
'I will go you once.'
Within ten minutes, when I had adjusted my Spencer rifle—a seven-shooter—and my Colt's revolver, with two cylinders ready for use in case of an emergency, I started. From the station onward was a lonely and dangerous ride of thirty-five miles, without a change, to the Sink of the Carson. I arrived there all right, however, and pushed on to Sand's Spring, through an alkali bottom and sand-hills, thirty miles farther, without a drop of water all along the route. At Sand's Springs I changed horses, and continued on to Cold Springs, a distance of thirty-seven miles. Another change, and a ride of thirty miles more, brought me to Smith's Creek. Here I was relieved by J. G. Kelley. I had ridden 185 miles, stopping only to eat and change horses.
After remaining at Smith's Creek about nine hours, I started to retrace my journey with the return express. When I arrived at Cold Springs, to my horror I found that the station had been attacked by Indians, and the keeper killed and all the horses taken away. What course to pursue I decided in a moment—I would go on. I watered my horse—having ridden him thirty miles on time, he was pretty tired—and started for Sand Springs, thirty-seven miles away. It was growing dark, and my road lay through heavy sage-brush, high enough in some places to conceal a horse. I kept a bright lookout, and closely watched every motion of my poor horse's ears, which is a signal for danger in an Indian country. I was prepared for a fight, but the stillness of the night and the howling of the wolves and coyotes made cold chills run through me at times, but I reached Sand Springs in safety and reported what had happened.
Before leaving I advised the station-keeper to come with me to the Sink of the Carson, for I was sure the Indians would be upon him the next day. He took my advice, and so probably saved his life, for the following morning Smith's Creek was attacked. The whites, however, were well protected in the shelter of a stone house, from which they fought the Indians for four days. At the end of that time they were relieved by the

appearance of about fifty volunteers from Cold Springs. These men reported that they had buried John Williams, the brave station-keeper of that station, but not before he had been nearly devoured by wolves.

When I arrived at the Sink of the Carson, I found the station men badly frightened, for they had seen some fifty warriors, decked out in their war-paint and reconnoitring the station. There were fifteen white men here, well armed and ready for a fight. The station was built of *adobe*, and was large enough for the men and ten or fifteen horses, with a fine spring of water within ten feet of it. I rested here an hour, and after dark started for Buckland's, where I arrived without a mishap and only three and a half hours behind the schedule time. I found Mr. Marley at Buckland's, and when I related to him the story of the Cold Springs tragedy and my success, he raised his previous offer of $50 for my ride to $100. I was rather tired, but the excitement of the trip had braced me up to withstand the fatigue of the journey. After the rest of one and one-half hours, I proceeded over my own route, from Buckland's to Friday's Station, crossing the western summit of the Sierra Nevada. I had travelled 380 miles within a few hours of schedule time, and surrounded by perils on every hand.

After the "Overland Pony Express" was discontinued, "Pony Bob" was employed by Wells, Fargo & Co., as a pony express rider, in the prosecution of their transportation business. His route was between Virginia City, Nev., and Friday's Station, and return, about one hundred miles, every twenty-four hours, schedule time ten hours. This engagement continued for more than a year; but as the Union Pacific Railway gradually extended its line and operations, the pony express business as gradually diminished. Finally the track was completed to Reno, Nev., twenty-three miles from Virginia City, and over this route "Pony Bob" rode for over six months, making the run every day, with fifteen horses, inside of one hour. When the telegraph line was completed, the pony express over this route was withdrawn, and "Pony Bob" was sent to Idaho, to ride the company's express route of 100 miles, with one horse, from Queen's River to the Owhyee River. He was at the former station when Major McDermott was killed, at the breaking out of the Modoc war.

On one of his rides he passed the remains of ninety Chinamen who had been killed by the Indians, only one escaping to tell the tale, and whose bodies lay bleaching in the sun for a distance of more than ten miles from the mouth of Ive's Cañon to Crooked Creek. This was "Pony Bob's" last experience as a pony express rider. His successor, Sye Macaulas, was killed the first trip he tried to make. Bob bought a Flathead Indian pony at Boise City, Idaho, and started for Salt Lake City, 400 miles away, where his brother-in-law, Joshua Hosmer, was United States Marshal. Here "Pony Bob" was appointed a deputy, but not liking the business, was again employed by Theodore Tracy—Wells-Fargo's agent—as first messenger from that city to Denver after Ben Holliday had sold out to Wells, Fargo & Co.—a distance of 720 miles by stage—which position Bob filled a long time.

"Pony Bob" is now, (at time of first publication), a resident of Chicago, where he is engaged in business.

CHAPTER 22

The Pony Express and its Brave Riders

During the winter of 1859, Mr. W. H. Russell, of our firm, while in Washington, D. C., met and became acquainted with Senator Gwin of California. The Senator was very anxious to establish a line of communication between California and the States east of the Rocky Mountains, which would be more direct than that known as the Butterfield route, running at that time from San Francisco *via* Los Angeles, Cal.; thence across the Colorado River and up the valley of the Gila; thence via El Paso and through Texas, crossing the Arkansas River at Fort Gibson, and thence to St. Louis, Mo.

This route, the senator claimed, was entirely too long; that the requirements of California demanded a more direct route, which would make quicker passage than could be made on such a circuitous, route as the Butterfield line.

Knowing that Russell, Majors & Waddell were running a daily stage between the Missouri River and Salt Lake City, and that they were also heavily engaged in the transportation of government stores on the same line, he asked Mr. Russell if his company could not be induced to start a pony express, to run over its stage line to Salt Lake City, and from thence to Sacramento; his object being to test the practicability of crossing the Sierra Nevadas, as well as the Rocky Mountains, with a daily line of communication.

After various consultations between these gentlemen, from time to time, the senator urging the great necessity of such an experiment, Mr. Russell consented to take hold of the enterprise, provided he could get his partners, Mr. Waddell and myself, to join him.

With this understanding, he left Washington and came west to Fort

Leavenworth, Kan., to consult us. After he explained the object of the enterprise, and we had well considered it, we both decided that it could not be made to pay expenses. This decision threw quite a damper upon the ardour of Mr. Russell, and he strenuously insisted we should stand by him, as he had committed himself to Senator Gwin before leaving Washington, assuring him he could get his partners to join him, and that he might rely on the project being carried through, and saying it would be very humiliating to his pride to return to Washington and be compelled to say the scheme had fallen through from lack of his partners' confidence.

He urged us to reconsider, stating the importance attached to such an undertaking, and relating the facts Senator Gwin had laid before him, which were that all his attempts to get a direct thoroughfare opened between the State of California and the Eastern States had proved abortive, for the reason that when the question of establishing a permanent central route came up, his colleagues, or fellow senators, raised the question of the impassability of the mountains on such a route during the winter months; that the members from the Northern States were opposed to giving the whole prestige of such a thoroughfare to the extreme southern route; that this being the case, it had actually become a necessity to demonstrate, if it were possible to do so, that a central or middle route could be made practicable during the winter as well as summer months.

That as soon as we demonstrated the feasibility of such a scheme he (Senator Gwin) would use all his influence with Congress to get a subsidy to help pay the expenses of such a line on the thirty-ninth to forty-first parallel of latitude, which would be central between the extreme north and south; that he could not ask for the subsidy at the start with any hope of success, as the public mind had already accepted the idea that such a route open at all seasons of the year was an impossibility; that as soon as we proved to the contrary, he would come to our aid with a subsidy.

After listening to all Mr. Russell had to say upon the subject, we concluded to sustain him in the undertaking, and immediately went to work to organise what has since been known as "The Pony Express."

As above stated, we were already running a daily stage between the Missouri River and Salt Lake City, and along this line stations were located every ten or twelve miles, which we utilized for the Pony Express, but were obliged to build stations between Salt Lake City and

Sacramento, Cal.

Within sixty days or thereabouts from the time we agreed to undertake the enterprise, we were ready to start ponies, one from St. Joseph, Mo., and the other from Sacramento, Cal., on the same day. At that time there was telegraphic communication between the East and St. Joseph, Mo., and between San Francisco and Sacramento, Cal.

The quickest time that had ever been made with any message between San Francisco and New York, over the Butterfield line, which was the southern route, was twenty-one days. Our Pony Express shortened the time to ten days, which was our schedule time, without a single failure, being a difference of eleven days.

To do the work of the Pony Express required between four hundred and five hundred horses, about one hundred and ninety stations, two hundred men for station-keepers, and eighty riders; riders made an average ride of thirty-three and one-third miles. In doing this each man rode three ponies on his part of the route; some of the riders, however, rode much greater distances in times of emergency.

The Pony Express carried messages written on tissue paper, weighing one-half ounce, a charge of $5 being made for each dispatch carried.

As anticipated, the amount of business transacted over this line was not sufficient to pay one-tenth of the expenses, to say nothing about the amount of capital invested. In this, however, we were not disappointed, for we knew, as stated in the outset, that it could not be made a paying institution, and was undertaken solely to prove that the route over which it ran could be made a permanent thoroughfare for travel at all seasons of the year, proving, as far as the paramount object was concerned, a complete success.

Two important events transpired during the term of the Pony's existence; one was the carrying of President Buchanan's last message to Congress, in December, 1860, from the Missouri River to Sacramento, a distance of two thousand miles, in eight days and some hours. The other was the carrying of President Lincoln's inaugural address of March 4, 1861, over the same route in seven days and, I think, seventeen hours, being the quickest time, taking the distance into consideration, on record in this or any other country, as far as I know.

One of the most remarkable feats ever accomplished was made by F. X. Aubery, who travelled the distance of 800 miles, between Santa Fé, N. M., and Independence, Mo., in five days and thirteen hours. This ride, in my opinion, in one respect was the most remarkable one ever made by any man. The entire distance was ridden without stopping to rest, and having a change of horses only once in every one hundred or two hundred miles. He kept a lead horse by his side most of the time, so that when the one he was riding gave out entirely, he changed the saddle to the extra horse, left the horse he had been riding and went on again at full speed.

At the time he made this ride, in much of the territory he passed through he was liable to meet hostile Indians, so that his adventure was daring in more ways than one. In the first place, the man who attempted to ride 800 miles in the time he did took his life in his hands. There is perhaps not one man in a million who could have lived to finish such a journey.

Mr. Aubery was a Canadian Frenchman, of low stature, short limbs, built, to use a homely simile, like a jack-screw, and was in the very zenith of his manhood, full of pluck and daring.

It was said he made this ride upon a bet of $1,000 that he could cover the distance in eight days.

One year previous to this, in 1852, he made a bet he could do the same distance in ten days. The result was he travelled it in a little over eight days, hence his bet he could make the ride in 1853 in eight days, the result of that trip showing he consumed little more than half that time.

I was well acquainted with and did considerable business with Aubery during his years of freighting. I met him when he was making his famous ride, at a point on the Santa Fé Road called Rabbit Ear. He passed my train at a full gallop without asking a single question as to the danger of Indians ahead of him.

After his business between St. Louis and Santa Fé ceased, his love for adventure and his daring enterprise prompted him to make a trip from New Mexico to California with sheep, which he disposed of at good prices, and returned to New Mexico.

Immediately upon his return he met a friend, a Major Weightman of the United States Army, who was a great admirer of his pluck and daring. Weightman was at that time editor of a small paper called the Santa Fé *Herald*. At their meeting, as was the custom of the time, they called for drinks. Their glasses were filled and they were ready to drink, when Aubery asked Weightman why he had published a damned lie about his trip to California. Instead of taking his drink, Weightman tossed the contents of his glass in Aubery's face. Aubery made a motion to draw his pistol and shoot, when Weightman, knowing the danger, drew his knife and stabbed Aubery through the heart, from which blow he dropped dead upon the floor.

The whole affair was enacted in one or two seconds. From the time they started to take a friendly drink till Aubery was lying dead on the floor less time elapsed than it takes to tell the story.

This tragedy was the result of rash words hastily spoken, and proves that friends, as well as enemies, should be careful and considerate in the language they use toward others.

In the spring of 1860 Bolivar Roberts, superintendent of the Western Division of the Pony Express, came to Carson City, Nev., which was then in St. Mary's County, Utah, to engage riders and station men for a pony express route about to be established across the great plains by Russell, Majors & Waddell. In a few days fifty or sixty men were engaged, and started out across the Great American Desert to establish stations, etc. Among that number the writer can recall to memory the following: Bob Haslam ("Pony Bob"), Jay G. Kelley, Sam Gilson, Jim Gilson, Jim McNaughton, Bill McNaughton, Jose Zowgaltz, Mike Kelley, Jimmy Buckton, and "Irish Tom." At present "Pony Bob" is living on "the fat of the land" in Chicago. Sam and Jim Gilson are mining in Utah, and all the old "Pony" boys will rejoice to know they are now millionaires. The new mineral, gilsonite, was discovered by Sam Gilson. Mike Kelley is mining in Austin, Nev.; Jimmy Bucklin, "Black Sam," and the McNaughton boys are dead. William Carr was hanged in Carson City, for the murder of Bernard Cherry, his unfortunate death being the culmination of a quarrel begun months before, at Smith Creek Station. His was the first legal hanging in the Territory, the sentence being passed by Judge Cradlebaugh.

J. G. Kelley has had a varied experience, and is now fifty-four years of age, an eminent mining engineer and mineralogist, residing in Denver, Colo. In recalling many reminiscences of the plains in the early days, I will let him tell the story in his own language:

> Yes, I was a pony express rider in 1860, and went out with Bol Roberts (one of the best men that ever lived), and I tell you it was no picnic. No amount of money could tempt me to repeat my experience of those days. To begin with, we had to build willow roads (corduroy fashion) across many places along the Carson River, carrying bundles of willows two and three hundred yards in our arms, while the mosquitoes were so thick it was difficult to discern whether the man was white or black, so

thickly were they piled on his neck, face, and hands.

Arriving at the Sink of the Carson River, we began the erection of a fort to protect us from the Indians. As there were no rocks or logs in that vicinity, the fort was built of *adobes*, made from the mud on the shores of the lake. To mix this mud and get it the proper consistency to mould into *adobes* (dried brick), we tramped around all day in it in our bare feet. This we did for a week or more, and the mud being strongly impregnated with alkali (carbonate of soda), you can imagine the condition of our feet. They were much swollen, and resembled hams. Before that time I wore No. 6 boots, but ever since then No. 9s fit me snugly.

This may, in a measure, account for Bob Haslam's selection of a residence in Chicago, as he helped us make the *adobes*, and the size of his feet would thereafter be less noticeable there than elsewhere.

We next built a fort of stone at Sand Springs, twenty-five miles from Carson Lake, and another at Cold Springs, thirty-seven miles east of Sand Springs.

At the latter station I was assigned to duty as assistant station-keeper, under Jim McNaughton. The war against the Piute Indians was then at its height, and we were in the middle of the Piute country, which made it necessary for us to keep a standing guard night and day. The Indians were often seen skulking around, but none of them ever came near enough for us to get a shot at them, till one dark night, when I was on guard, I noticed one of our horses prick up his ears and stare. I looked in the direction indicated and saw an Indian's head projecting above the wall.

My instructions were to shoot if I saw an Indian within shooting distance, as that would wake the boys quicker than anything else; so I fired and missed my man.

Later on we saw the Indian camp-fires on the mountain, and in the morning saw many tracks. They evidently intended to stampede our horses, and if necessary kill us. The next day one of our riders, a Mexican, rode into camp with a bullet hole through him from the left to the right side, having been shot by Indians while coming down Edwards Creek, in the Quakenasp bottom. This he told us as we assisted him off his horse. He was tenderly cared for, but died before surgical aid could reach him.

As I was the lightest man at the station, I was ordered to take the Mexican's place on the route. My weight was then 100 pounds, while now I weigh 230. Two days after taking the route, on my return trip, I had to ride through the forest of quakenasp trees where the Mexican had been shot. A trail had been cut through these little trees, just wide enough to allow horse and rider to pass. As the road was crooked and the branches came together from either side, just above my head when mounted, it was impossible to see ahead more than ten or fifteen yards, and it was two miles through the forest.

I expected to have trouble, and prepared for it by dropping my bridle reins on the neck of the horse, put my Sharp's rifle at full cock, kept both spurs into the flanks, and he went through that forest like a '*streak of greased lightning*.'

At the top of the hill I dismounted to rest my horse, and looking back, saw the bushes moving in several places. As there were no cattle or game in that vicinity, I knew the movements must be caused by Indians, and was more positive of it when, after firing several shots at the spot where I saw the bushes moving, all agitation ceased. Several days after that, two United States soldiers, who were on their way to their command, were shot and killed from the ambush of those bushes, and stripped of their clothing, by the red devils.

One of my rides was the longest on the route. I refer to the road between Cold Springs and Sand Springs, thirty-seven miles, and not a drop of water. It was on this ride that I made a trip which possibly gave to our company the contract for carrying the mail by stage-coach across the plains, a contract that was largely subsidized by Congress.

One day I trotted into Sand Springs covered with dust and perspiration. Before reaching the station I saw a number of men running toward me, all carrying rifles, and as I supposed they took me for an Indian, I stopped and threw up my hands. It seemed they had a spy-glass in camp, and recognising me had come to the conclusion I was being run in by Piutes and were coming to my rescue.

Bob Haslam was at the station, and in less than one minute relieved me of my mail-pouch and was flying westward over the plains. Some of the boys had several fights with Indians, but they did not trouble us as much as we expected; personally I only met them once face to face. I was rounding a bend in the mountains, and before I knew it, was in a camp of Piute Indians. Buffalo Jim, the chief, came toward me alone. He spoke good English, and when within ten yards of me I told him to stop, which he did, and told me he wanted '*tobac*' (tobacco). I gave him half I had, but the old fellow wanted it all, and I finally refused to give him any more; he then made another step toward me, saying that he wanted to look at my gun. I pulled the gun out of the saddle-hock and again told him to stop. He evidently saw that I meant business, for, with a wave of his hand, he said: 'All right, you pooty good boy; you go.' I did not need a second order, and quickly as possible rode out of their presence, looking back, however, as long as they were in sight, and keeping my rifle handy.

As I look back on those times I often wonder that we were not all killed. A short time before, Major Ormsby of Carson City, in command of seventy-five or eighty men, went to Pyramid Lake to give battle to the Piutes, who had been killing emigrants and prospectors by the wholesale. Nearly all the command were killed in a running fight of sixteen miles. In the fight Major Ormsby and the lamented Harry Meredith were killed. Another regiment of about seven hundred men, under the command of Col. Daniel E. Hungerford and Jack Hayes, the noted Texas ranger, was raised. Hungerford was the *beau ideal* of a soldier, the hero of three wars, and one of the best tacticians of his time. This command drove the Indians pell-mell for three miles to Mud Lake, killing and wounding them at every jump.

Colonel Hungerford and Jack Hayes received, and were entitled to, great praise, for at the close of the war terms were made which have kept the Indians peaceable ever since. Jack Hayes died several years since in Alameda, Cal. Colonel Hungerford, at the ripe age of seventy years, is hale and hearty, enjoying life and resting on his laurels in Italy, where he resides with his granddaughter, the Princess Colona.

As previously stated, it is marvelous that the pony boys were not all killed. There were only four men at each station, and the Indians, who were then hostile, roamed all over the country in bands of 30 to 100.

What I consider my most narrow escape from death was being

shot at one night by a lot of fool emigrants, who, when I took them to task about it on my return trip, excused themselves by saying, 'We thought you was an Indian.'

I want to say one good word for our bosses, Messrs. Russell, Majors & Waddell. The boys had the greatest veneration for them because of their general good treatment at their hands. They were different in many respects from all other freighters on the plains, who, as a class, were boisterous, blasphemous, and good patrons of the bottle, while Russell, Majors & Waddell were God-fearing, religious, and temperate themselves, and were careful to engage none in their employ who did not come up to their standard of morality.

Calf-bound Bibles were distributed by them to every *employé*. The one given to me was kept till 1881, and was then presented to Ionic Lodge No. 35, A. F. & A. M., at Leadville, Colo.

The Pony Express was a great undertaking at the time, and was the foundation of the mail-coach and railroad that quickly followed.

During the war J. G. Kelley was commissioned by Gov. James W. Nye as captain of Company C, Nevada Infantry, and served till the end of the war, after which he resumed his old business of mining, and is still engaged in it.

CHAPTER 23

The Battle of the Buffaloes

It was the afternoon of a day in early summer, along in 1859, when we found ourselves drifting in a boat down the Missouri. The morning broke with a drizzling rain, out of a night that had been tempestuous, with a fierce gale, heavy thunder, and unusually terrific lightning. Gradually the rain stopped, and we had gone but a short distance when the clouds broke away, the sun shone forth, and the earth appeared glistening with a new beauty. Ahead of us appeared, high up on the bluffs, a clump of trees and bushes.

As we drew near, a sudden caprice seized us, and shooting our boat up on the shelving bank, we secured it, and then climbed the steep embankment. We intended to knock around in the brush a little while, and then resume our trip. A fine specimen of an eagle caught our eye, perched high up on the dead bough of a tree.

Moving around to get a good position to pick him off with my rifle, so that his body would not be torn, I caught sight through an opening of the trees of an immense herd of buffaloes, browsing and moving slowly in our direction. We moved forward a little to get a better view of the herd, when the eagle, unaware to us, spread his pinions, and when we looked again for him he was soaring at a safe distance from our rifles.

We were on the leeward side of the herd, and so safe from discovery, if we took ordinary precaution, among the trees. It was a fine spectacle which they presented, and, what was more, we were in just the mood to watch them. The land undulated, but was covered for many acres with minute undulations of dark-brown shoulders slowly drifting toward us. We could hear the rasping sound which innumerable mouths made chopping the crisp grass. As we looked, our ears caught a low, faint, rhythmical sound, borne to us from afar.

We listened intently. The sound grew more distinct, until we could recognise the tread of another herd of buffaloes coming from an opposite direction.

We skulked low through the undergrowth, and came to the edge of the wooded patch just in time to see the van of this new herd surmounting a hill. The herd was evidently spending its force, having already run for miles. It came with a lessening speed, until it settled down to a comfortable walk.

About the same time the two herds discovered each other. Our herd was at first a little startled, but after a brief inspection of the approaching mass, the work of clipping the grass of the prairies was resumed. The fresh arrivals came to a standstill, and gazed at the thousands of their fellows, who evidently had pre-empted their grazing grounds. Apparently they reached the conclusion that that region was common property, for they soon lowered their heads and began to shave the face of the earth of its green growths.

The space separating the herds slowly lessened. The outermost fringes touched but a short distance from our point of observation. It was not like the fringes of a lady's dress coming in contact with the lace drapery of a window, I can assure you. Nothing so soft and sibilant as that. It was more like the fringes of freight engines coming in contact with each other when they approach with some momentum on the same track.

The powerful bulls had unwittingly found themselves in close proximity to each other, coming from either herd. Suddenly shooting up from the sides of the one whose herd was on the ground first, flumes of dirt made graceful curves in the air. They were the signals for hostilities to commence. The hoofs of the powerful beast were assisted by his small horns, which dug the sod and tossed bunches that settled out of the air in his shaggy mane.

These belligerent demonstrations were responded to in quite as defiant a fashion by the late arrival. He, too, was an enormous affair. We noticed his unusual proportions of head. But his shoulders, with their great manes, were worth displaying to excite admiration and awe at their possibilities, if they could do nothing more.

Unquestionably the two fellows regarded themselves as representative of their different herds, the one first on the ground viewing the other as an interloper, and he in his turn looking upon the former as reigning, because no one had the spirit to contest his supremacy and show him where he belonged. They sidled up near each other, their heads all the while kept low to the ground, and their eyes red with anger and rolling in fiery fury. This display of the preliminaries of battle drew the attention of an increasing number from either herd. At first they would look up, then recommence their eating, and then direct their attention more intensely as the combatants began to measure their strength more closely. And when the fight was on they became quite absorbed in the varying fortunes of the struggle.

At last the two huge fellows, after a good deal of circumlocution, made the grand rush. I reckon it would be your everlasting fortune if one of you college fellows who play football had the force to make the great rush which either one of these animals presented. The collision was straight and square. A crash of horns, a heavy, dull thud of heads. We thought surely the skull of one or the other, or possibly both, was crushed in. But evidently they were not even hurt.

Didn't they push then? Well, I guess they did. The force would have shoved an old-fashioned barn from its foundations. The muscles swelled up on the thighs, the hoofs sank into the earth, but they were evenly matched.

For a moment there was a mutual cessation of hostilities to get breath. Then they came together with a more resounding crash than before. Instantly we perceived that the meeting of the heads was not square. The new champion had the best position. Like a flash he recognised it and redoubled his efforts to take its full advantage. The other appeared to quadruple his efforts to maintain himself in position, and his muscles bulged out, but his antagonist made a sudden move which wrenched his head still farther off the line, when he went down on his knees. That settled the contest, for his enemy was upon him before he could recover. He was thrown aside and his flank raked by several ugly upward thrusts of his foe, which left him torn and bruised, all in a heap. As quick as he could get on his feet he limped, crestfallen, away.

The victorious fellow lashed his small tail, tossed his head, and moved in all the pride of his contest up and down through the ranks of his adversary's herd. How exultant he was! We took it to be rank impudence, and though he had exhibited some heroic qualities of strength and daring, it displeased us to see him take on so many airs on account of his victory.

But his conquest of the field was not yet entirely complete. As he strode proudly along his progress was stopped by a loud snort, and, looking aside, he saw a fresh challenge. There, standing out in full view, was another bull, a monster of a fellow belonging to his late enemy's herd. He pawed the earth with great strokes and sent rockets of turf curving high in air, some of which sifted its fine soil down upon the nose of the victor.

As we looked at this new challenger and took in his immense form, we chuckled with the assurance that the haughty fellow would now have some decent humility imposed upon him. The conqueror himself must have been impressed with the formidableness of his new antagonist, for there was a change in his demeanour at once. Of course, according to a well-established buffalo code, he could do nothing but accept the challenge.

Space was cleared as the two monsters went through their gyrations, their tossings of earth, their lashings of tail, their snorts and their low bellows. This appeared to them a more serious contest than the former, if we could judge from the length of the introductory part. They took more time before they settled down to business. We were of the opinion that the delay was caused by the champion, who resorted to small arts to prolong the preliminaries. We watched it all with the most excited interest. It had all the thrilling features of a Spanish bullfight without the latter's degradation of man. Here was the level of nature. Here the true buffalo instincts with their native temper were exhibiting themselves in the most emphatic and vigorous fashion. It was the buffalo's trial of nerve, strength, and skill.

Numberless as must have been these tournaments, in which the champions of different herds met to decide which was superior, in the long ages during which the buffalo kingdom reigned supreme over the vast western prairies of the United States, yet few had ever been witnessed by man. We were looking upon a spectacle rare to human eyes, and I confess that I was never more excited than when this last trial reached its climax. It was a question now whether the champion should still hold his position. It stimulates one more when he thinks of losing what he has seized than when he thinks of failing to grasp that which he has never possessed. Undoubtedly both of these animals had this same feeling, for as we looked at this latest arrival, we about concluded that he was the real leader, and not the other that limped away vanquished.

While these and other thoughts were passing through our minds, the two mighty contestants squared and made a tremendous plunge for each other. What a shock was that! What a report rolled on the air! The earth fairly shook with the terrific concussion of buffalo brains, and both burly fellows went down on their knees. Both, too, were on their feet the same instant, and locked horns with the same swiftness and skill, and each bore down on the other with all the power he could summon. The cords stood out like great ropes on their necks; the muscles on thighs and hips rose like huge welts. We were quite near these fellows and could see the roll of their blood-red fiery eyes. They braced and shoved with perfectly terrible force. The froth began to drip in long strings from their mouths. The erstwhile victor slipped with one hind foot slightly. His antagonist felt it and instantly swung a couple of inches forward, which raised the unfortunate buffalo's back, and we expected every instant that he would go down. But he had a firm hold and he swung his antagonist back to his former position, where they were both held panting, their tongues lolling out.

There was a slight relaxation for breath, then the contest was renewed. Deep into the new sod their hoofs sunk, neither getting the advantage of the other. Like a crack of a tree broken asunder came a report on the air, and one of the legs of the first fighter sank into the earth. The other buffalo thought he saw his chance, and made a furious lunge toward his opponent. The earth trembled beneath us. The monsters there fighting began to reel. We beheld an awful rent in the sod. For an instant the ground swayed, then nearly an acre dropped out of sight.

We started back with horror, then becoming reassured, we slowly approached the brink of the new precipice and looked over. This battle of the buffaloes had been fought near the edge of this high bluff. Their great weight—each one was over a ton—and their tremendous struggles had loosened the fibres which kept the upper part of the bluff together, and the foundations having been undermined by the current, all were precipitated far below.

As we gazed downward we detected two moving masses quite a distance apart, and soon the shaggy fronts of these buffaloes were seen. One got into the current of the river and was swept down stream. The other soon was caught by the tides and swept onward toward his foe. Probably they resumed the contest when, after gaining a good footing farther down the banks of the Missouri, they were fully rested.

But more probably, if they were sensible animals, and in some respects buffaloes have good sense, they concluded after such a providential interference in their terrific fight that they should live together in fraternal amity. So, no doubt, on the lower waters of the Missouri two splendid buffaloes have been seen by later hunters paying each other mutual respect, and standing on a perfect equality as chief leaders of a great herd.

CHAPTER 24

The Black Bear

My father, being one of the very first pioneers of Jackson County, Missouri, abundant opportunity was afforded me to become acquainted with the habits of wild animals of every description which at that time roamed in that unsettled portion of the country, such as elk, deer, bear, and panther.

Among these animals the most peculiar was the black bear, which was found in considerable numbers. Bears, in many respects, differ from all other animals; they are very small when born, and when grown the females, in their best state of fatness, will weigh from two hundred and fifty to three hundred and fifty pounds. The male bears weigh at their best much more; from four hundred to five hundred pounds. They are remarkably intelligent animals, and are very wild, wanting but little to do with civilization, for as soon as white people made their appearance in the regions of country inhabited by them, it was not long before they migrated to other portions of the country. To the early settlers of the new country bear meat proved of great value, being very fat, and on account of this great fatness particularly useful to them in the seasoning of leaner meats, such as wild turkey, venison, etc., which constituted much of the living of the early settlers or pioneers of the Mississippi and Missouri valleys.

The bear's life each year is divided into three distinct periods. From the first of April to the middle of September they live upon vegetables, such as they can find in the wild woods, fruits of every description, and meats of every kind, from the insect to the largest animal that lives; periwinkles, frogs, and fish of all kinds; all living things in the water as well as on the land. From the middle of September they cease to eat of the various things they have lived on during the summer, and take entirely to eating mast, that is, acorns, beech-nuts, pecans, chestnuts, and *chincapins*. On commencing to eat mast, they begin to fatten very rapidly. I should have remarked that during the summer months, the season in which they live on insects and meats of every variety, they lose every particle of the fat they had accumulated while eating mast. On account of his abstemious habits the prohibitionists should value the bear as emblematical of their order. Coming out of their long sleep the first of April, or when the vegetation has grown sufficient for them to feed upon, they commence to eat herbs, meats, and fruits of every kind. They are remarkably fond of swine at this period, and unlike the wolf, who seeks to catch the *young* pigs, the bear picks up the mother and walks off with her. She affords him a splendid opportunity for so doing, it being a trait of the mother hog, as it is of the mother bear, to fight ferociously for her young.

The strength of the bear is phenomenal. They can take up in their mouths and carry off with perfect ease an ordinary sized hog, calf, or sheep. During this season they frequent corn fields, devouring the corn when it comes to the size of roasting ears. Indeed there is little to be found that is edible by man or beast that the bear at some period of his life does not eat. When they commence eating mast, which is about the middle of September or the first of October, as stated, they eat nothing else until about the 15th to the 20th of December, by which time most of them become exceedingly fat; so much so, indeed, that in some cases it is difficult for them to run very fast, not half as fast as they could before becoming so fat. All of the very fat ones, about the middle of December, cease to eat or drink anything, make themselves beds and lie down in them, preparatory to going into their caves or dens for their long sleep.

They lie in these beds, which may be several miles from the caves in which they intend to take their winter sleep, several days, or sometimes a week, and by this temporary stay in the open air, nature is given time to dispose of every particle of water and food in the body. After this time has elapsed, they leave these temporary beds and go as straight as the crow flies to their intended quarters, which are generally caves in the rocks, if such can be found in the regions they inhabit. This sleep is taken when the animals are the very fattest. None but the very fat ones go through the period of hibernating. They do not lose one pound's weight during this sleep, unless it be in respiration, which is a very small quantity compared with the entire mass, for no excretions are made during that period.

Entering the caves they remain there from three to four months, this being their dormant or hibernating period, and for this reason they are known among hunters as one of the family of seven sleepers. Each makes his bed in the bottom of the cave by scratching out a large, round, basin-shaped place in the dirt; these beds after being once made remain intact, as the caves are invariably dry, and are used by the same bear year after year if he is not disturbed; and after his demise will be adopted by another of his kind. Some of these caves have been perhaps for ages during the winter time the abode of a number of these "seven sleepers."

In my opinion there is no animal in the world that is so healthy, and the meat of which is more beneficial to mankind, than is the meat of the black bear. The doctors invariably recommend it for patients who are troubled with indigestion or chest diseases. Bear's oil (for that is what it really is) is considered a better curative and much preferable on account of its pleasant taste, to cod-liver oil, which is very disagreeable.

In settling the Mississippi Valley, when bear's meat was such a factor in the way of food, each of the frontiersmen kept a pack of dogs—all the way from three to half-a-dozen—partly for bear hunting, which was a very exciting sport, in fact the most of any other game hunting. I have been long and well acquainted with the courage shown by dogs in hunting and fighting game, and there is nothing I ever saw a dog undertake that arouses his courage so much as a contest with a bear. The dog seems to think a fight with a bear the climax of his existence. One familiar with, and accustomed to, bear hunting can tell at long distances whether the dogs are having a combat with a bear or some other animal, by the energy they put into their yelping. When fighting a bear the dogs continually snap and bite at his hind legs, as this is the only way they have of exasperating and irritating him, as they dare not approach him in front.

The full-grown bear is able to stand off any number of dogs that can get around him. So strong are they that if they can get hold of a dog in their forearms or mouth, he is very likely to be killed. The large she-bear can take an ordinary sized dog in her forepaws and crush him to death, and they can strike with such force as to send the sharp nails of their paws fairly through the dog. On account of the adeptness with which bears use their forepaws, the dogs try constantly to be in their rear, and the bears are always trying to confront them. The bear in moving his paws to strike never draws them back, but invariably makes a forward movement, which is a surprise to the dogs, as it gives them no warning, hence the aim of the former to confront the enemy, and of the latter not to be confronted.

I have stood several times, when a boy, upon the doorstep of my father's log-cabin and watched the men and dogs in their chase after a bear, only a few hundred yards away. This was, of course, only a few months after the first settlers came into the country, for it was the habit of these bears to leave as soon as they knew the white people had come to stay.

Bears roam in the very thickest woods and roughest portions of the country, and it is difficult to find one so far away from the rough woods that he can not reach such locality in a very few moments after he is attacked; and unlike other game that was found on the frontier, instead of trying to get into the open prairie, where they can run, they make at once after being disturbed for the cliffs of the rivers and creeks and the canebrakes; in fact into the very roughest places they can find, and take the shortest cut to get to them.

Bears do not depend on the senses of sight and hearing for their protection as much as upon the sense of smell, by which they can distinguish perfectly their friends or enemies. The scent of man would strike terror to their hearts as much as the sight of him, and they scent him much farther than they can see him, especially when they are in the thick woods or canebrakes, where they often feed.

Frequently instead of fighting dogs on the ground, when tired, the bear climbs a tree, sometimes going up fifty feet, and there rests, lodged in a fork or upon a limb, surveying with complacency the howling pack of dogs, and they in turn, becoming more bold as the distance between their victim and themselves increases, defiantly extend their necks toward their black antagonist in the tree. Notwithstanding the bear's dread of the howling pack of dogs in waiting for their prey, if he sees a man he loses his hold and drops, falling among the dogs, sometimes falling on one or more and killing them.

I have known the hunter to be so cautious in showing himself that before he came near enough to shoot he would select the trunks of large trees, hiding behind them as he approached, until being near enough, and concealed from the bear by one of these trunks, he moved his head a little to one side to take aim; the moment he moved his head sufficient to do so, if the bear chanced to be looking that way, he would let go his hold and drop, showing that, after all, he knew where the real danger was.

It is very desirable in bear hunting that the bear should climb a tree and give his pursuer an opportunity to fire at him there, for while he is in the fight with the dogs it would be almost impossible for the hunter to shoot the bear without taking the chance of injuring or killing one or more of the dogs. The dogs are also in great danger when a bear weighing from three to five hundred pounds falls a distance of forty or fifty feet, be the bear dead or alive. No other animal that I know of could fall such a distance and not be more or less hurt, but bears are not injured in the least, being protected by their immense covering of fat, which forms a complete shield, or cushion, around the body.

The bear can stand on his hind legs just as easily as a man can stand on his feet, and in their fights with dogs they shield themselves by standing up against large trees, cliffs, or rocks, so that the dogs have no chance at them except in front. In this position they can stand off any number of dogs, and the dogs well know the danger of approaching from the front. No body of drilled men could act their part better than the dogs do, without any training whatever, which is a great proof of their intelligence.

The moment a bear shows that he is about to climb a tree in order to get out of the ground scuffle with his opponents, the dogs, and attempts to do so, the dogs with one accord pitch at him, until there are so many hanging to his hind legs that often he can not climb, and falls on his back to rid himself of and to fight them. He can fight when on his back as well as in any other position, for he embraces them in his arms, by no means gently.

He may try climbing a tree three or four times before he can sufficiently rid himself of the dogs; even then, perhaps, he may have one or two hanging to his legs, which he carries with him maybe ten or twelve feet up the tree, and the dogs, under the greatest excitement, keep perfect consciousness of the distance, and they are able to fall without being injured.

Let us now turn our attention to the mothers, or she-bears. They become mothers during the period of their hibernation, going into the caves at the time already mentioned when the other fat bears hibernate, and lie dormant until the time their cubs are born, which is about the middle of February. These require a great deal of the mother's attention, and she is faithful and follows her motherly instincts to her own death, if need be. After the cubs are born she goes once every day for water, which, with her accumulated fat, produces milk for the sustenance of her young, she having selected her cave near a stream of running or living water.

She does not eat a particle of any food from the first of December to the middle of April. By the time she leaves her bed, where she has been for four months in solitude, the cubs are sufficiently large to follow the mother, and should any danger threaten them, to climb a tree, which they are very quick to do, and if they do not do so at the bidding of the mother at once, she catches them up in her fore paws and throws them up against the tree, giving them to understand they must climb for their protection. The male bear is the greatest enemy the mother and the cubs have to look out for; for unless protected by the mother, he will seize and eat the cubs, during the season of the year when bears eat meat, but he is not disposed to hurt the mother bear, unless in a scuffle in trying to get hold of the young; therefore it is necessary for her to have her little ones with her every moment after they come out of the cave where they are born, and where they stay for more than two months before they are brought out into the sunlight.

Should danger threaten, and there is a small tree near, she will invariably make her cubs climb it, where they are safe, because the large male bear can not climb very small trees. If she is compelled to send her cubs up a large tree, she stands ready and willing to sacrifice her life for the protection of her young, and not in the annals of natural history can there be found a mother which shows such desperation in the protection of her young as does the mother bear.

Nothing daunts her when her cubs are imperilled, and neither man nor dogs in any number will avail in driving her from them. I have seen mother bears stand at the roots of trees up which their cubs had climbed, cracking their teeth and striking their paws, which sounded like the knocking of two hammers together, as warning to their enemies they would fight till they dropped dead, or killed their antagonist.

They all fast during the entire period of hibernation. Bears bring forth their young but once in two years, and nature has wisely designed it so. In order to protect the cubs from the male bear, and other enemies, the mother's constant presence and care are necessary until they are old and large enough to protect themselves. On this account she keeps them with her until they are over a year old, and they generally hibernate the first year with her, after which they leave her, to roam where they will.

As my knowledge of the bear was obtained by being brought up and living in the portion of the State of Missouri they inhabited, it

ALEXANDER MAJORS' FIRST BEAR HUNT.

was natural when I grew up that I became a bear-hunter. I have killed them at all times of the year; when in their caves, shortly after they have come out in the spring, and while in their beds, before going to their caves. I have traced them by their tracks in the snow from their temporary beds to their winter caves. On account of my own experience, and my association with the best and oldest bear-hunters, I have had good opportunities to learn the nature and habits of black bear. Although I have seen a great many bears of the Rocky Mountains, and have had some little experience with the cinnamon, the brown, and the silver-gray bear, I am not as familiar with their modes of life as I am with those of the black bear that were found in such numbers in the Mississippi Valley when the white people first emigrated to that country. Bears of the Rocky Mountains, and especially grizzly bears, are very much larger than black bears, and, as far as I have been able to learn from those who have hunted them, their meat, as food, does not compare with that of the black bear.

One of my personal experiences in bear hunting occurred about the 15th of December, 1839, in Taney County, Missouri, where I then lived. After a deep snow had fallen, I had provided myself with some bread, a piece of fat bear meat, and a little salt, and some corn for my horse, and unaccompanied, except by my horse and four dogs, I started out to try and kill a bear. On reaching that part of the mountains where I expected to find them, I came across a number of trails, and soon found one which I knew must have been by a very fat bear. Hunters know by the trail whether the bear is fat, for if fat he makes two rows of tracks about a foot apart, while a lean bear makes only one row of tracks, similar to that of a dog. I spent part of one day in tracking this animal, which I was sure would be well worth my pains.

While on this trail I was led to the deserted bed of one of the largest bears I ever saw, for I afterward had ample opportunity of judging of its size and weight. He had lain in his temporary bed during the falling of the snow, after which he had gone in a bee-line to the cave for his intended hibernation. Feeling sure he was such a large animal, I followed the trail four or five miles, going as straight as if I had followed the bearings of a compass. On a very high peak at the mouth of one of those caves, of which there are so many in that country, his trail disappeared. The openings of many of these caves are so small that it is often with great difficulty a large bear effects an entrance. However, though the openings are so small, the caves are broad and spacious. In these caves bears hibernate. This particular cave had a very small and irregular opening, so that I could not enter it with my gun; but, as is the custom with bear-hunters, I cut a pole ten or twelve feet long, sharpened one end, and to this tied a piece of fat bear meat, set fire to it, and made another attempt to enter the cave.

Finding I could not do this, on account of the opening being so irregular, I abandoned the idea of shooting him in his cave, and proceeded to kindle a fire at the mouth, and putting a pole across the opening, hung my saddle-blanket and a green buckskin that I procured the day before, when getting meat for my dogs, upon it. This covering drove the smoke from the fire into the cave, which soon disturbed the animal, so that he came and put the fire out by striking it with his paws. Instead of coming out of the cave as I supposed he would, after putting out the fire, he went back to his bed. He had gotten such draughts of the suffocating smoke that he made no other attempts to get to the mouth of the cave, where my four dogs were standing, ready, nervous, and trembling, watching for him, and I was standing on one side of the mouth of the cave, prepared to put a whole charge into him if he made his appearance. I waited a few moments after I heard him box the fire for him to return, but as he did not, I took the covering from the mouth of the cave and found the fire was entirely out.

I then rekindled it and replaced the coverings, and it was not long after until I heard him groaning, like some strong-chested old man in pain. I listened eagerly for his moanings to cease, knowing that he must die of suffocation. It was not, however, very long until all was still. I then uncovered the mouth of the cave to let the smoke out. It was some time before I could venture in; before I did so I relit my light, and going in I found my victim not twenty feet from the mouth of the cave, lying on his back, dead; and, as before stated, he was the largest animal of the kind I ever saw or killed. It took me seven or eight hours to slaughter him and carry the meat out of the cave, as I could not carry more than fifty pounds at a time and crawl out and in.

When I opened the chest of this big bear, I found two bullets. These were entirely disconnected with any solid matter. They had been shot into him by some hunter who knew precisely the location of a bear's heart, which is different from what it is in other animals. His heart lies much farther back in his body, being precisely in the centre of the same, while the heart of all other quadrupeds, and I think I have known all those of North America, lies just back of their shoulders; in other words, in the front part of the chest.

These bullets, from the necessity of the case, must have been shot into the animal when he was the very fattest, and when he was ready for hibernation, because they were not lodged in the flesh, but entirely loose in the chest, each one covered with a white film, and tied with a little ligament, about the size of a rye straw, to the sack that contained the heart. When the bear lay down, these bullets could not have been more than half or three-quarters of an inch from each other, for each one was covered separately, and had a separate ligament attaching it to the sack above alluded to; and the two ligaments, where they had grown to the sack, were not more than a quarter of an inch apart. I cut out the piece containing both the bullets, and taking it in my fingers reminded me of two large cherries with the stems almost touching at the point where they were broken from the limb.

What I have just described would indeed have been an interesting study to the medical fraternity, as perhaps there has never been anything like it. It could not have occurred in this particular way, except where the bear had gone through the preparation peculiar to him before hibernating, and after leaving his temporary bed he could lie dormant and give nature ample opportunity to restore the injury to the system which the bullet had caused. The above facts proved that it was just at the season of the year when the bear was ready to hibernate.

In this article at the outset, I mentioned the fact that the bear is a peculiar animal. Indeed he is the most peculiar of any quadruped with which I am familiar. He has many marked characteristics. He assumes in twelve months three different modes of life, each one thoroughly distinct from the other. He hibernates, during which time he abstains entirely from food and water. On coming out of this dormant condition he commences to eat food of every kind, peculiar to that season of the year. After living for months on anything and everything he can get, he ceases to eat any of these various things, and begins a totally different kind of diet, eating only mast—acorns and nuts of every kind. Another of their peculiarities is the cubs are not permitted to see the light for sixty days after being born, as they are in the dark solitude of a cave in the ground. Still another characteristic is the mother bear takes care of her young until they are fourteen months old, they hibernating with her the second winter of their lives.

The bear differs from other quadrupeds in being able to stand or walk on his two hind feet as well as on all-fours, and in this position he can make telling efforts at protecting himself. He climbs trees, and thus gets the mast by breaking the branches and picking off the acorns.

He is also so constituted that he can fall great distances, even from the top of a tree, without injuring himself in the least. The mother bear has, as far as I know, generally two, never more than three, cubs at a time; when young these cubs can be easily tamed, and become in time very devoted to their owner. They are very intelligent, so that with proper training they will learn the tricks any animal has been known to learn. When small they are great playmates for boys, and will wrestle with them and enter into sports with great intelligence. They are never dangerous until grown, and not then unless crossed or abused. Wild bears are not considered dangerous unless they are attacked and are unable to make their escape. Under no circumstances, as already stated, does the mother bear forsake her young when they are in danger. In teaching bears tricks, one lesson is sufficient, as they seem never to forget.

A friend of mine owned a pet bear which became so familiar about the place and so attached to all, that he could be turned loose with a chain several feet long dragging after him. He conceived the idea of scratching a hole beside the wall, where he could go and hide himself to take his naps. One day his owner wanted to show him to someone while he was asleep in his hole, and took hold of the chain, which was lying extended for some distance, and pulled the little bear out. This gentleman stated to me that this never occurred but once. After this, whenever the bear went to take his nap, the first thing he did after getting into the hole was to pull the chain in after him. His owner had a post set in the yard fifteen or twenty feet high, with a broad board nailed on the top. The bear would climb this post and lie down on the board. The first thing he did after lying down was to pull that chain up and put it in a coil at his side. His owner told me that one lesson sufficed to teach him anything. I have repeated many of these facts in order to bring them more clearly and forcibly to the mind of the reader.

CHAPTER 25

The Beaver

In the settlement of the Western States and Territories one of the sources of income, and the only industry which commanded cash for the efforts involved, was that of beaver trapping, the skin of the beaver selling as high as fifteen or twenty dollars. The weight of the beaver is from thirty to sixty pounds, and it is an animal possessed of great intelligence, as the amount and kind of work accomplished by it shows. It is a natural-born engineer, as connected with water; it can build dams across small streams that defy the freshets, and that hold the water equal, if not superior, to the very best dams that can be constructed by skilled engineers.

In making their dams the sticks and poles which they use in the construction of the same are cut with their teeth, of which they have four, two in the upper part of the mouth and two in the lower.

These poles they place across each other in all directions. They build their dams during the fall usually, and should they need repair, the work is done before the very cold weather commences, working only at night if danger is near.

In the month of October they generally collect their food, which consists largely of the cottonwood; this is cut in lengths of from two to six feet, the diameter being sometimes six inches, and carry it into their ponds made by the dams, and sunk in the deepest portion of the same. I should have stated that the higher up the stream they go, their dams are built correspondingly higher; hence a dam built at an altitude of 1,000 feet would not be built as high as one built at an altitude of 3,000 feet, in order to overcome the deeper freezing at that point, for in constructing these dams they must be of sufficient height to give plenty of room to get at their food in the water under the ice. The beaver does not eat a particle of meat of any kind. The popular idea is that as they are animals that live in and about the water, that they live upon fish, but this is not so; for, as above stated, their principal food is the bark and the tender-wood of the cottonwood, and they also eat of other barks.

They are one of the most cleanly animals that lives. They live in the purest water that can be found, generally selecting streams that take their rise in the mountains, and where they can have an abundance of water the year round to live in. They dam up the streams in order to make ponds of sufficient depth to swim in under the ice to obtain their food, for the bottom of this pond is their store-room during the winter months.

Beavers are exceedingly wild, seldom showing themselves, and from the bottom of their pond they make a tunnel leading to the house where they sleep, so that they can pass to the same unobserved by man or beast. When they make their ponds where the banks are low, they make their house upon the top of the ground, sometimes a rod or more from the edge of the pond, cutting timber of the size of a finger to two or three inches in diameter, placing the sticks in very much the same way as they do in building their dams, crossing and recrossing them so that it is quite a job to tear one of their houses to pieces; in fact no one but a man would undertake the task, and one that has never had any experience would find it very difficult to accomplish.

If one does it in the hope of catching the animal, he toils in vain, for he is soon scented, and the beaver takes refuge in the pond, passing through the underground tunnel. Where they find high banks, they start a tunnel several feet below the surface of the water and run it ascending, so as to reach a point in the bank six or eight or may be ten feet above the surface of the water underground, stopping before reaching the top of the ground, and at which point they take out dirt until they have a place sufficiently large for their bed. This kind of a house they much prefer to one made with sticks on the surface of the ground, as they are completely hidden from observation or the possibility of interruption from any one.

The beaver's feet are webbed for the purpose of swimming, and there are nails on his feet, so that he can scratch the earth almost equal to a badger. He has a paddle-formed tail, which on a large full-grown beaver is from ten to twelve inches long and from six to seven inches broad, and without any hair on it. These are tough and sinewy, and when cooked they make a very fine food, the flavour reminding one of pig's feet or calf's head. They make considerable use of their tail in performing their work as well as in swimming.

The beaver reproduces itself each year. The offspring are generally two in number, and these can be easily tamed.

The trappers in trapping for the beaver have to use great precaution in approaching the place where they intend to set the traps, often getting into the stream above or below and wading for some distance. If they walked upon the bank the beaver would scent them from the footprints. Beavers, like all other wild animals, dread the sight or scent of man more than anything else. In setting the traps the trappers invariably choose as deep water as they can find, so that when a beaver is caught he will drown himself in his struggles to get free from the trap; for if this does not occur, he has often been known to cut off, with the sharp chisel used in cutting timber, the foot that is caught in the trap, so that it is not infrequent when the trapper comes in the morning to find a foot of the beaver instead of the beaver himself, and often he catches a beaver with only three feet.

The beaver, considered as an engineer, is a remarkable animal. He can run a tunnel as direct as the best engineer could do with his instruments to guide him. I have seen where they have built a dam across a stream, and not having a sufficient head of water to keep their pond full, they would cross to a stream higher up the side of the mountain, and cut a ditch from the upper stream and connect it with the pond of the lower, and do it as neatly as an engineer with his tools could possibly do it. I have often said that the buck beaver in the Rocky Mountains had more engineering skill than the entire corps of engineers who were connected with General Grant's army when he besieged Vicksburg on the banks of the Mississippi. The beaver would never have attempted to turn the Mississippi into a canal to change its channel without first making a dam across the channel below the point of starting the canal. The beaver, as I have said, rivals and sometimes even excels the ingenuity of man.

Another of the peculiarities of the beaver is the great sharpness of its teeth, remaining for many years as sharp as the best edged tool. The mechanic with the finest steel can not make a tool that will not in a short time become so blunt and so dulled as to require renewed sharpening, and this, with the beaver, would have to be repeated hundreds of times in order to do service with it during the whole of its lifetime, which is from ten to fifteen years if it is permitted to live the allotted years of a beaver.

In one of my trips on a steamer of the Upper Missouri, one day while the boat's crew were getting their supply of wood, I took my gun and started along the river-bank in the hope of seeing an elk or deer that I might shoot. I came to a place on the river where the banks were very high, and I observed that a lot of cottonwood saplings from six to eight inches in diameter had been felled and cut into sections. I saw that it had been recently done, and I at first supposed that it had been done by some one with an axe, but when I reached the spot, I saw that it was the work of the beavers and that some of the wood had been dragged away. I followed the trail for a few steps, when I came to the mouth of a tunnel, and discovered that the timber had been dragged through it. The tunnel had an incline of about thirty-five degrees, and was as straight as if it had been made with an auger. This was in the month of October, at the time when it was their custom to stow away their food for the winter. They had no dam at this point, as the water was deep, and they were drawing the timbers down through the tunnel and sinking them in the deep water, so that they could have access to it during the period when the river would be frozen over.

The reason for the tunnel, of which I have spoken, was that the river-bank for some distance was high and almost perpendicular, and the beaver, being a very clumsy animal with short legs, his only alternative was to make a tunnel in order to get his winter food. They have a way of sinking the cottonwood and keeping it down in their pond or simply in the deep water when they do not make dams. This family of beavers evidently had their house far under the surface of the ground, for the place was admirably adapted for them to make such a home, the banks being so high above the water. One could see no trace whatever of the beaver, or have a knowledge of where he was, more than the opening of the tunnel and where the timber had been cut; indeed, one might pass hundreds of times and not be conscious that beavers were living right under one's feet. I picked up one of the chips which the beaver had cut, measuring about seven inches in length, and carried it home with me as a curiosity.

CHAPTER 26

A Boy's Trip Overland

Remembering my own love of adventure as a boy, I can not refrain from giving here a chapter contributed by my son, Green Majors, which will be found both instructive and interesting. He says:

At the inexperienced age of twelve years I was seized with a strong desire to go overland to Montana. For a number of years I had lived at Nebraska City, on the Missouri River, a starting point in those days for west-bound freight and emigrant wagon trains; and having so long seen the stage-coaches go bounding over the hills and rolling prairies, headed for the golden West, it was with a feeling of great satisfaction that on the morning of April 26, 1866, I was seated on top of one of those same coaches, as a fellow passenger with my father, Alexander Majors, bound for the Rocky Mountains, and Helena, Mont., in particular. To my boyish fancy the never-ceasing rocking to and fro of the overland coach of early days was a constant delight. Denver we reached in six days and nights of incessant travel. Rain nor shine, floods nor deserts, stopped us.

If a passenger became too sleepy or exhausted to hold on and sleep at the same time on the outside, he could get inside by submitting to the 'sardining' process. But inside, the clouds of dust and the cramped position necessary to assume made one at times feel like the coach were spinning round like a top in the dark. At Denver we laid in a big supply of luncheon material, for the next continuous ride, without a town, was for 600 miles, to Salt Lake City. However, before we reached Zion, our troubles were many, one of which was being caught in a violent snow-storm one dark night while bowling along over Laramie

Plains. Our driver and his mules both lost the road. He so notified us, and we got out to wade through the innumerable drifts to see if we could feel the hard-beaten trail with our feet. But it was of no use.

So for fear we might wander away from the emigrant road too far, or that he might drive over some precipice or into some hole or other in the blinding storm, we unhitched his four mules and tied each one with its head to a wheel, so there could be no runaway, and then all hands got back into the coach, tucked our wraps about us as best we could, and there we sat, like Patience on a monument, smiling at grief, with the wind whistling in all its many sad cadences through the flapping wings of that desolate coach, until the longest night I ever saw went by. Next morning we found two and a half feet of 'the beautiful' on the level, and the struggle to gain another station began. We tramped snow and broke trails for that coach to get through the drifts for about ten or fifteen miles, before we got to a lower altitude, out of the path of the storm, for all of which distance we of course paid the stage company 25 cents a mile fare, with no baggage allowance to speak of.

Not a great ways farther on, we struck the famous Bitter Creek country, a section that was the terror of travellers, because of poor grass, water that was foul and bitter, and alkali plains that were terrific on man and beast. At one place along Bitter Creek its water was as red as blood, at another as yellow as an orange; but generally its colour was a dark muddy drab, and highly impregnated with vegetable and earthy matter. I suppose Bitter Creek is the only place on earth where highwaymen had the cold-blooded nerve to charge travellers $1.50 for nothing but fat bacon, poorly cooked, and an inferior quality of mustard, as a meal's victuals, but the stage station-keepers had it there. By the time we finished our Bitter Creek experience we were proof against peril, so that subsequent floods in the *cañons* from melting snows in the mountains, sitting bolt upright with three on a seat to sleep over the rough mountain roads at night, and passing over long stretches of country with no water fit to drink, were trivial circumstances.

After a thirty-day siege of this sort of experience, we alighted on the gravelly streets of Helena, Mont., then a town of canvas houses and tents, and log huts. Helena at that time was the liveliest town I have ever seen in my life, either in America or Europe, over the whole of both of which I have since travelled. At that time her business houses were largely propped up on stilts, while underneath the red-shirted placer miner was washing the blue gravel soil for gold-dust. Her streets, in many places, were bridged over, to allow of the same thing. Sunday was the liveliest day in the week for business. The plainest meal at a restaurant cost $1.50, and bakery pies, with brown paper used for a crust, cost 75 cents each. Everybody had money, and nobody appeared to want to keep what he had. Gold-dust was the money of the country, no greenbacks nor coin being used. A pennyweight of the yellow dust passed for a dollar, but expert cashiers, at the gaming places and stores, were said to know how to weigh the article so deftly that $100 of it in value would only go $50 in distance.

However, wages were very high, and so was everything else, so that if a man were robbed pretty badly, he could soon recuperate his lost fortunes. There were no churches in Helena then, if, indeed, there were any in the Territory. The first Sunday after arriving there, I remember attending divine service in a muslin building, but the blacksmith's hammer next door and the lusty auctioneer's voice in the street made so much noise the congregation could not understand the divine's injunctions, so that church-going there, at that time, was attended with considerable annoyance. Everything was crude and primitive, everybody was cordial, generous, and open-hearted, and anything or anybody justly appealing to those roughly appareled yeomanry for aid or sympathy invariably opened the floodgates of their plenty and fired the great, deep, warm heart-throbs of their noble natures. But they were as prompt in meting out retributive justice to the wrong-doer as in loosing their purse-strings to a worthy applicant, and many were the wayward souls jerked into eternity through the deadly and inexorable noose of the ubiquitous vigilante, whose will was law, and the objects of whose adverse edicts were soon plainly told to recite their last prayers in the body.

Cattle-raising on the rich, nutritious bunch-grass of the broad valleys of the Territory also soon grew to be a very lucrative business, to supply the numerous placer-mining towns of Montana, a number of which were quite important and thrifty camps at that time. Farming was also followed to a limited extent. Inasmuch as potatoes, cabbage, and other vegetables were largely imported from Salt Lake, about five hundred miles, all sorts of soil products yielded handsome returns.

Montana has had her periods of depression as well as of prosperity. For after her then-discovered and easily accessible placer ground became washed out, which took several years, times there grew very dull, but not until something like $200,000,000 worth of gold had been washed from her auriferous gulches and hillsides. Quartz mining was rare in those days, because freight and everything else was so high that few had the means to engage in that kind of mining. From a State of such prosperous activity in the sixties, with a large and well-to-do population, in 1874-75 it grew so dull and so many had left the Territory that those remaining wished they could get away too. In the Centennial year of 1876, however, Montana's true era of prosperity dawned, when rich silver quartz was discovered at the now famous city of Butte, styled 'the greatest mining camp on earth.'

The Territory's business in every avenue soon rose from its low ebb to an affluent flood, all kinds and lines almost immediately feeling its vitalizing, stimulating influence. From an isolated mountain fastness it forthwith again became the theatre of activity and thrift, and the stream of precious metals that it again poured into the world's commercial channels not long after required the capacity of a line of railroad to handle its vast volume. Chicago, New York, Boston, and other Eastern centres recognised Montana merchants as among their heaviest and best-paying customers, again demonstrating that mining for the precious metals is the great vanguard of a rapid and substantial civilization.

The Utah & Northern was the pioneer railroad into her confines, but its business soon grew to such enormous proportions that the Northern Pacific followed in three or four years, and then Jim Hill swooped in with his Great Northern Road. So that that apparently isolated section has three transcontinentals now running east and west through her entire length, with the Chicago, Burlington & Quincy on her eastern border, impatient to share her immense traffic, and the Butte, Boise & San Francisco soon to give her a direct outlet to San Francisco Bay.

Sunrise in Camp.

But to return to the early days of Montana, certainly one of the grandest and richest sections of the Union. It is in this State that the muddy Missouri River has its source, although in the mountainous part of its course its water is as clear as crystal. Here, also, the broad and majestic Columbia has its inception, the heads of these two noble streams bubbling up out of her lofty mountains quite close together. And it is a striking coincidence that the same section that sends these two noble streams down through fertile fields to the sea, bearing on their mighty bosoms the wealth and water supply of empires, should also possess the largest and richest deposits of the precious metals that the world has ever known. But such is the case.

Speaking of precious metals recalls some of the 'stampedes' to newly discovered mining camps in early days. A 'stampede' is a panic reversed, usually instigated by the wild and rainbow-coloured statements of over-enthusiastic persons, and often those statements had utterly no foundation in fact. Men would rise from their beds in the middle of the night, if thought necessary, and with insufficient food, clothing, or implements, afoot or horseback, climb dark mountains or *cañons*, swim floods, tramp over alkali plains, or submit to any and all kinds of hardships, all for the sake of being among the first on the ground of newly discovered 'diggins.' *First come, first served,'* was the rule, and each man was determined, as nearly as possible, to be first served.

In the famous Sun River stampede, in the winter of 1866-67, with the mercury coquetting with the 30-degree-below-zero point, it was said men actually started out in their shirt sleeves to make a hundred-mile journey through the deep snow to the reputed new camp without food supplies to carry them through. And as it often proved in other cases, there wasn't a particle of truth in the reputed rich fields. Dame Rumour, that ever versatile and fertile-brained jade, had had an inning, and she batted hard, firing her hot balls of deception to all quarters of the field.

In those days buffalo were plentiful on the plains of Eastern Montana. I think I have seen from twenty to fifty thousand in a single herd there. They blackened the hills and plains with their shaggy coats, they swarmed the rivers in their peregrinations, and raised clouds of dust like a *simoon* in their journeys across the country. I have seen hundreds of them in a group mired down in the quicksands along the Upper Missouri River. Hunters walked on their backs and shot the fattest of them as trophies of the chase, and the ever ubiquitous, keen-scented wolves came and gnawed their vitals while they were yet alive, but helpless, in their inextricable positions. At that time bands of stately elk also abounded there.

Deer were plentiful, and the fleet-footed antelope bounded over every plain. Mountain sheep, whose tender meat was fat and juicy, climbed the terraced rocky cliffs in great numbers, while ducks, geese, pheasants, fool hens, and many other table fowl were to be had for a little effort on the part of the hunter. A fool hen is a species of bird weighing about two pounds, that is so foolish as to allow the gunner to lay aside his fire-arms and kill the whole flock with sticks and stones, so closely can it be approached without taking flight. Its meat is delicious.

Many volumes could be written on Montana's early reminiscences, her vast resources, her brilliant past, and her glorious prospective future. But the brief space allotted me precludes the possibility of detailed mention of people, places, or things, and I reluctantly stop sharpening my pencil. Montana has been great in the past, but her future will be much grander and greater still.

Chapter 27

The Denver of Early Days

Henry Allen was the first postmaster of Denver, so called, and charged 50 cents for bringing a letter from Fort Laramie. The first Leavenworth and Pike's express coach arrived there on May 17, 1859, having made the trip in nineteen days. This company reduced the postage rates on letters to 25 cents. The first postmaster of this concern was Mr. Fields, who was succeeded by Judge Amos Steck in the fall of 1859.

On June 6, 1866, Horace Greeley, of the New York *Tribune*, arrived in Denver by express coach *en route* to California, and addressed the citizens that same Monday evening. The next day he straddled a mule for the Gregory mines in company with A. D. Richardson, then a Western correspondent of the *Tribune*. On the 11th, they returned from Gilpin County mines, and published under Greeley's signature in a *News* extra his views concerning the extent and richness of the gold diggings which he had just witnessed with his own eyes. The circulation of this extra along the routes to the States soon caused another immense immigration to return there that fall.

On October 3rd the first election for county officers was held under provisional government. B. D. Williams was then elected to represent the new Territory of Jefferson in Congress.

The first marriage took place in Aurora (West Denver) October 16, 1859, Miss Lydia R. Allen to Mr. John B. Atkins, Rev. G. W. Fisher officiating. The first school ever started in Denver was by O. J. Goldrick, October 3, 1859, in a little cabin with a mud roof, minus windows and doors; and the first Sunday-school was organised October 6, 1859, by Messrs. Tappen, Collier, Adrian, Fisher, and Goldrick, in the preacher's cabin on the west bank of Cherry Creek.

The first theatre, called Apollo, was opened in Denver October 3,

335

1859, by D. R. Thorn's troupe from Leavenworth, with Sam D. Hunter for leading man and Miss Rose Wakely for leading lady. Old-timers will remember her well. She was considered the most beautiful lady that had graced Denver City in the first years of its existence.

The first election for territorial officers and legislative assembly occurred October 24, 1859, when R. W. Steele, a miner, was made first governor. Over 2,000 votes were cast in the twenty-seven precincts of the Territory at that election.

The first legislature assembled in Denver November 7, 1859, comprising eight councilmen and nineteen representatives. On New Year's, 1860, Denver had about 200 houses and Aurora (now West Denver) nearly 400, with a total combined city census of over 1,000 people, representing all classes, creeds, and nationalities; hence its cosmopolitan style from that day to this. Many brick and frame buildings, stores, hotels, shops, and dwellings were put up in both towns during 1860. One was the banking house of Streeter & Hobbs, corner of Eleventh and Laramie streets. The rate of interest charged by them at that time was from 10 to 25 *per cent* per month, according to the collateral security, and from 10 to 25 cents per hundred pounds was the rate from the Missouri River for freight by ox or mule train.

On the 8th of December, the day of the adjournment of the first legislature, an election was held by those in favour of remaining under the Kansas regime, and Capt. Richard Sopris was sent as representative in the Kansas legislature.

John C. Moore was elected the first mayor of Denver, December 19, 1859, under a city charter granted by the first provisional legislature. In the fall of '59 there were no particular politics there. The great question of the day was: "Are you a Denver man or an Aurorian?" Rivalry ran high between the two towns until the consolidation of Denver, Aurora, and Highlands, April 3, 1860. The first officers of the Aurora town company were W. A. McFadding, president, and Dr. L. J. Russell, secretary. Those of the Denver town company were E. P. Stout, president, and H. P. A. Smith, secretary. Strange to say, not a single one of these property holders is now living there, or is now the owner of a single lot in this large city.

I must not forget an event that happened in Denver then. A family arrived there from the East, consisting of father, mother, two daughters, and a son. One of the young Denverites took a fancy to one of the young ladies, but parents and son were opposed to the young man; yet he was not to be got rid of. One evening he took advantage of the absence of the parents and married the girl, and on the return of the parents in the evening the mother and son started to look for them, and threatened to kill the young man if they could find him. They found them at the Platte House, on Blake Street. The mother of the girl went to break in the door, but finally concluded not to do so, and left for her home. The parties are still living in Denver, and are well off and greatly respected.

On November 10, 1859, a lager-beer brewery was established by Solomon, Tascher & Co. It was said that the beer was drinkable. It was as innocent of malt and hops as our early whisky was of wheat or rye.

Thirty-three years ago next July the patriotic pioneers celebrated the Fourth of July in this city. It took place in a grove near the mouth of Cherry Creek. One Doctor Fox read the Declaration, and James K. Shaffer delivered an oration. There was music by the Council Bluffs band.

July 12, 1860, a series of murders and violence began there by desperadoes who had infested Denver during the summer. They tried to muzzle the mouth of the press, which bravely condemned their dastardly outrages, and as a consequence they raided the *Rocky Mountain News* and tried to kill its proprietor.

The first regular United States mail arrived there on August 10, 1860; P. W. McClure, postmaster. The first Odd Fellows lodge was instituted there on Christmas Eve, 1860.

The close of the year 1860 saw 60,000 people in the Territory, 4,000 of whom were in and around Denver.

At this juncture of time Denver was tolerably well favoured with the three great engines of civilization, to wit, schools, churches, and newspapers. There were three day schools, two or three newspapers, and the following church denominations, each with a place for holding services: Methodist Episcopal, Methodist Episcopal South, Roman Catholic, Presbyterian, and Protestant Episcopal. The latter denomination was well and truly cared for by the Rev. J. H. Kehler, who established St. John's Church in the wilderness, as he then called it. Therefore, to the praise of our pioneers let it be recorded that though then remiss in many of the modern enterprises, their liberality encouraged religion, morality, and popular education. They claimed that Whittier's apostrophe to Massachusetts might and should apply equally to Colorado in these regards:

The riches of our commonwealth
Are free, strong minds and hearts of health;
And more to her than gold or grain
The cunning hand and cultured brain.
Nor heeds the sceptic's puny hands,
While near the school the church-spire stands;
Nor fears the blinded bigot's rule,
While near the church-spire stands the school.

CHAPTER 28

The Denver of Today and Its Environs

The Denver of today, (at time of first publication), the capital of Colorado, has a population of 160,000, and it stands at an elevation of 5,196 feet.

In 1858 the Pike's Peak gold excitement caused a rush from the East to Colorado, and a camp was pitched at the junction of Cherry Creek and the Platte. From this small beginning sprang Denver, the "Queen City of the Plains." Beautiful in situation, with the great range of the Rocky Mountains towering in the west, and the illimitable plains stretching 600 miles to the Missouri River on the east, Denver is worthy of the attention and admiration of all who behold it. It is one of the greatest railroad points in the West, twelve railroads centring here and radiating to all parts of the United States, thus giving Denver almost unsurpassed facilities for transcontinental traffic. The foot-hills of the Rocky Mountains are only fourteen miles distant, and Long's Peak, James' Peak, Gray's Peak, and Pike's Peak are in plain view, connected by the gleaming serrated line of the Snowy Range. Parks, boulevards, opera houses, and costly and elegant public buildings and private residences are a few of the most obvious signs of wealth, cultivation, and luxury which are to be found in Colorado's capital.

Among the principal places of interest may be mentioned the Tabor Grand Opera House, erected at a cost of $850,000, and which is the finest building of its kind in America, having but one rival in the world, the Grand Opera House in Paris; the United States Mint; the County Court House, a most elegant and costly structure occupying an entire block with the buildings and grounds; the City Hall, University of Denver, St. Mary's Academy, Wolfe Hall, Trinity M. E.

Church, St. John's Cathedral, College of the Sacred Heart, Jarvis Hall, Baptist Female College, Brown's Palace Hotel, and hotels and business blocks, any of which would do credit to any of the metropolitan cities of the East. The city has extensive systems of street cars, motor lines and cables, is lighted by gas and electricity, has excellent waterworks, a well-disciplined and effective paid fire department, good police force, and telephone communication in the city and with suburban towns to the distance of 120 miles. The discovery that artesian wells can be sunk successfully has added much to the attractiveness of the city. The water is almost chemically pure, and is forced to a great height by hydrostatic pressure.

Denver is the objective point for a large tourist travel, and it is estimated that the arrivals during the year will average 1,000 daily. The climate is healthful and invigorating, and invalids find this an excellent place to regain their health. There is always some pleasing attraction to divert the mind. The theatres are open the year round, and the best companies and stars from the East appear upon their boards. The churches are presided over by clergymen of talent and culture. The newspapers are metropolitan in size and management. In a word, Denver is one of the most pleasant residence cities in the world. Rapid as has been the growth of this wonderful city, it is evident that it is but on the threshold of its prosperity, and that the future holds for it much more and greater success than has been vouchsafed it in the past.

Thirty-three miles south of Denver, on the Denver & Rio Grande Railroad, is Castle Rock. It is a picturesque little village, and derives its name from a bold and remarkable promontory which springs directly from the plain and under whose shadow the village stands. This promontory always attracts the attention of tourists, and is therefore worthy of special mention.

Perry Park is situated within half an hour's drive of Larkspur Station, and in natural attractions has few if any superiors in the State. Bountifully supplied with pure and sparkling water, and protected on the west by the Front Range of mountains, it forms a quiet and romantic resting-place for those who wish a pleasant summer's outing free from the annoyances of business. The park is filled with many remarkable rock formations equal in unique grandeur to those of the better known but not more attractive Garden of the Gods.

Palmer Lake is situated on the Denver & Rio Grande Railroad, about midway between Denver and Pueblo, the two principal towns of Colorado. It was formerly called "Divide," a very significant and appropriate title, as on the crest of this summit the waters divide, flowing northward into the Platte, which empties into the Missouri, and southward into the Arkansas as it wends its way to the Mississippi.

The traveller will enjoy a most delightful variety of scenery. On either side are rolling plains dotted with numerous herds of sheep and cattle, agricultural settlements with cultivated ranches, giving evidence of enterprise and thrift. Now and then we catch a glimpse of the river threading its way amid valleys and glens, while stretching away in the distance the cliffs and towering peaks of the Snowy Range, in their dazzling whiteness, appear like fleecy clouds upon the horizon, and form a striking contrast with the blue-tinted foot-hills, which, as we near them, appear covered with oak shrubbery, bright flowers, castled rocks, scattered pines, and quaking aspen glimmering in the sunshine. Gradually ascending the mountain pathway we reach the summit (2,000 feet higher than either Denver or Pueblo), and entering a gap in the mountains, before us lies Palmer Lake. Nestled here in this mountain scenery, sparkling like a diamond in its emerald setting, this lake is a delightful surprise to the tourist—a rare and unlooked-for feature in the landscape.

Glen Park, the Colorado Chautauqua, is within half a mile of Palmer Lake, in a charming park-like expanse between two mountain streamlets, and at the mouth of a beautiful *cañon*, fifty-three miles from Denver. One hundred and fifty acres are comprised in the town site. The park is at the foot of the Rocky Mountain range, and is sheltered at the rear by a towering cliff, 2,000 feet high, and on two sides by small spurs of the range. A noble growth of large pines is scattered over the park. A skilful landscape engineer has taken advantage of every natural beauty, and studied the best topographical effect in laying out the streets, parks, reservoirs, drives, walks, trails, and lookout points. It is a spot that must be seen to be appreciated, and every visitor whose opinion has been learned has come away captivated. There are building sites for all tastes. Some have a grand outlook, taking in a sweep of the valley for a distance of fifty miles.

Colorado Springs is the county seat of El Paso County, has a population of 12,000, and stands at an elevation of 5,982 feet. This delightful little city is essentially one of homes, where the families of many of the most influential business men of the State reside. It is a temperance town, with charming society, and an elegant opera house, built as a place of enjoyment rather than as an investment, by some of the most successful citizens. There are many points of scenic interest within an hour's ride of the city. Among them may be mentioned Cheyenne Cañons, Austin's Glen, Blair Athol, Queen's Cañon, and Glen Eyrie. No more delightful places can be found in which to enjoy the beautiful in nature and to breathe the health-giving and exhilarating air than these mountains and Pike's Peak. There are a number of smaller hotels and a good supply of comfortable and home-like boarding houses, in different parts of the town; also fine livery stables, where riding and driving horses and carriages of the best are furnished at reasonable rates.

Colorado City, the first Territorial capital of Colorado, and at present, (1893), a thriving railroad town, is situated on the Denver & Rio Grande Railroad, midway between Colorado Springs and Manitou Springs, seventy-eight miles from Denver.

Manitou Springs. Of all nature's lovely spots few equal, and none surpass, in beauty of location, grandeur of surroundings, and sublimity of scenery this veritable "Gem of the Rockies." As a pleasure resort it presents to the tourist more objects of scenic interest than any resort of a like character in the Old or New World; while its wonderful effervescent and mineral springs, soda and iron, make it the favourite resting-place for invalids. The great superiority of Manitou's climate is found in its dryness and the even temperature the year round. In summer the cool breezes from the mountains temper the heat, the nights always being cool enough to allow that refreshing sleep so grateful to all and most needed by the invalid.

There are more points of interest near Manitou than any other watering place in the world. The following is a partial list, with the distances in miles from town attached:

	Miles.
Ruxton Creek to Iron Springs and Hotel	1
Ute Pass to Rainbow Falls and Grand Cavern	1½
Red Cañon	3
Crystal Park	3
Garden of the Gods	3
Glen Eyrie	5
Monument Park by trail	7½
Monument Park by carriage	9
Seven Lakes by horse trail	9
Seven Lakes by carriage road	12
North Cheyenne Cañon	8½
South Cheyenne Cañon	9
Summit of Pike's Peak	12

In addition to these well-known localities there are scores of *cañons*, caves, waterfalls, and charming nooks which the sojourner for health or pleasure can seek out for himself.

The Garden of the Gods has been described and photographed more than any other place of scenic interest in Colorado, but words or pictures fail to give even the faintest idea of its wealth of gorgeous colour, or of the noble view which its gateway frames. The portals of the gateway spring from the level plain to a height of 330 feet, and glow with the most brilliant colouring of red. There is an outer parapet of pure white, and there are inner columns of varied hues, the whole suggesting the ruins of a vast temple, once the receptacle of the sacred shrine of the long-buried gods. Within the garden the rocks assume strange mimetic forms, and the imagination of the spectator is kept busy discovering resemblances to beasts or birds, of men and women, and of strange freaks in architecture.

Glen Eyrie is situated at the entrance to Queen's Cañon, and is a wild and romantic retreat, in which is built the summer residence of a gentleman of wealth, whose permanent home is now in the East. Within the glen, which is made sylvan by thickly growing native shrubbery, covered with wild clematis, are a great confusion of enormous pillars of exquisite, tinted pink sandstone.

Cathedral Rock and the Major Domo, which have gained a worldwide fame through pictures and descriptions, are to be found in Glen Eyrie, as are also "The Sisters," "Vulcan's Anvil," and "Melrose Abbey." These are all grand and impressive shapes of stone glowing with the most brilliant hues of red and pink, and cream and white, and umber.

Blair Athol is about a mile north of Glen Eyrie, and resembles the latter, with the exception of shrubbery and water. No residence has been erected here, as the difficulty of obtaining water has been too great to be successfully overcome. The quaint forms of rock and their brilliant colour, together with the frequent shade of evergreen trees, make this an interesting and attractive spot.

Bear Creek Cañon is reached by taking the road to Colorado Springs and turning to the right just before reaching Colorado City. This is a beautiful drive of five miles, at the end of which the Government trail to Pike's Peak carries the horseman and footman to the summit. The *cañon* is a picturesque wooded glen, with a dashing torrent and abounding in wild flowers. Bears are still frequently seen here, but they shrink modestly from forcing their attention upon strangers, and retire precipitately when made aware of the vicinity of callers.

The Cheyenne Cañons are favourite resorts for picnic and pleasure parties. Both these *cañons* give one a good idea of the gorges which abound in the fastnesses of the Rocky Mountains. They are deep gashes in the heart of Cheyenne Mountain, and display grand faces of magnificent red granite hundreds of feet in height. The Douglas spruce, the Rocky Mountain pine, the white spruce, and that most lovely tree of all, the *Picea grandis*, grow in great numbers in both *cañons*, while the Virginia creeper, two species of clematis (mauve and white), and other climbers add grace and charm to the scene. A stairway at the Seven Falls in South Cañon leads to the last resting place of "H. H." (Helen Hunt Jackson), who selected this spot for her grave. The stream in North Cheyenne Cañon is larger than that in the southern gorge, but the latter forms a magnificent cascade, descending 500 feet in seven leaps.

Seven Falls is the name given to the cascade referred to above, and it is well worthy the admiration its beauty always excites.

The Cheyenne Mountain toll-road is well worth seeing. It ascends the mountains about one-half mile south of the entrance to South Cheyenne Cañon, winding, with easy grades, through very fine scenery, and at times affording glimpses down in the *cañon* below.

The Seven Lakes are reached by means of the last described road. The lakes are picturesque, and such sheets of water usually are among the mountains, and there is a hotel for the accommodation of visitors.

"My Garden" is a very favourite resort, discovered by "H. H.," the authoress and poet. Take the Cheyenne road one and one-half miles from Colorado Springs, then follow due south past Broad Moor Dairy Farm half a mile, then through a gate across the "Big Hollow," and "My Garden" is reached, a lovely pine grove crowning the plateau, with an exquisite view of the range behind it.

Monument Park, Edgerton Station, sixty-seven miles south from Denver and eight miles northward from Colorado Springs and Manitou, is a pleasant day's excursion. "The Pines" is a comfortable hotel, situated in the centre of the park, one-half mile from the depot, commanding a fine view of Pike's Peak and Cheyenne Mountain Range; is open at all times for the accommodation of guests, and can furnish saddle-horses and carriages on premises. This park is chiefly remarkable for its very fantastic forms, in which time and the action of air and water have worn the cream-coloured sandstone rocks which the valleys have exposed, forming grotesque groups of figures, some of them resembling human beings, viz.: Dutch Wedding, Quaker Meeting, Lone Sentinel, Dutch Parliament, Vulcan's Anvil and Workshop, Romeo and Juliet, Necropolis, or Silent City, The Duchess, Mother Judy, and Colonnade. All of these, and many others too numerous to mention, are within easy walking distance of "The Pines."

A very pleasant drive can be taken to Templeton's Gap, which is situated just north of Austin's Bluffs, and is a sharp depression in the surrounding hills, characterized by quaint monumental forms of rock.

Ute Pass leads westward from Manitou over the range into South Park. It is now a wagon road cut in many places from the face of the cliff, the rocks towering thousands of feet above it on one side and on the other presenting a sheer descent of nearly as many feet down to where the fountain brawls along over its rugged channel. The pass was formerly used as a pony trail by the Ute Indians in their descent to the plains and in their visits to the "Big Medicine" of the healing springs—the name given Manitou by the aborigines. No pleasanter ride or drive can be taken than up Ute Pass. The scenery is grand and the view one of great loveliness.

Rainbow Falls are only a mile and a half from Manitou up the Pass, and are well worthy of a visit. They are the most accessible and the most beautiful on the eastern slope of the Rocky Mountains, and are visited by thousands of tourists every season.

The Great Manitou Caverns have added an attractive feature to the diversified wonders of nature surrounding Manitou Springs. The caverns are located one and a half miles from Manitou Springs. They were discovered by their present owner, Mr. George W. Snider, in the year 1881, but were only opened to the public in 1885.

The cog-wheel railroad to the summit of Pike's Peak, which was completed and put in operation in July, 1891, is the most novel railway in the world. When it reaches its objective point above the clouds, at a height of 14,147 feet above sea-level, it renders almost insignificant by comparison the famous cog-way up Mount Washington and the incline railway up the Rhigi in Switzerland. From its station in Manitou, just above the Iron Springs, to the station on the summit of Pike's Peak, the Manitou & Pike's Peak Railway is just eight and three-quarters miles in length. The cost of construction of the road was a half million dollars. While it could have been built for many thousands of dollars less by putting in wooden bridges and trestles, light ties and light rails, those in charge of the building of the road would not consent to the use of any flimsy material for the sake of saving any sum of money—a substantial road that would insure absolute safety being economical, as well as a guarantee for putting the road from the start on a paying basis.

The road-bed is solid and from fifteen to twenty feet wide, leaving fully five feet on each side of the cars. The culverts are solid masonry; the four short bridges are of iron girders resting on first-class masonry. There are an extra number of ties, which are extra heavy and extra long. The rails are standard "T" rails, with a double cog rail in the centre. This cog rail weighs 110 tons to the mile, which is unusually heavy. The rail is built in sections, each being put into a lathe and the teeth cut. The contract requires that each tooth shall be within the fifteenth part of an inch of the size specified. At intervals of every 200 feet the track is anchored to solid masonry to prevent any possibility of the track slipping from its bed.

The cars are designed to hang low, within eighteen inches of the rails. Each engine built by the Baldwin Locomotive Works has three cog and pinion appliances, which can be worked together or independently. In each cog appliance is a double set of pinion brakes that work in the cog, either one of which when used can stop the engine in ten inches, going either way, on any grade and at the maximum speed, eight miles an hour. The cars are not tilted, but the seats are arranged so as to give the passenger a level sitting. The engine pushes the cars instead of drawing them, which is of great advantage. And such is Denver today, and its attractive surroundings, changed from a border wilderness to civilization and grandeur within thirty years.

CHAPTER 29

Buffalo Bill from Boyhood to Fame

It may not be amiss just here, while writing of this "Land of the Setting Sun," its changes from savagery to civilization, to refer to one who has done so much to aid those who followed the Star of Empire toward the Rocky Mountains.

I refer to Col. W. F. Cody, known in almost every hamlet of the world as Buffalo Bill, one upon whom the seal of manhood has been set as upon few others, who has risen by the force of his own gigantic will, his undaunted courage, ambition, and genius, to be honoured among the rulers of kingdoms, as well as by his own people.

Nearly forty years ago, in Kansas, a handsome, wiry little lad came to me, accompanied by his good mother, and said that he had her permission to take a position under me as a messenger boy.

I gave him the place, though it was one of peril, carrying dispatches between our wagon-trains upon the march across the plains, and little did I then suspect that I was just starting out in life one who was destined to win fame and fortune.

Then it was simply "Little Billy Cody," the messenger, and from his first year in my service he began to make his mark, and lay the foundation of his future greatness.

Next it became "Wild Will," the pony express rider of the overland, and as such he faced many dangers, and overcame many obstacles which would have crushed a less strong nature and brave heart.

Then it became "Bill Cody, the Wagonmaster," then overland stage driver, and from that to guide across the plains, until he drifted into his natural calling as a Government scout.

"Buffalo Bill, the Scout and Indian Fighter," was known from north to south, from east to west, for his skill, energy, and daring as a ranger of mountain and plain.

With the inborn gift of a perfect borderman, Buffalo Bill led armies across trackless mountains and plains, through deserts of death, and to the farthest retreats of the cruel redskins who were making war upon the settlers.

Buffalo Bill has never sought the reputation of being a "man killer."

He has shunned difficulties of a personal nature, yet never backed down in the face of death in the discharge of duty.

Brought face to face with the worst elements of the frontier, he never sought the title of hero at the expense of other lives and suffering.

An Indian fighter, he was yet the friend of the redskin in many ways, and to-day there is not a man more respected among all the fighting tribes than Buffalo Bill, though he is feared as well.

In his delineation of Wild West life before the vast audiences he has appeared to in this country and Europe, he has been instrumental in educating the Indians to feel that it would be madness for them to continue the struggle against the innumerable whites, and to teach them that peace and happiness could come to them if they would give up the war-path and the barbarism of the past, and seek for themselves homes amid civilized scenes and associations.

Buffalo Bill is therefore a great teacher among his red friends, and he has done more good than any man I know who has lived among them.

Courtly by nature, generous to a fault, big-hearted and brainy, full of gratitude to those whom he feels indebted to, he has won his way in the world and stands to-day as truly one of Nature's noblemen.

One of the strongest characteristics of Buffalo Bill, to my mind, was his love for his mother—a mother most worthy the devotion of such a son. His love and devotion to his sisters has also been marked throughout his lifetime.

When he first came to me he had to sign the pay-roll each month by making the sign of a cross, his mark. He drew a man's pay, and earned every dollar of it.

He always had his mother come to get his pay, and when one day he was told by the paymaster to come and "make his mark and get his money," his face flushed as he saw tears come into his mother's eyes and heard her low uttered words:

"Oh, Willie! if you would only learn to write, how happy I would be."

Educational advantages in those early days were crude in the extreme, and Little Billy's chances to acquire knowledge were few, but from that day, when he saw the tears in his mother's eyes at his inability to write his name, he began to study hard and to learn to write; in fact his acquiring the art of penmanship got him into heaps of trouble, as "Will Cody," "Little Billy," "Billy the Boy Messenger," and "William Frederic Cody" were written with the burnt end of a stick upon tents, wagon-covers, and all tempting places, while he carved upon wagon-body, ox-yoke, and where he could find suitable wood for his pen-knife to cut into, the name he would one day make famous.

With such energy as this on his part, Billy Cody was not very long in learning to write his name upon the pay-roll instead of making his mark, though ever since, I may add, he has made his mark in the pages of history.

All through his life he was ever the devoted son and brother, and true as steel to his friends, for he has not been spoiled by the fame he has won, while today his firmest friends are the officers of the army with whom he has served through dangers and hardships untold, as proof of which he was freely given the endorsements of such men as Sherman, Sheridan, Gen. Nelson A. Miles, Generals Carr, Merritt, Royal, and a host of others.

Chapter 30

The Platte Valley

From the dawn of history to the present time, civilization has followed the valleys. From the Garden of Eden which was in the valley of the Euphrates to modern times the water courses have been the highways of civilization, and made the Tiber and the Thames, the Rhine and the Rhone famous in the annals of the world's progress. In our own country this fact has been especially illustrated. The valley of the Rio Grande del Norte was the pathway of the Spaniard in his march to the northward, and it is one of the curious facts of history that, before the Pilgrims had landed on Plymouth Rock, the adventurous cavaliers of Spain had penetrated the centre of the continent and discovered the sources of the great river in the Sangre de Cristo Mountains of Colorado.

It was along the Connecticut and the Hudson, the Delaware and the Susquehanna, the Ohio and the Mississippi, that the pioneers of the republic pushed their way westward and planted the civilization which has enjoyed so substantial and prosperous a growth. And when the pioneer resumed his westward march to the Rocky Mountains, his trains lay along the Missouri, the Arkansas, and the Platte, thus giving to the valley of the Platte an historic place in the records of the nation's advancement.

The Louisiana Purchase, within whose boundaries lay the great valley of the Platte and its tributaries, was completed in 1804, by President Thomas Jefferson. It was an act of statesmanship worthy of the man who had drafted the Declaration of Independence, and assured the young republic a future little dreamed of by the men of that day, but which we have lived to realise. Two years later, in 1806, Lieut. Zebulon Pike received an order to explore the newly acquired national possessions, and to find the headwaters of the Platte River. In pursuance of the order, Lieutenant Pike marched up the Arkansas to the Fountaine Qui Bouille, discovered and ascended the great peak which bears his name, entering the South Park from the present site of Cañon City by the Current Creek route. Aside from his discovery of the headwaters of the Platte, Lieutenant Pike's expedition was more largely devoted to the Arkansas and the Rio Grande than to this valley.

The second expedition up the Platte Valley was ordered in 1819 by John C. Calhoun, Secretary of War for President James Monroe, and was under the command of Major Stephen S. Long, of the corps of topographical engineers. Leaving Pittsburg, Pa., in April, 1819, Major Long proceeded westward and established his camp near the present site of Council Bluffs, Iowa, to which was given the name of Engineer Cantonment. Thence on June 6, 1820, with a number of scientists and a small detail of regular troops, he marched toward the mountains. On June 30th the party sighted the magnificent range of the Rocky Mountains, a view of which burst upon them in the full glory of the morning light. On July 3rd they passed, as Long's annals read, "the mouth of three large creeks, heading in the mountains and entering the Platte from the northwest." These were undoubtedly the Cache la Poudre, the Thompson, and the St. Vrain. On July 5th they camped on the present site of Fort Lupton, and on July 6th on the present site of Denver, at the mouth of Cherry Creek. Thence the party followed the valley to the Platte Cañon, and, proceeding southward along the base of the mountains, returned eastward along the Arkansas.

Twenty-two years later, in 1842, came Lieut. John C. Fremont, the famous pathfinder, who traversed the Blue toward the Platte, reaching the valley at Grand Island, a portion of the party going up the North Fork toward Fort Laramie, and the larger part marching up the South Fork to Fort St. Vrain, which had then been established a number of years, and had become a noted rendezvous for trappers, hunters, and plainsmen. The following year the intrepid explorer left St. Louis on his second expedition, travelling the valleys of the Kaw and the Republican, reaching the Platte at the mouth of Beaver Creek, and arriving at Fort St. Vrain on July 4, 1843. I quote the words of Lieutenant Fremont as prophetic of the future of the valley.

> This post was beginning to assume the appearance of a comfortable farm. Stock, hogs and cattle, were ranging about the prairie. There were different kinds of poultry and there was the wreck of a promising garden in which a considerable variety

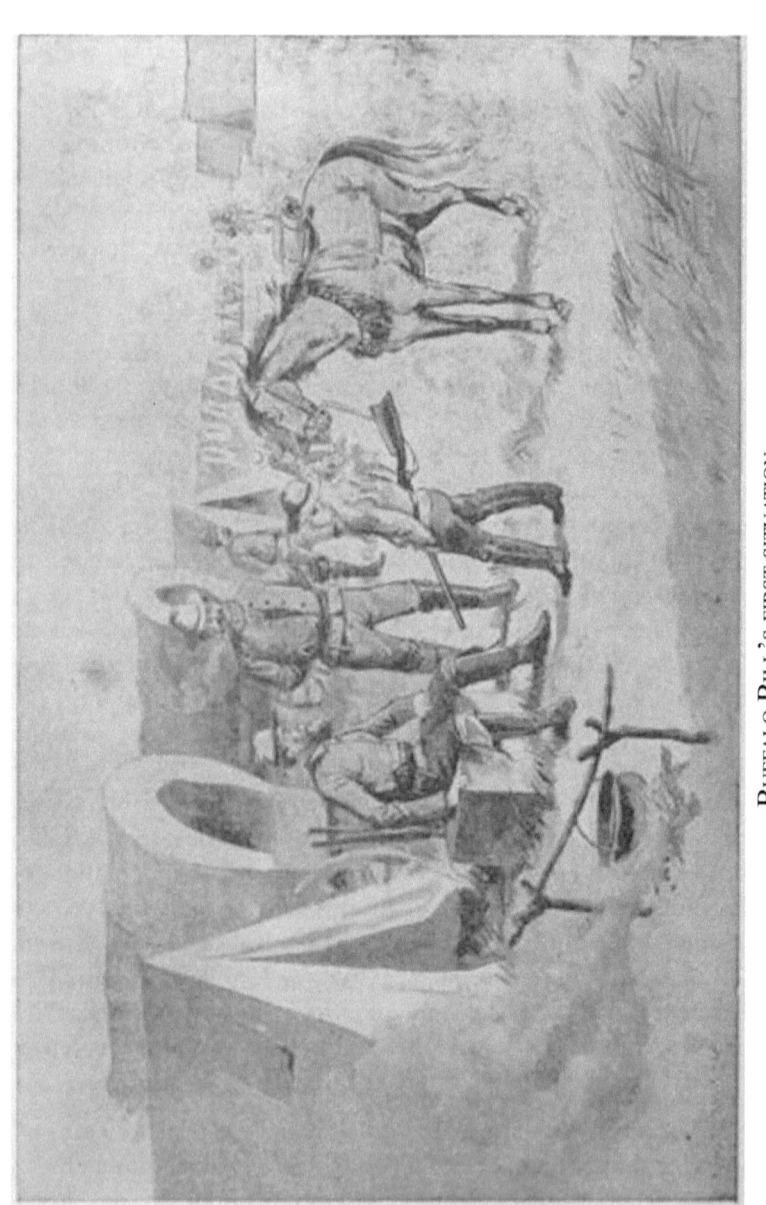

BUFFALO BILL'S FIRST SITUATION.

of vegetables had been in a flourishing condition, but had been almost entirely ruined by recent high water.

Between the dates of the expeditions of Long and Fremont three noted trading posts had been established along the Platte in the immediate vicinity of the spot on which we are now assembled. The first of these was Fort Vanquez, built by Louis Vanquez in 1832, at the mouth of Clear Creek, then known as Vanquez Fork of the Platte. The next was Fort Lupton, a portion of whose walls are still standing, and the third was Fort St. Vrain, built in 1840. These forts, as they were called, were trading posts at which a large traffic in skins and furs was conducted, and which became the headquarters of such famous frontiersmen as Kit Carson, Jim Bridger, Jim Baker, Jim Beckwourth, and others, who in those days constituted the vedettes of the civilization of the country. I have not time to dwell upon their exploits, but I note their names as indicating that we stand upon historic ground, and that here in this valley were planted the first germs of the prosperous growth which today enfolds it in every department of its social, industrial, and commercial life.

In 1847 the Platte Valley became the highway of the Mormons in their exodus from Illinois to Utah. Two years later its trails were broadened by the California pioneers *en route* to the shores of the Pacific to share in the golden discoveries of Sutter and his companions.

In 1857 came the expedition of Col. Albert Sidney Johnston marching to Utah to sustain the laws and authority of the United States.

But a greater movement was now organising to traverse and possess the valley of the Platte. In the fullness of time the crisis of its destiny had arrived. The year of 1859 dawned upon a nation fast drifting into the vortex of a civil war. The irrepressible conflict which for half a century had been going on between free and slave labour was nearing the arbitrement of arms, and absorbed all men's minds to the exclusion of events which were happening on the distant frontier. In the summer of 1858 Green Russell and a party of adventurous prospectors had discovered gold in Cherry Creek, a tributary of the Platte. The news spread, and grew as it spread, until the people living along the Missouri, which was then the frontier of the Republic, became excited over the richness of the discoveries.

They were ripe for adventure, desperate almost in their determination to re-establish the fortunes that had been wrecked by the financial panic of 1857, which had swept with disastrous effect along the entire borderland of the entire nation. In the spring of 1859 the march of the pioneers began. The Platte Valley was their grand pathway to the mountains, whose summits they greeted with exultant joy, and beneath whose protecting shadows they camped; here to make their homes, here to lay the foundations of the future State.

Thus in a little over half a century from the date of its purchase by the Federal Government, the Platte Valley had become the home of civilized man, and the work of its development begun. As gold was first discovered in this valley, so was quartz mining first begun on one of the tributaries in Gilpin County.

The first pioneer's cabin was erected in Denver; the first schoolhouse was built at Boulder; the first church was consecrated at Denver; the first colony located at Greeley, and the first irrigating ditches taken out, all within the Platte Valley. As the valley had been the route of Major Long and other of the early explorers, so, following in the train of the pioneer, came first the pony express, then the stage-coach, then the locomotive and the Pullman car. And it is a fact which I believe has never yet been published, that the last stage-coach of the great overland line was dispatched from the town of Brighton to Denver, thus associating its name with an act, insignificant in itself, but far-reaching in its importance, when it is remembered that that act marked the end of our pioneer period and ushered in the new growth of the railroad era.

We stand today, (1893), at the distance of three-fourths of a century from the date when the foot of the white man first trod the valley of the Platte. The names of Pike and Long are perpetuated by the two magnificent peaks which raise their summits to the clouds and stand as guardians of the plains below. Fremont lived to see his wildest dreams realised in the progress of the West, but whatever fame he may have achieved as a soldier and a statesman, his name will longest be remembered as the pathfinder of the Rocky Mountains. Wheat-fields now flourish where once stood the trading-posts of Vanquez and St. Vrain. The trails of the early explorers and of the pioneers of 1859 are almost obliterated, and grass is growing upon their once broad and beaten pathways. A happy, contented, prosperous people possess the land. A great line of railway now rolls the traffic of a continent along the valley where once the stage-coach and ox-trains of Russell, Majors & Waddell wended their slow and weary way. Thriving towns and villages and cities dot the plain, and reflect in the activity of their commercial life the industrial development by which they are surrounded.

CHAPTER 31

Kansas City Before the War

In August, 1838, there appeared in the far West a newspaper published at Liberty, in Clay County, Missouri, the only newspaper within many miles, a notice which read as follows: "Circuit Court of Jackson County, Missouri, at Independence, August term, 1838." Then followed a description of lands now included in what is known as the "old town" of Kansas City. Then continues:

> The above mentioned lands are situated in the county of Jackson, one and one-half miles below the mouth of the Kansas River, and five miles from the flourishing town of Westport. The situation is admirably calculated for a ferry across the Missouri River, and also one of the best steamboat landings on the river, and an excellent situation for a warehouse or town site. The terms of sale will be a credit of twelve months, the purchaser giving bond and approved security, with interest at the rate of 10 *per cent* from day of sale. All those wishing to invest capital advantageously in landed estate will do well to call upon Justice H. McGee, who is guardian for the heirs.
>
> James B. Davenport,
Peter Booth,
Elliott Johnson,
Commissioners.

The purchasers were William L. Sublette, John C. McCoy, William Gillis, Robert Campbell, and others, and the price paid for the entire tract, extending along the Missouri River from Broadway to Troost Avenue, containing 156 acres, was $4,220.

These gentlemen put their purchase into lots and blocks and called it "Kansas," but very little was done toward founding a city until some eight years later, when a new company was organised by H. M. Northup, who is still living; John C. McCoy, who died within the past few months; Fry P. McGee, Jacob Ragan, William Gillis, Robert Campbell, who have been dead but a few years respectively; Henry Jobe, W. B. Evans, and W. M. Chick, who have been dead much longer.

The first sale of lots was had in April, 1848, at which sale 150 lots were sold at an average price of $55.65 per lot.

The business of the city was confined almost entirely, for a number of years, to the levee, and was of the general character of that done in all river towns in their early history, pretty rough, pretty miscellaneous, and not altogether unmixed with "wet goods." Prohibition was an unknown element in social science, and the proportion of whisky consumed in the retail trade, compared with that of tea or coffee, was very like that described by Shakespeare in referring to Falstaff's "*intolerable deal of sack to the half penny worth of bread.*" But very few men of those days remain nowadays; yet, as I have said, H. M. Northup still lives, vigorous and active. Dr. I. M. Ridge still continues to practice his profession, although less extensively than forty years ago. John Campbell traverses our streets, but has long since turned his well-known and faithful old sorrel mule out to grass. William Mulkey looks hale and hearty, but has discarded his former buckskin suit, though he still maintains a portion of his farm in the centre of the city.

Once in a long while one of the old French settlers of those early days, or even an old plainsman, ventures into the busy city and looks about him in a bewildered sort of way for a day or two, and then disappears again into the nearest wilderness or prairie, as being far more congenial to his tastes and habits of life. Not all of them, however, are of this character and disposition. It is but a few weeks since I met one of our most noted pioneer plainsmen and freighters across the prairies of Kansas, Colorado, and New Mexico, in the earliest of the days I have been speaking of. In those times no name was better or more widely known than that of Seth E. Ward, the post trader at Laramie.

The descendants of most of the original owners of the "Town of Kansas," as it was first called, or "Westport Landing," as it was nicknamed later, still remain there, and are among its most prominent and respected citizens today.

Ten years later the "western fever" struck Ohio, and hundreds of young men of my acquaintance left there for Kansas and Nebraska. Omaha was a favourite objective point, and a town named Columbus was founded still farther west than Omaha, which was almost entirely colonized by people from Franklin County, Ohio. One of my friends, Dr. Theodore S. Case, also holding the rank of colonel, was studying medicine at the time in Columbus, Ohio, and resisted the fever until the following year, 1857, when, with a few books and a sheepskin authorising him to write M. D. after his name, and to commit manslaughter without being called to account for it, started for the West. He knew nothing of the West, but had a general idea that he would go to St. Louis, or Keokuk, or Des Moines, or Omaha, or Council Bluffs, or possibly to "Carson City," Kan.; for a sharper, originally from Columbus, had been out West and came back with a lithographic map of a city by that name, fixed up very attractively, and with all the modern improvements of court house, city hall, depots, churches, colleges, steamboats, etc., and he bought some $15 worth of lots on one of the principal thoroughfares of the city not far from the depot.

However, before he got as far west as St. Louis, he had learned the manners and tricks of such gentry, and did not go to "Carson City." By some accidental circumstance his attention was called particularly to the geographical location of Kansas City, and he at once determined to give it a look anyhow. There being no railroad nearer than Jefferson City at that time, he took the steamer Minnehaha at St. Louis, along with some other 299 fellows who were going "out west to grow up with the country," and four days afterward landed at Kansas City, May 1, 1857, almost thirty-five years ago.

The first view of Kansas City was by no means prepossessing, as it consisted principally of a line of shabby looking brick and frame warehouses, dry-goods stores, groceries, saloons, restaurants, etc., strung along the levee from Wyandotte Street to a little east of Walnut Street, the whole backed up and surmounted by a rugged and precipitous bluff, from 100 to 150 feet high, covered with old dead trees, brush, dog fennel and jimson weeds, with an occasional frame or log house scattered between and among them, and a few women and children, principally darkies, looking down at the boats.

To a young man, however, the levee, with its three or four steamers, huge piles of Mexican freight, prairie schooners, mules, greasers, Indians, negroes, mud clerks, roustabouts, Frenchmen, consignees, emigrants, old settlers, tenderfeet, hotel drummers, brass bands, omnibuses, etc., presented attractions not easily resisted. Notwithstanding all the tooting for hotels, there were really but two in the place, one on the levee, then known as the American Hotel, now remembered more familiarly as the "Gillis House," and the other the "Farmers' Hotel,"

Lee's Ferry, on the Colorado.

on Grand Avenue, between Sixteenth and Seventeenth streets. The first was technically known as the "Free State Hotel," having been built by the New England Aid Emigrant Society, and the other as the "Pro-Slavery," or "Border Ruffian House," as it was or had been the headquarters of the pro-slavery party in the border war of 1854 and 1856 between the free state and pro-slavery contestants for the possession of political control of the Territory of Kansas.

All travellers, however, who knew the ropes dodged both these hotels and took the omnibus for Westport, where two really good hotels were kept. To show the amount of travel toward Kansas at that time I may say that at the American Hotel alone there were 27,000 arrivals in the year 1856-57.

Such was Kansas City in early days and the experience there of a tenderfoot, but now an honoured citizen of what is really today a great city.

CHAPTER 32

The Graves of Pioneers

Many an Eastern city has more dead people than living. Instead of the West being young, the East is growing old. The antiquities of the Eastern cemetery are often more interesting to the Westerner than the life and energy of the living city. How the old names of Concurrence, Patience, Charity, Eunice, Virtue, Experience, Prudence, Jerusha, Electra, Thankful, Narcissa, Mercy, Wealthy, Joanna, Mehitable, on the tombstones of the old Puritan grandmothers have been supplanted by the new names of these modern times! And the old-time grandfathers—well, their names suggest a scriptural chapter on genealogy. These old-time names, with quaint and queer epitaphs, on less pretentious monuments than the costly ones now erected, make an interesting study, for the ancient dates and names show that the cemetery has a history from the earliest settlement. The ancestral bones from the Mayflower down to the present have been saved. It is true that the great Western cities now have costly, beautiful, and often magnificent monuments for the dead, for the modern cemetery is becoming aristocratic.

But for the reason it might be considered almost a sacrilege, the model of a typical New England graveyard, with its odd names and quaint epitaphs, would be an interesting historical study at the World's Fair. In fact it would be as much of a curiosity to millions of people in the West as Buffalo Bill's Wild West Show was in the East.

In all the cities of the West there are more live people than dead ones, which is not always true of the East, where the cemetery population is often larger. With the exception of some of the old Spanish mission cemeteries, those of the West are all new, unless one would wish to explore the ancient homes of the mound-builders and cliff-dwellers. A white man's graveyard is a new thing for the West. There are many thousands among the 17,000,000 people west of the Mississippi River who can tell of the days when Kansas City, Omaha, St. Paul, Minneapolis, Denver, Salt Lake, Galveston, Dallas, Helena, San Francisco, Portland, and Seattle hardly had a cemetery. Even St. Louis and New Orleans have been American cities less than a century.

But during all this time many millions have been added to the silent cities of the dead in the East, and the older the cemetery the more there is to it that is new to a Western tourist. One born in the West, on making his first trip to the East, finds almost as much of interest in a New England burial-ground, and often views it with as little reverence as does the Bostonian in gazing upon the mummies and antiquities of Egypt.

It is interesting to contrast the frontier funeral and burial-ground in the West with that of the East. The cemetery, the necessary but last adjunct to the organisation of a civilized community, follows in the wake of immigration and empire. No monuments mark the last resting-place of those buried in the first five great cemeteries in the far West. They are in the region of nameless and unknown graves.

Those five historic cemeteries, where thousands from the East and South died and fill unknown graves, are the Missouri River, and the Santa Fé, Oregon, California, and Pike's Peak trails. The trans-Alleghany, and later the trans-Mississippi pioneers, followed, in the main, the water-courses. There was no prairie-farming, and hence the term, "backwoodsman." It was a kind of a Yankee trick in the West, in later years, to leave the forests and begin ploughing the prairies, and save the time that had been hitherto used in log-rolling and clearing the river-bottoms for agriculture. The early trappers, hunters, and fur dealers followed up the Missouri River and its tributaries. Only with great difficulty could a corpse be concealed from wolves and coyotes, the latter animal always having been known as the hyena of the plains country.

Hence many an old hunter, when far from the borderland of civilization, has buried his "pard" in the Missouri River! Landsmen and plainsmen with a seaman's burial—a watery grave! The body wrapped in a blanket—when the blanket could be spared—and tied to rocks and boulders, was lowered from the drifting canoe into the "Big Muddy," as that river is commonly known in the West. Many an old hunter and trapper has been buried in the mighty rushing waters of the great Western river, even as the faithful followers of De Soto lowered his remains into the bosom of the Mississippi.

When it was necessary or convenient to bury the dead on land, the greatest precaution was taken to protect the body from wolves and coyotes, which were especially dangerous and ravenous when off of the trail of the buffalo. Rocks and large pieces of timber were placed on the newly made grave, but often these hyenas of the plains could be seen scratching and growling at this debris before the comrades of the dead man were out of sight. With these facts so well known, it is not strange that many in those early days preferred a burial in the rivers to that of the land. It seems almost paradoxical to thus find in the old trapper some of the instincts and traditions of the sailor. Far out on the plains cactus was often put in the grave, just over the corpse, as a protection against the wolves and coyotes.

The earlier expeditions starting from St. Louis went up the Mississippi a few miles, to the mouth of the Missouri River, and then followed the latter stream. For some time the old Boone's Lick country, now known as Howard County, Mo., and Old Franklin, was the frontier commercial head.

The town of Old Franklin, where was the original terminus of the old Santa Fé trail, when Kit Carson was only an apprentice to a saddler and harness-maker, is now the bottom of the Missouri River, for there a current of seven miles an hour has cut away the old town site.

But the pioneers became bolder. Instead of following the river they began to venture out from St. Louis overland, about the time of the old Boone's Lick settlement. It was considered a brave and hazardous journey to start from St. Louis overland in those days, for it was a village town, and all of the country to the west was a wilderness. It was about the year 1808 that the Workman and Spencer party started from St. Louis, and far out on the plains, before reaching the Rocky Mountains, one of the party sickened and died.

The Indians rendered what assistance they could in bringing herbs and such crude medicines as they used for fevers. The poor fellow died, and they dug for him a grave, which was among the first, if not the first, burial of a white man on the great plains of the West.

It was a novel sight for the Indians to see the hunters and trappers wrap up their dead comrade in a blanket, and put the body into a deep hole they had dug. They piled up brush and what heavy things they could find, and placed on the grave, carved his name in rude letters, and went on their way. But they had hardly resumed their journey before the wolves began to dig at the grave.

Were it not foreign to the purpose of this article, it would be interesting to relate at some length the fate of this expedition. The most of the party were slain in battles with the Indians, and Workman and Spencer are reported to have gone through the grand *cañons* of the Colorado River to California in 1809, but that remarkable feat is discredited by some, leaving honours easier with Major Powell, whose expedition through these *cañons* was in more modern times.

This lonely and desolate grave dug by the Workman and Spencer party is supposed to have been somewhere in what is now Kansas or Nebraska. It was the beginning of making graves on the plains and in the mountains, but time, wind, rain, and sand made them unknown.

Many thousands perished on the old-time trails to Santa Fé, the Rocky Mountains, and the Pacific Coast. Exposure, sickness, thirst, starvation, and massacre were the dangers the immigrants had to face. Many of their graves were marked with slabs, but the inscription was soon effaced. These graves are as unknown in the great ocean of plain, prairie, and mountain as though the pioneer dead had been buried at sea.

The most fatal days was when the cholera raged on the Western trails. Sometimes an entire train would be stricken and the captain would be compelled to corral the wagons until aid could be obtained from other caravans on the desert, then so called, or the teamsters recovered to continue the journey. Women sometimes helped to dig the graves and assisted in burying the dead, and have then taken the dead teamster's place at the wagon, driving the oxen until men could be employed.

With the opening of the Western trails for wagons, a larger number were buried in boxes made from rude pieces of lumber, or sometimes a part of the sideboard of the wagon was utilised for that purpose. The earlier expeditions were on horseback, and hence at that time the best that could be done would be to roll the body in a blanket. Only those in the East who have seen a burial at sea, although they may never have been on the plains, can realise the sadness and desolation of those who left their friends in the nameless graves of the old-time American desert. Many of the babies lived that were born on the California and Oregon trails, but the saddest of all was when the pioneer mother and babe were added to the thousands of nameless graves. The death-couch was a pile of straw and a few blankets in an old freight wagon. If the angels ever hover over the dying, there never would have been a more appropriate place for their ministrations. Nameless graves! Unknown!

Only the drifting sands and the ceaseless flow of the mighty Western rivers know the place of their nameless dead. These are the famous cemeteries of the far West. There are no granite shafts or beautiful emblems carved in marble. Heroic men and women! They died unknown to fame and honour, but they gave their lives that a new civilization and a new empire might be born in the far West. The brave men, North and South, who fell in battle, have their graves marked "unknown" when they could not be identified, but no one knows where sleep the thousands who died on these trails. Even a slab to the "unknown" could not be placed, for who knows the grave? Farmhouses, fertile fields, cities and towns, and the rushing railway car now mark the spot. The path of civilization and the rapid building of empire in the West is their only living monument.

During the cholera days there was a heavy loss of life on the Western steamboats. On the Missouri River some of the old boats had a burial crew. At night-time, when the passengers were hardly aware of what was going on, the boat would stop near a sand-bar. The bodies of those who had died during the day were taken to the sand-bar, where they were quickly buried. What would have been the use of putting up even a pine board, for the rising waters would soon have washed it away?

But this is not simply Western history. It is a part of the history of the North and the South, for those who came never to return were from those sections. In many an Eastern and Southern home it is as unknown to them as to the people of the West where sleep their dead on those old trails of the Western empire.

The emigrants and gold-seekers were population in transit. Their burial-places were as fleeting. With the building of new towns and cities were established cemeteries, but there still continued to be the thousands of unknown graves. A father, brother, husband, or son dies away from home. His name may not have been known, or if it was, the pencil-marks on the pine board soon lost their tracing in the weather-beaten changes that time brings. How often in my own experience in the mining camps I have seen men die far away from the tender and loving care of mother, wife, and sister. How terrible then is the struggle with death! The desire to live and to see the old home-faces again becomes a passion. In their delirium the passion becomes a reality.

In their feverish dreams I have seen the dying miner in his cabin fancy he was home again. He talks to his wife, and with words of endearment tells her that he has found a fortune in the mines. I never knew of a miner who, in the delirium of death, when he was talking of the mines, but what he was rich. He had struck the precious metal. He tells his people at home about it, and many a poor fellow has seemingly died content, founded on the fancy that he had a mine and that his wife and family would always have plenty. Out of many instances I will relate but one.

A young man from Galena, Ill., eleven years ago, (as at 1893), was taken sick and soon the fever was upon him. He grew rapidly worse, but bravely fought the pale reaper, for he wanted to see home again. But courage was not equal to the task. The poor fellow had to die, and when the fever was at its height, he imagined that he was with his wife and baby. How tenderly he spoke to his young wife. He thought he had a rich mine, and told her where it was located. Then he imagined that his pillow was his baby, and that he was running his fingers through the child's curly hair, and would fondle the child up to his bosom. As I gazed on the bronze and weather-beaten faces of those present in the cabin, I saw tears come into the eyes of some when the dying man was murmuring child-love talk to the baby.

At the time of the great Leadville rush, many came who never returned. Unknown, many of them sleep in their last resting place—in the gulches, on the mountain sides, and under the shadows of the pine trees and granite peaks. Exposure and not being prepared to guard against the sudden changes of climate caused many to die of pneumonia and fevers. The writer went through a hard attack of typhoid pneumonia in one of the mining camps. After the worst was over and I was conscious again, one of the boys said to me, "Hello, pard, when you were in the fever you thought you had found enough gold mines to have bought out the Astors and Vanderbilts."

The greatest number of deaths for a while seemed to come from what was known as the "sawdust gang." In the wild excitement of a new mining camp boom, people rush in by the hundreds and thousands. Many have only enough money to get there, and are compelled to sleep on the sawdust floor of the saloons. Thus they caught cold, which turning into pneumonia often proved fatal. And the cowboys—how often on the long Texas-Montana drives they have dug a hasty grave and with the lassos lowered their dead pard into it.

The sporting and theatrical element always have a swell funeral in the booming mining camps. The musicians from the dance-halls turn out, play dirges, and with due pomp and ceremony the funeral is conducted. The band returns from the new cemetery usually playing some lively air. The deceased has had a fine funeral and a good send off, and now to business. The dance-halls are crowded again, the music goes on, and men and women gamble, dance, and drink, unmindful of what has occurred.

Those were days of death, hell, and the grave. But what will not men undergo and dare for gold? They have braved anything for it in the past, and will in the future. Friendships and home ties are broken, and in the wild, mad rush for fortune, thousands of gold hunters have lost their lives, and fill nameless and unknown graves in the far West. There is something of romance in the death of a humble prospector searching for wealth on the mountain side. Whether rich or poor the old gold hunter often sees wealth ahead in his last hours. And, perchance, through the fading light on the mountain peaks, may he not see a trail leading to a city where the streets are golden? Who knows?

In 1849 and 1850, all along the trail of the overland freighters' route, were scattered unknown graves, clear into California, my dear father being one of the pioneers who died and filled an unknown grave. In the fall of 1850, on the east bank of the San Joaquin River, he died of cholera, and was buried, and his grave is unknown.

Another instance that I recall was of the death of one of the women of the party. She was buried at the South Pass, and they built a pen of cottonwood poles over the grave, placing her rocking chair to mark the spot, and which had her name carved on it.

CHAPTER 33

Silver Mining

My son Benjamin and I worked as contractors almost a year in 1868, upon the building of the Union Pacific Railroad, and we were present at the Promontory when the Union and Central Pacific roads met, and saw the gold and silver spikes driven into the California mahogany tie. It was regarded at that time as the greatest feat in railroad enterprise that had ever been accomplished in this or any other country, and it was a day that will be remembered during the lifetime of all that were present to witness this great iron link between the two oceans, Atlantic and Pacific. My calling as a freighter and overland stager having been deposed by the building of telegraph lines and the completion of a continental railway, I was compelled to look after a new industry, and as the silver mining at that time was just beginning to develop in Utah, I chose that as my next occupation, and my first experience in prospecting for silver mines was in Black Pine District north of Kelton some twenty-five miles, and I believe in the northwest corner of Utah.

The district proved to be a failure, but leaving it, I met with Mr. R. C. Chambers, who, upon acquaintance, I found to be a very pleasant gentleman. I left the camp and went to Salt Lake City, and wrote Mr. Chambers that I thought mines in the mountains were a better show for prospectors than the Black Pine District, and in a few days he came to Salt Lake City, and we then engaged in prospecting in the American Fork and Cottonwood districts, which lay in the Wasatch Mountains, twenty-five or thirty miles southeast of Salt Lake City. We had some success, but were not able to find anything in the way of bonanzas. We were connected with each other more or less until 1872, when a gentleman came to me one day in July of that year and told me that he had a bond upon McHenry mine, in Park District, and that the mine was a remarkably rich one. He desired me to telegraph to Mr. George Hearst of San Francisco to come to Salt Lake City and go and see the mine. He said that he wanted me to send the message because he knew Mr. Hearst, with whom I had become acquainted through Mr. Chambers, would come for my telegram, when he would perhaps pay no attention to his.

I sent the message, and received a reply forthwith that he would start at once for Salt Lake City. He arrived in due time, and we together went to the McHenry mine. Upon arrival we found it was not what was represented. We were thoroughly disappointed in our expectations. But while sitting, resting on a large boulder, a man by the name of Harmon Budden (who a day or two before had discovered and located the Ontario mine) approached us and spoke to Mr. Hearst. Mr. H. said he did not remember him, but Mr. Budden said he had previously met him in some mining camp in Nevada, and remarked that he had a prospect that he would like us to look at, only a short distance away. We went with him to the location. His shaft was then only about three feet deep, and when Mr. Hearst jumped down into the hole that he had dug, the surface of the ground was about as high as his waist, and he could jump in and out by putting his hands on the earth.

I saw that he was very much interested in the appearance of the ore, which at that depth and at that time did not show more than a streak of eight or ten inches of mineral. I was at that time what they called a "tenderfoot," and had not been in the mining business long enough to be an expert, and to my inexperienced eye there was nothing unusual in the appearance of the ore, but Mr. Hearst did see something, and he determined then and there to purchase the Ontario prospect, and arranged when we returned to Salt Lake City with Mr. Chambers to keep a watch over its development, and purchase it when he saw an opportunity to do so. Mr. Budden and his associates asked $5,000 for the prospect when we were there, but Mr. Hearst thought it might be bought for less, as it was nothing but a prospect.

But as the development of the mine progressed they raised their price for it $5,000 every time they were asked the terms, until at last it was up to $30,000, when Mr. Chambers purchased it for Mr. Hearst and his associates in San Francisco, Messrs. Tebis and Haggin. Mr. R. C. Chambers was made superintendent of the mine, and has remained its manager from that period until the present, he being one of the stockholders, as well as the superintendent. The mine has grown and developed until it is one of the great mines of the Rocky Mountain region, and under Mr. Chamber's supervision has been extremely successful and profitable to its owners. Its output, up to 1892, has been over $26,000,000, over $12,000,000 of which has been paid in dividends to the stockholders. This showed that Mr. Hearst was an expert, for he was really one of the best judges of minerals I ever met.

Utah has furnished the mining industry with some very remarkably rich silver mines, among them the Eureka, in Tintick District; the Eureka Centennial; the Chrisman Mammoth, a large gold and silver mine, and the Beck and Hornsilver, in the Frisco District; the Crescent; the Daly, in Park City District; and Ontario, as well as a great many smaller mines in the various parts of Utah. In Montana we have one of the greatest copper mines in America, called the Anaconda. It is the leading mine in Butte City, though they have many other remarkable mines in that district. Then there is the Granite Mountain, the Drumlummen, in Marysville District, also in Montana. But the greatest output from any mine yet discovered was the Comstock, in Virginia City, Nev. It has produced more millions of dollars than any other silver mine in the United States, its output being about one-third gold. The mining industry of the Rocky Mountain States and Territories is only in a fair way for development. The State of Colorado furnishes some very rich mining camps; also New Mexico and Arizona.

In Colorado there is the Central City and Black Hawk, and the adjacent mining district, from which there has been millions of dollars in gold extracted; also the Leadville, which has produced its millions in silver and lead; the Aspen District, with its Molly Gibson and other immensely rich mines. Then there is the Crede District, with its Amethyst and others, now producing large amounts of silver and some gold; the Silverton, where there are a great many rich mines being opened; the Ouray District and Cripple Creek, a newly discovered gold camp, with various others in that State too numerous to mention. Nearly all of the entire mining camps of the State produce both gold and silver in greater or less proportions, and with more or less galena or lead contained in the ores with the precious metals, and this great mining industry, when it is allowed to go on as it did before the demonetization of silver, will prove to be among the greatest and best paying industries in the whole Rocky Mountain region.

The Black Hills mining district of South Dakota is a very large mining camp, where millions and millions of dollars in gold and silver have been taken out, and where, no doubt, hundreds of millions more will be produced.

Idaho has also proven to be a very rich State in mineral wealth, both gold and silver, with many places where gold is washed out of the sands and gravel of the valleys.

Silver City, in New Mexico, has produced a great many millions in gold and silver, and at present seems to be a mining camp of great merit.

The mining industry of the mountains has, of course, been the means of influencing the building of numerous railroads through and into some of the most difficult mountain ranges; in fact wherever there has been a flourishing mining district the railway people have found a way, with capital behind them, to build a road to it, and it has now become apparent that a rich mining camp will have a railway connection sooner or later, no matter how difficult of access it may be. I think the men and the companies who have had the building of roads through and into the Rocky Mountains, and the interests of the country at heart, are deserving of great praise. No doubt, as many camps are discovered, it will be necessary to build many more roads than are now in existence, without which the mining industry could not be conducted with profit.

I may, in concluding this chapter on mining, speak of the great future there is for both Washington and Oregon as mineral States.

CHAPTER 34

Wild West Fruits

It is still within the memory of boys when it was almost universally agreed that nothing was more impossible than successful fruit raising in Colorado, with the exception of certain varieties of small fruits. It is easy to see how such a belief grew up, for even now in many places it requires ocular demonstrations to convince that, in parched valleys where frequently even cactus and sage-brush are but sparsely represented, fruit can be grown that in lustrous bloom and richness of flavour can not be surpassed in any country or climate. That such is the case, however, has already been so thoroughly proven, and the proof is being so persistently repeated year after year, and in widely separated localities, that to longer disbelieve or cavil is sufficient evidence either of ignorance or determination not to believe.

When travellers first crossed the prairies and followed the sandy or *adobe* river bottoms they could hardly be expected to think of the barren tracts as covered with orchards and gardens within a few years. Yet there were indices even then, and had not every mind been wholly absorbed in the search for gold, some one might have drawn a lesson from the laden plum and cherry trees that lined every foot-hill, *cañon*, and ravine, sometimes following the stream far out on the prairie. In the mountains, too, were raspberry patches, sometimes covering thousands of acres and yielding almost incalculable quantities of luscious fruit that, having no more appreciative pickers than bears and birds, annually decayed among the rocks and fallen logs.

There were, and still are, countless numbers of huckleberries, and in every part of the mountains grow more or less wild strawberries, raspberries, currants, gooseberries, thimbleberries, huckleberries, and numerous varieties of cherries, plums, and nuts. Considering these things it would not have required a great stretch of imagination of some old fruit man from the East to have foreseen something of the possibilities now beginning to be almost phenomenally realised in every part of the State.

A history of horticulture in the Centennial State has not yet been written, and it is impossible to say when and where the first domestic fruit was grown, or to whom is due the honour of having taken the initial step in the industry that from its rapid development and the enthusiasm already enlisted bids fair to outstrip all other pursuits in the State. In rapidity the growth has been much like that of our magic capital city, and as fruit is one of the things with which a luxury-loving people will not dispense, it may fairly be predicted that the infant industry, without any protection or coddling, will keep pace with the State and city.

It is not difficult to find good reasons for believing that its progress will not only exceed that of any other industry in the State, but that it will be out of proportion to that of the State itself. Irrigating is an expensive process, and whatever crop will bring the greatest return for the least outlay in that direction is the one to which the energy of the Colorado people should logically be directed. Not only can fruit be raised with much less water than any other crop, but a good yield in a single year after the trees are fairly well developed will reimburse the purchase price of the land and the other expenses, besides leaving a handsome profit.

If any one argues that only the southern half of the State can be relied upon for fruit, a visit to Larimer County will promptly and effectually convince him of his error. If he believes only in the western slope, let him follow the Arkansas River from several miles above Salida to where it enters Kansas, or the Platte from the foot-hills to Nebraska, examining the embryo orchards that enrich nearly every farm on his journey.

It is readily conceded that certain locations are, by nature, better adapted than others to certain kinds of fruits. To fit the varieties to the localities most suitable to their respective natures requires years of experiment. The fruit industry of Colorado is now in that experimental stage. To conduct the experiment so as to secure the best results, men of skill, long experience, and indomitable energy are necessary. Such men do not at present average one to the county. This fact does not reflect discredit on the men who are growing fruit. No one could realise the truth more fully than they do themselves. Hundreds of them who are succeeding with orchards scarcely knew one tree from another until they began putting them out on their farms.

The fact that so much has been accomplished without the experience and skill so essential to success in every country is the strongest possible evidence that the natural elements are here in the right combination and ready to do their part, and more, to win for the Centennial State a greater distinction as a fruit producer than has for years been hers as the silver queen. Just as sure as the conditions of climate and soil remain as they are, will this new industry eventually hold first place in every respect. In the immediate vicinity of the capital city, where only a few years ago was nothing but barren prairie, there are now hundreds of acres in orchards and vineyards. Apples, pears, plums, cherries, and numerous varieties of grapes are grown in abundance, and with such success that the fruit acreage is annually increasing. Up and down the Platte, on Cherry Creek and Clear Creek, on the prairie wherever water can be had for irrigating, farmers are putting out more and more in standard and small fruits. The never-failing demand for good fruit, to fill which California annually ships thousands of carloads, is encouragement enough, for it insures good prices without the trouble and expense of shipment.

Westward the same conditions are manifest, and the limited area of tillable land shows a yearly increasing number of fruit trees. Here close to the foot-hills a single acre, mostly in cherry trees, has yielded a cash return of $1,000 from one year's crop just harvested. It is but a matter of a few years until many another acre will yield as much or more, either English Morello cherry trees, as in this case, or from other varieties of standard fruits.

Boulder County has long been known as the home of small fruits. Last year the county furnished 184,300 pounds of grapes and 304,810 quarts of berries. In a walk through the streets of Boulder more grapes of the finer varieties, such as Delaware, can be seen than in the market of any other city in the State, without excepting even Denver in the present year. Nor is the county's output confined to small fruits, for in last year's report were 25,622 bushels of apples, 102 of peaches, and 143 of pears, besides 4,745 quarts of plums and 1,905 of cherries.

The same condition prevails in all the counties in the northwest part of the State, though, with the exception of the Greeley neighbourhood and the Platte Valley, the country is too recently settled to have made much progress in the culture of fruit. In the last few years the blight has been causing considerable discouragement in the Platte Valley and up the tributary streams in Larimer and Boulder counties.

Like other diseases, it has struck hard in a few specially valuable places, and in the riot of its march has caused more annoyance through fear than through actual ravages. It may thin out a few susceptible varieties of trees, but when it shall have run its course, the orchards that remain and those that will grow up in the future will be practically impregnable to its attacks. There are many varieties of fruits that will flourish just as well as apples and pears, and which the blight never touches. Men who are ready to drop the business when the fruit pest appears are not the ones who will win success. Many of the trees from which the finest apples are picked this year were badly blighted last year or the year before.

CHAPTER 35

How English Capitalists Got a Foothold

There are thousands, if not millions, of people in the United States who, if asked how they accounted for the fact that there are so many millionaires in the United States, could not give us a satisfactory explanation of the phenomenon.

It is a fact that there are hundreds who have amassed fortunes ranging from $1,000,000 to $100,000,000 each, within the last thirty years, and but very few people have any idea how they have made such immense fortunes in so short a time.

Not only our own people have made these vast fortunes, but hundreds of foreigners have accumulated immense wealth in this country, and now hold it. To give an idea of the immensity of these fortunes, I will call the attention of the reader to some well-known facts. First, to the fact, as is shown by Poor's Railroad Manual, that there is now about $5,500,000,000 of railroad bonds and floating debt, and there is about $4,500,000,000 of railroad stock, making a total of about $10,000,000,000, and this vast wealth is in the hands of comparatively few people.

Then there are national bonds to the amount of about $600,000,000. In addition to these are the bonds that have been issued by the States, counties, cities, towns, and school districts, amounting in the aggregate to probably $3,000,000,000. Then there are, according to the last census, about 9,000,000 of mortgages upon the farms, homes, and property of the people. The aggregate of these 9,000,000 of mortgages is probably not less than $5,000,000,000, and all of this vast amount of bonds, stocks, and mortgages draw interest, requiring about $1,000,000,000 each year to pay interest.

All of this wealth is in the hands of but a small percentage of the people, and what is incomprehensible to the masses is the fact that a very large *per cent* of it is in the hands of foreign capitalists. Of the $10,000,000,000 of railroad bonds and stocks, it is a conservative estimate to say that one-half of it belongs to foreign, principally English, capitalists. The question is often asked, How did they acquire this property? What did they give us in exchange for it? Was it gold, silver, or merchandise? If neither of these, what did we get? To prove that they did not send us either gold, silver, or merchandise in payment for at least $5,000,000,000 of our railroad bonds, we have only to refer to the report of the Secretary of the United States Treasury for 1891, and we find that since the close of the war, in 1865, our exports of gold, silver, and merchandise have exceeded our imports in the sum of $872,000,000; so that it is very clear that we have been sending them an enormous amount of money and merchandise over and above the amount we have imported from them, and whatever may have been received from the railroad bonds is still to be accounted for.

To understand how they have acquired this hold upon the resources of the country, imposing a burden on the people that is surely and certainly reducing them to the condition of paupers and serfs, we shall have to go back to the days of the war, and review the financial policy of the government, and point out how the laws have been framed exclusively in the interest of capital.

During the war the government issued many kinds of paper money, such as greenbacks, seven-thirty notes, one-year notes, compound-interest notes, and one, two, and three year notes, all amounting to nearly $2,000,000,000. This money was put in circulation by paying it out at its full face value to the soldiers, sailors, and creditors of the United States, but the government would not receive it back in payment of duties upon imports, but would receive it from any one who wished to purchase five-twenty government bonds, taking it at its face value.

The interest on these bonds was 6 *per cent*, payable in coin. This continued until February, 1863, when the laws were enacted that provided that after July 1, 1863, the paper money should not be received in exchange for bonds having interest payable in coin. The result of this was that shortly after the law went into effect the paper issued by the government rapidly depreciated, and very soon it was worth only about 40 cents on the dollar, but our soldiers were still compelled to take it at its full face value, that is, 100 cents on the dollar.

At the close of the war, in 1865, our government issued many hundreds of millions of their depreciated paper and paid it out to the soldiers, sailors, and other creditors of the government at its full face value, 100 cents on the dollar.

After the soldiers had been paid off in the depreciated currency of the government, and it had gone into general circulation, one of the most gigantic schemes ever concocted by the money-power was then devised.

The object was to destroy the money of the country, and issue in its place many hundreds of millions of dollars of government bonds drawing 6 *per cent* interest in coin, payable semi-annually.

During the winter of 1865-66, an agent of the Rothschilds went to Washington and secured the enactment of a law providing that any person might take any of the depreciated paper that had been issued by the Government for the purpose of paying off the soldiers and the other expenses of the war, and exchange it at its full face value for bonds of the United States drawing 6 *per cent* interest in coin, payable semi-annually, and that the money paid for such bonds should be destroyed within three years after the close of the war. By this means nearly $1,000,000,000 of the currency of the country was withdrawn from circulation and destroyed, and an equal amount of 6 *per cent* coin bonds were issued in place of the currency that was so destroyed.

No laws that were ever enacted, and no decrees that were ever promulgated by any tyrant that ever sat upon a throne, ever enabled a few to amass wealth as rapidly as they were enabled to do under the provisions of these laws.

Under the provisions of the laws of 1863 the currency was depreciated to less than 50 cents on the dollar, and under the law of 1866 hundreds of millions of dollars were bought up by the Rothschilds and other English and European bankers, at from 40 to 60 cents on the dollar, and were converted into five-twenty United States bonds drawing 6 *per cent* interest in coin, the interest to be paid semi-annually. This was equivalent to 12 *per cent* upon the actual cash paid for the depreciated paper with which they bought the bonds.

But this was only a part of the profit they were enabled to make. The interest was paid every six months in gold. The interest on $1,500,000,000 every six months was $45,000,000, and as the law that required the duties on imports to be paid in coin had never been repealed, gold was for many years at a high premium. The bondholders could take their $45,000,000 every six months to the gold-room in

Wall Street and sell it for 50 *per cent* premium. This was equivalent to 9 *per cent* on the face value of the bonds and 18 *per cent* on the coin they had paid for the currency with which they had bought the bonds.

But this was not all the profit they were enabled to make, for still other laws had been framed in the interests of capital and speculators.

Congress had assumed all the power that was claimed by the kings of old who claimed to rule by divine right; that is to give away the land of the nation to whomsoever they saw proper, and exempt it from all taxation for a term of years. In the exercise of this right they had given to individuals and corporations more land than there is in Great Britain; more land, in fact, than any king of England ever claimed to own. This land was given for the purpose of enabling these favoured corporations to build railroads for themselves (not for the people); the people had no interest in the roads, and could only use them on such terms as the railroad companies might dictate.

Railroad companies could not build railroads with land; it took money to build them; but the English bondholders had $50,000,000 or $60,000,000 coming in every six months for interest on their United States bonds, and they were willing to lend it to the railroad companies and take railroad bonds, secured by mortgage upon the railroad and their lands. Now, as there were a great many railroad companies that wanted to borrow money, they began to offer extra inducements to secure loans; they offered their bonds at 10, 15, and often 20 *per cent* discount. These railroad bonds usually drew 6, 7, and even 8 *per cent* interest, which was paid semi-annually. The profits made by these English capitalists were immense. Never in the world's history had such profits been made. The wildest dreams of John Law and the South Sea schemers were more than realised.

To fully understand this, let us take the actual results of one year's operations. The English capitalists, we will say, in 1867, invested $500,000,000 in the purchase of $1,000,000,000 of our depreciated currency. They took it to the United States Treasurer and exchanged it for United States bonds drawing 6 *per cent* interest in coin. At the end of six months they drew $30,000,000 in gold coin, and took it to the gold-room and sold it for $45,000,000 in greenbacks. Then they exchanged their greenbacks for railroad bonds at 20 *per cent* discount. They would thus receive about $54,000,000 of railroad bonds drawing 7 *per cent* interest. At the end of the next six months they would draw another $30,000,000 in coin and sell it for $45,000,000 in greenbacks, and exchange them for another $54,000,000 in railroad bonds.

They would also draw 7 *per cent* interest on the first $54,000,000 of railroad bonds, which, for six months, would be $1,840,000. The account of the first year would stand as follows: $500,000,000 in gold brought $1,000,000,000 of depreciated currency, and was exchanged for $1,000,000,000 of United States bonds; one year's interest on $1,000,000,000 amounted to $60,000,000. This was sold in the gold-room for $90,000,000 in greenbacks. Then the greenbacks were exchanged for railroad bonds at 20 *per cent* discount on the bonds. In this way at the end of the first year, for their investment of $500,000,000, they found themselves in possession of $1,000,000,000 of United States bonds, and $108,000,000 of railroad bonds, and $1,840,000 in cash for the first six months' interest on the first $54,000,000 of railroad bonds. Nor was this all the profit of the English capitalists, for in 1869 they secured the passage of a law by Congress pledging the government to pay not only the interest but the principal of the United States bonds in coin. This rapidly increased the value of the bonds, and in a few years they were eagerly sought for by English capitalists, and they rose to a premium of 25 *per cent* in gold on their full face value.

Within five years after the passage of the law of 1866, the bonded debt of the United States reached the sum of over $1,800,000,000. The interest was paid in coin, and was sold in the gold-room in Wall Street at a premium until 1878, and the profits realised upon the sale of this gold were simply enormous. These profits were promptly invested in railroad bonds at a discount of from 5 to 25 *per cent*.

In 1866 the bonded indebtedness of the railroads had got up to $2,165,000,000, and was in the hands principally of English capitalists, who had paid for them with the profits they had made on the United States bonds they had bought at a discount of from 40 to 60 *per cent*.

Not only the British capitalists made enormous profits, but our railroad corporations and speculators made still greater profits. For every dollar of the bonds they sold to the English capitalists they issued a dollar or more of the railroad stocks, so that in 1876 the amount of railroad stock reached the sum of $2,248,000,000.

From 1876 to 1890 the English and European capitalists continued to invest the interest they drew upon their government and railroad bonds in the new issues of railroad bonds, so that, in 1890, they had secured the enormous sum of $4,828,000,000 of railroad bonds, and it took $219,877,000 to pay the interest annually. During the same time the railroads had increased the amount of railroad stock to $4,495,000,000 and it took $80,000,000 to pay the dividends.

The railroad people not only made vast fortunes out of the $4,495,000,000 of watered stock (for it was in reality nothing but water, for the actual cost of building the roads was no more than was received from the sale of their bonds to the English capitalists), but they made hundreds of millions of dollars from the sale of the lands that had been given to them by the government, and had not cost them one cent, not even for taxes. They ran their roads through their lands for thousands of miles, and wherever they thought proper they would lay out towns and cities and sell the lots at fabulous prices.

They also induced towns, counties, and cities to issue millions of dollars of bonds and give to the companies, as a bonus, to run their roads through such towns and cities.

When we look at these facts, that are matters of history and can not be gainsaid, is it not plain to every man of common sense, that the policy of the government for the last quarter of a century has been in the interest of capitalists and speculators, and against the interest of the producing classes, who, either directly or indirectly, must pay the interest annually on this vast accumulation of wealth that is in the hands of the favoured few?

And to pay this vast amount of interest in gold, as these capitalists insist upon, and are trying to compel the people to do by using every means in their power to prevent the free and unlimited coinage of silver, will, in the near future, reduce the producing classes to the condition of serfs.

Chapter 36

Montana's Towns and Cities

The "Bonanza" State, young as she is today, has more towns and cities than such old and well developed States as Wisconsin, Illinois, or Minnesota had at a period in their history at which they might easily have expected to be far better developed, as regards population, than Montana could reasonably expect.

A half-century marks the time when the great Chicago of today was Fort Dearborn, planted, as it were, on a boundless prairie to watch a few blanketed Indians and traders at the mouth of the Chicago River. This was the nucleus of the great city—the second in rank of the many wonderful cities of the United States. Fifty years ago the pioneers of the Badger and Prairie States were doing what the old-timers and pioneers of Montana are doing today, building towns and founding cities. In the Eastern pioneer States where a few straggling hamlets were first fashioned by the efforts of the early emigrants, there are thousands of towns and cities, where the unpretentious log cabins and town sites were no more inviting than those of the early settlers of Montana.

Dating the first settlement of our State at twenty eight years ago, (at time of first publication), it may be said, without contradiction, that no Eastern State from its foundation to the twenty-eighth year of its age was half so marked or half so prosperous as Montana, with her hundred towns and cities at no greater age. If the State of Illinois has produced a Chicago at fifty years of growth, and Wisconsin a Milwaukee at a less number of years, and Minnesota the dual cities of St. Paul and Minneapolis in a much shorter time, what may not be expected of Montana, whose boundaries embrace probably the richest country in the world, and whose area equals that of the New England States and New York combined?

We see with open eyes what a half-century of American genius and Western enterprise has wrought; may we not see by a prophetic vision a grander half-century's work as the future of Montana? As certain as history repeats itself, the prospector's wickie-up will become the mining camp, the corral of the round-ups will furnish the location for rustic villages, the villages will become towns, and scores of towns will become cities, each one of which must be larger than the other, and one of which must be the great metropolis of the Northwest.

Following is a list of the towns and cities of the State, arranged in counties, together with the assessed valuation of those counties:

BEAVERHEAD COUNTY.—Assessed valuation for 1890, $3,175,949. County seat, Dillon; Bannack, Glendale, Redrock, Spring Hill, Barratts.

CASCADE COUNTY.—Assessed valuation, $12,383,864. County seat, Great Falls; Sun River, Cascade, Sand Coulee.

CHOTEAU COUNTY.—Assessed valuation, $5,364,264. County seat, Fort Benton; Chinook, Choteau, Harlem, Shonkin.

CUSTER COUNTY.—Assessed valuation, $6,350,915. County seat, Miles City; Rosebud, Forsyth.

DAWSON COUNTY.—Assessed valuation, $3,025,332. County seat, Glendive; Glasgow.

DEER LODGE COUNTY.—Assessed valuation, $7,359,589. County seat, Deer Lodge; Anaconda, Beartown, Blackfoot, Drummond, Phillipsburg, Elliston, Granite, Helmville, New Chicago, Pioneer, Warm Springs, Stuart.

FERGUS COUNTY.—Assessed valuation, $4,186,555. County seat, Lewiston; Cottonwood, Utica, Maiden, Neihart.

GALLATIN COUNTY.—Assessed valuation, $6,170,381. County seat, Bozeman; Three Forks, Gallatin, Galesville, Madison.

JEFFERSON COUNTY.—Assessed valuation,$4,917,382. County seat, Boulder; Jefferson City, Radersburg, Basin, Placer, Elkhorn, Whitehall, Alhambra, Clancy.

LEWIS AND CLARKE COUNTY.—Assessed valuation, $31,081,030. County seat, Helena; Marysville, Unionville, Rimini, Cartersville, Augusta, Dearborn, Harlow.

MADISON COUNTY.—Assessed valuation, $2,948,046. County seat, Virginia City; Fullers Springs, Sheridan, Twin Bridges, Laurin, Silver Star, Pony, Red Bluff, Meadow Creek.

MEAGHER COUNTY.—Assessed valuation, $5,239,882. County seat, White Sulphur Springs; Neihart, Castle, Martinsdale, Townsend,

Clendennin, York.

MISSOULA COUNTY.—Assessed valuation $8,815,854. County seat, Missoula; Demersville, Kalispel, Stevensville, Columbia Falls, Ashley, Grantsdale, Corvallis, Horse Plains, Thompson Falls, Camas Prairie.

PARK COUNTY.—Assessed valuation, $4,936,451. County seat, Livingston; Red Lodge, Cook City, Cokedale, Big Timber, Melville.

SILVER BOW COUNTY.—Assessed valuation, $32,426,794. County seat, Butte City; Melrose, Silver Bow, Divide.

YELLOWSTONE COUNTY.—Assessed valuation, $3,823,140. County seat, Billings; Park City, Stillwater.

WEALTH OF MONTANA.—Nothing speaks louder for the future of Montana than the figures that tell of her wealth and of the rapid increases which the last few years, as they rolled along one by one, have shown.

The increase during the last year has been no exception to this rule.

From a total assessable valuation of $116,767,204 in 1890, her wealth has increased to a total of $142,205,428 for 1891, a gain of over twenty-five millions. The valuation of the State, given by counties, is as follows:

County of		Valuation
County of	Beaverhead	$ 3,175,949
"	" Cascade	12,383,864
"	" Choteau	5,364,264
"	" Custer	6,350,915
"	" Dawson	3,025,332
"	" Deer Lodge	7,359,589
"	" Fergus	4,186,555
"	" Gallatin	6,170,381
"	" Jefferson	4,917,382
"	" Lewis and Clarke	31,081,030
"	" Madison	2,948,046
"	" Meagher	5,239,882
"	" Missoula	8,815,854
"	" Park	4,936,451
"	" Silver Bow	32,426,794
"	" Yellowstone	3,823,140
	Total	$142,205,428

But even this vast sum does not tell the whole story, for Montana's additional real wealth is not included in the assessable property of the State, as the vast millions of the intrinsic value of the silver, gold, copper, coal, and lead mines, and their precious output, are not assessable for taxation—only the improvements. So if the value of all of Montana's mines were put in the calculation of her wealth, what a vast amount of money-value would be placed to her credit. Of the hundreds of her gold and silver mines, two are valued at $25,000,000 each.

The above assessment value of $142,205,428 is made up of real estate, acre property, town lots, railroad rolling stock, road-bed and improvements, and personal property.

Montana's present ratio of population is not quite one person to the square mile, so with an assessment of over $142,000,000 with a population (according to the census of 1892) at 140,000, what will be the value of the State when its population shall have increased to ten persons to the square mile? The calculation is easily made—so within the next decade Montana's population may reach 1,440,000, and if the assessed value then is equal to the present wealth *per capita* of her citizens, the assessed value will reach the prodigious volume of $1,203,000,000—a calculation not unreasonable, since Montana's population in the last ten years increased 235 *per cent*.

CHAPTER 37

California's Great Trees

Not only is California the land of gold, the garden of fruit, and the home of the vine, but its rich soil is the footing for the greatest trees in the world. The redwoods of California are known all over the earth, and their fame is deserved, for they are the loftiest, the grandest trees that ever raised their crests to heaven, swayed in the breeze, and defied the storm. Though usually spoken of as the redwoods, these big trees are of two varieties. The redwood proper is the *Sequoia sempervirens* of the botanist, and the sister tree is the great Washington *Sequoia*, Wellington *Sequoia*, or *Sequoia gigantea*, being known by all three names, the last being the most correct. Another forest giant of a different nature to either, and yet commanding attention, on account of its giant size and age, is the *Pinus lambertiana*, the great sugar-pine of California. These three are the greatest trees on earth.

To single out the largest individual tree, it is probable that the *Sequoia sempervirens* would have to be awarded the palm; while to the greatest number of very large trees, the palm would have to be awarded to the *Sequoia gigantea*. Redwood trees (*Sequoia sempervirens*) are found only on the Coast Range, and *Sequoia giganteas* only in the Sierra Nevada Mountains. There are no redwoods south of Monterey County or north of Trinity County. The trees are different in foliage, and in their cones the *Sequoia gigantea* has a larger, more compact, firm cone than the *Sequoia sempervirens*, the cone of which is small and split open, though the similarity in form of the cones is noticeable. It is not generally known that "*sequoia*" is the name of the genus, just like oak, cypress, maple, and hence that the *gigantea* and *sempervirens* are species of the same genus. The name *sequoia* comes from Sequoyah, a Cherokee Indian chief of mixed blood, whose wisdom raised him as much above his fellows as the redwoods tower above other trees.

As to the age of the trees, it is conceded by botanists that the concentric rings interpret their annual growth. Objection has been taken to this on the ground that the distance between the rings varies very much in different trees of the same species. This fact has, however, no weight. The closer the rings the thriftier the tree, and their distance apart has no more to do with their age than a man's height or weight have to do with his age. Differences in soil and location account for the closeness of the rings, but, unquestionably, every added ring represents an added year of growth. In some cases there are but six or eight rings to the inch, in others thirty to forty. The ages of the big trees in the Calaveras and Mariposa groves range from 1,000 to 4,320 years of age.

One can scarcely conceive what this means; and the historic incidents of the days when these trees were already old may help to convey an idea of their age. When Carthage was founded some of these trees were centuries old; before Solomon built his temple, or David founded Judea, some of these forest giants fell crashing to earth, and have lain prone there ever since. All through the ages of Christianity the changing winds have shaken their tapering tops, and have swayed their crests in the gentle zephyrs, or rocked them to and fro in the gale, and now man, the pigmy, with his piece of jagged steel, his span of life three score years and ten, comes along, cuts through the forest giant, and the growth of thousands of years, that has defied storm and tempest, falls a victim to the pigmy.

The largest stump extant is in Mill Valley, Marin County, half an hour's ride north of San Francisco. This remnant of a great tree belongs to the redwood family; is, in fact, a genuine *Sequoia sempervirens*. How high it may have been it is impossible to say. Its circumference now is 135 feet, and measures across, on an average, 43 feet 6 inches. The saplings which stand round the ruin measure from 3 to 10 feet in diameter. The largest standing tree is the "Mother of the Forest," in the Calaveras grove. It now measures, without the bark, at the base 84 feet, and the full circumference, with the bark, which was stripped off in 1854 for exhibition purposes, was 90 feet. Its height is 321 feet, and the tree is estimated to contain 537,000 feet of inch lumber, allowing for saw cuts.

Close to it, prone upon mother earth, lies the "Father of the Forest." When standing, it is accredited with having been 400 feet high, with a circumference at the base of 110 feet, and he unquestionably was once king of the grove. "The living and representative trees of the

Calaveras groves," says J. M. Hutchings, in "The Heart of the Sierras," "consist of ten that are each 30 feet in diameter, and over seventy that measure from 15 to 30 feet at the ground." About six miles to the southeast of the Calaveras grove (in Calaveras County, Cal.) is the South grove. It contains 1,380 *Sequoias*, ranging from 1 foot to 34 feet in diameter.

In the Mariposa grove, in Mariposa County, Cal., there are many large trees, among them the "Grizzly Giant," measuring 91 feet at the ground, and 74 feet 6 inches three feet six inches above the ground, and is 275 feet high. Many very large trees and many interesting facts might be mentioned relative to them.

The *Sequoia gigantea* in the Sierras, in addition to the differences in cone and flower from the *Sequoia sempervirens*, has this one that, while the former grows only from seeds, the latter grows from both seeds and suckers, though mainly from the latter. The *Sequoias* of the Sierras rise to a height of 275 or even 350 feet, and are from 20 to 30, or even in rare cases 40 feet in diameter.

CHAPTER 38

The Flowers of the Far West

For centuries the rose—the queen of flowers—has been a never ceasing inspiration to poets and writers. Every bard has sung his lay to the majesty of this peerless flower.

Every ancient country has its rose traditions. Fashions do not assail the rose, only in specialty and variety.

The unanimity characterizing its nomenclature is but another feature in the unvarying and universal popularity of the rose.

All research fails to reveal the white rose as known to the ancients; the Greek word "*rodon*," ruddy, being used synonymously by all countries.

It was the flower dedicated to love—to Cupid and Venus. Cupid bestowed it as an emblem upon Harpocrates, the god of silence, to bind him not to betray the evil of his mother, Venus. In consequence the rose became symbolical of silence, and was gracefully distributed on the guest-table as a delicate reminder that all confidences should be respected. Comus, deity of the table, Hebe and Ganymede, nectar-bearers to the gods, were crowned with roses. The rose is typical of youth as well as beauty.

During the greatest opulency of the ancient empires its purity was often sullied by effeminacy and sensuality.

Who has not heard of the roses of the valley of Cashmere? Who has not longed to behold their exquisite perfection? Who, in contemplating the forms and colours, the lights and shadows of Flora's choicest blooms, has not found language failing in fineness to express the delicate eloquence of the rose? Who, in cultivating it, has not felt solicitude and affection for these creatures of the garden? Who has not had his anger excited in beholding a bud ruthlessly torn by sacrilegious hands and has not looked upon the broken stem as he would upon a bleeding artery? Who, in cultivating roses, has not spiritually felt the better for it? The subtlety of its fragrance, the grace of its form, the perfect harmony of its tones appeal to the imagination like music to the soul. In the whole range of nature's variety and completeness nothing so satisfies the idea of perfection as the rose. 'Tis grace idealized and the quintessence of beauty in its flowing lines and curves.

The relative position of the rose to its stem suggests majesty; its colour in contrast to its leaves, completeness; the unfolding of its petals, grace; its tintings fulfil that aesthetic delight, harmony; its fragrance, the sublimated breath of a fairer existence. In all candour, does it not more than satisfy the degree superlative?

Nature has richly endowed the earth with roses. Every country can offer its wild-rose tributes on Flora's shrine, with but one single exception, and that Australia. There are over eighty varieties of the wild rose known, the greater number being indigenous to Asia.

With experimenting and cultivating, varieties of roses have multiplied by hundreds; and rose culture, like everything else in this nineteenth century, has become a science.

Roses are like children, requiring warmth and affection. In a mild climate, where the seasons do not vary greatly in regard to temperature, the rose outvies tradition itself, and unfolds and matures with a regularity quite astonishing.

California climate is nature's elected home for roses. In almost any portion of the State removed from the immediate harsh influences of the coast, roses revel, from the tiniest boutonniere rose, with its pert little face, to that great lusty fellow, big as a large saucer and as hardy as a cabbage.

To the old residents, no rose in California appeals more to the poetical sense than the old Castilian, one of the oldest varieties in the State, and one now greatly despised by its more fortunate and voluptuous sisters. The fragrance of this rose is incomparable, its colour an intense glowing old pink, its foliage painfully disappointing. Having such a vigorous and healthy trunk and lusty system of roots, the Castilian is employed largely to graft other stock upon.

An ideal climate should produce nothing but ideal forms. This natural and just hypothesis is amply proven in presenting the full array of California roses as evidence. What better class of evidence could be desired?

There are several general groups into which California roses are usually divided: Tea roses, Bourbon roses, hybrid perpetual roses, China or Bengal roses, moss and climbing roses.

Of these classes, but several can be mentioned. Roses, as a theme, are practically inexhaustible, and the few kinds that appeal most strongly to the writer's sympathies will receive a passing word.

A rose-covered cottage, the material expression of peace, lowliness, beauty, and picturesqueness; a picture that most of us mirror in our minds in youth as connected with great and simple happiness. Many of the old Spanish houses of California are overrun with climbing roses. These old houses, simple in style of architecture, broad and square in appearance, are inviting abodes for the clinging loveliness of California's climbers.

Some fine April morning take a little trip to San Rafael, one of San Francisco's suburban villages. In this hill-girth town blooms the fairest rose of all the climbers. Some call it the "San Rafael Rose," others the "Beauty of Blazenwood."

The trunk rises bare and sturdily from the ground; as it approaches the top of a porch it spreads and bursts forth into a cloud of tawny yellow loveliness. Each rose presses hard upon its neighbour until special fancy is lost in the bewildering mass of bloom.

In this rose, the palest cream tint to the richest glowing apricot tones are observable. Frequently here a dash of colour almost vermilion is discovered; there a long slender-necked bud thrusts forth its head, as in derision to its closely-packed companions.

These roses are not very double, and a mass of their bloom presents features of ragged, wild grace; the vivid colours enthral, hasty steps are slackened to gaze at this golden corona of smiling April.

The brilliant William Allen Richardson, the mellow-toned and sweet-breathed Salina Forrester, the lusty-growing and superb bearing Reve d'Or, the daintily flowering and enamelled-leaved single white Cherokee, the prolific blooming and tiny-flowered Lady Banksia, and California's old stand-by, the Lamarque, a profusely bearing, many petalled white rose, perfect in all stages of development, and very handsome foliage.

In many of the old towns of California may be seen rose trees of really enormous size.

The writer saw a Duchesse de Brabant rose tree in Colusa County at least nine feet high and thirty feet or more in circumference. It was covered with hundreds of silvery pink roses; the trunk looked scraggy, and was probably twelve inches in circumference. Such a case is rare, however.

The Loretta is a rose of exquisite texture, of a creamy tone, and petals as clear-cut and dainty as a cameo. Too much praise can not be showered upon this long-stemmed vigorous grower. Such a galaxy of beautiful roses, each clamoring for recognition, that the only way to render justice is to stop right short and write nothing more.

The La France roses, Perle de Gardin, Marie Van Houtte, Archduc, Charles Catharine Mermet, Homer, Papa Gontier, Jacqueminot, and hundreds of others that nothing short of a book can satisfy their vanity and express their many graces.

The western coast of Europe and the western coast of America have about the same annual mean temperature—50° Fahrenheit, with a limit of 51° 30" of north latitude.

The Pacific Coast has greatly the advantage over western Europe, in that the extremes of heat and cold are nearer together, a characteristic that is attributable to two paramount causes: Firstly, the Japanese current emanating from the Indian Ocean. The main body of this heated water sweeps toward the west coast of America, turns easterly and southerly, helping to produce a delightful insular climate along the coast of Oregon and California. Secondly, the mountain barriers upon the east and north; the sheltering influences of the Sierra Nevadas and Cascade mountains as they reach the coast of Alaska encircling its southern and western coasts, thus cutting off the polar winds that would otherwise flow over Oregon and California.

The State possesses three distinct climates, that of the coast, valleys, and mountains, similar in the matter of seasons, but otherwise totally dissimilar.

Degrees of latitude have no bearing upon fruit culture in California, for it is an ascertained fact that fruits ripen earlier in the north than in the south of the State.

Horticulture and geographical situations have nothing in common. In other regions one is quite dependent upon the other, but in California horticulture laughs at geographical boundaries.

These surprising conditions depend wholly upon topography, and consist not in parallels of latitude, but by topographical curves varying in direction and governed by deposit and natural formation, altitude, rainfall, and temperature.

What is known as the Citrus Belt of California is a great valley lying between the Coast Range on the west and the Sierra Nevadas on the east, and runs in a direction northwest to southeast, and extends from Red Bluff on the north to the Tejon Mountains on the south.

The total area is about 17,200 square miles. This great valley contains about one-half of all the fruit trees and a third of all the vines in the State. Within the limits of this belt to the northernmost boundaries, in favoured spots the orange flourishes side by side with the apple.

Immense tracts of this great valley are used for agricultural and pasturage purposes, and, as yet, orchards occupy but an insignificant area of this immense valley.

Several characteristics of the California climate and soil conjoin not only to produce glorious flowers, both wild and cultivated, but the greatest possible variety of fruits and berries. The abundant heat, almost perennial sunshine, and dry atmosphere, together with the fine adaptability of the soil and the great length of the growing season, join forces to produce fruits of superior size and excellence. The trees are amazingly prolific bearers, and also produce mammoth fruit.

All conscientious horticulturists resort to the "thinning out" process in order to preserve the quality and size of what they allow to remain on the trees.

The fruit industry in California, in spite of the immense crops matured every year, is but in its infancy. Millions of trees and vines are not yet in bearing, or only yielding third, fourth, and fifth year crops.

Since the formation of the Fruit Growers' Union in 1881, when the first law was enacted to protect California horticulturists, there has been steady progress and practical expenditure of brains and money to further the interests, in every way possible, of the fruit growers of California.

Horticulture has been reduced to a science by disseminating knowledge and a hearty coöperation of fruit growers to extend the interests of the State in every way possible.

The history of horticulture in the State of California almost up to the present time has been one of experimenting, ascertaining the adaptability of the soil to certain kinds of fruits, and testing what European and Eastern trees do well in this climate, for many varieties make utter failures, while others are improved beyond recognition.

Californians have had to learn also that a horticultural precedent has been established here, independent of what obtains in other countries. Although ideas and methods have been gleaned from abroad, application to local and special needs have metamorphosed them to a great extent. Hap-hazard planting in California is humbug unless wedded to Yankee shrewdness.

Know your soil and its elements, the atmosphere, heat, and moisture and exposure; then ascertain what fruits do well under those limitations.

Clear your land, plough and sow a crop of something to mellow up the soil, the next year plant your young trees. Climate will be your fellow-worker and steadfast friend. Nine-twelfths of the year a man can sit down and watch nature work. The man who complains of climate in California should be banished from this paradise, for even the golden fruit of Hesperides would be but clay to one whose birthright is discontent.

What will constitute California's future glory will be the division of the lands into small holdings of from twenty acres up to about two hundred acres; where owners give their personal supervision; where the excellence of the fruits should be the consideration, over and above the profits; where men who resort to practices in the business that cheapen the standard of fruits should be forced out of the market; where every man works for the good of the whole; where the pride of the horticulturist, and not the greed of the speculator, obtains, and where the specialist and student flourish. If these conditions will not make California the greatest fruit-producing country on earth, then human ingenuity is at fault, and not climate.

Many a tourist in coming to San Francisco, and it might be said it is the exception when it is not so, has wondered if California fruits can make no better showing than the sour, half-ripened fruit he partakes of; last, but not least, the prices he pays for this fruit are so incredulously high that he wonders if it can be possible he can be eating imported fruit, and not the production of the California soil. Then he compares his experience here with that abroad; at the forts along the Mediterranean for a cent or two he can entirely satisfy a robust appetite with luscious fruit.

California fruit growers are so busy at present over their export trade that home consumption is relegated to the leavings, under the same principle a cobbler's children have no shoes.

Great things are expected of the olive industry of this State. Although the last returns showed but little over eleven thousand gallons of oil from the last crop, there are thousands upon thousands of young trees not yet in bearing. The oil produced is of a superior quality, and leads the sanguine to believe that the olive crown will yet rest upon our brows.

Fruit curing is, and will continue to be, one of the first industries of the State. The figures for the season just passed will aggregate

48,700,000 pounds of dried fruit, nearly four-fifths of which will represent French prunes; this is but a mere bagatelle to what the crop will be several years hence.

The prune industry is centred in Santa Clara County; the biggest prune orchard in the State is now in the Salinas Valley, San Luis Obispo County. In this orchard there are 300 acres of prune trees planted in a body, representing 324,000 trees. Prune trees make such quick returns, four-year-old trees bear heavily.

All temperate zone and semi-tropical fruits are raised with equal facility. Berries do superbly; strawberries, however, are too often forced.

Fruits in California, where irrigation methods are too much employed, depreciate in quality; the fine flavour is sacrificed for the early ripening—a too frequent method of producers, that should be cried down. Flavour is what makes fine fruit. Size and beauty do much in their way, but flavour is the nectar of the gods. Size and beauty constitute the shell, flavour is the subtle spirit that animates it.

In many localities the orchards are merely cultivated, that is, ploughed and harrowed three or four times a year, but never irrigated artificially. In portions of the State where midsummer irrigation is required, and where the country presents a level surface, as in Yolo County, whole orchards are flooded with an abundant supply of water.

The raisin of late years has received a greater impetus than any other fruit in the State. The ease with which raisin vines are propagated, the early profits, immense crops, and excellent prices induce hundreds to engage in the industry. About a thousand acres are set to raisin vines. Fresno County is the centre of this industry. Over 50,000,000 pounds were produced this year, and one-third only of the vines are in bearing.

The orange crop was enormous; lemons, figs, apricots, nuts, pears, peaches, and cherries each and all have made excellent records for themselves.

The shipping record for the year 1890 was 16,191 car-loads, which would make a continuous train of cars 123 miles long.

The report of the State Board of Horticulture says: "It is a significant fact that while our wheat output has not materially increased from 1880 to 1890, our fruit output has increased more than thirty times, and is growing with great rapidity. While the showing here made still keeps California in the front rank of wheat-growing States, being third in the rank, it demonstrates the great advantages of the State as a fruit-producing country.

"In 1880 our exports of fruit brought us probably about $700,000, while they now amount to about $20,000,000. This wonderful result has brought with it what is above all computation, to wit: the demonstration that fruit-growing in this State is very profitable, and is almost absolutely safe from frosts and other drawbacks, and has practically no limit."

CHAPTER 39

Colorado

It is a mistake to believe that, because Colorado has a high elevation, the mercury in the thermometer drops down below zero in the winter season and stops there, and that the snow mounts up with the altitude. The fact is that the average precipitation of moisture at Denver during the entire year is only 14.77 inches. With such a slight precipitation there is practically no danger of snow blockades on the railroads, save at a few points exposed to drifts, and these points have been amply protected. This is especially true of the through line of the Denver & Rio Grande Railroad from Denver to Salt Lake City and Ogden.

Facts speak louder than words, and the fact is that travel over "the Scenic Line of the World" has gone on with less interruption from snow during the last five winters than it has on the plains lines, which are popularly supposed to be more free from such delays than the mountain systems.

A winter's residence in Colorado will banish forever the false impression that this is a boreal region, given over to inclemency and snow-drifts. There is more sunshine in Colorado than in Florida; there is less snow than in any State east of the Missouri River. A single trip over the Denver & Rio Grande Railroad from Denver to Ogden, in midwinter, will disabuse the mind of the tourist or transcontinental traveler of the erroneous notion that mountain railroads suffer from delays by snow to any greater extent than do the trains upon the less attractive, and by far more bleak, plains.

The glories and pleasures of a summer trip by rail through the Rocky Mountains have been lauded *ad infinitu*m, and, indeed, too much can not be said in this direction; but winter adds new grandeur to the scene, lends a new charm to the massive bulwarks of the gigantic ranges, and introduces a new element of variety and beauty to these unsurpassed and unsurpassable wonders of nature. These sights can be enjoyed, these wonders witnessed, with no dangers of delay and no anticipation of vexatious detentions. There are those, however, who, knowing that the Denver & Rio Grande Railroad climbs great passes over the mountains, are apprehensive of snow blockades at these points. Here facts come to the rescue. The trains are not delayed, for the exposed places of this character have been amply protected, and the experiences of years prove that delay of trains from snow is a rarer event on this mountain-climbing system than on the level, and in fact more exposed, lines of the East.

For the benefit of those who are unacquainted with the peculiarity of the mountain-base climate, it may be well to mention some of its characteristics. In summer the days are seldom hot, and it is rare to see the thermometer reach 90° at Manitou. The farther one moves eastward from the foot-hills, the greater are to be found the extremes of temperature. Omaha, although much lower in elevation, experiences far greater extremes of heat and cold.

In the dry air of the Colorado plateau the feeling of heat and cold is much less marked. One is not oppressed at all by a temperature of 90°, nor does almost any amount of cold produce the chilliness in the open air, which is really the distressing and objectionable feature of a low temperature. The nights in summer are always cool and refreshing.

It must not be supposed that the climate of Colorado is an equable one, or that there is a distinct dry and rainy season, as in California and on the Pacific Coast. The contrary is true. The diurnal range of temperature, as in all high countries, is great; and there are rains throughout the warm parts of the year and snows in winter, but both are moderate in quantity.

A glance at the reports compiled by the United States Signal Service shows the remarkable fact that 340 out of 365 were "sunny days" in Colorado.

It is not necessary to add an elaborate argument. The conclusion is self-evident and inevitable. The winter climate of Colorado, on the whole, presents advantages for the invalid and the pleasure-seeker that can not fail to command attention. The Denver & Rio Grande is not alone a summer road. Its trains run on schedule time all the year round, and give to the travelling public all the comforts, conveniences, elegancies, and luxuries to be found on any line, with the added attraction of scenery the grandest in the world.

Climate and health go together so closely associated that they have become almost synonymous terms. So beneficial have been found the climatic influences of Colorado that her fame as a sanatorium has become world-wide, and this reputation has been so well-founded in recent years that thousands of people from all parts of America and Europe—from many parts of the world, in fact—are now coming annually to Colorado for recuperation or permanent residence. The dryness and lightness of the air, and its invigorating character, together with the almost constant prevalence of sunshine, impart new energy to the well and a fresh lease of life to those whose constitutions are impaired. All the conditions of life to the newcomer in Colorado are fresh and inspiring, and even wasted and shattered constitutions are restored to vigour. This is illustrated daily by the experiences of thousands who have sought the benign influences of Colorado climate with scarcely a hope, in the beginning, of recovery. These climatic influences are especially beneficial to persons suffering from all kinds of lung diseases, except to those in the last stage of consumption. That the climate itself is a preventative of consumption is evidenced in the fact that phthisis does not originate here.

The places of peculiar advantage in seeking health are the towns and cities on the plains, and parks and pleasure resorts on the mountains. The plains in some instances are the most beneficial for a permanent residence, while in other cases the mountains are preferable. There are not exceeding an average of sixty-five cloudy days per year in Colorado, while there are scarcely twenty days that the sun is all the day invisible at any given point. Summer weather usually continues till October, and the autumn till January. Usually the winters are mild, followed by an early spring. In summer the temperature rarely reaches 90° and is normal at 70°. Colorado climate is beneficial not to consumptives alone, but persons of kidney and liver and kindred diseases are benefited both by climate and the mineral waters which everywhere abound in the State, and are especially numerous and available on the Denver & Rio Grande Railroad lines.

The supply of coal in Colorado is inexhaustible, the lignite or brown coal area extending from St. Vrains on the north to the Raton Mountains on the south, about 220 miles in length and varying from twenty to twenty-five miles in breadth, along the eastern base of the mountains. Large portions of this field have been swept away by floods resulting from melting glaciers. The principal developments of this vast field have been made in the vicinity of Trinidad and Walsenburg, Cañon City, Coal Creek, Colorado Springs, Golden, Loveland, Erie, and Boulder. Lignite also exists in North Park and at various points on the divide between North and Middle parks. Jet, or the black variety of coal, occurs in seams from one-half to six inches in width in the shale about Cañon City and Little Fountain Creek. The most important mines of bituminous coal are the Trinidad group and the mines at Crested Butte. Anthracite coal appears to be confined mainly to the coal basins in the Elk Mountain. Native coke is found near Crested Butte, where a dyke of lava has intruded the coal strata. Official geological surveys give a coal-bearing *strata* of 40,000 square miles, or one-third of the entire area of the State. In 1873, when coal-mining began to take shape as an industry, the output was 69,977 tons; today the output is 2,373,954 tons, which comparison gives the reader some idea of the rapidity of its growth.

It has been said, with a great deal of truth, that all of Colorado is a health resort. With its gorgeous peaks and lovely valleys, its beautiful cities on the plains, its forests and its streams, its broad green parks and charming crystal lakes amid the mountains, with its sunshine and pure air, it is certainly a land for man's health and pleasure. The most desirable resorts in the world are upon the lines of the Denver & Rio Grande Railroad. Only eighty miles from Denver, or five miles from Colorado Springs, and nestling at the foot of Pike's Peak, is situated Manitou, that delightful resort for health and pleasure seekers, as popular to-day as Newport or Saratoga, attracting tourists from all parts of the United States and Europe. It has wonderful effervescent and medicinal springs, and is surrounded by more objects of attraction than any other spot in the world, including the Garden of the Gods, Glen Eyrie, Red Rock Cañon, Crystal Park, Engleman's Cañon, Williams Cañon, Manitou Grand Caverns, Cave of the Winds, Ute Pass, Rainbow Falls, and Bear Creek Cañon, all places of great attraction to the visitor.

Palmer Lake is a local pleasure resort. Poncha Springs, five miles from Salida, are the noted hot springs—altitude, 7,480 feet—a great health resort. Wagon Wheel Gap, in the picturesque San Luis Valley; hot springs of great curative qualities. It is a favourite health and pleasure resort; the best place in the West for trout fishing. Glenwood Springs is a fine town and a watering place and health resort, having extensive hot springs of great curative properties. Formerly the Mecca of the Indians. Elevation 5,200 feet. Twin Lakes, a beautiful body of crystal water, a pleasure resort and place of entertainment; fine boating and fishing; near Leadville, and reached by the Denver & Rio Grande. Trimble Hot Springs, nine miles from Durango; hot springs noted for remedial qualities. Ouray, hot and cold mineral springs; summer resort. The Great Salt Lake, the famous hot springs of Albuquerque, and numerous other attractions are reached by the Denver & Rio Grande.

The number of irrigable acres in Colorado is placed at 35,000,000 in round numbers, an area fully one-seventh larger than the State of New York. Ten years ago there were but 600 miles of irrigating ditches; now, including canals and laterals, there are 34,000 miles, and $9,500,000 have been expended in their construction. With these figures one can not but be impressed with the possibilities of the future, and believe with the most enthusiastic in the ultimate reclamation of the so-called arid land. It has been by the aid of irrigation that agriculture has been made to vie with mining as the chief industry of the State, and in the future, through its agency, the waters of the mountains will be more generally distributed by reservoir systems. The first of these reservoirs is now being constructed on the line of the Denver & Rio Grande Railroad, between Castle Rock and Palmer Lake. It will irrigate a large portion of the divide country. Of so vast an extent is this reservoir that the projectors contemplate the erection of a hotel and the various appurtenances of a mountain resort. When the government puts into execution its vast plan of irrigation the seed so modestly planted ten years ago will have its fruition. The number of square miles and the acreage under irrigation are found in the following table:

	Sq. Miles.	Acres.
San Luis Valley	3,096	1,981,440
Southwestern Colorado	1,080	691,200
Grand River Valley	360	230,400
Gunnison and Uncompahgre Valleys	720	460,800
Northwestern Colorado	1,980	1,267,200
North Central Colorado	720	460,800
Small areas	3,600	2,304,000
Eastern Colorado	41,868	26,795,520
	54,000	34,560,000

In addition to these irrigated lands may be placed the Arkansas Valley, from Pueblo to the Kansas State line, and the country between Cherry Creek and the foot-hills, and from Cherry Creek Cañon to

Denver. During the past twelve months there has been an increased activity in this sort of construction. It is a record unprecedented in irrigation, and taken in connection with the organisation of new companies, this fact indicates no limit to this species of development.

Even the people of Colorado do not comprehend that in this State may be grown fruit of a superior quality to that raised in the orchards of California. The pears and peaches are more luscious, and all the boasted varieties of California grapes are here grown successfully. The truth of these statements was satisfactorily demonstrated at the recent State fair in Pueblo, and by the fruit exhibit made by the Bureau of Immigration and Statistics at Chicago last fall. The apple, for luxurious growth and flavour, is without a superior in any State, and the orchards of this fruit alone aggregate half a million trees. The success with which grape culture has been conducted indicates for the future a great vintage industry. Fruit-tree planting is progressing at an enormous rate. It is profitable. In 1891 the number of trees planted was 200,000, the yield of apples was 60,000 bushels, and the largest yield from a single orchard of 2,000 trees was 15,000 bushels.

The yield last year almost doubled that of the year previous. Strawberries, raspberries, blackberries, gooseberries, and currants are prolific, and for size and flavour are unsurpassed. They grow on the highest mountain and in the lowest valley, and the yield is from 3,000 to 6,000 quarts per acre. One of the most profitable of the recent plantings, in the direction of fruit-plants, is that of the watermelon. In the Arkansas Valley they grow in great abundance, and are of superior merit to the Georgia melon. In fact most varieties of fruit indigenous to the temperate zone are successfully grown in Colorado. Fruit culture is no longer an experiment; it is a great success, and in the future will take its place as a distinctive and most profitable industry.

Colorado's future as a great manufacturing State is assured. In her hills, upon her mountain sides, on the plains, and in the valleys, her deposits of raw material abound, both in variety and richness, second to no other State in the Union. In fact she stands alone in this respect. At present these resources are undeveloped; the surface has been merely touched, and yet this superficial view reveals to the observer possibilities beyond conception. As this empire, of which Colorado is the geographical centre, becomes settled more thickly, the demand upon these resources will increase, and with this increasing demand manufactures will multiply, and soon every article known to the trade will be furnished direct from her vast deposits. Not only will she supply the wants of her own and contiguous territories, but in time markets remote will come to Colorado for supplies.

The abundance of the raw material and the economy in manufacturing will level competition, and the high quality of the product will place her supreme in the world's commercial marts. The results of last year, aggregating $50,000,000 in the reported values of the manufacturing product in eighteen cities, give some conception of Colorado's manufacturing future; and it has only been a very short time since, in the whole breadth of the State, when not a single article was manufactured, and everything used was shipped from eastern cities at enormous prices. Within the past year the following manufactories have been added: A paper-mill, a match factory, a cotton-mill, a woollen-mill, a boot and shoe factory, an overall factory, and a knit-underwear establishment. The manufactured product of 1892 will not fall below $75,000,000.

Colorado continues to be the paradise of the sportsman. Its myriads of streams teem with mountain-trout; the forests are, as ever, the domain of the elk, deer, and other game; and its many lakes, while abounding in fish, are the haunts for the wild feathery tribe, and offer great attraction for both rod and gun. Everywhere on the various lines of the Denver & Rio Grande the tourist and the pleasure-seeker at home may find a field of sport to his liking. Should he choose a day of recreation after small game, he may stop off in the valleys among the farms, and a bag of birds and rabbits will be his trophy. For elk and deer he may follow the valley of the Upper Arkansas, deploying to the near-by hills, or go to the valleys and mountains of Southern Colorado, or follow the line of the Denver & Rio Grande down to Gunnison, or cross the range to Glenwood, and search the wooded hills and the glens and valleys of the Yampa and the Grand; thence southward, via Ouray, he may follow the Dolores from the San Miguel to the San Juan and Muncos, following the footsteps of the Indians, now departed, upon their favourite hunting-grounds.

For the angler, as has been stated, fish are abundant in all the streams and lakes reached by the Denver & Rio Grande; but for the best sport and most enjoyable entertainment Wagon Wheel Gap, on the Rio Grande del Norte, in Rio Grande County, is conceded to be the choice of all places. This is both a pleasure and a health resort, affording at the same time rest and recreation for the sick and weary, and rare amusement for the invalid and the tourist alike. At this point the finest of mountain-trout are always abundant, and the angler may enjoy himself with the speckled beauties to his heart's content. The

Gunnison River likewise abounds in fine trout, and there are many points of advantage on this as many other streams along the line of the Denver & Rio Grande.

Ores are found under all conceivable conditions in Colorado, and, as a rule, in sufficient quantities to admit of their profitable extraction. In the metamorphosed granite mountains of the main range the typical fissure veins, with well-defined and nearly perpendicular walls, are found often aggregated in great numbers, and universally mineralized to a profitable degree. In the *trachytic* and *porphyric* districts rich fissures also prevail, running very high in silver as a rule, while occasionally the precious metals are associated with such quantities of lead or copper ore that the base metals more than pay all cost of mining and treating the ore. In other sections, again, where there have been large overflows of porphyry upon the carboniferous or *silurian* limestone, great deposits of silver lead ore are found, often covering many acres of ground like vast coal-beds.

To this latter class belong the mines of Leadville, which in the past ten years have yielded over $100,000,000. Also the mines about Aspen, Robinson, Red Cliff, Monarch, White Pine, and Rico. Wherever the deposits, however, and whatever the character of the mineral, the result is the same—an increase in the wealth of the State where developed. A number of valuable and important discoveries of gold and silver have been made this year (1892). The enormous deposits of silver at Crede promise to make it a rival of Leadville, while the immense gold-fields at Cripple Creek, near the line of this road, will add millions of dollars to the yellow metal wealth of the country. Rico, in the San Juan country, will produce millions of dollars more this year than ever before in its history. The quantity of the precious metal and the prosperity of the mining sections are only measured by the energy of the communities themselves and the extent of the capital employed. The record of the mining industry last year can be gleaned in the subjoined table:

	1889.	1890.
Silver, ounces	21,119,613	25,788,819
Gold, "	194,908	4,016,229
Lead, tons	3,166,970	3,932,814
Copper, pounds	3,127,739	2,422,000

The estimate for 1889 does not include the metals contained in the ore shipped out of the State, while that for 1890 does include them.

Colorado has exceeded every other section in the growth of her farming industry. This growth has been phenomenal. In 1880 the State imported 500,000 bushels of wheat, 2,000,000 bushels of corn, 500,000 bushels of potatoes, 1,000,000 bushels of oats, and 100,000 tons of hay. Last year there were produced in the State about 10,000,000 bushels of cereals, and instead of importing, the State exports; and in eastern markets Colorado wheat and oats command a premium. So great has been the development that authorities on agriculture assert that the agricultural output exceeds that of mining, which assertion is contradicted by mining people. But be this as it may, no other section presents a parallel to the rapid advance of agriculture in this State. One-half of the 66,880,000 acres of land in Colorado is estimated as agricultural land, of which 12,000,000 acres can be turned to the plough. There are now 2,000,000 acres under cultivation. The remarkable feature of this progress is the success attained by the "rain belt," which only a few years since was considered irreclaimable land. All over the State farming has been profitable, and by the contiguity of markets prompt returns for the products are the rule. This has induced immigration, and is one of the contributory causes of the influx of settlers into every section where cheap lands may be obtained.

IRON.—The largest deposit of iron in Colorado is in Gunnison County, and when taken in connection with the fact that in this locality cheap fuel abounds, it is a deposit of magnitude unequalled anywhere in this country. By this fortuitous combination of deposits, No. 1 Bessemer pig iron can be produced at Gunnison for a cost not exceeding $12 per ton, or 50 *per cent* less than the price at Pittsburg. The deposit is near Sargent, on the Denver & Rio Grande Railroad. With an outcrop that is enormous and high in grade, it extends at intervals for a mile on the mountain side. A number of openings have been made, one of which is a tunnel run across the vein ninety-seven feet and an open cut exposing a face of forty feet all in solid iron. There are about fifty acres in the five iron claims which compose the White Pine deposit. There are iron beds on Gold Hill and Cebolla Rivers.

At the latter place the iron lies in an immense ledge of unknown depth. Iron abounds in other portions of the State, especially in Chaffee County, where the Colorado Coal & Iron Company of Pueblo have been drawing material for the manufacture of railroad iron, merchant bar, and steel. Iron and steel can be manufactured as cheaply in Colorado as in any other section of the United States, and the advantages that contribute to the State's superiority in this respect are the increasing demands, which can not be affected by the overproduction of the East and South; no rival point west of the Rocky Mountains claiming competitive facilities and an advantageous position as the geographical centre of a vast territory; an intelligent class of lab or; an abundance of building material and the most extensive fields of coking and fuel coal, and the only anthracite found west of Pennsylvania.

The annual production of 1,000,000 tons of crude pig iron, representing a value of say $14,000,000, the evolution of that 1,000,000 tons of pig iron into its higher products of bar iron, and steel, and sheets, and plates, and machinery, and cars, and locomotives, and pipes, and ploughs, and other farm implements, and all the long list of appliances and commodities of iron and steel, aggregating in value, at a lower estimation than can be legitimately placed, more than $50,000,000, means more for Colorado than many of her most sanguine advocates have anticipated.

CHAPTER 40

The Surgeon Scout

While dwelling upon the scenes and incidents of my life upon the frontier, and speaking of those with whom I came in contact, I wish to refer to one whose meeting with me toward the latter days of overland travel began with a sincere friendship that has lasted until this day, and will continue to the end of our lives.

The person to whom I refer is Dr. D. Frank Powell, an army surgeon in those days, and whose gallant services as an officer and scout, as well as his striking appearance, gained for him the border cognomens of "White Beaver" (by which he is as frequently called as by his own name) and "The Surgeon Scout," "Mighty Medicine Man," and "Fancy Frank."

Doctor Powell was the firm friend of Buffalo Bill, and his valuable services, rendered as a scout, guide, and Indian-fighter, made him famous as the Surgeon Scout.

His dash and handsome style of dress also gained for him the name of "Fancy Frank," while the other two appellations by which he was known were gained by his skill and service as a surgeon and physician.

When the Indians were stricken with an epidemic of smallpox, although at the time at war with the whites, Surgeon Powell conceived the idea of boldly entering their village and checking the dread disease.

Leaving the fort upon his perilous mission, Surgeon Powell made his way alone to the Indian country, and rode forward at sight of them, making signs of peace.

The astonished redskins received him with amazement, but, assured that he was in their power, they listened to the bold proposition he had to make them, and which was that he would check the epi-

D. FRANK POWELL. "WHITE BEAVER."

demic then raging or forfeit his own life.

Struck with the boldness of the man, whom they knew so well as the comrade of Buffalo Bill, and who spoke their language fluently, the chiefs listened to all he had to say and then put him to the test.

Then it was that the strange circumstance occurred of a pale-face foe and medicine man vaccinating the Indians, young and old, all except the medicine men of the tribe, who would have nothing to do with him.

The result of Doctor Powell's work was that the dread disease was soon checked, and under his care many desperate cases of sickness were cured, and he became the ideal of his friends, who held a grand powwow, and presented him with a robe of sixteen white beaverskins—the white beaver being a sacred animal among them.

Nor was this all, for they made him a mighty medicine man, or chief of their tribe, and bestowed upon him the name of "White Beaver," which he uses today in connection with his own name.

A resident now of La Crosse, Wis., Doctor Powell has a large practice there, resides in an elegant home, and is for the fourth time mayor of that beautiful city, and one of the most popular men in the State, socially and politically.

The doctor has been a most extensive traveller, in this country and abroad, and yet each year, for a couple of weeks, entertains as his guests the tribe of Winnebago Indians, of whom he is still the medicine chief, and who make a pilgrimage to see him, consult him as to the affairs of their people, and show him devoted respect during the time they are encamped upon his grounds, where he has a place set apart for them.

A handsome man, of splendid physique, one who has known a strange life of adventure, he is yet as gentle as a woman, and ever generous to those with whom he comes in contact; and this tribute to his worth as a man and skill as physician and surgeon he most justly deserves.

Conclusion

A summing up of the happenings that occurred or transpired in every decade, commencing with the twenties and ending with ninety.

There was but little occurred of very great note west of the Mississippi during the twenties. The State of Missouri was admitted into the sisterhood of the States in the beginning of the twenties; after that there was very little of note that transpired during the twenties, with the exception of a few Indian scares on the frontier of Missouri, which, as a rule, were brought about without any real cause, and some trapping expeditions going west to the Rocky Mountains to trap for beaver fur, and also trading expeditions to Santa Fé, in New Mexico. With those exceptions, everything went along as quiet and almost as calm as a summer morning.

In those days the entire community west of the Mississippi River, as well as the States east of it, were self-sustaining, producing all that they consumed in clothing and food, in their own homes, and I might say that this state of things also existed during the term of the thirties. Very little of note occurred outside the regular course of events save the Blackhawk war upon the Upper Mississippi and the appearance of steamboats in the Missouri River, as far west as the west border of the State of Missouri, which commenced in the early thirties, and became a very large source of transportation and passenger travel, and there was also, in the commencement of the thirties, some Mormon elders that came to the county of Jackson, in Missouri, bringing with them the revelations of their prophet Joseph Smith, and claimed that they had been sent to that county by the direction of the Lord to their prophet to establish the Zion of the Lord, or a "New Jerusalem," and, of course, a new church, which has since kept its existence until the present time, with its headquarters now in Salt Lake City, Utah.

With the arrival of steamboats in the Upper Missouri, farmers commenced to raise hemp and other commodities that they could ship to St. Louis and New Orleans upon the steamers, which was the commencement of the people in that State to market the surplus that they could produce upon their farms; but the advantage of this trade or business only applied to the farmers and producers living in the river counties (I mean the counties located on the river), as it was too costly to haul their products upon wagons and with teams for any great distance; so the steamboat transportation could only be very beneficial to the counties, as above stated, the interior portions of the State having to plod along very much as was the case before steamboats came into use. There was no finer passenger travel ever inaugurated than the accommodations that travellers enjoyed as passengers upon those floating palaces, and I have lived to see them come and go, so far as their operations upon the Missouri is concerned. The Missouri afforded nearly 3,000 miles of water navigation, measured by the windings of the river. I have travelled on steamboats from its mouth, or St. Louis, to the head of navigation at Fort Benton, in Montana.

Now, commencing with the forties, there was nothing of great moment happened until the great freshet of '44, which was the largest flood that has been known in the Missouri, about the mouth of the Caw, in the last seventy-five years, and I think that there never has been in the history of the country as great a flood in the Missouri at that point. In '46 the Mexican War came up, and produced quite a stir among the business men upon the west border of the Missouri, as at that time there was no Kansas and Nebraska, the whole country being called "the Indian Territory" west of the State of Missouri.

The Santa Fé trade, by this time, had become a regular annual business, and men had learned how to outfit wagons and teams so as to carry large amounts of merchandise and Government stores from the Missouri River to Santa Fé, N. M. and when General Donathan organised his regiment of troops, by the authority of the Governor of the State of Missouri, to march to Santa Fé, N. M., he found no trouble, neither did the government, in securing all the transportation necessary to meet any emergency that might arise, with a plain and well-beaten road the entire route that they had to travel, this road having been opened by the merchant-trains in previous years.

In '47 the Mormon leader, Brigham Young, with a company of his elders and members of the church, left the Missouri River in the early spring and travelled 1,000 miles into the interior of the country, and

THE RETREAT ON THE COLORADO OF MAJOR JOHN D. LEE, THE MORMON.

formed a colony in that year in Salt Lake Valley, and named the city that they found Salt City, which proved to be a halfway house, as we might call it, between the Missouri River and the Pacific Coast, which proved of great advantage to the emigrants who left the Missouri in the spring of '49 to reach the gold-fields of California; for it was in '49, or rather the winter of '48, when the placer gold in California was discovered, and it was on this account that '49 became one of the most eventful years of the forties, the Mexican War having closed, and peace negotiations established in '48, which gave the United States the entire domain of the Pacific Coast lying north of the line now dividing Old Mexico from the United States. There were vast numbers of brave and daring citizens from almost every State in the Mississippi Valley who attempted to reach California by the overland route, and at no time, not even during the Mexican War, up to '49, had there ever been any overland travel to compare with that of '49.

Tens of thousands of emigrants or gold-hunters left the west border at that time, outfitting themselves, some with ox-teams and some with mules and the best wagons that could be found in the market, loaded to the guards with supplies of food and clothing to make the trip and return, for at that time none of them expected to remain or make their homes in California; if so, it must have been a very small percentage of the number. Many of them died with cholera on the way; the large majority, however, reached their destination, but many of them through great suffering and privation from one cause or another.

One of the misfortunes that attended the majority of them was want of experience in travelling their animals; they started off in too big a hurry, and pressed their teams too much at the outset, the result of which was, many of their animals died from fatigue, caused by over-travelling, long before they reached the Pacific Coast, the result of which was to leave on the road, or rather in the road, often the valuables that they had secured in the outset for their comfort and preservation when they reached the land of gold.

The year '50 was also a very fatal year to emigration, for it did not cease with '49, but the success of the "forty-niners" in gathering gold proved to be a great inducement to the country to continue the movements of '49 in the way of outfitting and emigrating to the Pacific Coast; in fact, it continued in a greater or smaller degree during the entire fifties; but in the year '50, as in '49, there were great numbers died with cholera. It was fatal among the emigrants from their starting point from Missouri till they would reach the Rocky Mountains, after which time the cases of death from cholera were very few compared with what they suffered upon the plains before reaching the mountains.

There were but few cases that occurred after they reached the Sacramento Valley in California. Instead of returning, as the most of the gold-seekers intended to do on leaving their homes, they found California a delightful climate, with rich and fertile valleys, and many, very many of them concluded, after having a year's experience in the country, to become citizens, and a little later in the fifties, there were a great many people in the Western States who sold their homes and started with their families for the golden shores of the Pacific—in other words, for California—in view of adopting that State for their future homes. I was acquainted with numbers who did so, and who I have since met at their homes in California, who were delighted with the change that they made, and it is a very common thing now, after the country has been settled so many years, to find numbers of people there who think that California is the only country fit to live in.

Returning to the fifties, there was nothing of great note happened until the admission of Kansas and Nebraska in 1854, when floods of emigrants, mostly from the Northern States, passed into those Territories. A number, however, were from the Southern States, and held pro-slavery views.

In '56 what is known as the Kansas war occurred, from the invasion of men from Missouri and other States.

In '57 and '58 the Mormon war occurred, when Gen. Albert Sidney Johnston was sent to Utah with an army of 5,000 regulars.

In 1859 the great Comstock mine was developed, and it added to the currency of the world between one and two hundred millions of dollars in gold and silver. Also in '58 began the Pike's Peak excitement, which resulted in the settlement of Denver.

In 1860 the election of Abraham Lincoln was followed, in '61, by the breaking out of the Civil War.

In '62 the initial steps for the establishment of the Union and Central Pacific railroads were taken, and the idea was fulfilled in '69. Daily stages were put on in 1859 from the Missouri River to Denver and Salt Lake.

It was during the sixties that the telegraph was established across the continent, following in the track of the Pony Express.

Gold was discovered in Montana in the sixties, resulting in the settlement of that Territory.

During the seventies and eighties, the most important happenings in our country were the remarkable growth of the railroad interests.

www.ingramcontent.com/pod-product-compliance
Lightning Source LLC
Chambersburg PA
CBHW021956160426
43197CB00007B/150